Professional and Ethical Issues in Psychology

Foundations of Practice

Professional and Ethical Issues in Psychology
Foundations of Practice

Walter B. Pryzwansky, Ed.D.
Robert N. Wendt, Ph.D.

W. W. Norton & Company
New York • London

Manufacturing by Haddon Craftsmen

Library of Congress Cataloging-in-Publication Data

Pryzwansky, Walter B., 1939–
Professional and ethical issues in psychology:
foundations of practice / Walter B. Pryzwansky, Robert N. Wendt.
p.   cm.
"A Norton professional book."
Includes bibliographical references and index.
ISBN 0-393-70285-5
1. Psychologists—Professional ethics.   2. Psychology—Moral and
ethical aspects.   I. Wendt, Robert N.   II. Title.
BF76.4.P78   1999
150' .23—dc21   99-26042   CIP

W. W. Norton & Company, Inc., 500 Fifth Avenue, New York, N.Y. 10110
www.wwnorton.com
W. W. Norton & Company Ltd., 10 Coptic Street, London WC1A 1PU

1 2 3 4 5 6 7 8 9 0

To

Kathy

WBP would like to thank his best friend and wife, Kathy, for her continued
support, understanding, and encouragement during his entire career.

and

Judy

BW would like to thank his best friend, Judy, for her balance, support,
and patience. These are indeed the best years.

Contents

Acknowledgments

Many people have helped nurture this idea, which grew out of an APA symposium and the authors' experiences with that organization. We appreciate the positive response to an earlier book and the encouragement to develop our original plan. The immediate, enthusiastic support of W. W. Norton vicepresident Susan Munro was a critical factor in moving it ahead. Associate editor Regina Dahlgren Ardini was incredibly thorough and helpful in editing our material. Cadie Blalock was her usual efficient and committed self in insuring that drafts were typed accurately on what became a harried schedule. Thanks also to Lisa Bell, who was very helpful and skilled in the final preparation of many chapters. Sue Martin's able assistance, especially in proofreading, was greatly appreciated. We thank a number of graduate assistants at the University of Toledo for their library efforts, with special thanks to Roger Fortner, Brian Sullivan, and Gene Wright for their persistence and extra effort.

Finally, we thank our wives for their understanding and encouragement throughout this project.

Preface

The growth of psychology as a profession has resulted in developments in training, credentialing, professional practice guidelines, and accreditation of training programs at various levels. At the same time, external forces have exerted pressures to establish and/or enhance regulatory systems of this profession, as well as others. These influences have originated in the legislative, legal, and service domains.

This book addresses the history and current situation of professional psychology. We hope prospective and practicing psychologists will turn to it for current information and for a context in which to place professional needs or questions as they arise. This book is designed for two audiences, practitioners and psychology students, and it is relevant as a text for both undergraduate and graduate professional and ethics courses. Students considering a career in psychology will find considerable detailed information about the profession.

The application of psychological knowledge to personal, interpersonal, and societal problems has grown dramatically since World War II. Concurrently, with a burgeoning of applied psychology specialties, the discipline of psychology has shifted significantly, from being primarily an exclusively academic/scientific discipline to being more an applied profession. Led by clinical psychology, other specialties, including counseling, industrial/organizational, and school psychology, have established themselves. These have been followed by the forensic and neuropsychological specialties. As a result, not only have professional psychologists emerged as a force in industrial, healthcare, mental health, and educational settings, but psychology also now produces more Ph.D.s than the "hard" science areas. This shift to a "blended" field also has created numerous internal changes.

The purpose of this book is to inform the reader about the foundational areas of practice in the psychology profession. This material should be helpful to those aspiring to join the ranks of psychologists, as well as to seasoned practitioners. The information is as current as possible and in some instances concerns embryonic developments and trends.

"Foundations of Practice," our subtitle, is meant to encompass the essential components that define professionals in general. Generally, these components include the established credentials of the field, standards of training and practice, formal organizations, and professional ethics. Chapters present the existing positions, standards, and/or documents with which all applied psychologists should be familiar. Given the diversity of psychology practice, some readers will no doubt wish more or less emphasis on a particular topic or issue; here we can only say that we have tried to be both balanced and concise.

We begin the book with an overview of opportunities for careers in professional psychology and the myriad professional organizations that represent the diversity of the profession. Next, we present the training orientations that have evolved and the premises that underline each perspective. This discussion is linked to the regulation chapter, in that both programs and individual practitioners need to be accountable to their communities. Several chapters follow that deal with professional ethics and their application, along with legal considerations. We emphasize the professional's obligation to lifelong learning and professional development. Finally, we consider some of the impending issues and challenges facing professional psychology.

The reader is encouraged to read the original sources referred to in this text and to keep up with relevant issues, especially when pursuing membership in an organization or applying for a professional credential. Because changes are taking place rapidly in the field, certain information or criteria may change. This book is intended only as an introduction. If we have sensitized readers to the important aspects of their professional lives and made them think about becoming involved in the profession's development, then we will have reached our objective.

Professional and Ethical Issues in Psychology

Foundations of Practice

Chapter 1

Historical Foundations of Professional Psychology

WHAT IS A PROFESSION?

The observation that "professions are more numerous than ever before" is as true today as when Hughes (1963) made it over 30 years ago. Many occupations have become "professionalized" and more are joining that quest everyday. Professionalization movements attempt to change the status of the occupation. This is accomplished partially through education (prolonging preparation as the profession matures) and recruitment of the best and brightest. At the same time, the members of the profession strive to be more objective in dealing with cases; that is, they suspend personal investment to insure that it does not influence their actions or advice, while remaining deeply interested in providing optimal service using the best information (Hughes, 1963). As occupations become more organized, people work in increasingly complicated organizations. Yet, in spite of such trends, very few occupations will truly achieve the authority of established professions (Wilensky, 1964).

Theology, medicine, and law are recognized as our earliest professions—and, indeed, professions that many other occupations identify as their standard on this evolutionary path. Originally, these three professions were very similar in their practice; in fact, one individual might provide all three types of service. However, as these roles became more distinct, characteristics of each profession emerged. Most definitions of a profession include the following: the existence of a formal professional member organization, systematic training, a code of ethics, regulation of its members as they provide a service, and, most importantly, a body

1

of knowledge "to profess." Sheldon (1995) reasons that, as our society has moved from being an "agricultural society" to a "knowledge society," it has also become a "professional society." He envisions, as a result of this evolution, greater movement in the direction of specialization within professions. Thus, one might conclude both that the number of professions will increase and that currently existing professions will become increasingly complex. Sheldon goes on to define professional behavior as a derivative of the social contract between professional groups and the community and to point out that such an understanding is considered indispensable in our society. Professional behavior, according to Sheldon (1995, p. 227), has the following four attributes:

1. A high degree of generalized and systematic knowledge.
2. A primary orientation to the community interest rather than to individual self-interest.
3. A high degree of self-control achieved through codes of ethics that have been internalized during the process of work socialization and through voluntary association with organizations that are operated by the professionals themselves.
4. A system of rewards (monetary and honorary) that signify work achievement and thus are ends in themselves rather than means to some end of individual interest.

Many have contended that the existence of professionals has a negative impact on society (see Sinclair, Simon, & Pettifor, 1996, for a summary). They have expressed concern that too much power and status are assigned to groups that are self-regulating and restrictive in terms of potential competition. For example, Sarason (1996) notes that in the 1960s community groups striving to change the schools began to see public school system professionals as part of the problem. He argues that "circumscribed power" is inherent in the concept of the *professional*, since it would be inappropriate for those who do not have the knowledge and skills obtained within systematic training contexts to determine the actions of professionals. But this power is constricted by numerous forces. In public schools professionals experience power struggles not only among themselves, but also with the ultimate decision-makers within the school and, increasingly, external groups (e.g., parent organizations, federal and state legislatures, community and business groups, special constituent groups) who demand to be included in decisions. Similar struggles are taking place in medical settings, where the power of physicians has been steadily eroded. According to Sarason, professionals have difficulty sharing responsibility with nonprofessionals because such collaboration may require change and compromise.

Kultgen (1988) writes of a "social contract," suggesting that professionals must form true "moral communities" if they desire to be a positive force in society. Their ethics should be socially responsible, and viable accountability mechanisms should be in place to regulate their behavior.

PSYCHOLOGY AS A PROFESSION

History

Most writers cite 1879 as the year psychology became a separate and distinct discipline, shedding its cocoon of biology and emerging from that discipline, as well as the discipline of philosophy, to stand on its own. That year Wilhelm Wundt founded the first psychological laboratory labeled as such in Leipzig, Germany. While the biological roots of psychology remain evident in basic, general psychology texts and in the research of some psychologists, the discipline's uniqueness has obviously been established in this century.

In the beginning, most psychologists were employed in institutions of higher learning, teaching and performing research. Yet, it was not long before psychologists began to apply their knowledge in settings other than academia. In 1896, Lightner Witmer established, in Philadelphia, the first psychological clinic for the treatment of children's educational problems (Napoli, 1981). Witmer is also credited with coining the term *clinical psychology*. By the early twentieth century, the Binet Intelligence Test was being used to make school placement decisions for children. Then, during World War I, government officials asked psychologists to assist in the selection of armed services recruits. Napoli (1981) identifies the first three applied areas of psychology to be clinical, educational, and industrial. The emergence of the specialty school psychology was associated with Arnold Gesell, who was given the official title of school psychologist in 1915 by the Connecticut State Board of Education (Fagan & Delugach, 1985). It was not until after World War II, however, that the term *school psychology* gained favor as a way to differentiate it from other specialties in what had become known as the mental health movement.

Almost from its beginnings, the new discipline counted both scientists (researchers) and practitioners (professionals) among its members. Some saw its potential as a science and urged that its emphasis be directed toward the development of new knowledge; others were primarily interested in applying that knowledge to practical problems. Napoli (1981) has noted that the first constitution of the American Psychological Association (APA), written in 1894, defined its purpose as "the advancement of Psychology as a science" and limited its membership to those who were "engaged in this work." Almost before the ink was dry on that document, psychologists began debating and clarifying terms—a process that continues today. In spite of the existence of APA, a Society of Experimental Psychologists was organized in the 1920s, while the establishment of yet another organization, the American Association of Clinical Psychologists, was contemplated in 1917. Manifestations of such tension are not surprising when one considers that the basic researcher and the applied practitioner lay claim to the same title, "psychologist," even though their training and objectives of employment reflect very significant differences. The practice-research dichotomy is similar to the distinction between medicine and biology or chemistry.

There are some, nevertheless, who have argued that the bifurcation of psychology is unnecessary and somewhat overstated. For example, in 1949, the report of the Boulder Conference, which will be discussed in chapter 4, recommended that a scientist-practitioner model of training and practice be adopted for clinical psychology. The basic premise of that model is that the applied psychologist (i.e., practitioner, professional) is well grounded in the scientific knowledge base of the parent discipline and also contributes to that knowledge base through applying it to real-world problems. The scientist's investigations can be described as *basic* (versus *applied*) research, although that distinction has also been challenged.

In spite of the struggles noted here, psychologists could claim to be unique in that they were the only occupational group wherein the science and practice constituencies use the same title (Napoli, 1981). It is difficult (and perhaps meaningless) to pinpoint the beginning of psychology as a *profession* versus psychology as a *science*. The early interest in and efforts to apply the new science have already been noted. However, if we accept the common features of most definitions of a profession, it is hard to say just when psychology became "professionalized." As mentioned earlier, in 1917 a group considered forming an association of clinical psychologists. In 1937, the New York State Association of Consulting Psychologists reorganized itself into the Association of Consulting Psychologists (ACP). This organization was concerned with professional issues on a national level and, in particular, licensing and ethics. Consequently, we can assume that, at the very least, by 1937 the profession of psychology had truly been developed. We will be returning to the definitional features of a profession in chapter 5. Here let us look at two critical identifiers of a profession: need and autonomous responsibility.

It has been argued (Dörken & Rodgers, 1976) that, if psychology is to be a profession, the profession and the public it serves must be able to identify the unique field of need that is being served, rather than accepting a validated body of knowledge as its primary defining parameter. Fox, Barclay, and Rodgers (1982) argue that professional psychology should be considered "that profession which is concerned with enhancing the effectiveness of human functioning" (p. 307).

They do not define the "field of need" in a monopolistic way, in the sense that psychology is the only profession that will deal with problems of illness. Rather, they note that it is "the only profession that consistently focuses its efforts on solving problems through alterations in patterns of behavioral coping" (p. 308). The ultimate concern of professional psychologists is "all problems involving human coping skills and human coping effectiveness" (p. 308). It would seem safe to say that most people would agree with this conceptualization.

It can also be assumed that the professional will deal with the entire field of need, "even when effective solutions to the problems presented are uncertain" (Dörken & Rodgers, 1976, p. 290). Dörken and Rodgers argue that the responsibility for making decisions regarding problems where the solution(s) is less than apparent and the knowledge base wanting is what truly defines a profession. They claim "that where a body of knowledge is adequately validated and adequately comprehensive to serve a field of need, then experts in that knowledge are basically technicians rather than professionals" (p. 289). According to Dörken and Rodgers, psychology's commitment to validate procedures and scientifically research approaches can be construed as a commitment to a technology rather than a profession. Such an orientation leads to the technician serving and contributing to the informational needs of other professionals. The contributions of psychology to education, law, and medicine are of this highly specific type. This decision regarding focus also affects, then, the degree of independence assumed by the practitioner.

The issue of professional autonomy has been addressed formally by organizations serving psychology. The American Psychological Association published its first official position on relations with other professions in 1954. It asserted that APA had full responsibility for overseeing the evolution of professional psychology, while staking the claim of an autonomous profession for psychology, except where social responsibility is a factor (Saccuzzo & Kaplan, 1984). The most controversial statement in the 1954 report was one that said psychologists should conduct psychotherapy only in "genuine collaboration" with physicians. This position had actually come out of the Boulder Conference (Raimy, 1950). Four years later (APA, 1958), this clause was replaced with a statement saying that psychologists could conduct independent psychotherapy when appropriate. Furthermore, APA pledged legal support for psychologists who were challenged for engaging in such a practice. The most recent affirmations of the principle of autonomous functioning appear in the APA *Ethical Principles of Psychologists* (1992a), as well as the *General Guidelines for Providers of Psychological Services* (1987a) and *Specialty Guidelines* (1981) (see chapters 6 and 7). For example, the *General Guidelines* state that "psychologists pursue their activities as members of the independent, autonomous profession of psychology"(p. 719).

Fillmore Sanford, then executive secretary of the APA, reviewed the obligations of psychology as a profession in 1951. In an attempt to promote its development, he proposed the following 16 principles/criteria (pp. 668–670):

1. A good profession is one that is motivated by a sense of social responsibility.
2. A good profession is one sufficiently perceptive of its place in society to guide continually its practices and policies so they conform to the best and changing interests of that society.
3. A good profession is one that is continually on guard lest it represent itself as able to render services that are beyond its demonstrable competence.
4. A good profession is one that is continually seeking to find its unique pattern of competence and that concentrates its efforts on the rendering of the unique service based on its pattern of competencies.
5. A good profession is one that devotes relatively little of its energy to "guild" functions, to the building of its own in-group strength, relatively much of its energy to the serving of its social function.
6. The good profession is one that engages in rational and non-invidious relations with other professions having related or overlapping competencies and common purposes.
7. A good profession is one that devotes a proportion of its energies to the discovery of new knowledge.
8. The good profession is one in which there are good channels of communication between the discoverers of knowledge and the appliers of knowledge.
9. The good profession is one in which its discoverers of knowledge are not relegated to positions of second-rate status.
10. The good profession is one that is free of non-functional entrance requirements.
11. The good profession is one in which preparatory training is validly related to the ultimate function of the members of the profession.
12. A good profession is one in which the material benefits accruing to its members are proportional to social contributions.
13. The good profession is one whose members are socially and financially accessible to the public.
14. The good profession has a code of ethics designed primarily to protect the client and only secondarily to protect the members of the profession.
15. A good profession is one that facilitates the continuing education and training of all its members.
16. A good profession is one that is continually concerned with the validity of its techniques and procedures.

Bernstein and Nietzel (1980) used this list to retrospectively assess the progress made by psychology toward appropriate professional goals and came away with a positive conclusion. For example, criteria 3, 4, 13, and 14, which are concerned with ethical behavior, are covered by the *Ethical Principles of Psychologists and Code of Conduct* (APA, 1992a). Training standards are dealt with in criteria 10, 11, and 15. Chapter 4 of this book spells out the standards and validation procedures psychology currently employs to insure the adequacy of training programs. While continuing professional education remains the least monitored area, mechanisms are in place to enhance professionals' efforts in this area. Over the past few years psychology has reached out to other helping professions in a constructive way, resulting in professional liaisons and collaborative efforts (criteria 6) (e.g., Millon, 1983). The remaining criteria deal with the profession's responsibilities to society (1, 2, 5, and 12) and the promotion of the science and "applied science" of psychology (7, 8, 9, and 16). We looked briefly at the latter issue when considering the dual nature of psychology as a science and profession. Keeping the channels open between researchers and clinicians remains a challenge for our profession. Finally, psychologists seem sensitized to their social responsibility, partly because the field of psychology has the advantage of being relatively young and thus can learn from the struggles of other, older professions. Also, by the very nature of the discipline and the values it espouses, psychology has always approached its objectives with social responsibility in mind. While it remains for other, more objective observers outside the discipline to make the final judgment, we see the current standards and literature of the psychology profession as positive in this regard.

The Future of Professions

Before looking at the future of psychology, let's look at the challenge(s) faced by all professions in this technological age. At one point professionals could lay legitimate claim to a specific knowledge base that gave them status and decision-making influence. Now technology has made information readily accessible in an understandable form, so that consumers can be in a position to make an informed decision; sometimes they know as much as highly specialized professionals. This has the potential to change the profession-client relationship dramatically, making the clients equal partners or collaborators with the professional, and certainly better judges of the quality of professional services than ever before. As a result, the assumed status of belonging to a profession is diminishing; now that status must be earned by providing quality service. The cost-consciousness of the 1990s has added to the pressure on the professions, particularly as former aides or support personnel gradually have taken over certain services within their respective professions or become independent providers. For example, nurses may prescribe medicine in certain states, and under managed care social workers and counselors may be seen as providing comparable services to doctoral-level psychologists or psychiatrists, with a reimbursement fee established for all providers at the level of the provider with the fewest years of training. The customization of services has reinforced this trend. For example, if a professional's work is seen as X number of sets of competency, apart from an integrative knowledge of how these sets interact or need to be seen as a system, then the client/consumer purchases the set that makes the most sense to him/her at the most economical rate. Thus, the service is conceptualized as a "product," and market values dominate the professional practice.

The effects of this shift in how we think of professionals have been experienced in the education of professions as well. Frankford and Konrad (1998) describe a typical crisis for medical education in terms of whether medical educators can respond to market imperatives and create new forms of practice. They argue that the new medical care delivery organizations serve as a threat to *traditional educational autonomy*, since external agents are demanding provisions of certain kinds of education. In addition, the very notion of *professionalism* is under stress, since professionals are increasingly caught between the values of market-oriented organizations and their obligation to patient interests. Frankford and Konrad conclude that traditional individualistic professional autonomy is no longer viable and must be reformulated, for the vision of professionalism "must stress the intrinsic value of work" that contributes to the social good (p. 142). If sense of identity were to permeate the commitment to work, individual autonomy would be replaced by professional responsiveness. The control of work would rest in a collegial group open to the larger normative environment rather than a professional society. Therefore, the implication for training is that educators must incorporate "responsiveness to lay values" (p. 143) to further their students' competence in "knowing in action" and "reflection in action."

CHANGES IN THE PROFESSION

Professional Training

Peterson concluded in 1985 that professional schools and the professional doctorate (i.e., Psy.D.) have become established in American psychology. However, Fox, Barclay, and Rodgers (1982) found that three impediments stood in the way of professional psychology's growth and development. First, they noted the lack of a single agreed-upon definition of the profession and its scope. Second, with respect to the education of professionals, they identified two troublesome features: (a) training settings that were so uncontrolled and variable that uniformity of training was lacking and professional identity was hard to establish; and (b) practicum experiences that take place in service delivery systems controlled by professionals other than psychologists. Finally, the absence of a credential by which the practitioner can be unambiguously defined was noted as a problem plaguing the profession of psychology.

Let us begin with a description of some developments related to graduate training in psychology—both research-oriented and applied programs (these will be described in detail in chapter 4). Over the past few years, a number of groups within the field have called for a national conference on training to consider an effort similar to Flexner's (1915) work early in the century, which revolutionized medical education. The last conference on graduate education in psychology was held in 1958 and was known as the Miami Beach Conference (Roe, Gustad, Moore, Ross, & Skodak, 1959). A number of conferences have specifically addressed professional training. Most notable was the Shakow report (1947), which recommended graduate training in clinical psychology based on the need for psychological assessment and therapy in Veterans Administration hospitals. This report was the first to emphasize scientific and professional areas of functioning. The Boulder Conference (Raimy, 1950) specifically addressed training of clinical psychologists, as did the Chicago Conference (Hoch, Ross, & Wender, 1966), which stressed alternatives to the scientist-practitioner model. A conference focusing on school psychologists' training was also held in the 1950s (Cutts, 1955), as well as a conference at Stanford University that emphasized the need for community mental health programs (Strother, 1956).

The Vail Conference (Korman, 1976) was notable for its endorsement of the professional degree in psychology (Psy.D.) and was followed by a conference to address several issues related to the practitioner model of training programs (Watson, Caddy, Johnson, & Rimm, 1981). As a result, the APA Education and Training Board directed its Committee on Graduate Education and Training to consider professional training. At their planning meeting, they noted that at least three philosophical issues undergird all education and training concerns: "(1) continuity and change in education; (2) independence and responsiveness to society; and (3) diversity and homogeneity of values and of professional activities of functions" (Brickman, 1985). The committee outlined 12 topic areas that they thought should be fully discussed and reviewed by the field prior to a national conference (they recommended a time frame of two years for such discussion). Arranged into categories in table 1.1, these 12 topic areas or issues form a comprehensive list of considerations that the profession faces in determining the future shape and direction of graduate training in psychology. Subsequently, a national invitational conference to address issues of graduate education in psychology occurred in June 1987. Since then there have been one national conference on internship training and two national conferences on postdoctoral training. These conferences will be dealt with in later chapters. Suffice it to say that education and training issues have received high priority in the decade of the nineties.

Table 1.1
ISSUES IN GRADUATE EDUCATION

I. Professional Role Issues
1. Is the primary mission of the department to train a practitioner-investigator-educator or is some level of integration expected among the three roles?

II. Educational Content and Process Issues
2. Should there be a core curriculum or should the curriculum be individualized?
3. What should the structure and content be at the undergraduate, graduate, and postgraduate levels?
4. Do we train generalists or specialists?
5. Where should graduates operate on the technological transfer continuum, i.e., moving knowledge from the basic or applied research stage to practical application?
6. How should psychology grow—increased specialization based on societal needs?

III. Educational Milieu Support System Issues
7. How diffuse or centralized should program quality control be allowed to exist?
8. What role should societal and financial support play in training?
9. How do we (psychology) apply the instructional methods we have developed to our own educational programs?

IV. Student Issues
10. How should recruitment and retention policies and procedures be arranged to achieve our objectives?
11. How is effective socialization to be realized?

Data from Brickman, 1985.

Changing Gender Composition of Psychology

In 1986 an APA committee reported on changes taking place within the field of psychology that have now become common knowledge (Howard et al., 1986). For example, the production of academic/research psychologists had declined by 40% from its peak in the 1970s, the number of new psychology Ph.D.s graduating from departments rated in the top quartile had dropped, minorities represented only 10% of the doctorates, and women made up the majority of psychology doctorates and outnumbered males by 2 to 1 among undergraduate psychology majors. The majority of new Ph.D. recipients were trained as health service providers from programs in a variety of administrative settings.

Over the past three decades the number of women entering all areas of psychology has steadily increased. By 1990 women made up 50% of the doctoral level graduates (Kohout, 1991). A mid-1980s study on the decrease in the number of men entering the field concluded that psychology, especially academic psychology, was losing its "attractiveness to males" (Howard et al., 1986, p. 23). As a result of such observations, the APA established the Task Force on the Changing Gender Composition of Psychology (APA, 1995a) to study this gender shift and provide interpretations, predictions, and suggestions for action. In studying the causes of this change in distribution of the sexes, this task force pointed out concurrent changes in the sociopolitical arena, the expansion of the field in terms of work settings and activities, and the changing focus of psychology. Psychology is not unique, in that the percentage of women earning doctoral degrees in all fields has risen significantly since 1971, although the increase in psychology has been especially dramatic. This gender shift is seen particularly in the practice areas of psychology—clinical, counseling, and school psychology. By 1991 the percentage of women in all subfields of psychology was 31% greater than 20 years earlier, with school (46%) and developmental (63%) psychology reporting the highest percentage change. The percentage of psychologists working part-time has increased slightly (11%). Although some reports suggest women remain more open to part-time work, there are indications that women from certain specialties prefer full-time employment.

The task force report concluded that the gender shift is the result of a complicated mix of factors. It pointed out warning signs in terms of decreased attractiveness for *both* men and women in certain subfields of psychology. As external regulations increase and autonomy declines, professional fields become less attractive, and as an area becomes "feminized" it becomes less attractive to men. The changes in academia and private practice, as well as societal skepticism of professional and scientific communities, have contributed to this vulnerability. The task force found no dramatic gender differences in terms of employment, primary work activity, or earning power. Beyond these findings, no "clear causal conclusions" could be drawn, particularly concerning social and economic changes over which the discipline has no control.

Denmark (1998) examined the status of women in psychology international-ly and found, not surprisingly, that "the United States has achieved greater gen-der equity over time than have other countries without a loss of status occurring within the discipline" (p. 472). Thus, she concluded that status is linked to the opportunity structure existing in the larger social context. Problems of sexism and antifeminism still existed internationally, although improvements had been noted in many areas.

Supply and Demand

For the past few years there has been growing concern that the profession is train-ing too many psychologists for the opportunities that exist in the traditional healthcare and human services sector. Those concerns are supported by the fact that in the last few years 100–300 doctoral students have not been placed in internships at the time of the uniform notification day in February. Against a backdrop of the high productivity of some professional psychology programs, with the number of graduates holding steady or growing slightly, and managed care companies' tendency to choose master's level mental health workers over doc-toral psychologists, the Association of Psychology Post-Doctoral and Internship Centers, along with APA, and the Association of State and Provincial Psychology Boards, and the Canadian Council of Professional Psychology spon-sored a 1997 Supply and Demand Conference (APPIC/APA, 1998).

One of the unavoidable findings of the conference was that data are sketchy at best regarding a number of questions in the area of supply and demand. For example, estimates of the number of students unplaced in internships range from 3 to 17%. Nevertheless, while no one has a firm figure, what was a non-concern only a few years ago has become a major worry among students. Similarly, stu-dents seem pessimistic regarding job employment, while available federal data report that psychologists, in comparison with professionals in many other fields, are well employed. It's not clear if the concern is that jobs take longer to find rather than being unavailable. Students' worries may also reflect the fact that, while traditional areas of practice (e.g., individual private practice) are less open, opportunities abound in other areas and emerging psychology roles have not been promoted and capitalized upon in recent years. The conference report rec-ommended systematic data collection efforts.

The conference also addressed the timing of internship experience (see chap-ter 4). Should internship continue to be at the predoctoral degree stage (to insure quality control) or should it follow graduation (to enable students to find better jobs and pay while completing supervisory requirements usually associated with the internship)? Any change would involve states and jurisdictions responsible for licensure, since licensing laws now call for an internship; such changes would not be easy given anticipated political hurdles. The participants did endorse the concept that licensure be granted following the completion of the degree requirement and an internship; a postdoctoral supervisory experience was also endorsed.

Finally, the conference recommended systematic data collection in the supply and demand areas, including doctoral program data concerning the internship and employment situation of students, years to degree, percentage of students finding or not finding internships, etc. The discipline was asked to track the number of students in bachelor's, master's, doctoral, internship, and post-doctoral programs and to make available to students an informational analysis of graduates in emerging roles. Such a longitudinal database would be invaluable in terms of describing the career lifecycle.

The Specialization of the Psychology Profession

In 1947, when the American Board of Professional Psychology (ABPP), a national, independent board certification credentialing body, was incorporated, American psychology recognized three specialty areas of psychology. Psychologists voluntarily applied to meet the training and examination criteria for one of three specialties: clinical, counseling, or industrial-organizational psychology. Although individuals and groups began to petition the ABPP to consider other specialty areas almost immediately, it was not until 1968 that a fourth specialty practice area, school psychology, was recognized (Pryzwansky, 1998)—and then not until concurrent APA accreditation of school psychology doctoral programs was approved. While groups continued to petition ABPP, the field did not take any further steps until the late 1980s. By this time, the growth in knowledge leading to subject differentiation among psychology professionals was being reflected in practice. As a result, some argued for the planful evolution of the field, while others maintained the viability of a generic, clinical (i.e., applied) professional training as either sufficient or foundational. Others point to the typology of the current model of specialties recognized within ABPP board certification as the direction for professional psychology (Weins, 1993). Terms such as *fields, generic specialties* (e.g., clinical, counseling, industrial-organizational, and school psychology), *specialties, special proficiencies,* and *practice competencies* began to emerge. Fundamentally, the research and subject areas were expanding, and that phenomenon was reflected in practice.

Thus, in the 1980s the APA established several task forces to address the issues involved in recognition of specialties and to propose criteria and a plan for such recognition. At that time, ABPP had viable petitions from groups where training programs and practitioners existed in sufficient numbers to warrant consideration of board certification if a credentialing system were in place for those specialties. Consequently, adopting the criteria and model that evolved from the APA task forces, ABPP recognized two additional psychology specialties in 1985 (Pryzwansky, 1998). These were clinical neuropsychology and forensic psychology. Subsequently, ABPP has recognized five additional specialties: behavioral, health, psychoanalysis, family, and rehabilitation psychology for board certification with group psychology currently in the final stage of recognition. Finally, in 1995 APA established the Commission for the Recognition of Specialties and Proficiencies in Psychology (CRSPP). While ABPP retains the authority to recognize specialties seeking to offer board certification, it has placed a moratorium on recognition per se and advises groups to pursue CRSPP recognition initially. Within the CRSPP framework, *specialty* status is granted to those areas of professional psychology that demonstrate distinctiveness with respect to the population they serve, the problems they address, and the techniques or methodologies they employ. In essence, the CRSPP criteria and procedures build on the APA task forces and ABPP materials. Proficiencies are considered to be circumscribed aspects of practice that focus on a particular problem, patient population, or treatment procedure. Taken together with specialties, designation of specialty and proficiency informs the public about the nature and scope of services that psychologists provide as well as the knowledge base they have.

APA has recognized the following *specialties* based on CRSPP recommendations: clinical, counseling, industrial-organizational, school, clinical child, clinical health, clinical neuropsychology, and psychoanalytic psychology. In addition, APA has recognized the following four proficiencies: treatment of alcohol and other psychoactive substance abuse disorders; biofeedback; applied psychophysiology; and geropsychology.

It is important to recognize that psychologists in various specialties share a common core of training and as a result have overlapping skills and functions. In some instances, the specialties of clinical, counseling, and school psychology will be considered foundational training for a specialty that is defined only at the postdoctoral level, where students undertake in-depth training in a specialty, pursue training in a subspecialty area of practice, or emphasize in-depth training in service to a particular population or with a particular intervention strategy. Not surprisingly, some specialties share proficiencies.

Chapter 2

Careers in Applied Psychology and Allied Helping Professions

Most students who decide to major in psychology want to be of service to people, and, although psychology as an undergraduate major provides the foundation for study in other areas, such as law, business, medicine, education, or law enforcement, entry into the helping professions (i.e., professions where direct service to clients is the primary role) requires at least a master's degree.

The purpose of this chapter is to provide an overview of graduate-level careers in psychology and the allied professions. For some students the allied professions provide viable career options to the traditional psychology programs where an undergraduate psychology degree is necessary, such as clinical and counseling psychology, and also serve, albeit indirectly, as an introduction to the considerable variety of helping professionals in the community.

The chapter begins with an overview of the process of applying to graduate psychology programs. Then we describe applied areas of specialization in psychology as defined by the American Psychological Association (APA), including the specialties of clinical psychology, counseling psychology, neuropsychology, industrial/organizational psychology, psychoanalytic psychology, and school psychology. In addition, a number of proficiency areas are discussed. Finally, allied areas that also offer opportunities for state licensure and employment as a helping professional, including counseling and social work, are reviewed.

GRADUATE STUDY

The undergraduate bachelor's degree, a liberal arts degree, is intended to provide for the development of the knowledge base or skills to become a helping professional. Some undergraduate programs have specific areas or tracks to help students prepare for graduate study, and most provide a broad foundation of psychological knowledge. Often, psychology can be combined with other programs, such as business, which enhances employment options after graduation. Undergraduate students need to anticipate further graduate study and position themselves to continue their academic career. They should:

1. Make certain that they have a high grade point average (GPA). A GPA of at least 3.5 on a 4-point system is needed for the more competitive clinical and counseling psychology programs, and 3.0 for school psychology, counseling, and social work programs. Graduate programs are especially interested in the GPA over the last two years in psychology-related courses.

2. Have a high score on the Graduate Record Exam (GRE) or the Miller Analogies Test (MAT), depending on the program requirement. Some programs require only the General Aptitude Section (Verbal, Quantitative, Analytical); however, most psychology departments also want a psychology specialty score. Preparation for the examination is essential. Take a study course or purchase self-study booklets and take the practice examinations. For the GRE psychology subject section, thoroughly study an introductory text, a history and systems text, and texts from any major areas in which you have not taken courses (e.g., perception, development). The examination should be taken in the fall of the year before you wish to begin graduate study. The test can be taken by paper and pencil (offered infrequently; six- to eight-week wait for results) or by computer (offered as often as once a month at authorized facilities; results within ten days; current version does not allow for returning to items once answered). Information on these tests is available at most college student services offices or from the Educational Testing Service, Princeton, NJ 08540 for the GRE, and the Psychological Corporation, 555 Academic Court, San Antonio, TX 78204 for the MAT.

3. Develop relationships with professors who will be able to give positive recommendations for graduate study. Volunteering to assist with projects is a good way to learn about research methodology while getting to know the professors. Students who assist with specific research projects usually find the professor is able to write more meaningful letters of recommendation than when they only take one or two of the professor's classes.

4. Get involved in honor societies such as Psi Chi (psychology). This organization provides programs for students and faculty and is a source of professional and social contacts. It should be emphasized that, while doctoral programs have very high admission standards, students with lower GPAs or

GREs can find graduate programs if they are willing to explore options other than clinical or counseling psychology programs.

Upon graduation, working in an entry-level position in a helping role, such as a case manager in a community mental health center, provides valuable experience. Such job-related experiences enhance an application for a master's program; indeed, graduate programs prefer students with some work experience in addition to their undergraduate degree.

APA-accredited programs leading to a doctoral degree usually take students after the bachelor's degree. These programs take five years, which includes a yearlong internship at an APA-approved site, as well as in most instances a master's thesis and a doctoral dissertation. Coursework includes basic foundation courses in physiological, developmental, cognitive, and social psychology, as well as courses in experimental design and statistics. In the second year, students take various applied courses in testing and measurement, psychological assessment, psychotherapy, and advanced seminars. After the completion of coursework students are typically required to take comprehensive written examinations over several days' time.

In addition, there are professional master's degree programs that lead to licensure or certification. They may be offered within professional schools, psychology departments, or departments of education. Although the APA accredits doctoral-level programs, accreditation by the Council for Accreditation of Counseling and Related Educational Programs (CACREP) or the National Association of School Psychologists (NASP), among others, assures a high quality nondoctoral program that meets external standards. Counseling, social work, and school psychology programs take typically two years to complete. They emphasize applied courses and internship experiences and provide career opportunities at the master's or educational specialist level for students who do not wish to pursue a doctoral degree. Professionals with these degrees perform many of the same tasks as doctoral-level psychologists. Students might also become licensed as professional counselors or marriage and family counselors or become certified as school psychologists and work independently in schools, private practice, or mental health agencies. The academic requirements for these licenses include master's degrees in a variety of fields, including clinical or counseling psychology, school psychology, counselor education (e.g., community, mental health, school counseling), rehabilitation counseling, and social work. After completing the master's degree, students will have opportunities to pursue the doctoral degree at a later time, although they need to be aware that many doctoral programs look more favorably on master's degree programs that require a master's thesis rather than a project or comprehensive examination.

Ultimately, however, the decision will have to be made whether to pursue graduate study in order to be able to perform many of the activities that are the most interesting and rewarding, such as assessment, consultation, and psychotherapy, in a setting that affords autonomy and independence. Psychology has defined itself as a doctoral-level profession; therefore, graduate study is essential in order to receive licensure and entry-level professional positions. The APA and state licensing laws maintain that the title "psychologist" be reserved for doctoral-level individuals. The doctoral degree in psychology applicable to applied psychology may be a Ph.D. in clinical counseling or school psychology, an Ed.D. in school or counseling psychology, or a Psy.D. in one of these areas from a professional school of psychology. Entrance into programs that are accredited by the APA is often extremely competitive, usually requiring very high GPAs, GREs greater than 1200, plus excellent letters of recommendation. Thus, gaining entrance into graduate school can be quite difficult. In some areas of study, the number of applicants far exceeds the positions available. Clinical psychology programs, for example, accept only about 10% of their applicants, and some of the smaller programs as few as 2% of their applicants. As a result, many students apply to a large number of programs in order to enhance their probability of acceptance. There are other areas of psychology and the allied professions that may have fewer applicants, but these, too, require a strong undergraduate record.

Graduate study is usually more interesting and demanding than undergraduate degree programs. On the one hand, the course content is highly relevant to one's career decision and there is less emphasis on rote memorization; on the other, greater self-motivation, higher scholastic expectations, and a greater workload, which requires conceptual integration and writing skills, are standard in graduate programs. The average length for a master's program is two years (longer if you are in a part-time program), while doctoral programs are usually four or five years in length. Graduate school can be very stimulating if you are bright and inquisitive and have a strong desire to help people. As a career, psychology can be rewarding and may produce a comfortable income. In 1994, Wiggins indicated that the average beginning salary for a doctoral-level psychology graduate was between $28,000 and $55,000, depending on the area of training and specialization. These figures have most likely increased since then.

The APA has an excellent publication, *Graduate Study in Psychology*, which is updated annually and is quite helpful regarding application procedures and information about specific programs. Deciding upon a career choice should be made after careful consideration and investigation. An important first step is to carefully examine your motives for entering the field and look at your particular interests and experience. Do you want to work with people? Are you more interested in children or adults? What aspects of your undergraduate work did you find particularly stimulating? What kind of people and situations have provided you with the most satisfaction? What are your strengths, limitations, and growth potential? (Remember, some of us are "late bloomers"!) After careful self-examination, look for career specialties that match your interests and abilities. Talk to faculty and psychologists. Sternberg (1997) has written an excellent book published by the APA about career opportunities that have developed as a result of psychology's diversification the past 20 years.*

The next step is to explore specific programs with regard to the specialty you want to emphasize. It is extremely difficult to switch graduate study from one institution to another. Therefore, it is important that the program has a specialization that is consistent with your goals. At the same time, it is helpful to learn about the emphases of the faculty and the program and what the program is looking for in a student. Here the program itself is the best source of information. Most programs have a brochure that describes the program philosophy and objectives, as well as admission procedures. The better the "fit" of the student with the program, the more likely admission will be gained and the higher the satisfaction with the graduate school experience.

When applying to programs, be realistic about your chances for acceptance. Because of the time and expense involved in the application process, apply only to programs where you meet the minimum requirements. At the same time, it is a good idea to apply to a number of schools where you would be comfortable in case your first choice results in a rejection. It is important to apply for the degree level that you ultimately wish to obtain. Many psychology doctoral programs admit only students at the bachelor's level and so having a terminal master's degree from one institution may not enhance your application for a doctoral program at another school. At other institutions doctoral study may be available after completion of the master's degree. The decision to pursue a master's versus the doctoral degree is best made as early as possible to avoid the frustration of having to repeat coursework.

Applications

Admission deadlines for the fall semester are usually in early January. We advise writing to programs requesting information and application materials one full

*Sternberg, R. (Ed.). (1997). *Career paths in psychology: Where your degree can take you.* Washington, DC: American Psychological Association. This book includes chapters on 14 different graduate-level careers in psychology, each written by a distinguished professional from that area. Important aspects of each career area are presented, as well as the variety of settings and organizations that cut across all the areas.

year before you intend to begin study. The APA *Graduate Study in Psychology* (p. xi) has developed an excellent set of recommendations regarding the application itself:

- File all applications on time. Late or incomplete applications will not be considered.
- Submit all applications neatly typed. Messy, unprofessional-looking applications are likely to give members of the admissions committee negative impressions about you.
- If you are asked to prepare a biographical statement or to write an essay, take this assignment seriously. Write it carefully, prepare drafts, ask your faculty advisor and friends for their comments, and proofread it after you have typed it.
- Choose your references carefully. Letters of recommendation are important and will do you the most good if they are written by psychologists who know you and think highly of you.
- Be courteous to your references. Ask them in advance if you may use their names as references on your application. Furnish them with a copy of your biographical statement and with honest information about your overall GPA and psychology GPA. Tell them about your career plans, your previous experiences, and your work history; in short, tell them anything that might be useful to them in writing about you. Remember many reference writers are busy and may not have time to write your letter for several weeks; don't ask them at the last minute. Be sure to provide references with the appropriate recommendation form used by the graduate program. Include envelopes that you have stamped and addressed to the program to help ensure that the letters will reach the appropriate destination.

Increasingly, programs are asking students to travel to the campus for a personal interview as part of the selection process. Doctoral programs in clinical, counseling, and school psychology are the most likely to request personal interviews. Students are expected to pay for their own travel and lodging costs. Some programs allow for telephone interviews when it is prohibitive for the student to come to the university. Each program has different policies relative to the interview process.

Financial aid is often available in the form of graduate research or teaching assistantships, which provide free tuition, and a stipend for 20 hours per week of assisting with research projects or teaching undergraduate classes. Other financial assistance includes Perkins Loans (formerly National Direct Student Loans), Stafford Loans, or supplemental loans. Clinical psychology students are also eligible for Health Education Assistance Loans (HEALs). In addition, many universities have graduate scholarship programs that provide assistance with tuition costs. Contact the university student loan office as well as the department regarding financial aid opportunities.

Most psychology programs have established April 15 as the deadline for allowing students to make a decision regarding acceptance and financial aid for the fall semester. Students need to be aware that this deadline is firm; although they can decline or change their mind prior to April 15, after that date they have made a commitment.

An important step in the decision-making process relative to graduate school involves what area of specialization is most appealing This decision will ultimately determine which graduate programs are most appropriate for a particular student. Below are adaptations from the archival descriptions of the areas of specialization recognized by the APA.

AREAS OF SPECIALIZATION
Archival Description of Clinical Psychology

Clinical psychology is a general practice and health service provider specialty in professional psychology. Clinical psychologists assess, diagnose, predict, prevent, and treat psychopathology, mental disorders, and other individual or group problems to improve behavior, adjustment, adaptation, personal effectiveness, and satisfaction. What distinguishes clinical psychology as a general practice specialty is the breadth of problems addressed and of populations served. In research, training, practice, and education, clinical psychology focuses on individual differences, abnormal behavior, mental disorders and their prevention, and lifestyle enhancement.

Parameters that Define Professional Practice in Clinical Psychology
Populations. Clinical psychology services involve the application of psychological principles to the assessment and alleviation of human problems in individuals, groups, families, and communities. Clinical psychologists focus on services to individuals of all ages and may work with a single individual or with groups or families from a variety of ethnic, cultural, and socioeconomic backgrounds who are maladjusted or suffer from mental disorders. Populations include those with medical problems and physical disabilities, as well as healthy persons who seek to prevent disorder and/or improve their adaptation, adjustment, satisfaction, and personal development.

Problems/Issues. As a general practice specialty, clinical psychology focuses on the understanding, assessment, prediction, prevention, and alleviation of problems related to social, cognitive, emotional, biological, psychological, and behavioral maladjustment; distress, disability, and mental disorder; and, therefore, of necessity, enhancement of psychological functioning and prevention of dysfunction.

Procedures. Many clinical psychologists engage in formal diagnostic assessment, administering and interpreting tests of intelligence, personality, and cognitive and neuropsychological functioning. They also interview clients relative to social, medical, and developmental histories and integrate the data in order to develop a diagnosis and establish treatment plans or make referrals to outside specialists (APA, 1998a). Assessment procedures include direct observation; milieu measures; physiological measures; analysis of archival data; structured and unstructured interviews; measures of intelligence and achievement; objective and projective personality tests; functional analysis of behavior and behavioral rating scales; tests of cognitive impairment and higher cortical functioning; and batteries of techniques consisting of one or more of the above.

Intervention procedures from a variety of theoretical orientations include group therapy, couples therapy, family therapy, and individual psychotherapy, as well as personal enhancement interventions. Clinical psychologists also develop, supervise, administer, and evaluate skills training programs, inpatient intervention programs, and community prevention and intervention programs, among others.

Consultation regarding the breadth of problems addressed is provided to industry, nursing homes, legal systems, healthcare professionals, educational personnel, social service agencies, public policy makers, rehabilitation centers, and other institutions.

Supervision is provided to psychometricians, biofeedback technicians, psychological technicians, other persons who provide psychological services, healthcare professionals from other disciplines, and psychology trainees in practicum, internship, and postdoctoral settings. Clinical psychologists also supervise clinical research and perform teaching, clinical supervision, and administrative activities.

Research, a core activity of clinical psychology, includes the development and validation of assessments and interventions related to cognitive, intellectual, emotional, behavioral, physiological, interpersonal, and group functioning; basic research in prevention, personality, psychopathology, and behavior change and enhancement; program evaluation; and the review, evaluation, critique, and synthesis of research.

Knowledge Base

Preparation for entry into the specialty begins at the doctoral level and serves as a basis for advanced postdoctoral training in clinical psychology or in one or another of the advanced specialties that build on its knowledge and application bases. The substantive areas of basic psychology in which clinical psychologists must have both theoretical and scientific knowledge include the biological, social, and cognitive/affective bases of behavior and individual differences. In addition, clinical psychology focuses especially on two areas: (1) personality and its development and course and (2) psychopathology and its prevention and remediation. This emphasis includes the full span of psychopathological disorders and conditions—etiologies, environments, degrees of severity, developmental levels, and the appropriate assessments, interventions, and treatments that are associated with these conditions. Understanding of diversity, of cultural context, and of ethical principles is an integral part of the knowledge base of all aspects of clinical psychology.

Psychological assessment requires knowledge of the developmental and sociocultural normative expectations for the individual(s) assessed. The assessment of cognitive, affective, behavioral, attitudinal, and/or psychophysiological functions of individuals and groups is used to identify and measure unique characteristics that may require modification or amelioration to facilitate performance and social competence. Knowledge includes theoretical and applied principles of measurement and assessment, administration and scoring, and interpretation of results across diverse populations.

The knowledge base of interventions requires mastery of theories of psychotherapy and psychotherapeutic methods and awareness of current literature on effectiveness and emerging interventions. In addition, clinical psychology is built on knowledge of principles of behavioral change, clinical decision-making, and the professional and ethical concerns surrounding clinical practice. Clinical psychology practitioners have a knowledge base that includes both patterns of normal and deviant development across the life span and awareness of cultural characteristics relevant to the populations served.

Consultation utilizes knowledge of consultation models in clinical psychology; the theoretical and empirical bases of assessment, diagnosis, and intervention; and knowledge of the roles and functions of other professionals with whom clinical psychologists interact, such as physicians, attorneys, and educators.

Supervision requires knowledge of the empirical, clinical, and theoretical bases set forth in the rich and extensive literature on clinical supervision as a professional activity.

In order to become a clinical psychologist, one must have a Ph.D. and be licensed as a psychologist at the independent practitioner level by a state or provincial board. Licensure is necessary in order to assume the title of psychologist and establish a private practice and to be employed in medical/psychiatric hospitals or government and community agencies. Clinical psychologists are usually trained in the scientist-practitioner model, with a strong emphasis on research. Training programs are housed in departments of psychology that offer the Ph.D. (APA, 1998a).

Archival Description of Counseling Psychology

Counseling psychology is a general practice and health service provider specialty in professional psychology. It focuses on personal and interpersonal functioning across the life span and on emotional, social, vocational, educational, health-related, developmental, and organizational concerns. Counseling psychology centers on typical or normal developmental issues, as well as atypical or disordered development, from individual, family, group, systems, and organizational perspectives. Counseling psychologists help people with physical, emotional, and mental disorders improve well-being, resolve crises, and alleviate distress and maladjustment. In addition, practitioners in this professional specialty provide assessment, diagnosis, and treatment of psychopathology.

Parameters that Define Professional Practice in Counseling Psychology

Within the context of life span development, counseling psychologists focus on healthy aspects and strengths of the client (individual, couple, family, group, system, or organization), environmental/situational influences (including the context of cultural, gender, and lifestyle issues), and the role of career and vocation on individual development and functioning.

Populations. Client populations served by counseling psychologists can be organized along three dimensions: individuals, groups (including couples and families), and organizations. Counseling psychologists work with individual clients of all ages, such as: children who have behavior problems; late adolescents with educational and career concerns or substance abuse problems; adults overcoming disabilities, making career shifts, or facing marital or family difficulties; older adults dealing with retirement. They work with groups in a variety of settings toward achieving solutions to many of these problems, as well as toward enhancing personal and interpersonal functioning. Counseling psychologists also consult with organizations and work groups to help provide a work environment conducive to human functioning and to enhance the ability of organizations to increase productivity and effectiveness.

Problems. The problems addressed by the specialty of counseling psychology are varied and multifaceted and are addressed from developmental (life span), environmental, and cultural perspectives. They include, but are not limited to:

- educational and vocational career/work adjustment concerns
- vocational choice and school–work–retirement transitions
- relationship difficulties, including marital and family difficulties
- substance abuse problems
- learning and skill deficits
- stress management and coping
- organizational problems
- adaptation to physical disabilities, disease, or injury
- personal/social adjustment, personality dysfunction, and mental disorders

Knowledge Base

Building upon a core knowledge base of general psychology (i.e., the social, bio-logical, individual, and cognitive/affective bases of behavior; history and systems of psychology) common to the other applied specialties within professional psy-chology, the skillful and competent practice of counseling psychology requires knowledge of personality, psychopathology, human life span, learning (cognitive, behavioral), consultation and supervision, methods of research and evaluation, social and organizational psychology, career development and vocational behav-ior, individual and group interventions (counseling/psychotherapy), individual differences (including racial, cultural, gender, lifestyle, and economic diversity), and psychological measurement and principles of psychological/diagnostic and environmental assessment.

Procedures. The procedures and techniques used within counseling psycholo-gy include, but are not limited to: clinical supervision; crisis intervention; psy-chodiagnostic training; disaster and trauma management; test construction and validation; behavioral and psychotherapeutic interventions; individual, family, group and systemic counseling; and methodologies for quantitative and qualita-tive inquiry. Intervention techniques have as their focus change in client feel-ings, cognitions, and behavior and may be preventive, remedial, or skill-enhanc-ing. The intervention procedures range from short-term or time-specified to long-term.

Professional preparation for the specialty of counseling psychology occurs at the doctoral and postdoctoral level. Compared to clinical psychology training, counseling psychology training usually places somewhat less emphasis on formal assessment and greater emphasis on group, couple, and family therapy. Counseling psychology programs may be in departments of psychology or depart-ments of counseling, which most likely will be in schools or colleges of educa-tion. However, other alternatives to traditional university settings are schools of professional psychology, which offer a doctor of psychology degree (Psy.D.) with an emphasis on clinical theory and training. Many professional schools offer specialties in clinical and counseling psychology (APA, 1998d).

Clinical/Counseling Work Settings

Most clinical and counseling psychologists engage in independent practice, at least on a part-time basis. Independent or private practice blends several types of activities and work; however, psychotherapy is usually the major component. Psychotherapy can include individual therapy with children, adolescents, and adults, group therapy, and marital and family therapy. Psychological testing is also a major component and includes vocational tests, intelligence tests, personality inventories, and neuropsychological tests. Private practice may involve solo or group practice or independent contracting as a consultant to an organization. The solo practice is the most common for psychologists, although with the advent of managed care there is greater movement toward group practice with other professionals such as psychiatrists and social workers, in HMO-type settings. Independent contracts may be with a business, hospital, nursing home, community mental health center, etc.

This means that psychologists need to have, in addition to their clinical abilities, business skills in relation to marketing and managing the complexities of a private practice. This includes office rental, staff employment, payroll and taxes, collections, billing insurance and clients, and budgeting additional office expenses. Insurance billing alone becomes problematic, since literally hundreds of different plans exist with varying requirements for precertification for initial sessions and continuation of treatment. This can mean extensive time spent providing written documentation or in telephone conversations with insurance company reviewers.

The complexities of private practice can be overwhelming for beginning psychologists; yet the level of prestige, independence, and income potential is relatively high, which makes private practice a goal of many psychologists. Glidewell and Livert (1992) report that psychologists in private practice are emotionally better off than psychologists who work in clinics, hospitals, and mental health centers. Boice and Myers (1987) indicate that, in comparison to psychologists in academic settings, those in private practice have significantly less job-related stress and fewer health and mental health concerns. There is greater professional autonomy and variety, with the independence to develop interests, specialties, and one's personal schedule. Private practitioners have greater income potential than psychologists who work in hospitals, universities, or mental health centers. The major problems seem to be time pressures and isolation. Professional self-doubt, maintaining the therapeutic relationship, and scheduling hours around client availability seem to be the heaviest stressors. Hellman, Morrison, and Abrahamowitz (1987) reported that psychologists having moderate caseloads, in contrast to either light or heavy caseloads, had the least stress.

It does need to be noted, however, that managed care has had a significant impact on earnings of psychologists in general and beginning practitioners in particular. Not only is reimbursement for services lower than ten years ago, but beginning practitioners must also consider strategies to become members of provider panels and develop referral sources. For entry-level psychologists developing a private practice has become more difficult. Often psychologists need to consult or contract on a fee-per-service basis to an organization while they develop their practice.

Other employment settings, on a full-time or part-time basis, include hospitals, nursing homes, health maintenance organizations, and medical and community mental health clinics. Employment settings also include schools, private industry, government agencies, and university counseling and health centers. Contract work for providing training, consulting, or direct services is also available in the above settings.

Clinical and counseling psychologists may teach full-time or part-time in a university setting. Full-time academic positions involve securing a tenure track position at a university, beginning as an assistant professor, with promotion to associate professor with tenure in four to seven years, and full professor in another five to eight years. Academic positions provide flexibility and independence as well as a great deal of job security once one has tenure. Expectations relative to research, teaching, and professional service determine advancement. Research requirements for promotion and tenure vary from institution to institution. In clinical training programs, teaching will mainly be at the graduate level, with strong clinical research expectations, while at four-year colleges undergraduate teaching and public service are emphasized. Applicants need to be clear about the institutional expectations when they accept a position and understand that their publication record will be crucial in determining their academic mobility and marketability. In academic settings one may also have the opportunity to assume administrative duties, such as department chair, associate dean, or dean of the college, or provost or vice president of the institution. Most professors' salaries are paid on a nine- to ten-month basis, and currently starting salaries for assistant professors are in the $35,000 to $40,000 range. Full professors are generally paid between $60,000 to $100,000, even more in rare instances, depending on the institution. Base salaries are usually supplemented by summer grants, summer teaching, book royalties, outside consulting, and part-time private practice.

Academic positions can vary considerably, since positions are available for clinical/counseling psychologists in programs other than APA-accredited psychology programs. Some may teach in other departments in the university (e.g., counseling, educational psychology, human resources, child and family studies); some are administrators of specific programs (e.g., advising, student affairs). They may also be employed in university counseling centers.

University health clinics and counseling centers have mental health staff who provide services to students in distress. Many students are dealing with developmental issues (separation from family, identity and intimacy issues, etc.), as well as relationship problems. More serious problems relative to depression and eating disorders may be dealt with in short- or perhaps long-term therapy. Individual and group therapy are the most commonly provided services. Career counseling is also provided. Outreach programs to students on campus might include alcohol and substance abuse prevention and crisis intervention in cases of student violence, suicide, or death. The work in counseling centers is varied, since students present a wide range of problems and cultural and ethnic backgrounds.

Community mental health centers employ psychologists on a full- or part-time basis. Psychologists may provide direct services to clients, program assessment and evaluation, and increasingly, supervision of master's-level clinicians. The centers usually deal with a wide variety of severe psychological disorders and provide a variety of programs for specific populations, such as, for example, sexual offenders. The variety of problems, age groups, and types of programs allows clinicians to specialize in a number of different areas. Some mental health centers provide services only to the severely mentally ill or to adolescents and children. They often serve poor, minority, and other clients who are not able to access private practitioners. Since they rely on local and state funding, pay is low and may be uncertain.

Archival Description of Clinical Health Psychology

Clinical health psychologists apply scientific knowledge of the interrelationships among social, cognitive, behavioral, emotional, and biological components in health and disease to the promotion and maintenance of health; the treatment, prevention, and rehabilitation of illness and disability; and the improvement of the health care system. The distinct focus of clinical health psychology is on physical health problems. The specialty is dedicated to the development of knowledge regarding the interface between behavior and health and to the delivery of high-quality services based on that knowledge to individuals, families, and healthcare systems.

Parameters that Define Professional Practice
in Clinical Health Psychology

Clinical health psychologists adhere to the biopsychosocial model and work in a broad range of healthcare settings with other healthcare providers.

Populations. The client populations served by health psychologists are defined by physical symptoms or physical illness experienced by persons of all ages. Populations include, but are not limited to, persons with pain, stroke, asthma, headache, cancer, pregnancy, infertility, arthritis, injury, diabetes, obesity, hypertension, hemophilia, organ failure, Raynaud's disease, dental disease, osteoporosis, physical disability, premenstrual syndrome, terminal illness, sickle cell disease, cardiovascular disease, irritable bowel syndrome, acquired immune deficiency syndrome, as well as those individuals at risk for these problems and those who desire to develop/maintain a healthy lifestyle. Patients, family members, and healthcare providers are also recipients of clinical health psychology services.

Problems/Issues. Problems addressed by the specialty of clinical health psychology include, but are not limited to:

1. psychological conditions secondary to diseases/injury/disability (e.g., depression following myocardial infarction, family issues in chronic illness or death, body-image concerns secondary to burns, surgery, amputation)
2. somatic presentations of psychological dysfunction (e.g., somatization disorders, chest pain in panic attack)
3. psychophysiological disorders (e.g., tension and migraine headache, irritable bowel syndrome)
4. physical symptoms/conditions responsive to behavioral interventions (e.g., vasospasms, anticipatory nausea, urinary and fecal incontinence)
5. somatic complications associated with behavioral factors (e.g., mismanagement of diabetes, noncompliance with medical regimens)
6. psychological presentation of organic disease (e.g., steroid-induced psychosis, hypothyroidism presenting as depression)
7. psychological and behavioral aspects of stressful medical procedures (e.g., pain, lumbar puncture, wound debridement, cardiac catheterization)
8. behavioral risk factors for disease/injury/disability (e.g., smoking, risk-taking, weight gain/loss, substance abuse)
9. problems of healthcare providers and healthcare systems (e.g., physician-patient relationships, staff burnout, care delivery systems)
10. advisability of learning to develop and maintain healthy lifestyles

Some psychologists specialize in wellness issues. Emphasis on lifestyle changes and general wellness issues involves a holistic view of mind-body interactions and personal growth. Meditation, stress reduction, diet and exercise, and self-exploration are positive steps clients can take to improve their personal health.

Procedures. Practitioners have in-depth expertise in assessment, intervention, and consultation, as they relate to this specialty, as well as skills in interdisciplinary collaboration with other healthcare providers. A broad array of specialized procedures exist, including, for example, family therapy, group therapy, biofeedback, relaxation training, staff consultation, counseling for health promotion, Sickness Impact Profile, Family Environment Scale, Type A Structured Interview, Multidimensional Pain Inventory, Millon Behavioral Health Inventory, Psychosocial Adjustment to Illness Scale, quality of life measures, psychophysiological monitoring, skills training to promote adaptive coping, crisis intervention at the time of diagnosis/change in health status, cognitive behavioral therapies for pain, headache, improving compliance, and preparing for stressful medical procedures. Practitioners are also skilled in working in a broad array of healthcare settings with other healthcare disciplines.

Knowledge Base

Clinical health psychology has extensive intradisciplinary as well as interdisciplinary foundations in the health sciences. The specialty integrates knowledge of social, cognitive, affective, biological, and psychological aspects of health and disease with that of behavior. Health psychologists maintain a broad understanding of anatomy, biology, pharmacology, psychoneuroimmunology, and human physiology and pathophysiology. They also understand how learning, memory, perception, cognition, and motivation influence health behaviors, as well as how they are both affected by and can affect response to physical illness/injury/disability. Knowledge of the impact of culture, social support, health policy, physician-patient relationships, and the organization of healthcare delivery systems on health and help-seeking is also fundamental, as is knowledge of diversity and minority health issues, individual differences in coping, emotional and behavioral risk factors for disease/injury/disability, human development issues in health and illness, and the impact of psychopathology on disease, injury, disability, and treatment. The health psychologists also have special expertise in health research methods and awareness of the distinctive ethical and legal issues associated with their practice. Education and training for clinical health psychology has been addressed in the 1983 Working Conference on Education and Training in Health Psychology (Stone, 1983). Students interested in health psychology should consult *Doctoral Programs in Health Psychology* published by the Division of Health Psychology (Division 38) of the APA. This guide lists programs and their areas of specialty. Practitioners can be board-certified in health psychology by the American Board of Health Psychology, an affiliated board of the American Board of Professional Psychology (APA, 1998b).

Work Settings in Health Psychology

Training for health psychology takes place in healthcare facilities, including hospitals and medical treatment facilities, where psychologists work in the field of behavioral medicine, often with clients exhibiting physical pain, chronic illness, and psychological reactions to illness and suffering. Currently there are approximately 50 clinical internship sites in the United States and Canada that offer specialized training in health psychology. A list of these programs is available from the Division of Health Psychology of the APA (Division 38). Interest in health psychology has grown considerably over the past 15 years and is related to the interest in wellness and the psychological relationships to illness and injury. Increasingly, psychologists have moved into positions in hospitals and other medical facilities, and, at the same time, there has been a strong movement within the profession to secure hospital privileges for psychologists.

Archival Description of Clinical Neuropsychology

Clinical neuropsychology combines principles of assessment and intervention based upon the scientific study of human behavior as it relates to normal and abnormal functioning of the central nervous system. The specialty is dedicated to enhancing the understanding of brain-behavior relationships and the application of such knowledge to human problems.

Parameters that Define Professional Practice in Clinical Neuropsychology

Clinical neuropsychology has extensive intra- and as interdisciplinary foundations and is characterized by activities in a number of scientific and professional domains. The practice of clinical neuropsychology addresses psychological or behavioral manifestations of neurochemical, neurological, neuropathological, and pathophysiological changes in brain disease and the full range of aberrations in the central nervous system that may arise during development.

The three primary developmental domains include basic experimental research in physiological and cognitive psychology, the development of quantitative and qualitative neuropsychological principles and procedures for clinical practice, and the syndromal analysis of the behavioral consequences of central nervous system lesions. The specialty's growth has been influenced by the introduction of formalized procedures for accrediting educational programs and individual competencies.

Populations. Clinical neuropsychologists serve adults with such neurological disorders as neoplasms, head trauma, degenerative diseases, cerebrovascular accidents, infectious and inflammatory diseases, demyelinating disease, and various forms of dementing illness. Psychiatric patients include those with somatoform disorders of pseudoneurologic character; depression as a component of, or to be differentiated from, dementia; psychosis as a pseudodementing disorder and as a differential diagnostic entity to be distinguished from behavioral disturbances in selected neurological populations such as partial complex seizure disorders.

General medical and surgical populations include candidates for kidney transplant or dialysis; candidates for cardiac surgery, including transplants; chronic pain patients with a neurological versus functional basis; and older individuals who may have some neuropsychological deficits associated with an early dementing illness that may complicate medical or surgical management.

Children with learning disabilities of developmental or organic basis are referred from pediatricians, pediatric neurologists, and the schools. Recently there has been a marked expansion of practice in the areas of neuropsychological evaluation and treatment of all types of pediatric neurological patients.

In addition, patients who are chemically dependent (especially polydrug users and alcoholics), AIDS dementia cases, and victims of environmental toxin exposures constitute a growing referral base.

Problems. Clinical neuropsychologists function primarily on referrals from health, education, and legal professionals; agencies and institutions; and in response to needs of other service systems (e.g., courts, schools, military installations, chemical treatment facilities, and extended rehabilitation and general care facilities). Primary employment settings are estimated to be almost equally divided between hospital-medical centers, private practice, and a combination of (salaried) hospital or clinic-based employment and private practice.

Referrals can be for assessment or intervention. Neuropsychological assessment typically includes, but is not limited to, the following: differential diagnoses between psychogenic and neurogenic syndromes and between two or more suspected etiologies of cerebral dysfunction; evaluating spared and impaired functions secondary to a cerebral cortical or subcortical event; establishing neurobehavioral baseline measures for monitoring progressive cerebral disease or recovery; comparing the efficacy of pre- and postpharmacologic, surgical, or behavioral interventions. Interventions include designing procedures for utilizing available functions to compensate for impaired functions; retraining of the impaired function to a higher level of adaptive effectiveness; environmental (ecological) manipulation to enhance adaptive effectiveness; and formulating rehabilitation strategies.

Procedures. Clinical neuropsychological services include neuropsychological assessment, cognitive remediation and intervention, agency and institutional consultation, education and counseling for individuals and families, and selected psychotherapies or behavior therapies as appropriate for neurologically involved individuals.

Knowledge Base

Differentiation of clinical neuropsychology from other psychological specialties is reflected in the distinction between generic and specialized competencies. Generic applied competency requires a foundation in psychological science with a predominantly clinical emphasis, although such training may be obtained through other generic avenues if a clinical internship is included. Over the past few decades, the roles of clinical, counseling, and school psychologists have converged so that there is a substantial overlap in generic applied knowledge and competency attained in related programs at the predoctoral and internship levels. Clinical neuropsychology involves the building of specialized competencies upon the generic applied knowledge and competency base obtained in a generic applied predoctoral program of a health-related nature.

The generic knowledge base for clinical neuropsychology includes general consultation skills; the structure and process of interviewing; intellectual, aptitude, interest, and personality measurement; selected psychotherapy and counseling interventions; and a consumer-patient education orientation, including ethics. Specialized competence includes effectiveness in comprehensive history-taking; identification of neurobehavioral problems/issues to be addressed; application of a wide range of neuropsychological assessment procedures to multiple populations; test construction and validation; remedial and supportive intervention design and implementation; individual and agency consultation; and consumer education/ethics, specifically in a neuropsychological context. Such specialized competency is achieved by means of sets of skills anchored to the above parameters of practice in the settings outlined above. While there is overlap with the other health-related specialties in terms of generic applied competence, there is the elaboration, extension, and refinement of neurobehavioral applications, which involve additional foundations in experimental, cognitive, and physiological psychology, as well as in the clinical neurosciences. Such extensions of knowledge and application are obtained by specialty track programs at the predoctoral and internship levels and/or by postdoctoral preparation in a specialized clinical neuropsychology program (APA, 1998c).

Archival Description of Industrial and Organizational Psychology

Industrial and organizational (I/O) psychology is a general practice specialty of professional psychology with a focus on scientifically-based solutions to human problems in work and other organizational settings. In these contexts, I/O psychologists assess and enhance the effectiveness of individuals, groups, and organizations.

Parameters that Define Professional Practice in I/O Psychology

Whether serving as consultants to organizations or employees, I/O psychologists provide a range of psychological services, including: job and task analyses; leadership and team development; management consultation and coaching; human resources planning and policy analyses; design and evaluation of organizational development and intervention strategies; development and validation of personnel selection, job classification, training, and employee and career development policies and procedures; analyses of employee morale and job satisfaction, organizational climate, productivity, job performance, and appraisal systems, and personnel turnover.

Populations. I/O psychological services are provided to and within a broad range of organizations in the public and private sector, such as health, labor, research, business, education, government, community, and industry. I/O psychologists also provide services as experts to legal and quasi-legal bodies in regard to the application of psychological principles and science to the workplace.

Problems. I/O psychologists recognize the interdependence of individuals, organizations, and society, as well as the impact that factors such as national and international law and government regulations, organized labor, consumer awareness, skill shortages, and the changing nature of the workforce have on work-related organizations. Specific examples of problems addressed by I/O psychologists in this context are (the list is illustrative rather than exhaustive): organizational restructuring; workplace stress and safety; employee motivation and performance; adaptation to job redesign or expansion, employee turnover, absenteeism, and productivity; adaptations to organizational changes and technology; adverse impact of selection or promotion; and succession planning and development of managers and executives.

Procedures. Research methods are an integral part of the I/O psychologist's practice, providing the foundation for problem definition, analysis, and solution in organizations. Some of the procedures and techniques common to the practice of I/O psychology are:

- *Assessment:* analyzing job content; assessing consumer preferences and reactions; measuring organizational structure, climate, productivity; validating measures and tests used for employee selection, promotion, classification, evaluation, and identification of management potential
- *Intervention:* developing compensation systems; conducting executive/employee development efforts; designing performance appraisal systems and work environments; formulating and implementing training and development programs; and integrating human resource function with overall business mission and strategy
- *Consultation:* conducting process consultation, needs analysis, and management consultation and coaching; maximizing organizational policies and procedures; and providing expert testimony or review of human resource systems and policies
- *Evaluation:* determining utility and effectiveness of human resource policies and procedures; evaluating organizational interventions, training and development, selection and compensation systems; evaluating and optimizing person-job effectiveness; and job and task analysis

Knowledge Base

Education and training in I/O psychology are typically offered and completed at the doctoral level. The requisite education and training are rooted in the foundations of psychological science, which include (a) biological bases of behavior, (b) cognitive-affective bases of behavior, (c) social bases of behavior, and (d) individual differences. A strong foundation in research methods, psychological and behavioral measurement, and advanced statistical theory and methods is also required.

In addition to core knowledge and skills, advanced specialty education and training are required in the following competency areas: career development; consumer behavior; consulting and business skills; attitude theory, measurement, and change; job and task analysis and classification; individual, group, and organizational assessment methods; leadership and management theory and evaluation; theory of organizations and organizational development; training theory, program design, and evaluation; job evaluation, performance appraisal and feedback, work motivation and compensation; ethical, legal, and other professional issues in the practice of I/O psychology; and effects of health and work stress in organizations and of human factors and performance in work.

In addition to the psychological science foundations on which these core and advanced areas of competency are based, the knowledge base of I/O psychology is also influenced by the evolving knowledge bases in other disciplines, such as law, business, ergonomics, physiology and medicine, and labor and industrial relations. Inasmuch as a substantial degree of I/O psychology practice in organizations involves negotiated union contracts, federal, state, or local law and regulations, and ethical issues raised by the nature of consultative services with organizations, knowledge of these issues is also essential to effective practice in this specialty.

The I/O psychologist has completed a doctoral program with an emphasis in I/O psychology. He or she often works in a management consulting firm or independent consulting practice; in a university, teaching and doing research; or in a combination of such settings. Licensure by a state board of psychology differs from state to state; however, licensure is most likely required for work in an independent consulting practice. Bachelor's-level positions are available in human resource departments, and master's-level positions are sometimes available in research and grant projects in local and state agencies or in smaller business firms. These positions mainly involve the integration of psychological theory and techniques to improve job satisfaction and productivity in business and industry (APA, 1998e).

Income is highest for I/O psychologists who are employed by insurance and financial institutions. Consulting firms also pay at a high rate. Academic institutions and governmental agencies pay less well. Generally, I/O psychologists have a higher rate of income than clinical/counseling psychologists. The employment outlook is quite good, especially when the psychologist has particularly strong quantitative research skills. Advancement is attainable in most settings. Primary employment is in universities (33%), followed by business and industry (20%), management consulting firms (17%), and independent consulting practices (10%). The remainder work in federal government positions or in health organizations.

Archival Description of Psychoanalytic Psychology

Psychoanalytic psychology is a specialty of professional psychology distinguished by its body of knowledge and methods of treatment. Its theories of personality cover social behavior, human development, abnormal and normal behavior, and even artistic functioning. Cognitive processes, affective reactions, and both conscious and unconscious processes are part of its purview. One of its most noteworthy and historically distinctive features is its focus on implementing long-term, intensive, psychotherapeutic activity, employing such interventions as dream interpretation, attention to free association, and analysis of the therapist-patient relationship to achieve character transformation. Psychoanalytic methods have been used in group therapy, milieu therapy, short-term therapies, and marital and family therapy.

Parameters that Define Professional Practice
in Psychoanalytic Psychology

Populations. Psychoanalytic treatment began over 100 years ago with the treatment of individuals with hysterical paralysis and what we would now call dissociative disorders. It has since expanded to include a large variety of forms of individual psychopathology presented by children, adolescents, and adults. In some of its variants, it has expanded from a sole focus on the individual to the treatment of couples, families, and groups. Psychoanalytic psychology is rich in its treatments and studies of these populations. Such study is long-term, often of many years' duration, and extremely detailed. Populations of interest are not restricted to living humans; biographical analyses of historical figures and human productions, such as works of art and literature, have also been subject to psychoanalytic investigation.

Problems. The breadth of problems addressed by psychoanalytic psychology matches the diversity of the populations it studies. While applicable to most problems of human adaptation, it is distinctive in several ways: (a) It provides a systematic explanation of unconscious processes. (b) A huge literature on attachment has grown out of psychoanalytic work on infant and child development, a literature that explores child psychopathology as well as the vicissitudes of various kinds of attachment and attunement between parents and children. In addition, patients who have entrenched character pathology or have proven resistant to alternative forms of treatment often require a more intensive form of intervention over a longer period of time. It is in the area of character pathology (such as has been found in borderline personality disorders and the other severely crippling disorders of the self) that psychoanalytic psychology has been a leader, both in theoretical writing and clinical procedures.

Procedures. In all of their manifestations, the techniques employed by psychoanalytic psychologists deal with the dynamic unconscious, transference, and their relationship to psychological functioning. The applications range broadly, depending on patient characteristics, characterological issues, and type of population. Some intervention techniques employed include: use of empathy, play therapy, dream analysis, free association, attention to the patient/psychologist relationship and its disturbances, and investigation of significant present and past relationships.

Knowledge Base

Specialist training in psychoanalytic psychology is entered only postdoctorally. Such training is intensive, comprehensive, and quite broad, typically stretching out for several years, and is conducted in formal training institutes developed for this purpose. Courses and seminars focus on theory building in psychoanalysis and the specific content of the various psychoanalytic personality theories: traditional Freudian theory, the British school of object relations, contemporary theories of the construction of the self and its disorders, and ego psychology, which focuses on patterns of normal development. The theory and tactics of interpersonal psychoanalysis are also studied. Findings of empirical research within the specialty are studied, including its limitations and as yet unanswered questions. The techniques of intensive psychoanalysis are taught, accompanied by specialized seminars in dream interpretation, transference and countertransference, and the unique challenges posed by the disorders of the self. Special attention is paid to analytic theories of gender and sexuality.

Psychoanalytic training includes a focus on current controversies that exist in the specialty, along with completion of supervision and a personal training analysis that provides rich knowledge about the use of the psychoanalytic psychologist's self as tool in the work to be done (APA, 1998f).

Archival Description of School Psychology

School psychology is concerned with the schooling process and the science and practice of psychology with children, youth, families, and learners of all ages. School psychologists' basic education and training prepare them to provide a range of psychological assessment, prevention, intervention, health promotion, program development and evaluation services, with a special focus on the developmental processes of children and youth within the context of schools, families, and other systems.

School psychologists are prepared to intervene at the individual and system levels and to develop, implement, and evaluate preventive programs. In these efforts they conduct ecologically valid assessments and intervene to promote positive learning environments within which children and youths from diverse backgrounds have equal access to effective educational and psychological services to promote healthy development.

Parameters that Define Professional Practice in School Psychology

School psychological services are provided in a broad array of settings, such as schools, workplace, school-based and school-linked health centers, and medical, social service, or correctional facilities. School psychologists recognize schools as a crucial context for development. They know effective instructional processes and understand classroom and school environments, as well as the organization and operation of schools and agencies. They also apply principles of learning to the development of competence both within and outside school; consult with educators and other professionals regarding social, affective, cognitive, and behavioral performance; assess developmental needs and develop educational environ-ments that meet those diverse needs; coordinate educational, psychological, and behavioral health services by working at the interface of those systems; intervene to improve organizations and develop effective partnerships between parents and educators and other caretakers. An essential role of the school psychologist is synthesizing information on developmental mechanisms and contexts and trans-lating it for adults who are responsible for promoting the healthy growth and development of children and youth in a wide range of educational contexts.

Populations. Consistent with an emphasis on the development of competence, school psychologists provide services to learners of all ages and the systems and agencies that serve them and their families. Among the populations served are:

- individuals from birth to young adulthood who have mental disorders, learn-ing or behavior problems, or specific disabilities that affect learning, behav-ior, or school-to-work transitions; and those who experience chronic or acute conditions of childhood and adolescence that influence learning and mental health
- families who request diagnostic evaluations of learning disabilities and social problems and assistance with academic and behavioral problems at home and at school
- teachers, parents, and other adults who wish to enhance their ability to pro-vide healthy relationships and environments that promote learning and development
- organizations and agencies that aim to promote contexts that are conducive to learning and development

Problems. Among the problems addressed by school psychologists are:

- educational and developmental problems related to school achievement and school adjustment, social or interpersonal problems related to learning or behavior; specific disabilities and disorders that affect learning, behavior, or school-to-work adjustment; chronic or acute situations of childhood and adolescence that influence learning or mental health, such as personal or school crises or mental disorders first noticed in infancy, childhood, or ado-lescence
- adverse social conditions that threaten healthy development in school and community, such as violence, teenage pregnancy, substance abuse, and juve-nile delinquency
- problems of instructional and learning environments that affect the func-tioning of the school-age population

Procedures. In addition to those procedures typically associated with the general practice of psychology, school psychologists employ the following:

- assessment of cognitive abilities, achievement, personality, developmental status, and social and emotional functioning using interviews, observations, and performance assessments to understand learning and behavior problems
- diagnostic assessments to support eligibility for and delivery of services within statutorily regulated contexts that integrate diagnostic information from other professionals to support recommendations for educational modifications and community services
- primary prevention programs to reduce the incidence of school violence, sexual abuse, and teenage pregnancy, and to promote children's well-being through more appropriate educational and classroom accommodations; secondary prevention programs to assist students who have mild or transitory problems that interfere with school performance, such as poor peer relationships, learning or behavior problems in the classroom, and adjustment to adoption, death, or divorce
- crisis intervention services that support children following death, abuse, violence, natural disaster, or a student's suicide
- consultation with teachers, parents, and agency administrators; supervision of psychological services staff concerning children's behavior and academic and social problems; design and direction of professional development programs for teachers and comprehensive and integrated service delivery systems
- consultation with physicians and other professionals concerning the school functioning and learning of children with, for example, substance abuse, chronic illness, learning disorders, attention-deficit/hyperactivity disorder, and physical or genetic conditions
- educational evaluation services, including development of appropriate measures of child behavior in classroom contexts; analysis of academic achievement using standardized tests, performance assessment, self-reports, and other appropriate methods; evaluation of individualized educational plans; observation and measurement of teacher and parent behaviors; and evaluation of instructional and organizational environments

Knowledge Base

School psychology has evolved as a specialty area with core knowledge rooted in psychology and education. School psychologists possess advanced knowledge of theories and empirical findings in developmental and social psychology, developmental psychopathology within cultural contexts, and in the areas of learning and effective instruction, effective schools, and family and parenting processes.

School psychologists conceptualize children's development from multiple theoretical perspectives and translate current scientific findings to alleviate cognitive, behavioral, social, and emotional problems encountered in schooling.

A strong foundation in measurement theory and applications of advanced statistical methodology is required in order to design or evaluate innovative classroom programs, educational and psychological interventions, comprehensive and integrated service systems, and standardized and nonstandardized measures in emerging assessment areas for individuals from culturally or linguistically diverse backgrounds.

School psychologists are accountable for the integrity of their practice. They protect the rights of children and their families in research, intervention, and psychological assessment. Their work reflects knowledge of federal law and regulations, case law, and state statutes and regulations for schools and psychological services. They appreciate the importance of the historical influences of state, federal, community, educational, and organizational dynamics on the social, emotional, and academic functioning of children and youth in educational settings.

Professional preparation for the specialty of school psychology occurs at the doctoral level (APA, 1998g). The entry level for the school psychologist is generally completion of the master's degree with two years of graduate coursework plus an internship. The second year may lead to the Education Specialist Degree, which in many respects approaches the complexity of doctoral-level training (Cobb, 1989). Some school psychologists also hold a doctoral degree, which is usually four years or more of graduate training, including a yearlong internship. Certification is through the state department of education, which allows for employment by a local board of education. A license by a state board of psychology is required to work outside an educational setting, with only limited licenses offered in some states for nondoctoral-level psychologists.

School psychology training programs can be found in departments of psychology or in colleges of education in a variety of departments, including counseling, educational psychology, or special education. The program should meet the training standards set forth by the APA or the National Association of School Psychologists (NASP). The location of the department is usually determined by historical factors (wherever the program was initially developed in that particular university), since school psychology involves the integration of a number of different disciplines.

School psychology and clinical psychology have many commonalities. In some respects school psychology may be perceived as "clinical child psychology in the schools." The psychological assessment of children and behavioral and therapeutic interventions have evolved from clinical psychology. However, over the years, with increasing emphasis on consultation theory and practice, psychoeducational interventions, and prevention, school psychology has moved away from its clinical origins. Still, both clinical and school psychology operate from a scientist-practitioner model in training and practice.

Work Settings in School Psychology

School psychologists typically perform diagnostic evaluations of students, consultation with parents, teachers, and administrators, and individual and group therapy with children and adolescents. They work closely with intervention assistance teams in schools and design and implement behavioral and academic interventions. They might also conduct research and design programs that meet the needs of children. Consultation to school administrators and school boards is an important aspect of their duties. They also make and coordinate referrals to medical, vocational, and mental health resources, and follow up in the school setting with those children who have been referred. Conoley (1992) sees the role of the school psychologist evolving from traditional testing and placing of children into special education classrooms, to the prevention of problems for the school and community. The school psychologist provides links between the school, families, and community agencies. Increasingly, more time is spent developing and collaborating with teams of school professionals to deal with school-wide and individual problems.

Employment opportunities in school psychology are quite good and job security is very high. School psychologists often serve a number of schools, have considerable flexibility, and, with the magnitude of school and children's problems, find their creativity challenged.

Forensic Psychology

Forensic psychology involves the practice of psychology as related to law and the legal system. Forensic psychologists apply psychological principles to legal issues. Their expertise is often essential in court. Forensic psychology is an area of specialization offered in graduate programs and internship training where emphasis is on diagnosis, treatment, and court testimony regarding criminal behavior. Expert testimony is given in criminal and court cases resulting from psychological assessment of individuals regarding criminal and legal issues of insanity and competency to stand trial and assessment of dangerousness. They may consult with legal firms regarding jury selection, trial strategy, witness testimony, and preparation of cross testimony. They also may be involved in custody and disability evaluations, as well as consultation with insurance companies. Some forensic psychologists are trained in both psychology and law.

PROFICIENCY AREAS

As of 1998 the APA awards certificates of proficiency based upon successful completion of a written examination in the following areas: treatment of alcohol and other psychoactive substance abuse disorders; biofeedback; applied psychophysiology; and geropsychology. The attainment of these and other areas of proficiency are independent of the formal graduate program. These proficiencies are a mechanism for psychologists to inform consumers, referral resources, and third-party payers that they possess the knowledge and experience associated with the practice in a given area. Substance abuse treatment, as well as several additional areas of practice emphasis, such as divorce mediation, sports psychology, and sex therapy, are briefly presented in order to reflect the breadth of practice within psychology and to provide a perspective on the increasingly diverse career options in psychology.

Substance Abuse Treatment

Because of the high prevalence of addictive disorders in the general population, most psychologists deal with substance abuse disorders either in private practice or a treatment facility. Licensed psychologists do not need any additional certification to specialize in substance abuse, although training in graduate school, workshops, and supervised clinical work is required.

Clients who need detoxification are usually treated in an inpatient facility. Private practitioners conduct substance abuse screening, provide interventions, and refer clients for the appropriate level of healthcare. Clients who are stable in sobriety are good candidates for individual and family therapy; improving coping skills and relations with family members can assist in preventing relapses.

Divorce Mediation

Psychologists often work with couples and individuals going through separation and divorce. One of the goals of therapy is to assist with the emotional effects of separation and divorce. Divorce mediation is also a semiformal proceeding where property settlement, the distribution of assets, and child custody arrangements issues can be settled without the traditional adversarial process inherent in the legal system. Divorce mediation training is available through extensive workshop offerings by private institutes to psychologists who wish to include this as part of their practice.

Sports Psychology

Athletes in our culture deal with a number of developmental, emotional, and psychological stressors. Sports psychologists assist athletes in their training and competition. They are involved in working with athletes at the high school, college, and professional levels, focusing on attitudes, concentration, motivation, psychological reactions, and the stress of competition. Because there are no formal graduate training programs in sports psychology, psychologists tend to develop individualized means of securing the necessary training and experience.

Sex Therapy

Psychologists may specialize in working with couples and individuals who experience sexual difficulties related to intimacy issues or specific sexual dysfunctions, such as impotence or lack of desire. Knowledge about the physical and medication aspects of such dysfunctions is crucial and, therefore, consultation with medical professionals is an important aspect of working with these problems. Sex therapists may also work with sex offenders in regard to assessment for the courts or treatment in private practice. They may also specialize in working with married couples and/or with gay and lesbian individuals and couples. In many respects dealing with sexual issues is a subset of couple therapy.

Since graduate programs in psychology offer minimal training relative to sexual issues and dysfunctions, postgraduate training is needed. Additional certification is not required for licensed psychologist. The standards set forth for certification by the American Association of Sex Educators, Counselors, and Therapists (ASECT) are helpful in establishing credibility as a sex therapist.

RELATED ALLIED PROFESSIONS

Counseling

Historically, the counseling movement was related to vocational and career guidance. In 1913 the National Vocational Guidance Association was founded to help advance the career guidance movement. During the first half of the century, career guidance services were offered in many high schools and colleges. Since the early 1950s, however, the counseling profession has undergone major changes and shifts, from a primary concern with career guidance for adolescents and young adults to the development of effective counseling approaches and the provision of services to a wider variety of clients. The counseling process itself has also changed, and the theoretical underpinnings of counseling have been redefined. Moreover, the counseling profession has matured and, through licensure and professional association efforts, a professional identity for counselors has been defined.

The greatest influence on the counseling profession was Carl Rogers, whose client-centered approach to therapy emphasized the client-counselor relationship and influenced the profession to adopt a substantive theoretical base in the provision of services to a wider variety of clients and problems. In the 1950s, the American Personnel and Guidance Association (APGA) was founded. Since that time APGA has changed its name to American Association for Counseling and Development (AACD) and more recently to American Counseling Association (ACA).

Since the 1960s a number of innovative counseling approaches have been adopted, including behavioral counseling, gestalt therapy, rational emotive therapy, reality therapy, and others. Since the 1970s counselors have also been employed in a wide variety of work settings, including elementary schools, community mental health agencies, substance abuse treatment programs, employee assistance programs, crisis treatment centers, and private practice.

Counseling as a profession has also been active in regards to licensure; in 1998, professional counselors are licensed in 44 states. Licensure is required in order to use the title of counselor and to work in private practice. In 1981, the Council for Accreditation of Counseling and Related Educational Programs (CACREP) was established to develop criteria, evaluate, and provide accreditation for counselor education programs. Currently, about 20% of the programs meet the CACREP standards. The National Board of Certified Counselors (NBCC) was established in 1982 to certify counselors in general practice.

The majority of counselor education programs are at the master's degree level, although licensure requirements and standards set by Council for Accreditation of Counseling and Related Educational Programs (CACREP) go considerably beyond a typical master's degree program and, as such, many programs are two full years in length. While counseling can be viewed as an area of applied psychology, most programs are housed in colleges of education. Most counselor education programs have areas of specialization within the master's degree program, which might include school counseling, community counseling, employee assistance, rehabilitation counseling, and marriage and family counseling.

School Counseling

School counselors may be employed at elementary, middle, or high schools. In addition, counselors are also employed in vocational schools and colleges and universities. School counselors usually have a master's degree and are certified by a state board of education. A few states, such as Ohio, also require a certificate to teach and a specified number of years of teaching experience.

Many elementary schools employ school counselors, although in some instances counselors are assigned to more than one school, depending upon the size of the schools. They are responsible to the school principal and will often work with other specialists, such as school psychologists, school social workers, or speech therapists. They provide small group counseling and counseling services to individual students, and conduct counseling-related classroom presentations. Referrals are made by parents, principals, classroom teachers, or students themselves, and cover a wide range of problems, from hurt feelings to serious behavior problems. Crisis intervention, due to serious family problems or death of a schoolmate, friend, or family member, is an important aspect of the position. Small group counseling may deal with social or interpersonal skills or specific issues, such as divorce. Classroom presentations may involve special developmental topics, such as stress management, career awareness, or communication skills.

Consultation is an important part of the role of elementary counselors. School counselors also spend a great deal of time consulting with teachers and principals relative to problems with individual children and classroom management. They will frequently consult with parents relative to parenting issues. They will also coordinate guidance materials for classroom teachers and be responsible for group testing and other school related programs.

The functions of the school counselor working in a middle school are similar to those in an elementary school, but with a shift in emphasis. Middle school counselors who are dealing with emerging adolescent issues usually spend more time in individual and group counseling than in consultation. They need to assist students in planning their high school programs and help them see the link between the high school curriculum and various career options. They often deal with referrals regarding delinquent behavior, substance abuse, sexuality, and potential dropouts, as well as general emotional issues surrounding puberty.

All high schools employ counselors who assist with vocational and educational exploration. They are usually assigned a specific group of students for class scheduling and general advising. They must be knowledgeable about the high-school curriculum, college admissions, financial aid, scholarships, vocational training programs, and special-education placement. They also must deal with students who have personal problems, such as relationship problems with peers and parents, as well as issues of delinquency, sexuality, and substance abuse. School counselors are also assigned scheduling, administrative, and record-keeping duties, which take time away from counseling individual students.

Counselors are also employed in vocational high schools as well as post-high-school vocational programs. Their role is similar to that of high school counselors, assisting with the evaluation of students' skills and interests, the selection of appropriate programs, and, if necessary, the remediation of reading and math skills. They are also involved in developing employability skills and the placement of students and graduates in work settings. Some personal counseling is done upon request when behavior is interfering with work training.

Most colleges and universities employ master's level counselors in student-services positions, for example, housing, career placement, academic advising positions, and admissions and financial aid offices. The counselors do not do personal counseling; personal and career counseling are provided by counseling centers, which are usually staffed by doctoral level counselors or clinical psychologists, although some community colleges employ master's level counselors. Counseling centers also provide a number of programs for students, such as substance abuse, and crisis intervention services for individuals or larger groups in cases of campus-wide emotional events, such as significant death(s) or violence.

Community Counseling

Community agencies, most of which are publicly funded, provide a variety of services to a wide range of clients. The most prevalent are community mental health centers, which offer diverse programs for the seriously mentally disturbed, including residential and case management services; treatment of juvenile and adult offenders; alcohol and substance abuse treatment; job and career services; and general outpatient services for children and adults. Services will differ from agency to agency, depending on the funding source and the mission of the agency. Most agencies employ a wide variety of professionals, including counselors, psychiatrists, psychologists, and social workers, and additional support personnel such as case managers. Often a team approach is emphasized, with counselors and social workers usually providing individual, group, and family counseling, as well as educational and career counseling.

Counselors need a state license in order to practice and secure employment. Licensure usually requires a master's degree in community counseling (48 semester hours) or mental health counseling (60 semester hours), including courses in assessment, diagnosis, psychopathology, and intervention of emotional and mental disorders. There are also internship requirements, and many states require supervision for at least two years beyond the attainment of the degree prior to being licensed to function independently. Counselors graduating from CACREP accredited programs will find that most state licensing boards will automatically accept their coursework as meeting the academic requirements for licensure as a professional counselor.

Marriage and Family Counseling

Marriage and family counselors are employed in community agencies and private practice. A license is required to practice counseling or marriage and family therapy. While marriage and family therapy is employed across many disciplines, it is a recognized CACREP specialty within the counseling profession. Program approval is available through CACREP or the American Association of Marriage and Family Therapy (AAMFT). The AAMFT, founded in 1942, is the largest organization devoted to the specialty, with over 22,000 members, and has developed training and competency standards. In addition, Division 43 (Family Psychology), a division within APA, was formed in 1984 and has increasingly attracted psychologists who work with families.

While the beginnings of marriage and family counseling can be traced back to the late 1950s and 1960s, the real growth occurred in the late 1970s and 1980s. It differs from group and individual counseling in theory, technique, and clientele.

Because the family is a system over generations, myths, rules, power, sex roles, and emotional attachments have led to theories and techniques that are specific to working with couples and families. Moreover, marriage and family counseling concentrates on making changes in systems as well as individual behavior, whereas group and individual counseling focuses on inter- and intrapersonal changes. The rise in marriage and family counseling corresponds to the changes in the composition and structure of the American family and to emerging issues related to ethnicity, single parenting, remarried families, etc. In marriage and family counseling, involvement of all family members is seen as crucial, and the emphasis is on helping individuals through resolving marital and family conflicts.

Community agencies commonly deal with family problems and frequently seek to employ counselors with training in dealing with families. Counselors may also develop family enrichment programs in areas such as parenting or couple communication. The efficacy of dealing with multiple family members is appealing to cost-conscious agencies and insurance companies.

Private Practice

Counselors who wish to engage in private practice usually begin by working in a community agency and then move into private practice on a part-time basis prior to considering full-time practice. They usually affiliate with a group practice that includes a mix of psychiatrists, psychologists, and social workers; in this way they can establish a referral base while sharing expenses and learning the basics of the business end of practice. Building a private practice referral base is essential for financial success. It sometimes can be more difficult for nondoctoral level practitioners to establish themselves with insurance and health maintenance organizations (HMO) and the general public.

Employee Assistance Counseling

During the past 10 years, many companies and businesses have established employee assistance programs (EAPs), which are designed to assist employees who have mental health or career problems. Drug and substance abuse among employees is also a major concern, and the value of rehabilitation has become important to most employers, in light of the cost of training new employees.

EAP counselors generally have a master's degree in counseling; they usually work with employees on a short-term basis and then make a referral to a private practitioner or community program (e.g., substance abuse treatment). Individual problem assessment, individual counseling, developing and maintaining good referral sources, developing and offering educational programs to employees, and consultation with management regarding mental health problems are the main functions of most EAP counselors.

Rehabilitation Counseling

Rehabilitation counseling is a very specialized area of counseling. Graduate education support was established and enacted by Congress in 1954; federal funds were provided to train counselors to work in state and federal vocational rehabilitation agencies. Training today is more broad-based and less job-specific and exists at the bachelor's, master's, and doctoral levels. Bachelor level programs exist in over 40 colleges and universities throughout the United States and prepare individuals for entry-level positions in a variety of settings. These are primarily caseworker and interviewing positions in public and private agencies that are concerned with rehabilitation, job placement, and health and welfare. Bachelor programs also prepare students for graduate study in a variety of counseling programs.

Master's level training is considered to be the entry level for the rehabilitation counselor. Currently, there are over 75 master's degree programs in the United States, which range in length from one to two years. Graduates have a broad selection of agencies and client types to select from when considering employment.

Doctoral level programs were also established in the 1954 legislation and are primarily designed to prepare individuals for faculty positions at colleges and universities and administrative and research positions, as well as clinical positions in a variety of settings, such as hospitals, mental health centers, or private practice. The approximately 38 doctoral programs are housed in special education, counselor education, counseling psychology, or other departments that offer a specialization in rehabilitation counseling.

The certification board is the Commission on Rehabilitation Counselor Certification (CRCC), a division of the Bureau for Rehabilitation Certification (BRC). The CRCC is designed to assure that individuals meet the standards of educational preparation, supervised experience, and national examination. It awards several types of certification, including the certified rehabilitation counselor (CRC). Typically, at the master's level rehabilitation counselors will be licensed by the state under the counselor licensing law.

Two separate bodies accredit rehabilitation counselor education programs. The Commission on Accreditation of Rehabilitation Facilities (CARF) maintains standards to identify facilities and institutions that offer high-quality services to its clients. The Council on Rehabilitation Education (CORE) was established in 1971 to ensure quality education in rehabilitation counselor training programs. CORE reviews and provides program accreditation.

Rehabilitation counselors work with individuals who have a variety of disabilities. Such disabilities may include:

- arthritic conditions
- blindness/visual impairments
- cancer
- cardiovascular disorders
- cerebral palsy
- developmental disabilities
- eating disorders
- epilepsy
- hearing impairments
- mental illness
- mental retardation
- psychiatric disabilities
- pulmonary disorders
- renal failure
- speech disorders
- spinal cord injury
- substance abuse disorders

At the same time, the counselor needs to be aware of the client's social, racial, ethnic, and cultural background, which makes rehabilitation counseling a highly individualized process.

Counselors may be employed in nonprofit agencies, insurance companies, state vocational rehabilitation agencies, and state agencies that serve individuals who are blind or have visual impairments. Examples of nonprofit agencies are sheltered workshops, vocational training centers, addictions treatment programs, and halfway houses. While case coordination remains a major function, counselors in such agencies also do some individual and, more often, group counseling. Rehabilitation counselors employed by insurance companies deal with worker's compensation and personal injury claims and provide testimony in court hearings. Counselors in state agencies tend to engage in case coordination and make referrals for evaluation, intervention, and training.

The outlook for employment continues to be favorable, considering the increased and continuing need for vocational counseling, training, and placement for an expanding population of individuals who are disadvantaged and disabled.

Social Work

Graduates of accredited programs in social work are either at the bachelor's (BSW) or master's level (MSW). Programs are accredited by the Council on Social Work. Social workers are called caseworkers, school social workers, clinical social workers, psychiatric social workers, or social service workers, depending on the setting and state. Some states, such as Ohio, have licensure for social workers, which protects the title and practice of social work. In addition, the National Association of Social Workers has an examination and certification process for master's level social workers through its Academy of Certified Social Workers (ACSW), which provides the assurance of quality.

A BSW program provides a general orientation to the practice of social work and prepares individuals for beginning professional practice. Social workers with a BSW are often hired by social service agencies, most notably public welfare agencies. These agencies provide programs such as food stamps, Aid to Families with Dependent Children (ADFC), or Supplemental Security Income (SSI), designed to supply income for the poor, blind, aged, and persons with disabilities. Social workers also work in child services programs assisting unwed mothers and adoptive or foster parents. They may interview applicants and determine eligibility for assistance, perform an intake assessment of the client's problems and make recommendations for specialized services, or provide case management services in regard to financial, medical, or psychological aspects of their clients' lives. In addition, probation officers in the court system are usually at the BSW level.

The practitioner with an MSW is considered to be able to function in autonomous practice in a wide variety of settings. The MSW program is typically two years of study, specializing in clinical practice in a healthcare facility or administration of a public agency. There are approximately 100 graduate social work programs in the United States. Some states require licensure in order to practice.

Social workers are employed in a wide variety of settings where they provide direct social work services. These include healthcare facilities, such as hospitals, hospices, or extended care facilities for the elderly. Social workers attend to the psychosocial needs of patients. They tend to work in multidisciplinary teams (e.g., with nurses, physicians, nutritionists) and are involved in working with the patients and their families regarding medical treatment, discharge planning, and coordinating referrals for additional treatment.

They also may work in mental health centers, providing direct counseling services to clients and their families. They may work in inpatient, outpatient, partial hospitalization, or crisis programs. Traditionally, social workers have provided the link between the home, the family, the center, and other community resources. Additionally, they may provide aftercare services in psychiatric hospitals and residential treatment programs.

Social workers are also employed in schools, where they provide individual counseling services to students with social, behavioral, or emotional problems, along with group and community level interventions. They are employed by the school district and coordinate the provision of community services to families enrolled in the schools.

Social workers also work with clients in chemical dependency programs. There are a variety of treatment models for substance abuse; however, social workers generally provide education, outpatient care, emergency care, and inpatient programming. Many addicted people have additional problems with employment, food, and housing; also, they may have a second diagnosis of schizophrenia or another mental illness, so that treatment requires considerable coordination with other community resources.

The corrections system also employs social workers to provide individual and group counseling services to offenders in prisons, training schools, and probation and parole programs for the purpose of rehabilitation. BSW social workers may be employed as probation officers who meet with clients at regular intervals and provide monitoring and counseling as needed; social workers at the MSW level are also employed by courts, police departments, and alternative treatment programs for both adult and juvenile offenders.

Finally, an increasingly large number of social workers are entering private practice, where they provide a wide range of counseling services. Most often they are affiliated with a diverse group of practitioners, including psychiatrists and psychologists. They may practice independently or under supervision, depending upon the availability or access to HMO panels and insurance reimbursement for services.

Social workers are employed in diverse settings throughout the social services system. The BSW is the entry level; however, some of the positions held by BSW social workers may also be open to bachelor level graduates of psychology programs. Finding these positions requires a great deal of investigation. A good starting place is the university's or college's career services department. At the MSW level, social work positions are usually job-specific and require a social work degree and license. In these settings social workers and psychologists often work closely together.

SUMMARY

There is considerable opportunity for entry into the helping professions. The diversity within psychology is matched by that in the allied professions, including counseling and social work. Far too often students and professionals lack knowledge about the various specializations within their own field as well as others. Since appreciation usually comes from understanding, the information in this chapter is highly relevant to practicing professionals as well as aspiring students. Given the opportunities, students and professionals alike need to evaluate realistically their aptitudes and interests when decisions are made about enrolling in or developing a specialty. It is important to note that, while differences between specialties are highlighted within and by each profession in order to establish a professional identity, the similarities relative to the helping process far outweigh the differences. While some areas may enjoy more prestige and current opportunity, all the helping professions provide a context for great personal and professional satisfaction.

Chapter 3

Professional Organizations

Americans of all ages, all conditions, and all dispositions constantly form associations. They have not only commercial and manufacturing companies, in which all take part, but associations of a thousand other kinds, religious, moral, serious, futile, general or restricted, enormous or diminutive. The Americans make associations to give entertainments, to found seminaries, to build inns, to construct churches, to diffuse books, to send missionaries to the antipodes; in this manner they found hospitals, prisons, and schools. If it is proposed to inculcate some truth or to foster some feeling by the encouragement of a great example, they form a society. Wherever at the head of some new undertaking you see the government in France, or a man of rank in England, in the United States you will be sure to find an association. (Alex de Tocqueville, *Democracy in America*, 1835)

As noted in chapter 1, an important defining characteristic of professions is their organization of members in formal ways. Such entities, known as societies, academies, or associations, assist in further promulgating the profession, establishing its standards, and even promoting its scientific development. Their goals can be comprehensive and expansive or quite specific. Colgate (1983) makes the distinction between professional and trade associations in that the ultimate goal of trade associations is "increased income from its product or service [and] the goals of professional societies are commonly considered to point more towards the expansion of knowledge or the establishment of professionals standards" (p. 5). Scientific or learned societies are formed by individuals with a common background in a subject/discipline and promote operation of knowledge in that area. Colgate also notes that lobbying has become an important function of the contemporary organization. Reports are made to the membership on governmental developments that might affect it and viewpoints of the members are presented to representatives in the federal government. Moore (1970) argued that the attributes of professionalism should be regarded as a scale rather than in a cluster; as such, the attributes would have values. Each scale would then have its own subset of scale values. According to Moore, the subscales of the organization's attributes follow the order of recognizing a common occupational interest, and then establishing control to maintain standards of performance, and, finally, controlling access to the occupation. Moore perceives the utility of organizations in several ways: for example, they provide a formal means of communication among their constituents, represent professional organizations with various outside interests, as well as promote the profession through activities ranging from public relations to enforcing ethical codes.

Scientific societies started in Europe with the Renaissance, the first being the Academica Secretorum Naturae in Naples in 1560. McClellan (1985) has written a historical account of scientific societies in the eighteenth century, a time when such societies grew exponentially and were quite significant until the French revolutionary era. The American Philosophical Society, which is the oldest American scientific society, was founded by Benjamin Franklin in 1743 (Colgate, 1983). The 1983 edition of the *Encyclopedia of Associations* (Akey, 1983) contains 17,644 entries. Colgate (1983) reported that 2,300 professional and learned societies are listed among the 5,800 national trade and professional associations in that encyclopedia. The largest percentage of associations (30%) had their offices in Washington, DC. Approximately 45 psychology organizations could be identified, ranging from the large American Psychological Association to a number of small psychology organizations such as the American Psychological Society, Society for Experimental Psychology, Society for Engineering Psychology, and the Psychometric Society. It is interesting to note that the latest edition of the *Encyclopedia* (Maurer & Sheets, 1998) now lists 23,000 nonprofit American membership organizations of national scope. In their recent survey they found that 7 of 10 Americans belong to at least one association, with 25% belonging to more than one.

One intent of this chapter is to present the characteristics and structure of the more representative organizations that psychologists join, with special emphasis on the American Psychological Association (APA) because of its size and influence. Also, knowing the structure and operation of psychology's major association should help understand smaller associations. In addition, the significance of organizations for individual professionals will be addressed, along with other pertinent questions. The Web site is noted when available.

DO ORGANIZATIONS MATTER?

The value of organizations to their respective professionals as well as individual members has been both prized and maligned by professionals. Certainly, the opportunities for professional and personal exchange are an obvious advantage; in current jargon, they stimulate "networking" experiences. Regular interactions with colleagues can be valuable in terms of professional rejuvenation. The sharing of ideas, both in formal and informal contexts, takes place at association meetings/conventions. Newsletters and journals also provide information regarding current developments in the specialties of the profession. At the same time, many of the guild responsibilities are more than the self-protectionism that some would argue is their only, or primary, reason to exist. Promotion of scientific, educational, and applied standards facilitates the integrity of the profession while contributing to its evolution. However, association activities require monetary resources that may be primarily derived from membership dues; thus, the individual professional interested in such goals becomes obliged to join the organization if it is to remain viable.

Organizations engage in a variety of activities, particularly the larger their constituencies become. The professional, therefore, needs to assess what the organization does for the profession and not simply the direct benefit that is received to him or her. If the profession requires representation and maintenance, then membership is not an unreasonable obligation for each professional.

Often, the letters-to-the-editor section of organization newsletters contain public notice of individuals who have terminated their membership because of a specific action or lack of responsiveness of the organization to an issue. Like society in general, organizations must serve a pluralistic membership. The APA is one such example, wherein various specialties are represented; also, given its size, members of various political persuasions can be found. It would seem then, that single-issue decisions of the organization can often be questioned as the criterion for a decision to terminate (or join) membership in an organization.

Aside from the general question of organizational membership, some choices obviously need to be made from a plethora of association options. National versus regional and/or state choices sometimes represent the most obvious competing interests. Where issues can take on dimensions unique to a state, then a powerful state organization is obviously necessary. A national group can be a valuable, formidable ally to the state organization, and serve to prevent a parochial view from dominating an issue. On the other hand, national associations' resources cannot be expected to be matched by state organizations, particularly those in states with small populations. Likewise, the national organization can forge a unity among the professionals while serving to eliminate the waste of time, money, and energy accompanying activities that "reinvent the wheel." Yet, if more federal power (and decision-making) is shifted to the states in the coming years, then a different alignment of state organizations to national organizations may have to evolve.

The generic versus specialty issue (see chapter 1) is reflected in this question as well. Should psychologists judge the organization by what it does for his or her specialty, or even whether it deals with applied versus scientific concerns? On the other hand, are the two emphases so intertwined that efforts done on behalf of one automatically and inevitably benefit the other? Are the needs and priorities of each camp better served by its own group? Must there be one overarching organization? In fact, psychologists are always weighing the answers to these and other questions.

Another concern that has been voiced by some is that organizations have become closed groups, run by the same people (organizational "groupies") who are inaccessible except where their agendas are concerned. The larger the organization, and the more limited one's mentorship in relation to professional organizations, the greater the likelihood of such alienation developing. Ironically, organizations subsist on volunteer help, and very often bemoan the reality of the low percentage of the membership that express interest in becoming involved at the committee level. Generally, degree of involvement in an organization is limited only by the member's interest and time commitment.

Arguments also abound that organizations can become out of touch with the membership and therefore preoccupied with the goal of self-perpetuation. While such concerns are possible, the solution is all too obvious for that situation to exist over a long period of time. More likely it is the frustration over the slowness with which some organizations respond that is behind such a charge. While a legitimate issue, the potential for sound policy to develop under considered review, insulated from the zeitgeist, may be the most important service that an organization can offer a profession.

In fact, the last decade has seen episodes of budget deficits, cutbacks in employment, threats to viable private practice in the health service arena, and meager salary increments for state employees among other developments, which have resulted in professional organizations competing for their members' dollars in a way never experienced before. At the same time the knowledge explosion has led to specialization of practice, which has focused a professional's identity and led him or her to seek affiliations that support a targeted practice. At the same time, the cost of credentialing has increased. So, in contrast to generic national (i.e., APA) and state psychological associations, the more "niche" type organizations hold greater attraction. The rising costs of belonging to an organization force professionals to make tough choices, and self-interests are beginning

to take precedent. Ironically, the criticisms noted in other chapters have resulted in some professionals taking a second look at the organized aspects of their
own profession. Thus, joining the professional organization is no longer more or
less a given, a development that in the long run could possibly undermine the
profession and the professional.

Organizations do serve the function of keeping the professional "connected"
to the discipline and its many facets. This advantage comes at a cost, wherein the
benefits are not always measured in terms of immediate impact on the individual
and perhaps should not be judged solely with that criterion in mind. Workshops
and readings are one form of continuing professional development, but staying
abreast of the current evolution of the psychology discipline is more of a challenge, but can easily be done within a national organization such as the APA.
Similarly, the state organization keeps one immediately connected to developments more relevant to the local practice of psychology. Regional or local associations within the state are equally important to maintain a contextual focus,
and usually involve minimal resource commitment. Lastly, professional organizations can provide a valuable educative resource for the public as well as a service;
the APA's and state psychological organizations' volunteer disaster response services is one example.

Representation and advocacy of the profession are not minor commitments of
national and state organizations even though, again, the immediate direct benefit to individual members may be less clear at times; rather, the individual psychologist must build on those contextual benefits. Yet, at times, this level of
organization does take an advocacy for individuals when circumstances of the situation have import for a larger cadre of psychologists. However, in spite of this
rationale for professional commitment to a national and state organization, there
are a variety of services offered to the members. Beyond the national and state
organizational commitment, the individual should obviously make specialty-ori-
ented decisions that meet his or her needs.

AMERICAN PSYCHOLOGICAL ASSOCIATION

Considered the major psychology organization in the United States because of its
size (155,000 members) and resources (the 1997 operating budget was approximately $60.5 million; the 1999 budget was approximately $90 million), the APA
has a comprehensive set of objectives touching upon all facets of the psychology
profession. The purpose of the APA, as described in its literature, is to "advance
psychology as a science and a profession, and as a means of promoting human
welfare by the encouragement of psychology in all its branches in the broadest

and most liberal manner; by the promotion of research in psychology and the improvement of the qualifications and usefulness of psychologists through high standards of ethics, conduct, education, and achievement; by the establishment and maintenance of the highest standards of professional ethics and conduct of the members of the Association; by the increase and diffusion of psychological knowledge through meetings, professional contacts, reports, papers, discussions, and publications; thereby to advance scientific interests and inquiry, and the application of research findings to the promotion of the public welfare" (APA, 1998i, p. 1). Since its founding in 1892 at a meeting convened by G. Stanley Hall at Clark University, the APA has grown into a large, complicated organization representing the scientific and professional arms of psychology. The structure as it is known today came about during 1942–1945, when 12 organizations representing specialized interests in psychology reorganized with the APA. A rather elaborate governance structure and an equally complex central office operation (500 employees) now exist within the association. The former includes elected representatives of the membership who hold their terms for a prescribed period, while the latter are salaried administrative officials and staff selected by and responsible to the elective governing body. Central office provides staff for all boards and committees, runs one of the largest scientific publishing houses in the world, invests in stocks, manages real estate (the APA owns two office buildings), and interacts with private, state, and federal agencies and organizations.

Membership

The APA has two basic membership categories, member and associate, with other categories (fellow, dues exempt) also recognized, along with an affiliate status (international affiliate, high school teacher affiliate, student affiliate). The qualifications vary with each of the categories, as does the cost of membership. Also, member dues provide the APA with only 18% of its operating expenses. Each membership category is briefly described below.

1. The minimum standard for *full membership* is a doctoral degree based in part on a psychological dissertation, or other evidence of proficiency in psychological scholarship. The degree must also have been received from a program that is primarily psychology in content and conferred by a regionally accredited graduate or professional school.
2. Individuals with a master's degree in psychology from a regionally accredited university may apply for *associate membership*. While initially associates may not vote or hold office in the association, after five consecutive years of membership they may vote.

3. The status of *fellow* is titular, recognizing unusual and outstanding contributions or performance in the field of psychology. Fellow nominees must have been members for one full year, hold a doctoral degree in psychology, and have at least five years of experience beyond that degree. The nomination for consideration of such status must come from one of the APA divisions (of which the individual is a member) and be supported by evidence put forward by the division to support the "unusual and outstanding contribution." At least three fellows of that division need to endorse the nominee. Following nomination by the division and evaluation by the APA Membership Committee, the names of those individuals recommended for election are forwarded to the APA Board of Directors for review and nomination to the Council of Representatives (C/R). Election by the C/R is required for fellow status to be conferred. Individuals may hold fellow status in several divisions by meeting the procedures and criteria for such status in that division. Once the C/R has elected a member fellow in a division, subsequent fellow status in other divisions is conferred at the division level. At times, one hears the designation of "old fellow," which simply refers to the individual in one division who has been awarded such recognition in another division.

4. *Dues exempt* status is open to members who have reached the age of 65 and have been members for 25 years. Also, members who have been judged to be permanently and totally disabled qualify for this membership category.

5. *Affiliates* include (a) international affiliates, (b) high school teacher affiliates, and (c) student affiliates. Subscriptions to any of the APA's journals or other publications are available at the special rate charged to these members.

The *student* affiliates are a large group (62,000) made up of approximately two-thirds graduate students. Their membership entitles them to the APA *Monitor, American Psychologist*, a journal credit, reduced journal rates, discounts on APA books, consumer service discounts, and the APA *Graduate Student (APAGS) Newsletter*. They are eligible to participate in the Insurance Trust plans, including professional liability insurance; there is an internship insurance for students and healthcare insurance. The APA also publishes the popular *Graduate Studies in Psychology and Careers in Psychology* noted in chapter 4, along with career resource booklets such as "Is Psychology the Major for You? Planning for Your Undergraduate Years," "Career Path in Psychology," and "How to Manage Your Career in Psychology." All of these publications are available from the APA order department, (800) 374-2721, as is the free booklet "Psychology: Scientific Problem Solvers—Careers for the 21st Century." Finally, the APA

Science Directorate sponsors an annual competition for graduate student travel awards for students to present their research at the APA convention. There is also a minority student fellowship awards program.

Members and associates are entitled to participate in a low-cost insurance program in several areas of coverage. Programs are tailored to the needs of psychologists. By having access to the many programs and services of the Insurance Trust, members are eligible for life, health, and professional liability insurance, as well as income protection. The Trust is a separate for-profit entity which provides insurance protection plans for APA members. Insurance brochures and applications can be obtained from the Trust office. The APA negotiates premium rates and refunds and makes modifications as necessary.

The members also receive the official journal of the association, *American Psychologist* (which publishes empirical, theoretical, and practical articles), along with the official newspaper, *APA Monitor* (which reports news about psychology and psychologists along with listings of employment opportunities). All publications are monthly and included as part of the membership dues. Members also receive a discount on APA books and consumer services discounts such as special car rental rates, hotel rates, and office products.

For further information and applications (specify the type of membership or affiliation desired) write to: Membership Office, APA, 750 First Street, N.E., Washington, DC 20002-4242.

Governance Structure

The APA organization is represented in figures 3.1 and 3.2. The following discussion provides the essential facts about the structure and functioning of this professional organization and serves as an example for understanding other organizations. Names of officers, boards and committees, and representatives of APA appear each year in the archival issue (August) of the *American Psychologist*.

Divisions

After becoming an APA member, an individual may apply for membership in one *or more* of the APA's 50 divisions. The divisions have their own standards for election to membership which tend to be more specialized than those of the APA. Divisional affiliation is not required by APA membership to be retained. The divisions are listed in table 3.1.

As part of the major reorganization of the APA in 1945, divisions were created to recognize differences in interest among psychologists. A division may be established whenever 1% of the association petitions for it and the Council of representatives (C/R) approve. Division officers are elected according to the

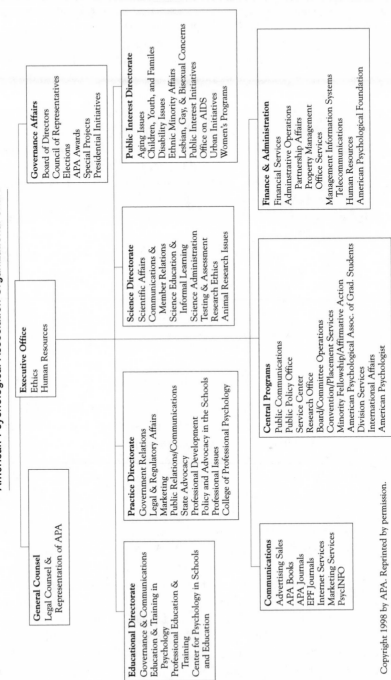

Figure 3.1
American Psychological Association Organizational Chart

Executive Office
Ethics
Human Resources

General Counsel
Legal Counsel &
Representation of APA

Governance Affairs
Board of Directors
Council of Representatives
Elections
APA Awards
Special Projects
Presidential Initiatives

Public Interest Directorate
Aging Issues
Children, Youth, and Familes
Disability Issues
Ethnic Minority Affairs
Lesbian, Gay, & Bisexual Concerns
Public Interest Initiatives
Office on AIDS
Urban Initiatives
Women's Programs

Science Directorate
Scientific Affairs
Communications &
   Member Relations
Science Education &
   Informal Learning
Science Administration
Testing & Assessment
Research Ethics
Animal Research Issues

Finance & Administration
Financial Services
Adminstrative Operations
Partnership Affairs
Property Management
Office Services
Management Information Systems
Telecommunications
Human Resources
American Psychological Foundation

Practice Directorate
Government Relations
Legal & Regulatory Affairs
Marketing
Public Relations/Communications
State Advocacy
Professional Development
Policy and Advocacy in the Schools
Professional Issues
College of Professional Psychology

Central Programs
Public Communications
Public Policy Office
Service Center
Research Office
Board/Committee Operations
Convention/Placement Services
Minority Fellowship/Affirmative Action
American Psychological Assoc. of Grad. Students
Division Services
International Affairs
American Psychologist

Educational Directorate
Governance & Communications
Education & Training in
   Psychology
Professional Education &
   Training
Center for Psychology in Schools
   and Education

Communications
Advertising Sales
APA Books
APA Journals
EPF Journals
Internet Services
Marketing Services
PsycINFO

Copyright 1998 by APA. Reprinted by permission.

Figure 3.2
Boards and Committees of the American Psychological Association

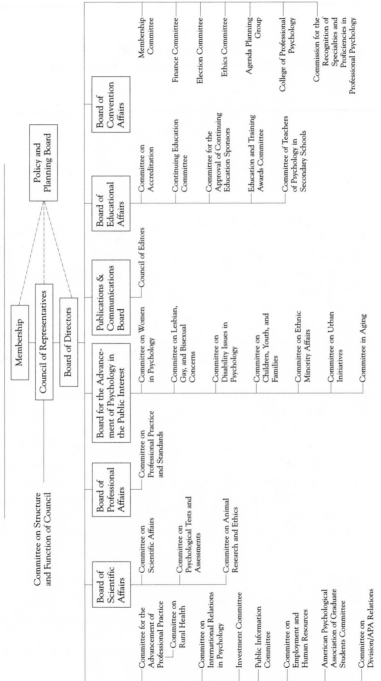

Copyright 1998 by APA. Reprinted by permission.

Table 3.1
DIVISIONS OF THE AMERICAN PSYCHOLOGICAL ASSOCIATION

1. General Psychology
2. Society for Teaching Psychology
3. Experimental Psychology
5. Evaluation, Measurement, and Statistics
6. Behavioral Neuroscience and Comparative Psychology
7. Developmental Psychology
8. The Society of Personality & Social Psychology
9. Society of Psychological Study of Social Issues
10. Psychology and the Arts
12. Clinical Psychology
13. Consulting Psychology
14. The Society for Industrial & Organizational Psychology, Inc.
15. Educational Psychology
16. School Psychology
17. Counseling Psychology
18. Psychologists in Public Service
19. Military Psychology
20. Adult Development and Aging
21. Applied Experimental and Engineering Psychologist
22. Rehabilitation Psychology
23. Society for Consumer Psychology
24. Theoretical and Philosophical Psychology
25. Experimental Analysis of Behavior
26. History of Psychology
27. Society for Community Research and Action: Division of Community Psychology
28. Psychopharmacology and Substance Abuse

29. Psychotherapy
30. Psychological Hypnosis
31. State Psychological Association Affairs
32. Humanistic Psychology
33. Mental Retardation and Developmental Disabilities
34. Population and Environmental Psychology
35. Psychology of Women
36. Psychology of Religion
37. Child, Youth, and Family Services
38. Health Psychology
39. Psychoanalysis
40. Clinical Neuropsychology
41. The American Psychology–Law Society
42. Psychologists in Independent Practice
43. Family Psychology
44. Society for the Study of Lesbian & Gay Issues
45. Society for the Psychological Study of Ethnic Minority Issues
46. Media Psychology
47. Exercise and Sport Psychology
48. Peace Psychology
49. Group Psychology and Group Psychotherapy
50. Addictions
51. The Society for the Psychological Study of Men and Masculinity
52. International Psychology

Note: There are no Divisions 4 and 11.

bylaws of the division at the time officers of the APA are elected; ballots are mailed to the division membership on or about May 15. The president and president-elect serve for one year and the secretary/treasurer for three years. The list of division officers appears each year in the archival issue (August) of the *American Psychologist*.

Divisions are represented on the C/R according to the apportionment ballot results described in the next section. The apportionment is done annually so it is conceivable that a representative may not serve a full term.

Divisions typically charge dues to members in order to provide such services as a newsletter or journal.

Council of Representatives (C/R)

The C/R is the body with legislative power over most business of the APA. It is made up of elected representatives from the divisions and state/provincial associations. The number of seats for both groups is determined by apportionment ballots sent to the membership each year. Individual APA members may allocate their 10 votes among divisions and/or state/provincial associations. A division or state/provincial association receives one council seat for each 1% of the annually allocated seats. An additional 48 are divided among divisions and state or provincial associations according to the number of memberships they were allocated in that process. The individual representatives are then elected at the division or state/provincial association level. Finally, the APA Board of Directors are also members of the council.

The C/R is a major link between division and APA activities. The C/R's legislative year begins at the end of the annual adjourned business meeting in January (the beginning, incidentally, of C/R terms of office). The adjourned meeting is considered to be a continuation of the meeting held at the annual convention. The terms of APA officers and members and chairs of boards and committees begin at the same time as those of the newly seated council members. The APA reimburses some expenses of council members so that they may attend these two meetings; the sponsoring division or state association may cover some of the rest. It is interesting to note that members of the C/R have formed coalitions and caucuses, representing groups with common concerns. Current groupings include the Women's Caucus, Public Interest Coalition, Scientist/Practitioner Coalition, Research/Academic Coalition, Coalition of Applied/Professional Psychologists, and the State Psychological Association Caucus. The C/R members are listed each year in the archival issue of the *American Psychologist*. To be eligible to serve as a council representative, one must be a member of the APA, a member of the group one represents (e.g., division), and serve as representative of only one voting unit. A council member

who has served for six consecutive years is not eligible for election or reappoint-
ment for a period of one year.

The C/R elects individual APA members who serve (a) on the APA's standing boards/committees and continuing committees, and (b) as representatives for
organizations that report through the APA Board of Directors. Nominations are
solicited from the membership (see the January-February APA *Monitor*), the
divisions, state associations, and each board and committee. Approximately
1,200 nominations are received each year, with 100 names appearing on the ballot from which 45 selections are made. The APA Subcommittee on Nominations
of the Board of Directors submits the list of candidates, selected according to
stated criteria, to the APA Board of Directors, who approves the final ballot and
sends it to the C/R.

Items for the C/R agenda come from the annual reports of divisions, items
sent forward by APA boards/committees, and new business introduced by council representatives. Further, upon petition of 50% of APA members, business can
be brought before the C/R.

Board of Directors

The Board of Directors (BD) serves as the administrative agent for the C/R, and
has the authority to take actions necessary for the conduct of the association's
affairs between council business meetings. The Board of Directors consists of an
executive officer, three officers (the president, president-elect, past president),
and six other members, who are elected by and from the C/R during the immediately preceding year. Directors serve three-year terms. The treasurer and
recording secretary are nominated by the Board and elected by the C/R; they
become Board members and serve a five-year term. The executive officer is
appointed by the Board of Directors and also serves a five-year term.

Policy and Planning Board

Provision for the elected Policy and Planning Board, consisting of nine members,
is in the *Bylaws* (APA, 1998i). It is mandated that this board make recommendations on current and long-term policy of the APA and "extensions and restrictions of the functions of the Association, its Divisions, or State/Provincial
Associations, that are consonant with the purpose of the Association" (APA,
1998i, p. 26). It is unique among boards in that it can make recommendations
directly (a) to the voting members of the APA, (b) to the APA Board of
Directors, or (c) the C/R.

Committee on Structure and Function of the Council

The APA Committee on Structure and Function of the Council is the only continuing committee that reports directly to the C/R. The mission of this six-member committee is to (a) receive, review, and initiate recommendations, suggestions, and complaints about council function and operations; and (b) give continuing attention to the development of procedures by which the council can be kept informed about the history and nature of problems or issues currently facing the APA.

Boards and Committees

Figure 3.2 lists six selected boards with the committees that report through them. Procedures for election to these boards/committees have been outlined earlier.

There are four entities that report to Council through the Board of Directors that warrant mention. The Agenda Planning Group has oversight for the two consolidated meetings of boards and committees. It prepares a crosscutting agenda to insure that all participants view common business items. The College of Professional Psychology and the Commission for the Recognition of Specialties and Proficiencies in Professional Psychology are described in chapter 5. Finally, the Committee on Division/APA Relations serves in a facilitator role, promotes leadership development, and mediates disputes. Given its direct relationship to professional practice, we have chosen to use the Board of Professional Affairs as an illustrative example of board functioning.

Board of Professional Affairs (BPA)

The BPA is "responsible for developing recommendations for and monitoring the implementation of APA policy, standards, and guidelines for the professions of psychology" (APA, 1998i, p. 27). A nine-member board, the BPA has oversight responsibility for committees, task forces, and work groups that report to it. Among the work groups (WG) of BPA is the WG on Expanding the Role of Psychology in the Health Care Delivery System. The Committee on Professional Practice and Standards, and the Advisory Committee in Colleague Assistance also report to the board.

Associated with the Practice Directorate, the BPA coordinates its work closely with the other governance group associated with this directorate, the Committee for the Advancement of Professional Practice. APA members who are licensed health care psychologists and provide services in the health or mental health field, or who supervise those who provide such services, pay a special assessment. These funds support the operation of the committee, the Office of Professional Practice, and special projects recommended to the APA Board of Directors by the committee. The eleven-member committee oversees the Office of Professional Practice. In order to ensure the responsiveness of the committee to the needs of the assessed groups there is the Liaison/Consultation Group for

Professional Practice, consisting of 106 delegates—a delegate from each state, district, and provincial psychological association affiliated with APA and each division of APA, wherein at least 50% of the division members pay the annual assessment.

Central Office

The program and business activities of the APA are coordinated at the association's central office in Washington, DC (see figure 3.1). A paid staff headed by the executive officer is responsible for these activities. The major operating offices include Communications, Governance Affairs, General Counsel, Central Programs, Finance and Administration, and the four Directorates of Practice, Service, Education, and Public Interest. Governance Affairs provides administrative support to the Board of Directors and the C/R. General Counsel is responsible for all aspects of legal counsel and representation of APA. Finance and Administration is responsible for processing and recording all accounting/financial transactions that occur within the APA general fund, Insurance Trust and other affiliated entities. The Communications Office informs the public and policymakers about psychology and the APA. Thus, the coordination and service functions are widespread and interface with the membership, the governance structure, and the public. Research and operational responsibilities are handled by central office staff. In addition to coordinating the annual APA convention, the central office is the site of more than 100 meetings of the governance body.

Publications

To fulfill the objective of publishing and distributing knowledge about psychology, the APA Office of Communications is responsible for the following areas: marketing, publications, advertising sales, publishing support, the APA Monitor, PsycINFO, and PsycNET Internet Program. PsycINFO is a family of interrelated information services providing access to the literature in psychology. Twenty-nine periodicals plus a variety of books, brochures, and pamphlets are available from the APA.

As noted earlier, the American Psychologist is published monthly; the APA dues include a subscription to this journal. In addition to the scientific and professional articles that appear therein, the journal is important for other regularly published information. For example, the August issue serves as the organization's archival issue. Each August issue lists the elected officers, board and committee members, subcommittees and task forces, officers (and secretaries) of each state psychological association, addresses for state and provincial boards as well as agencies that offer licensure or certification of psychologists. The proceedings of the APA Council of Representatives, along with the treasurer's and executive officer's yearly reports are also included. Major policy statements of the organization, such as *Ethical Principles of Psychologists*, usually appear initially in the August issue.

The April issue lists the annual APA Awards, including:

1. Distinguished Scientific Contributions
2. Distinguished Scientific Awards for the Applications of Psychology
3. Awards for Distinguished Profession Contributions
4. Awards for Distinguished Contributions to Psychology in the Public Interest
5. Distinguished Scientific Awards for an Early Career Contribution to Psychology
6. Distinguished Contribution to Research in Public Policy
7. Distinguished Education and Training Contributions
8. Distinguished Contributions to the International Advancement of Psychology

The March through July issues provide detailed information about the annual APA convention, including preregistration application and advanced hotel registration materials. The December issue lists APA-accredited doctoral training programs in school, clinical, and counseling psychology, along with accredited predoctoral internship training programs; a supplement to that listing appears in the archival issue (August).

The official newspaper, the *APA Monitor*, is published monthly and sent to members as part of their membership dues. It contains timely information, including association highlights, conference information, membership activities and awards, national and international job listings, and information about new APA book titles. The *Monitor* contains theoretical and application-based articles concerned with current trends in psychology, public interest initiatives, and educational and medical aspects of the profession. Sections occurring monthly include Practice, Science, and the Judicial Notebook, a section devoted to ethical issues in practice. There is ongoing correspondence between the editors and readers concerning current theories and topics. Many editions of the *Monitor* are devoted to special issues, providing readers with a knowledge foundation in the area as well as editorial and reader contributions. A multiyear schedule of conventions, meetings, and workshops is provided along with a continuing education calendar of APA sponsored events.

Table 3.2 lists the journals and periodicals published by the APA. All journals are available to APA members at a discount. Some of these journals are published with divisions and, therefore, may be available as part of the division's assessment. Clearly, *Psychological Bulletin* (evaluative reviews), *Psychological Documents* (abstracts), *Psychological Review* (theoretical papers), and *Contemporary Psychology* (book reviews) serve as reference materials. In addition, *PsycSCAN* is a quarterly publication that helps professionals and students keep up to date in the areas of applied psychology, clinical psychology, developmental psychology, and learning disabilities/mental retardation. The material included in *PsycSCAN* is designed for researchers and based on abstracts from special subscriber-selected journals.

The APA also publishes an annual *Membership Register*, as well as a detailed *Membership Directory* every four years; the latest Directory was published in 1997. The *Publication Manual* is the guide to preparing manuscripts for publication in APA and related journals. Public information materials are also available, such as the booklet detailing functions entitled *Psychology as a Health Care Profession*. Career information can be found in a booklet entitled *Careers in Psychology*. For undergraduates, several excellent publications are available, for example, *The Psychology Major: Training and Employment Strategies; Graduate Study in Psychology and Associated Fields* (a comprehensive survey of more than 600 graduate programs (see chapter 4); *Preparing for Graduate Study: Not for Seniors Only* (a how-to sourcebook); and *Library Use: A Handbook for Psychology* (a how-to handbook).

Annual Convention

The annual APA convention is held in August with more than 10,000 members in attendance. The location differs each year, and the dates and locations of the upcoming six conventions can be found in the calendar of each issue of the *American Psychologist* and the *Monitor*. Similar information regarding regional, state, and international psychological meetings as well as psychological workshops, conferences, and related association meetings are also included.

One of the largest conventions in the United States and the world's largest meeting for psychologists, the APA week-long program features more than 3,000 presentations in the form of lectures, workshops, symposia, invited addresses, poster sessions, and other forums. Of special note is the Master Lecture Series on Psychology, which consists of two-hour lectures dealing with a different area of psychology each year. The lectures are taped for distribution and also are available in book form. The G. Stanley Hall Lecture Series consists of five two-hour lectures designed to update the teaching of introductory psychology; they are also available in book form. Each division is allotted convention time for business meetings and for the presentation of papers relevant to their interests. A call for papers is distributed to the membership in the fall issues of the *Monitor* with

Table 3.2
JOURNALS AND PERIODICALS PUBLISHED BY THE APA

American Psychologist
Behavioral Neuroscience
Clinician's Research Digest
Contemporary Psychology
Developmental Psychology
Experimental and Clinical Psychopharmacology
Health Psychology
Journal of Abnormal Psychology
Journal of Applied Psychology
Journal of Comparative Psychology
Journal of Consulting and Clinical Psychology
Journal of Counseling Psychology
Journal of Educational Psychology
Journal of Experimental Psychology: Animal Behavior Processes
Journal of Experimental Psychology: Applied
Journal of Experimental Psychology: General
Journal of Experimental Psychology: Human Perception and Performance
Journal of Experimental Psychology: Learning, Memory, and Cognition
Journal of Family Psychology
Journal of Personality and Social Psychology
Neuropsychology
Neuropsychology Abstracts (previously *PsycSCAN: Neuropsychology*)
Professional Psychology: Research and Practice
Psychological Abstracts
Psychological Assessment
Psychological Bulletin
Psychological Methods
Psychological Review
Psychology and Aging
Psychology, Public Policy, and Law
PsycSCAN: Psychoanalytic Abstracts
PsycSCAN: Applied Psychology
PsycSCAN: Behavior Analysis & Therapy
PsycSCAN: Clinical Psychology
PsycSCAN: Developmental Psychology
PsycSCAN: Learning Disabilities and Mental Retardation

directions for proposing papers for consideration. In addition to the above emphases, films, exhibits, and a placement service are also provided. Orientations are provided for new members. Finally, in addition to the separate APA book-store, a large exhibitors' hall is associated with the convention wherein publish-ers, credentialing bodies, and related groups exhibit.

Career Development and Career Building

In addition to the career planning materials available to graduate students noted above, the APA offers employment services and professional advancement resources. At each annual convention there is a placement center that matches psychologists interested in new employment with employers with job vacancies. There is also a resumé referral service, which allows members to post resumes to a database available to employers seeking psychologists. Hundreds of job open-ings appear each month in the *Monitor;* job seekers may also place notices. There is also an ethnic minority job bank service. Finally, The APA Practitioner's Toolbox Series, an eight-volume series, helps practitioners manage the dynamics of an evolving marketplace. Titles include "Building a Group Practice" and "Marketing Your Practice."

The APA also provides opportunities for continuing education (CE). There are more than 50 CE workshops during the annual convention, involving 4- and 7-hour sessions. In addition, the APA has a system for reviewing and approving workshops given throughout the United States and Canada. Such programs are eligible to meet the mandatory CE requirements in most states. These programs facilitate the psychologist's ethical responsibility to remain current with knowl-edge and practice developments in the discipline. Finally, independent study programs, based on APA publications, allow members to design individualized programs to complete at their own pace. There are 33 independent study pro-grams available at this time.

For first-time convention-goers, studying the program before attendance will help alleviate what can be an overwhelming experience, as will attending pro-grams designed to help maximize conference attendance. No doubt, one's initial attention is drawn to the scholarly presentations—however, division business and C/R meetings are open to members and their attendance is welcomed; such attendance helps understand how the organization functions and the important issues and developments in the interest areas.

Advocacy

In January 1986, the APA Council of Representatives established the interim

Advisory Committee for Professional Development. This committee works to establish a permanent Office of Professional Development, which generates and allocates funds to advance the professional practice of psychology at the state and federal levels. Among its activities, the office surveys state psychological associations to identify issues of concern and to develop and implement professional psychology's position on changes in the healthcare system. Thus, services to state association and marketing objectives have been established. In 1998, a special assessment was charged to APA members who are licensed healthcare psychologists to support such efforts.

Finally, the APA C/R has set up the Psychology Defense Fund to finance special projects and legislative actions at the state level. It does not overlap with federal legislative activities of the Association for the Advancement of Psychology (AAP; see below). The fund is separate from the APA budget and supported by individual contributions as well as contributions of APA divisions, state affiliates, and other groups. Examples of the awards they have made include grants to psychologists in suits over confidential or ethics issues, a research project to review statutes, and court decisions on the legal status of psychology, state by state.

Restructuring

By now, the size and complexity of the APA should be obvious. Along with this growth has naturally come a variety of subdisciplines and special interest groups. The tensions existing in psychology's early beginnings (see the first chapter) have not only increased, but are now intertwined with an even more complicated set of agendas promoted by a variety of constituencies among the membership. As a result, in the 1980s the APA has increasingly found itself ineffectual in doing business. To confront this challenge, the APA C/R tried to divide its work between two bodies, or forums, as they were called. Basically, the forums included researchers and academicians in one group and practitioners in the second. The notion that was followed was simple in design, that is, each group/forum would conduct business relevant to its respective interests. A number of factors arose to defeat this initial attempt to reorganize. At the 1985 APA convention, a task force set up to study APA structure made rather sweeping recommendations. Basically, the organization has remained the same, and the practitioner-scientist tension, while more subdued now, still can be identified in many discussions. This was a factor that lead to the establishment of the scientifically oriented *American Psychological Society*.

http://www.apa.org

AMERICAN PSYCHOLOGICAL FOUNDATION

The American Psychological Foundation was established in 1953 to promote psychology and to help extend its benefits to the public through three programs: education, research, and public policy. It was established by APA "to create an instrument to contribute financially to the continued development of psychology" (Matarazzo, 1998), and its assets now total $4 million. In 1998 it invested more than $23,000 in education scholarships and $60,000 in research grants and awards. It annually awards the Gold Medal Awards for Lifetime Achievement in Science Practice and Application Psychology, a Distinguished Teaching in Psychology Award, and several other awards.

THE ASSOCIATION FOR ADVANCEMENT OF BEHAVIOR THERAPY

Founded in 1966, the Association for Advancement of Behavior Therapy (AABT) is an interdisciplinary group active in the behavioral and cognitive sciences interested in understanding human behavior and helping to intervene with personal and social problems and issues. A goal is to further research, theory, and practice in the sciences There is a board of directors (president, past president, president-elect, secretary/treasurer, and three representatives-at-large), as well as five coordinators, who are responsible for education, membership, convention, and professional affairs and publications. The staff includes an executive director. There are also over 30 active special interest groups covering a variety of interests such as specific behavior change techniques, focal target problems and populations, particular work settings, central theoretical concerns, and salient change agent issues. Almost all distribute a newsletter and conduct educational activities.

The Educational Affairs office of the AABT offers a broad range of professional consultations, as well as peer review services such as assembling briefs and depositions in legal proceedings involving behavior modification procedures and programs. The Professional Affairs office monitors state and legislative activity that may have an impact on behavior therapy and make information available to government policymakers. Similar functions are pursued vis à vis other mental health organizations and insurance carriers.

Publications of the AABT include the magazine/newsletter The Behavior Therapist, which is devoted to the publication of original experimental or clinical research that advances the theory and practice of behavior therapy. It is available to members at a discount. (*Behavior Assessment,* a journal that deals with assessment as well as research/methodological issues, was formerly an AABT publication, but is now published solely by Pergamon Press.)

Membership in the AABT is at the full, associate, or student level. Full membership is open to all persons who agree with the purposes and objectives of the organization and are either professionals in good standing in the American Psychological Association or American Psychiatric Association or who are: (a) practicing behavior clinicians, (b) engaged in research or activities pertinent to the "development and advancement" of behavior therapy or (c) "interested in acquiring professional knowledge and competence in some aspect of the behavior therapies with a view toward eventual participation" (AABT, 1984, p. vii). Individuals who do not meet the membership criteria, but whose credentials are otherwise acceptable to the membership are eligible for associate membership. Student membership is open to students at the bachelor's, master's, or doctoral level. There are 4,500 members.

An annual convention is held, which includes workshops, institutes, symposia, exhibits, poster sessions, invited addresses, and fundamentals courses. While the AABT does not have continuing education requirements, credits are available for the fundamentals courses, preconvention institutes, and workshops.

Finally, the AABT geographical affiliate groups engage in activities determined by their membership. Almost all of these groups hold meetings and distribute newsletters.

http://server.psyc.vt.edu/aabt

ASSOCIATION FOR BEHAVIOR ANALYSIS

An international organization, the Association for Behavior Analysis (ABA) grew out of the Midwestern Association of Behavioral Analysis, which had been organized to establish a separate identity for the behavioral analysis group of the larger psychological community. A major purpose is to "provide a forum for the discussion of issues and the dissemination of information pertinent to the interests of the membership by means of an annual convention. It is an interdisciplinary group of professionals, paraprofessionals, and students interested in the experimental, theoretical, and applied analysis of behavior" (ABA, 1985, p. i).

The ABA is organized around an executive council standing committee, select committee, and special interest groups. The executive council includes the president, past presidents, president-elect, secretary/treasurer, four council members, two affiliate representatives, and two honorary council members. The standing committees are affiliate, membership, certification, international development, membership recruitment, and education and evaluation. There is a convention staff.

Membership is limited to one class of members; minimum requirements are a master's degree in psychology or in a related field and demonstrated competence in either the experimental or applied analysis of behavior (demonstrated by a minimum of a year's supervised work in either area, and a graduate project, thesis, or dissertation in one of the areas as well). Applicants who do not meet those criteria must demonstrate their competency in behavioral analysis by submitting evidence of at least two years of supervised experience or of having made significant contributions to knowledge in behavioral assessment by research publications or other means. There is also a student affiliate class of participants. Sustaining supporting and emeritus status is recognized through a varying membership rate. The *ABA Newsletter* is sent to the membership.

An annual convention is held, which includes a business meeting. Papers, workshops, seminars, symposia, poster sessions, invited addresses, and preconvention institutes make up the program. The ABA is supported by the APA to sponsor continuing education programs in psychology, which is done through the workshops. A placement service is also offered, along with exhibits.

http://www.wmich.edu/aba

ASSOCIATION OF BLACK PSYCHOLOGISTS

Founded in 1968 by Black psychologists across the country, the Association of Black Psychologists' (ABPsi) goal is to actively address the problems and expected needs of Black psychologists and the larger Black community. The purposes of this organization of more than 1300 members are to promote and influence the profession of American psychology, influence as well as affect social change, and develop programs that can assist in solving problems of Black communities and other ethnic groups. Membership is limited to persons who (a) hold a college or advanced degree in psychology, related behavior sciences fields, or an experiential equivalent in psychology, (b) are working in the field of psychology, or (c) are students in psychology. There is a student division within ABPsi.

The association's quarterly *Journal of Black Psychology*, the monthly *Newsjournal-Psych Discourse*, voting privileges, and convention discounts are included with membership.

http://www.abpsi.org

BRITISH PSYCHOLOGICAL SOCIETY

The British Psychological Society (BPS) was founded in 1901 and incorporated by Royal Charter in 1965. It "exists to promote the advancement of the study of psychology and its applications, and to maintain high standards of professional education and conduct" (BPS, 1998). BPS currently has 27,000 members. Membership categories and criteria are complex and include affiliateship as well as graduate, foreign, and student affiliateships. The BPS is divided into 13 sections and 8 divisions. The *sections* exist where members have decided to pool and exchange scientific interest and knowledge. They are open to society members with an interest in the area. The sections are: psychotherapy; psychobiology; social psychology; cognitive psychology; developmental psychology; occupational psychology; psychology of women; sport and exercise psychology; consciousness and experiential psychology; education; history and philosophy; and mathematical, statistical, and computing. The *divisions* cater to the professional interests of members; participants must be elected to the division. Divisions include: health psychology; clinical psychology; counseling psychology; occupational psychology; educational and child psychology; criminological and legal psychology; and Scottish Division of Educational and Child Psychology and the Division for Teachers and Researchers in Psychology. There are also six branches in Great Britain, which hold meetings and conferences.

Training and practice of psychologists in Great Britain is somewhat different than in the United States, and this difference is reflected in the requirements for BPS membership. In 1987 BPS was authorized to maintain a Register of Chartered Psychologists. The title *chartered psychologist* is granted only to applicants who are eligible for *graduate membership* of the Society and have a minimum of three years' postgraduate training in psychology and pass a qualifying examination set by the Society. Chartered recognition is of importance to applicants who want to practice psychology professionally. Chartered psychologists and members agree to abide by the Society's code of conduct. If a chartered psychologist wishes to use a specialist title (clinical, counseling, forensic, educational, occupational) he or she must meet the regulations governing their use. A Register of 8500 chartered psychologists, including their qualifications and work addresses, is now available throughout the United Kingdom.

In addition to its monthly bulletin, *The Psychologist* (free to all members), the BPS publishes 11 journals, which are available to members at a reduced rate.

There is an annual conference held in early April and an additional London Conference in December. The different regional offices and sections also hold conferences and produce newsletters.

http://www.bps.org.uk

CANADIAN PSYCHOLOGICAL ASSOCIATION

The Canadian Psychological Association (CPA) represents the professional and scientific interests of all psychologists in Canada. Founded in 1939, it currently has a membership of more than 4,200 members and through its affiliations represents over 12,000 psychologists in Canada. The objectives are: "to lead, advance and promote psychology as a science and as a profession for the benefit of humanity; to provide leadership in psychology in Canada; to promote a sense of identity among psychologists; to promote the advancement, dissemination, and practical application of psychological knowledge; to develop standards and ethical principles for education, training science and practice in psychology" (CPA, 1998).

The CPA's board of directors includes officers as well as two directors representing practitioners, two directors representing scientists and scientist-practitioners, and four others elected as at-large members. The Association is organized into 23 sections and two interest groups (psychophysiology and disaster/trauma). The sections include criminal justice; brain and behavior; and clinical, education, military, industrial/organizational, developmental, and counseling psychology. The CPA accredits doctoral programs and internship in professional psychology (clinical psychology, counseling psychology, clinical neuropsychology). There is an agreement with the APA for a simplified accreditation procedure for programs during concurrent accreditation from each association. The CPA maintains an active lobbying presence in the Canadian government.

Members of the CPA must have at least a master's in psychology or the equivalent thereof and be a resident of Canada or the United States. In most circumstances, a sponsor must endorse an application for membership. The APA and CPA have reciprocal agreements for membership. An APA member may join the CPA for one-half of the CPA dues; the same arrangement exists for CPA members joining the APA. In addition, there are student memberships for graduate and undergraduate students, international affiliate memberships, and special affiliate memberships for persons who are actively interested in psychology but who are not psychologists. Fees for members cover subscriptions to two journals: *Canadian Psychology*, and a choice of either *Canadian Journal of Experimental Psychology* or the *Canadian Journal of Behavioral Science*. The third journal may be subscribed to for 85% off the regular subscription rate. In addition, all members and affiliates receive the quarterly newspaper *Psynopsis*. Publications are in both French and English. The Association also offers professional liability insurance and a benefit program for members.

In addition to the publication of three quarterly journals, the CPA holds annual conventions and presents an annual award for "Distinguished

Contributions to Canadian Psychology as a Science" and "Distinguished Contributions to Canadian Psychology as a Profession," among others.
http://www.cpa.ca

The Human Factors and Ergonomics Society

The Human Factors and Ergonomics Society is the largest society in the field of ergonomics. Incorporated in 1957, HFES is now an interdisciplinary organization of professionals interested in the human factors field, that is, discovering characteristics of human beings that are applicable to the design of systems and devices of all kinds. An executive council and executive director are responsible for the operation of the organization.

There are approximately 60 local chapters in the United States, Canada, and Europe and 20 technical groups that promote special interests ranging from computer systems to the aging. While the majority of the 5,000 members are psychologists and engineers, membership includes a wide range of professions. Members are required to have a bachelor's degree and either three years of experience in human factors work or two years of advanced graduate work. Membership decisions are made by a committee, which may waive requirements for exceptional candidates. There are also associate and student memberships available.

The organization meets as an international body in the fall to allow members to present research developments and provide a forum for discussion of important issues.

Several publications are offered by the society, including the journal *Human Factors*, the *HFS Bulletin*, the magazine *Ergonomics in Design*, and the *HFS Directory and Yearbook*, all of which are free to members. There are also videotapes and films available for members to borrow.

Awards are made annually to recognize outstanding achievement in the field. Representation before Congressional committees is also provided to promote the interests of human factors professionals.
http://www.hfes.vt.edu

National Association of School Psychologists

Established in 1977, the National Association of School Psychologists (NASP) now has a membership of 20,000 school psychologists (individuals working or holding credentials as a school psychologist). There are also international, student, and associate or training school psychologist (nonvoting) membership categories. The mission of NASP is "to promote educationally and psychologically healthy environments for all children and youth by implementing research-based, effective programs that prevent problems, enhance independence, and promote optimal learning. This is accomplished through state-of-the-art research and training, advocacy, ongoing program evaluation, and caring professional service" (NASP, 1997). Members receive the newspaper *Communiqué* eight times a year, and the quarterly journal *School Psychology Review*. NASP publishes books and monographs, as well as videos and position papers, which are available free or at a discount to members. NASP publications include *Best Practices in School Psychology*, *Children's Needs: Psychological Perspectives*, and *Attention Disorders in Children*.

A recent reorganization of the governance structure of the organization is underway and will receive final approval in 2003. An executive council consists of five officers, four senior delegate representatives, four program area managers (professional development, information services, professional standards, and advocacy), and an executive director. The delegate assembly consists of representatives from four geographic regions who set policy for the organization.

http://www.naspweb.org

PSYCHONOMIC SOCIETY

The objective of the Psychonomic Society is to "promote the communication of scientific research in psychology and allied sciences" (Psychonomic Society, 1997). Members hold a doctorate and are qualified to conduct and to supervise scientific research in psychology or allied sciences. They must have published significant research to be nominated for member status. Society membership is now 2,500. Recommendation for membership is initiated by one of the members, with election conducted by the governing board. Associate membership status is available. Associates must also hold the doctorate.

A governing board supervises the general affairs of the Society. The board consists of 12 members and the ex-officio secretary/treasurer; terms are for six years. The board elects a chairman (one-year term) and the secretary/treasurer (three-year term). Each year the membership-at-large nominates persons for the board. The names of the six persons receiving the greatest number of nominations make up the ballot for that year.

The society publishes the following journals: *Psychobiology; Psychonomic Bulletin & Review; Animal Learning and Behavior; Memory and Cognition;*

Perception and Psychophysics; Behavior Research Methods; Instruments &
Computers. An annual scientific meeting is held, with members presenting
papers or sponsoring nonmember presentations. The annual business meeting is
also held at this time.

http://www.psychonomic.com

SOCIETY OF BEHAVIORAL MEDICINE

A relatively new organization, the Society of Behavioral Medicine was established in 1978. It is an interdisciplinary group whose focus is the relationship
among health, illness, and behavior. Most of the members are psychologists and
physicians, but persons from other disciplines are encouraged to join. There are
approximately 1,500 members, and it is anticipated that the organization will
continue to grow.

Membership includes subscriptions to two journals, *Annals of Behavioral*
Medicine and *Behavioral Medicine Abstracts*, a membership directory, and discounts on monographs and registration fees.

http://socbehmed.org/sbm/sbm.htm

SOCIETY FOR RESEARCH IN CHILD DEVELOPMENT

Since its founding in 1933, the Society for Research in Child Development
(SRCD) has functioned to support and advance research in the scientific study
of child development. There are approximately 5,000 international members
from the practice and human development community.

The Society is governed by a council of 13 members. These include four officers (president, president-elect, past president, and secretary); six elected members; and three members appointed by the council. The length of term is stag-
gered and varied among the council members.

Membership is open to any individual actively engaged in research or teaching
in human development or any of the related basic sciences. Levels of membership
are Full, Spouse, Student/PostDoc, and Undergraduate Affiliate Basic or Plus.

Three journals are published by the society: *Child Development, Child*
Development Abstracts and Bibliography, and *Monographs of the Society for Research*
in Child Development. In addition, there is a newsletter, a membership directory,
and a review series. The Society has established ethical standards for research
with children. The SRCD holds a biennial meeting.

http://www.journals.uchicago.edu/SRCD/About.html

AMERICAN PSYCHOLOGICAL SOCIETY

Founded in 1988, the American Psychological Society (APS) is devoted solely to scientific psychology. APS aims "to advance the scientific discipline of psychology and the giving away of psychological knowledge in the public interest" (APS, 1998). It has over 15,000 members. The board has five officers as well as three members-at-large. Membership is open and includes a subscription to the *APS Observer Newsletter*, its flagship journal *Psychological Science*, and *Current Directions in Psychological Science*. A substantive monthly newsletter of approximately 65 pages, the *Observer*, includes "International Psychology" and "Psychology in Perspective" sections, and a "Teaching Tips" section which provides the "latest in practical advice on the teaching of psychology" at two- and four-year colleges and universities, including content and methods. In addition, an employment bulletin, meeting calendar, and profile of an organization are included, as well as the "Student Notebook" section. *Psychological Science* provides authoritative articles across all of scientific psychology's subdisciplines. *Current Directions* provides concise, informative reviews on emerging trends, issues, and controversies. APS holds an annual four-day convention; a number of psychology-orientated and related organizations hold some type of session in conjunction with their convention. For example, the American Association of Applied and Preventative Psychology (AAAPP) holds its convention in conjunction with APS, and the Society for Personality and Social Psychology (APA's Division 8) holds its annual meeting just prior to the APS convention. AAAPP is an organizational affiliate of APS, with approximately 1,000 members interested in research-oriented applied and preventative psychology. A Biological Basis of Behavior conference is held in conjunction with APS's annual convention. Finally, the annual APS Teaching Institute offers a special blend of cutting-edge psychological research and proven teaching techniques. A member benefits program exists which includes liability insurance to meet the needs of scientific psychologists.

One of the primary reasons APS was founded was to provide a distinct presence for scientific psychology in Washington, DC, through governmental relations and advocacy. For example, APS advocated for separate offices for behavioral and social science at the National Institutes of Health.

http://www.psychologicalscience.org

INTERNATIONAL ORGANIZATIONS

The International Association of Applied Psychology

The largest and oldest international psychology organization, the International Association of Applied Psychology (IAAP) has 80 countries represented among its membership. Founded over 60 years ago (1920), its objective is to increase communication among the world's psychologists. In serving psychologists both in and out of academia, the IAAP strives to put psychologists in touch with one another so that they can share findings and views and avoid duplication of work. The officers include a president, vice president, past president, and general secretary/treasurer. There are currently 13 divisions, which provide newsletters, activities, and networks of contacts for psychologists doing applied research. Examples of divisions are: Applied Gerontology; Organizational Psychology; Psychological Assessment; Environmental Psychology; Psychology and National Development; Educational, Instructional, and School Psychology; and Clinical and Community Psychology.

There are two types of membership in the IAAP. Full members must be members of a national psychological society. Associate members hold a degree representing a substantial education in psychology and employment in psychological work. The dues include a subscription to the IAAP quarterly publication, *Applied Psychology—An International Review*. The IAAP also publishes the *European Journal of Work and Organizational Psychology*. Quadrennial international congresses are conducted by IAAP; the twenty-fifth congress will take place in Singapore in 2002.

http://www.iaapsy.org

International Society for Developmental Psychobiology

In 1967, the International Society for Developmental Psychobiology was founded to promote research on the development of behavior in all organisms. The Society has been associated with the American Association for the Advancement of Science and the Society for Neuroscience and is now a member of the Federation of the Behavioral, Psychological, and Cognitive Sciences. There are nearly 300 members in this organization; its primary function is to provide a forum for sharing research through an annual convention and by publishing a journal, *Developmental Psychobiology*. The officers include a president, secretary/treasurer, past president, president-elect, program coordinator, representative to the federation, and three board members.

In order to be a member, an advanced degree (Ph.D., Ed.D., M.D.) is required as well as at least two publications on topics related to psychobiology. Students engaged in this line of research are also eligible for membership. Membership includes subscription to the Society's journal and membership in the Federation of Behavioral, Psychological, and Cognitive Sciences. Also published are a newsletter, membership directory, and a program and proceedings of the annual meeting.

http://www.psychology.uiowa.edu/isdp

TRAINING PROGRAM ASSOCIATIONS

Council of Graduate Departments of Psychology

The Council of Graduate Departments of Psychology (COGDOP) is an association of chairs of departments of psychology or their equivalents (e.g., departments or schools with a current APA-accredited program). Their objectives include (a) promotion of the development of psychology by providing forums for discussion of education, training, and research; and (b) establishment of a mechanism to interact with and make recommendations to various levels of APA governance and central office operations, government agencies, foundations, and other organizations. The executive board consists of six elected representatives. Their annual meeting is scheduled for the winter, and a second meeting is scheduled annually, concurrent with the APA convention.

National Council of Schools and Programs of Professional Psychology

The National Council of Schools and Programs of Professional Psychology (NCSPP) is an organization of professional schools and programs in psychology. Founded in 1976, its mission is the "progressive improvement, enhancement, and enrichment of professional education and training" (Peterson, Abrams, Peterson, & Strickler, 1997, p. 373). Membership is reserved for those programs accredited by the APA (n=33), although an "associate" category (n=12) is available for those programs at some stage of the accreditation process. Most recently the NCSPP endorsed an educational model, which includes a curriculum and a pedagogy of integrative experiences among its five elements (see chapter 4 for a complete description).

The NCSPP is governed by an Executive Committee, which includes a president, president-elect, past president, and secretary/treasurer as well as, in order to insure diversity, the chair of the Ethnic-Racial Diversity Committee and the chair of the Women's Issues Committee. Besides these two standing committees, the work of the organization is done by about 10 committees whose chairs are appointed by the president. These other committees include, for example, the Education and Training Committee, the Accreditation Issues Committee, and the Membership Committee. NCSPP has recently hired a part-time executive director.

The NCSPP meets twice annually. One meeting is scheduled for two days before the APA meetings. The second meeting is the mid-winter conference. This meeting typically lasts four days in a different city every year.

Specialty Training Councils

There are four councils representing the psychology specialties of clinical (Council of University Directors of Clinical Psychology), counseling (Council of Counseling Psychology Training Programs), health (Council of Health Psychology Training Programs), and school (Council of Directors of School Psychology Programs). The program representative for each of the councils is the director/chair/coordinator. Their annual meetings are usually held at the same time as the APA convention. In addition, a mid-winter meeting is scheduled, when the three councils meet with APA staff and interact around common issues.

Recently, a council of chairs of Training Councils has been formed and promotes formal communication and collaboration among the specialty councils for the first time. The specialty councils are joined by the Association of Counseling Center Training Agencies, Association of Directors of Psychology Training Clinics, Association of Medical School Psychologists, Council of Program Directors in Community Research and Action, VA Headquarters Psychology Training Advising Committee, Canadian Council of Professional Psychology Programs, NCSPP, and APPIC.

Academy of Psychological Clinical Science

An academy of doctoral programs dedicated to developing empirical evidence regarding clinical practice and promoting its application is the Academy of Psychological Clinical Science. Their focus is on the science end of the scientist-practitioner model. In 1997 the Academy consisted of 30 clinical psychology training programs dedicated to the advancement of clinical science and its application (Academy of Psychology Clinical Science, 1997). The goals of the Academy include fostering the training of students for careers in clinical science research so that they can skillfully produce and apply scientific knowledge. They promote the application of knowledge in a way that is consistent with scientific evidence.

Chapter 4

Education and Training

For over 30 years, professional psychology doctoral education has followed the scientist-practitioner model conceptualized at the Boulder Conference (Raimy, 1950). That is, the practicing psychologist embodies the attributes of a scientist in that he or she contributes to the knowledge base as a researcher. At the same time, the careful evaluation and application of that knowledge would be reflected in his or her specialty practice. This is a theoretical underpinning of a professional psychology program's doctor of philosophy (Ph.D.) degree.

The emergence of the practitioner approach to training (Korman, 1974) as a viable alternative has resulted in the increasing acceptance of the doctor of psychology (Psy.D.) degree. The practitioner model subscribes to most of the values in the scientist-practitioner model (Korman, 1974), but endorses this model as an additional form of professional training that signifies a basic service orientation. Thus, in place of the Ph.D. dissertation, the Psy.D. project allows for greater flexibility in defining the appropriateness of the project so that it is relevant to the professional role for which the candidate is preparing to enter. Advocates of this model (Peterson, 1976) argue that it is a challenge to train professional psychologists thoroughly except through explicitly defined professional programs. While professional schools (versus universities) may find it difficult to promise that graduates of their programs would contribute to the knowledge base upon which the practice is based, a liberally defined scholarly inquiry would be embraced. Similarly, some aspects of the scientific method are seen as applicable to professional practice, but not always possible or even warranted.

The need for the Psy.D. degree is argued by Peterson (1976), who says that Psy.D. programs are defined "comprehensively so that the knowledge base and the range of skill extend from biological psychology through organizational psychology" (p. 795). Ph.D. training programs, with their emphasis on scholarly inquiry, cannot be as broad in professional skills training; they train only one form or another of a professional application, for example, behavioral therapy or consultation. Korman (1974) summarized all of the recommendations of the Vail Conference, such as a "career-lattice" concept of training, the desirable charac- teristics of professional training, continued professional training throughout one's career, training of minority groups and women, as well as service delivery systems and the social context. Meanwhile, Perry (1979) argued for the contin- uance of the Boulder Conference model of training because alternate models are unnecessary or undesirable; he also states that quality of training is the real issue. Barlow, Hayes, and Nelson (1984) noted (1) the basis of the training model is both research and practice, (2) the research must be a vital part of the applied psychology field, (3) the profession can find people capable of doing both, and (4) involvement with the clinical practice brings one in contact with the impor- tant research issues and will provide financial support for later efforts.

Attainment of a doctorate degree represents the *entry* level in the psychologi- cal profession as it is defined by the APA—the level at which independent prac- tice may begin. However, a perennial issue in the profession has been the role and status of master's or specialist's degree-trained (60 semester hours) individuals. It is argued that they often engage in roles that are similar to those of doctorate- trained psychologists, particularly in public agencies and institutions. Also, after building years of experience with certain populations, these master's- or special- ist's-degree professionals may be more competent in certain areas than the new doctorate recipient. Finally, the qualification for independent practice in the pri- vate sector highlights the critical issue in the master's versus doctoral discussion: What should be the minimum training and supervised practice (if any) for func- tioning independently? Nonetheless, while recognizing that this question has yet to be resolved, this chapter will concentrate primarily on doctoral training.

DEGREE OPTIONS

Doctor of Philosophy

The Ph.D. is traditionally a research-oriented degree, so it is not surprising that professionally-oriented Ph.D. programs have been established and supported with less than enthusiastic endorsement within the university community. Typically, the Ph.D. programs exist in departments of psychology, side by side with such research-oriented Ph.D. programs as experimental psychology, physio- logical psychology, and developmental psychology. They may also be located in schools of education, where they frequently train the specialties of counseling and school psychology, but here again, the research expectation exists. Thus, the initial scientist-practitioner identification of professional psychology serves it well in terms of representing the dual identity of the discipline while serving as an underlying rationale for the placement of a professional program within this research-oriented degree. However, the tension still exists and a number of Ph.D. professional psychology programs in departments of psychology train researchers in clinical practice, as contrasted to the goal of training practitioners (albeit with a scientist-practitioner degree). In fact, such tensions led to the Vail Conference deliberations noted above. Ph.D. programs in the university setting may also be located in schools of medicine among other departments or units.

Doctor of Education

The doctor of education (Ed.D.) degree is typically offered through schools of education and is available for school psychologists (and in some rare instances, counseling psychologists) (Fagan & Wise, 1994). Although some school psychology programs are located in schools of education because educational psychology programs had originally been housed there, such a placement facilitates collaboration between psychologists and educators. Although the Ed.D. degree may be the only doctoral degree offered in the school of education, both the Ph.D. and Ed.D. may be available. Generally, there is little difference between the Ph.D. and Ed.D. degrees in school psychology, although the Ed.D. is generally recognized as a professional degree. The education field itself is struggling to differentiate Ed.D. and Ph.D. training, and thus all Ph.D. programs within Ed.D. departments reflect that lack of clarity. Discussions to resolve this problem focus primarily on the nature and objective(s) of scholarship training as well as the emphasis on training experiences related to practice.

Doctor of Psychology

The doctor of psychology degree is available at some universities but is usually offered through freestanding institutions. In 1974 the National Council of Schools and Programs of Professional Psychology (NCSPP) was established as an organization of primarily Psy.D.-oriented programs endorsing education for practice as their objective of training. Scientific and professional elements of education and training are incorporated in the curriculum, which should reflect the six core professional competency areas endorsed by NCSPP. These areas are relationship, assessment, intervention, research and evaluation, consultation and education, management and supervision. "All professional psychology graduates are expected to function as local clinical scientists" (Peterson, Peterson, &

Abrams, 1994, p. 4) who are knowledgeable of research and who can use theory and scientific research in their practice. Research training helps to develop and enhance critical thinking skills; thus, inquiry within the local context of professional psychology practice, while different than the general practice of science, recognizes the uniqueness and constraints of the context when science is applied to the immediate problem.

The NCSPP standards for education in professional psychology have evolved from resolutions dealing with attitudes, aptitudes, values, and diversity of women passed at seven conferences since the Vail Conference. The primary goal of this education and training is "preparation for the delivery of human services in a manner that is effective and responsive to the individual and societal needs, [and that] recognizes and values human diversity" (Peterson et al., 1994, p. 10). Education is based on the premise that all of professional psychology is relationship-centered and therefore education of the personal and professional selves of students is emphasized. Fox (1994) argues that professional psychology must have a "single, comprehensive definition" and that the definition should be accepted by the profession, drive the education and training of the professional, and be readily understood by the public. Without that definition, and without a uniform professional curriculum, professional psychology's development is hampered.

Ph.D. versus Psy.D.

In order to facilitate the development of psychology as a profession, Shapiro and Wiggins (1994) made the radical proposal that the doctor of psychology degree should identify psychologists who provide health services and the doctor of philosophy degree should describe the academic—or research—psychologist. They feel that the current dual definition of the Ph.D. is too confusing! They note that almost 70% of the APA membership identifies their activities as health services and that the number of programs awarding the Psy.D. has grown to 40, graduating 13% of all doctoral graduates in the profession. The use of the Psy.D. degree, then, would represent an important truth-in-labeling shift for the discipline that would parallel the M.D. in medicine, the D.D.S. in dentistry, and the J.D. in law. Shapiro and Wiggins recommend that a credential review be established, as has been done in other fields, wherein current practitioners holding the Ph.D. would be awarded the Psy.D.; thus, they could self-identify as Ph.D. and Psy.D. Subsequently, the Ph.D. degree would be reserved for individuals qualified to enter a career in research and scholarship, and all practitioners, current and in training, would hold the Psy.D.

Shapiro and Wiggins continue an argument begun in 1967 (APA Committee) that led to the endorsement of the Psy.D. degree during the Vail

Conference (Korman, 1974). Since the Ph.D. is still used in the scientist-practitioner programs, this suggestion presents serious logistic and political challenges in spite of its rational appeal to some. It should be noted that the scientist-practitioner model of training for practitioners is still a viable approach in spite of its challenges both within the university context and in practice (see Barlow et al., 1984, and Lambert, 1993, for a detailed presentation of this model).

Others take a much more micro view of this discussion. For example, Nelson (1995) argued that it is that "unique perspective about human behavior in myriad interdisciplinary contexts" and the particular problem-solving skills that bind psychologists of all types and help the field experience its growth and success. Consequently, he argues that all training programs must devote more attention to the four constructs of critical thinking capabilities, strategies of inquiry and observation, measurement theory and method, and learning how to learn as a psychologist.

The scientist versus practitioner and the scientist-practitioner versus practitioner splits continue, and represent the differences in practice objectives and training strategies of programs. Stricker & Trierweiler (1995) believe a "local clinical scientist model, which encourages the application of scientific knowledge and the scientific attitude to the local clinical setting," is the bridge (p. 1001). "Local" means that an observation may not be generalizable beyond the immediate setting, so that while events appear unique, a scientific attitude of inquiry should prevail since they may be subject to more general rules. Thus, for the local clinical scientist to practice without having fully supportive evidence is not unethical, but it is unethical to engage in practices that contradict scientific evidence. Similarly, Peterson (1995) argues that researchers should consider "conceptions of professional work that emphasize reflection in action and disciplined inquiry, rather than psychotherapy and psychodiagnosis as defining features. Education for practice is neither science nor art, but a profession in itself" (p. 975). There does appear to be a scientist-practitioner split, but practitioners seem to be doing more to understand scientific findings and translate them into practice than scientists are doing to understand the problems faced by clinical practitioners (Beuther, Williams, Wakefield, & Entwistle, 1995). In closing, it is important to note that the tension between science and practice appears to exist in many disciplines where professional training is involved; what makes professional psychology unique is its early identity roots in science.

GRADUATE STUDY IN PSYCHOLOGY

A recent study of graduate programs (based on data in the 1996 edition of APA's

Graduate Study in Psychology) provides a comprehensive picture of current characteristics of psychology training as well a trend in the United States and Canada. Norcross, Hanych, and Terranova (1996) reported on 2,023 graduate programs, both master's and doctorate, research and professionally orientated. Half of these programs offer the doctorate. Two-thirds of the departments (N=559) housing these programs were labeled psychology departments, with the majority (54%) of the programs established since 1960. The percentage of women who were in full-time faculty positions in the doctoral programs was 30%, and approximately 10% were members of a racial or ethnic minority (the percentages were similar in master's programs). The percentages were higher among part-time faculty. Norcross and colleagues noted a decline in the number of applications programs received from 1979 to 1992, but also that the number of programs doubled during this same period. Following are several general conclusions:

1. Admissions to a graduate program requires at minimum the equivalent of a rigorous undergraduate minor in psychology.
2. The average verbal plus quantitative GRE score is 1000 for master's departments and 1100 for doctoral programs; average undergraduate GPAs are 3.2 and 3.5 respectively.
3. Increasing one's research experience and productivity were seen as the better of several strategies to influence acceptance into a doctoral program.
4. The match between the applicant's interest and program credentials is most critical given the number and diversity of the available programs; applicants and advisors were strongly urged to study the differences among programs and the implications for available graduate study support.

Henderson, Clarke, and Reynolds (1996) reported that in terms of psychology doctorates the number of graduates rose from 954 in 1965 to 3118 in 1985, when it leveled off; the number of graduates in 1995 was 3,267. They also noted that in 1995, of the three major applied psychology areas (clinical, counseling, and school), more women earned the doctoral degree than men.

DESIGNATION OF PROGRAMS AS PSYCHOLOGY PROGRAMS

For a number of years, there have been calls for development of a formal mechanism that would identify/designate a training program as a "psychology" program. State psychology licensing boards, in particular, find themselves in a peculiar position of having to judge whether a program is indeed a psychology program, and not, for example, psychological in nature, when transcripts carry a different program title (e.g., human development). Applicants for licensure, and sometimes faculty, argue for the program's validity on the grounds that it is indeed "psychological in nature." Similarly, students applying to graduate school may have questions regarding the nature of a program, as do other consumer groups and federal or state agencies. While various accreditation mechanisms exist, there currently is no nationally agreed-to-criteria by which all programs wanting such recognition could be reviewed. Without a designation process, the field faces the prospect of a definition evolving from case law, policies of other independent organizations, and federal and state statutes and regulations. As a result, students may not always be assured that programs meet the educational requirements. Finally, users of psychological services (clients, legislators, school district personnel directors, etc.) cannot assume that the person claiming to be a psychologist will have the educational background to provide safe, effective, and appropriate service.

As a result, the APA has been considering a plan for the designation of graduate programs in psychology. In 1985, the Council of Graduate Departments of Psychology opposed such an effort on several grounds. Philosophically, it was argued that the time was not ripe for standardization given the rapid changes in the field. Practically, academic freedom seemed to be at risk and the process was seen as a threat to accreditation. Also, programs feared that if they were not designated, whatever the reason, they might face lawsuits of various types. After much discussion, the APA Council of Representatives voted at their August 1985 meeting to suspend their discussions of designation (and the recommendations being made by a task force) until the task force on the structure of APA made its final report. Subsequently, the Association of State and Provincial Psychology Boards (ASPPB) and the National Register have decided to collaborate on a psychology program designation plan.

There are several sources for identifying psychology programs. First, there is the APA accreditation process discussed in chapter 5. Second, the APA (1996a) publishes the *Graduate Study in Psychology*, which lists more than 600 programs. This publication is organized into four sections:

1. Departments and Schools of Psychology and APA-Accredited Programs Offering the Doctoral Degree
2. Other Departments Offering the Doctoral Degree (e.g., College of Education, Department of Child Study)
3. Graduate Departments of Psychology Offering Less than the Doctoral Degree
4. Other Graduate Departments Offering Less than the Doctoral Degree

APA-accredited programs, it should be noted, are listed in Section I even if their departments are not labeled as psychology departments. Within each section, institutions are listed alphabetically by state, and alphabetically for Canada. In addition, a "List of Programs by Degree Offered" is also provided and includes valuable locator assistance to the reader.

The information presented in *Graduate Study* is provided voluntarily by the psychology programs and includes data on requirements, facilities, and financial assistance. For institutions and programs that did not provide information, only the institution's name, department, address, telephone number, and chairperson's name are listed. Otherwise readers can expect to find the following information on the department:

- university name, department, address, and telephone number
- APA accreditation status
- department overview (year that information was provided, chairperson, faculty size)
- programs and degrees offered
- application information
- student information (e.g., numbers, dropout information)
- degree requirements
- admission requirements
- tuition for full-time study
- housing and daycare
- financial assistance
- special group considerations (e.g., the number of women and minority faculty, special programs available to people with physical disabilities, teaching opportunities)

It is important to keep in mind that information is supplied by the programs and there is no policy board or peer review process to insure the accuracy of the programs' reports.

The *Graduate Study* also contains the 1978 APA policy on reserving the titles of "Professional Psychology," "School Psychologist," and "Industrial Psychologist" for those who have completed doctoral training in psychology. Likewise, the 1976 APA policy for psychologists who wish to change their psychology specialty is included; this policy indicates that such respecialization training should involve more than practicums and/or internship, it should meet all of the doctoral training requirements of the specialty, and a certificate should be awarded upon completion of the training.

The APA also publishes *Getting In: A Step-by Step Plan for Gaining Admission to*

Graduate Study in Psychology, which explains how to select programs and apply to graduate school. Likewise, the APA Public Interest Directorate offers a number of free publications that provide information on course offerings dealing with opportunities available to women, ethnic minorities, lesbians, and gays. Those publications are: *Survival Guide to Academia for Women and Ethnic Minorities; Directory of Selected Scholarships, Fellowships, and other Financial Aid Opportunities for Women and Ethnic Minorities in Psychology and Related Fields; Graduate Faculty Interested in the Psychology of Women;* and *Graduate Faculty Interested in Lesbian and Gay Issues.*

The third source for identifying psychology programs is *Designated Doctoral Programs in Psychology*, published annually by the Council for the National Register of Health Service Providers in Psychology. The listing was designed to facilitate the National Register's review of individual applications for listing in the *National Register*; the list did not include all the programs that meet their stated guidelines. These guidelines were originally developed in 1977 at the Education and Credentialing Psychology Meeting, a group of invited psychologists representing invited organizations and divisions as well as related APA boards and committees. In 1985 the American Association of State Psychology Boards (now known as the ASPPB) and the National Register approved a joint designation system that remains in place today. This list of designated psychology programs contains those programs that have applied for review by the ASPPB/NR Joint Designation Committee and either clearly meet criteria 2 through 10 used to identify doctoral programs as a psychology program (see table 4.1) or have received APA/CPA accreditation (criterion 1). It is important to note that a determination of the educational quality of the programs is not intended by this designation. These criteria incorporate the above-mentioned 1977 meeting recommendations and are now used in various ways by credentialing bodies. In addition to providing concise information to prospective graduate students, the listing facilitates the work of psychology licensing boards and the National Register as they review the educational training background of individual applicants. All applied programs meeting the criteria are encouraged to apply for listing regardless of specialty. There were 424 doctoral programs listed in the 1997 edition; one-third demonstrated their adherence to criteria 2 through 10 of the ASPPB/NR Joint Designation Committee. Recently (1996), the Joint Designation Committee has begun requesting updated information from one-third of the designated programs on a rotating three-year cycle.

The *Educational Reporting Service—EPPP Performance by Designated Doctoral Programs in Psychology* is a related ASPPB publication that provides annual aggregate data on the performance of graduates from the designated programs (where programs have three or more candidates taking the examination) on the Examination for the Professional Practice of Psychology (EPPP) (see chapter 5).

Table 4.1
ASPPB/NR GUIDELINES FOR DEFINING "DOCTORAL DEGREE IN PSYCHOLOGY"
(as developed by the Education and Credentialing in Psychology meeting in 1977)

The following criteria will be used to identify doctoral programs as psychology programs:

1. Programs that are accredited by the American Psychological Association are recognized as meeting the definition of a professional psychology[1] program. The criteria for accreditation serve as a model for professional psychology training.

OR
All of the following criteria, 2 through 10

2. Training in professional psychology is doctoral training offered in a regionally accredited institution of higher education.[2]
3. The program, wherever it may be administratively housed, must be clearly identified and labeled as a psychology program. Such a program must specify in pertinent institutional catalogues and brochures its intent to educate and train professional psychologists.
4. The psychology program must stand as a recognizable, coherent organizational entity with the institution.
5. There must be a clear authority and primary responsibility for the core and specialty areas whether or not the program cuts across administrative lines.
6. The program must be an integrated, organized sequence of study.
7. There must be an identifiable psychology faculty[3] and a psychologist responsible for the program.
8. The program must have an identifiable body of students who are matriculated in that program for a degree.
9. The program must include supervised practicum, internship, field, or laboratory training appropriate to the practice of psychology.
10. The curriculum shall encompass a minimum of three academic years of full-time graduate study. In addition to instruction in scientific and professional ethics and standards,[4] research design and methodology, statistics and psychometrics, the core program shall require each student to demonstrate competence in each of the following substantive content areas. This typically will be met by including a minimum of three or more graduate semester hours (5 or more graduate quarter hours) in each of these 4 substantive content areas:

Table 4.1 (continued)

a) biological bases of behavior: physiological psychology, comparative psychology, neuropsychology, sensation and perception, psychopharmacology

b) cognitive-affective bases of behavior: learning, thinking, motivation, emotion

c) social bases of behavior: social psychology, group processes, organizational and systems theory

d) individual differences: personality theory, human development, abnormal psychology

In addition, all professional education programs in psychology will include course requirements in specialty areas.

[1] Reference to "professional psychology" in guidelines 1 and 2 refers to psychology as a profession. The term is not intended in the more restrictive sense of applied or practice areas of psychology, since the intent is for a generic designation system.

[2] Guideline 2 refers to an institution with regional accreditation in the United States, an institution with provincial authorization in Canada, or in other countries, an institution that is accredited by a body which is deemed by the ASPPB/National Register Joint Designation Committee to be performing a function equivalent to that of U.S. regional accrediting bodies.

[3] There must be an identifiable psychology faculty on site sufficient in size and breadth to carry out its responsibilities.

[4] In reference to "instruction in scientific and professional ethics and standards," it is understood that a course of three or more graduate semester hours (five or more graduate quarter hours) or its equivalent is highly desirable; substantial instruction in these issues is required. It is also understood that guideline 10 includes the requirement of a minimum of one year's residency at the educational institution granting the doctoral degree.

From Council for the National Register of Health Service Providers in Psychology (1997). Reprinted with permission.

And finally, the July or August issue of the *American Psychologist* lists APA accredited programs.

INTERNSHIP TRAINING

Recently, APA boards and committees have been discussing a proposal to change the one-year internship from a predoctoral to a postdoctoral requirement. A working group of the Board of Educational Affairs has addressed the implications of such a change for training, licensure, and accreditation policy. Not surprising, the group found differences of strong opinions within and between communities of doctoral training programs and internship training programs. A majority of university-based clinical psychology program directors, as well as medical school or university health service centers, favor the postdoctoral internship. In contrast, directors of counseling and school psychology programs, professional schools of psychology, and the APPIC Board are in favor of the predoctoral internship. The proposal has generated arguments of funding, quality of training, licensure problems, accountability implications, and the surprising fact that the median number of *practicum* hours for most students is 1500 prior to the predoctoral internship. Nonetheless, the working group decided that it would be more sensible to begin to examine in depth the construct of "supervised practice experience" at different stages of education and training and consider a period of time for a reasonably controlled experimentation in the timing of internship training rather than recommend a decision on the placement of the internship. Thus, the relatively new graduate student in professional psychology will want to monitor the discussions and developments as they become expressed in various professional publications.

Two articles that provide more information on this debate are by Belar and colleagues (1989), who discuss the 1987 National Conference on Internship Training, which reached consensus on the purpose and nature of the predoctoral internship, and more recently, by Stedman (1997), who reviews the literature since 1974 on the subject of predoctoral internship. The 1987 internship conference (Belar et al., 1989) adopted a policy statement defining internship training as "a two-year process; one year is predoctoral and one year is postdoctoral" (p. 61). It also decided that all internship training should take place within APA-accredited internship programs, should be funded at levels commensurate with experience, and should occur after the completion of the dissertation. The delegates to this conference specified requirements for a core set of requirements, proposed a collaborative relationship between the internship program and the graduate program, increased the number of practicum hours in direct provision of a range of psychological services to 450 out of a total of 900 hours, with at least 300 hours in formal supervision, and called for the broadening of the sources for funding. Finally, they recommended that 500 hours of the predoctoral internship year be spent in direct patient/client contact with a minimum of four hours per week of face-to-face supervision (three of which should be scheduled on an individual basis).

POSTDOCTORAL EDUCATION AND TRAINING

Currently there is considerable interest in postdoctoral training, which has led to formal actions on several fronts. This interest is partly the result of a "lifelong" learning philosophy. The technological information phenomenon, which has contributed to an ever-expanding information base, taxes an individual's capacity to keep abreast of his or her professional "area" let alone other related areas. Also, in most states professional psychologists must document at least a year of postdoctoral supervised experience before obtaining licensing (which has led a minority of psychologists to argue that all professional training should be postdoctoral, as noted above).

In a study of postdoctoral education and training programs for research and practice (Wiens & Baum, 1995), based in large measure from listings in the APA *Monitor*, 229 programs responded with the surprising figure that 1,276 psychology fellows/residents were being trained in programs ranging in size from 1–99 participants. While one year of a postdoctoral supervised experience is required for permanent licensure in most states, it is noteworthy that formal postdoctoral training is this widespread. It has been reported that while in 1985 only 28 states required postdoctoral experience for permanent licensure, in 1995 that number rose to 46 (Stewart & Stewart 1998). Yet, there was wide variability in the number of hours constituting a training year. Stewart and Stewart also report that through October 1996 there were 439 sites providing a total of 1,107 full-time training slots, with neuropsychology and rehabilitation offered most frequently (27%).

Two major, but separate, postdoctoral training conferences and one significant postdoctoral program accreditation effort have taken place. Following the 1987 conference on predoctoral internship training in professional psychology, in 1992 the Association of Psychology Postdoctoral and Internship Centers (APPIC), the American Board of Professional Psychology, American Psychological Association, Association of State and Provincial Boards, and the National Register of Health Care Providers in Psychology cosponsored a conference on postdoctoral training in professional psychology. Among the actions taken by the conference, a definition of the postdoctoral residency was proposed as "an organized education and training program" based on a doctoral program in professional psychology (including completion of a doctoral internship) with the objective "to develop advanced competency and expertise for the professional practice of psychology" (Larsen et al., 1993, p. 8). In addition to this definition, a policy statement regarding the nature of the program was included (a minimum of two hours per week of supervision, a minimum of two supervisors per residency year). The conference also called for periodic review and accreditation of the postdoctoral residency programs and evaluation of field training programs.

In 1995 the APA Conference on Postdoctoral Education and Training in Psychology was directed to "study postdoctoral education and training extant across different areas of psychology and identify postdoctoral education models, directions, and mechanisms for quality assurance which may be needed by individuals entering the discipline of psychology in the twenty-first century" (APA, 1995b, p. vii). Thus, this conference was much broader in scope and discipline then the 1992 conference. The term "postdoctoral education" was used to cover the broad continuum of training from informal self-development activities (i.e., self-study) to formal postdoctoral training in practice and/or research. Also unique to this conference was a resolution that its goal was to bring together teachers, researchers, and practitioners in psychology to foster integrative thinking across those perspectives rather than seek consensual resolutions. Six general issues were confronted by the conference participants in dealing with challenges of training, practice, and postdoctoral education: (1) models for education and training beyond the doctoral degree, (2) societal needs, changing demographics, and national policies, (3) the expanding knowledge and skills base, (4) the impact of changing technology, (5) evaluation and lifelong learning, and (6) funding for recommendations. Recommendations were made to the APA in each of these areas, along with recommendations relevant to the individual psychologist as well as the community of psychologists represented by the conference participants. For example, lifelong learning was seen as the personal responsibility of all psychologists. The APA was charged with developing strategies for creating structures that would promote interactions between the scientific and practitioner communities within psychology and with other disciplines; the idea of peer review of research training programs (as opposed to accreditation) was proposed; and postdoctoral and continuing education programs in teaching were advocated.

Finally, the Interorganizational Council of Credentialing Organizations (IOC) met to develop criteria and procedures of accreditation of postdoctoral residencies (see chapter 5 for a more complete description of the ad hoc group's influence). Subsequent involvement of the APA Committee on Accreditation resulted in their adoption of the IOC materials and initiation of accreditation of programs at this level of training.

In summary then, American psychology has seen a flurry of activity related to education and training. The result has been a greater consensus as to what constitutes professional graduate training in psychology. At the same time, the number of programs and graduates have increased. Given the supply-and-demand outlook for psychologists (to be discussed later) and the regulation changes that have taken place, it may be that professional psychology is approaching a period in its history when even greater integration of the training sequence and more standard curriculum will be the result.

Chapter 5

Regulation of the Psychology Profession

Professions are organized groups of individuals that represent and advance the development of the group. One of the most important characteristics seems to be that they promote standardized training in knowledge and skill areas to stated criteria; furthermore, that objective is also promoted and monitored by a formal establishment. It has been argued that in psychology the training leads to "a way of thinking based on a scientific background and body of knowledge shared in common with other psychologists, augmented by special skills and knowledge based on education and training in the specialty area" (Bardon, 1981, p. 209). Finally, it has been noted that virtually all professions have codes of ethics that emphasize public service. While such altruistic considerations of the professional are considered critical to their definitions, Hogan (1979) notes that some writers have also included the business motivations of the profession.

In marketplace terms, Beales (1980) points out that professionals are unique in that they generally fill two roles, "the consumer's agent and a principal in the transaction" (p. 125). Given that the professional not only diagnoses, that is, sells information, but also recommends treatment or service that he or she can deliver, the dual role represents a conflict of interest. The problems confronting the consumer include the risk of misdiagnosis, excessive diagnosis leading to unnecessary or inappropriate treatment, and low quality treatment. The need for regulation rises as the need to protect the consumer increases, such as when it is difficult to assess the quality of the service. Regulation addresses this problem by dealing with the quality of production inputs—the quality of the professional.

In addition, training programs (such as preservice academic and practicum training, internships, and postdoctoral residencies in psychology) can voluntarily submit to a peer review of the adequacy of their preparatory education. While an internal review mechanism usually exists, the peer review is conducted by a professionally recognized accrediting body using criteria developed and sanctioned by the discipline. Typically, such reviews lead to a formal *accreditation* status, with subsequent reaccreditation and sanction provisions as a part of the obligations for such recognition.

Credentialing is the mechanism, then, by which a professional regulates his- or herself or is regulated. It can take place at several levels and implies that a relationship exists between the credential and the competency of the practitioners within the profession. In fact, some authors have conceptualized the construct for competence to vary as a function of the particular credential that is held (Koocher, 1979).

This chapter describes the various types of regulatory mechanisms that exist in psychology. The value of the credential is the validation purpose it serves for the public, that in fact the bearer of the credential has fulfilled requirements and training to participate in the profession. It also provides a feedback mechanism to the training programs in the sense that examinations must also be passed, and the success rate of the programs' graduates become public record. Accreditation also serves as a quality index for individuals, as they decide to enter either the training phase for the profession or the profession itself.

PSYCHOLOGY CREDENTIALS

Graduate Degree

The most basic credential is often overlooked in credentialing discussions. The graduate degree stands for what might be argued as the most important element of any profession. Graduate programs are academic in nature, and one should be able to assume that programs advertising their intent to train professionals will maintain high standards for graduation. The degree, then, serving as one of the psychology credentials, has potentially the most credibility for insuring the entry-to-the-field competence of the novice professional. Longitudinal samples of the graduate's behavior under increasingly demanding conditions, which involve direct and indirect evaluations, support this conclusion. However, this premise is based on the assumption that the professional degree is not strictly academic, but also contains sequenced, supervised professional practice (i.e., practica and internship). Certainly, we can expect that a professional degree serves to confirm that the entry-level knowledge and skills expected of the professional psychologist have been mastered to some minimum criteria as determined by the experienced, even expert, professionals doing the training.

Doctoral-level training in psychology is often designated by award of the doctor of philosophy (Ph.D.), doctor of psychology (Psy.D.), or doctor of education (Ed.D.) degree as noted in chapter 4. Ph.D. programs have typically embraced a *scientist-professional* (subtle differences in the meaning of this hyphenated concept are embodied in terms such as scholar-professional, scientist-practitioner, or practitioner-scientist) model of training for a number of years, as adopted at the Boulder Conference (Raimy, 1950). More recently, the Vail Conference endorsed a recommendation that the highest professional degree be the Psy.D. (Korman, 1974b). The Vail Conference participants reasoned that where "primary emphasis in training is on the direct delivery of professional services and evaluation and improvement of those services, the Psy.D. degree is appropriate." Thus, the Ph.D. was conceptualized as appropriate when the primary training emphasis is on the development of new knowledge in psychology.

In addition to departments of psychology in universities, professional programs in psychology exist in a variety of organizational settings, such as medical schools, colleges of education, freestanding schools of professional psychology, and autonomous professional schools in academic settings, all of whom may award one or two of these degrees or a related degree, as noted in chapter 4.

Licensure

Licensure represents the mechanism by which state governments protect the public health, morals, safety, and general welfare of their citizens (Council of State Governments, 1952). The state identifies a regulatory agency to carry out this function by establishing a separate board for the occupation or profession. In fact, licensing laws are estimated to affect 20–30% of the work force, with the number of licensed occupations or professions numbering 500 (Hogan, 1979). Generally, the occupational or professional groups seek this type of legislation with the purpose of protecting the public from harm by incompetent, unethical, or unscrupulous practitioners. This goal is accomplished by establishing entry requirements and mechanisms for regulating professional conduct.

Perhaps the most commonly identified credential, licensure, remains the least understood credential because of confusing terminology and the mixed purposes and functions for which it was envisioned. There are at least three types, or levels, of licensure acts. Technically, a *licensing* act not only grants the use of professional title to individuals meeting established criteria, but also restricts the practice in the profession as defined therein. Thus, the often-used synonymous term, a *practice* act, may be used. It is the most restrictive of the three types of regulation. *Certification*, on the other hand, usually is established primarily to restrict the use of title (or derivatives of the title, such as "psychological" in the case of psychology) and is not concerned with the restriction and/or protection of professional practice except where the person wishes to use the title *psychologist*. These acts are in fact referred to as "title" acts or permissive laws. While both of these forms of licensure laws are mandatory (in the sense that the practitioner is required to hold the credential in order to practice), a more voluntary type of credential called *registration* has received some attention. It requires no criteria, such as passing an exam or meeting minimum educational or other prerequisites, before permission is granted to practice. A registration law proposal has been made for psychotherapists in which the practitioner would file relevant information with the state (e.g., education, experience, intended field of practice, methods, goal of treatment, fees, success rates, etc.), and a board of registration would be responsible for disciplinary enforcement (Hogan, 1979). In this model, practitioners would be required to provide the client with sufficient information (full disclosure) of their service and the practice, subject to direct evaluation by the client.

Most psychology licensing laws tend to be *generic*, that is, psychologists are credentialed without reference to specialty practice area or a distinction of whether they have applied training. *Specialty* designation may take several forms. For example, the term "clinical psychology" may be used wherein any specialty of applied/professional practice is implied rather than the specialty of clinical psychology per se. Then again, the term "clinical health psychology" may be used in a specific specialty manner, with different education and training requirements stipulated. In general, however, licensing boards that have moved toward "specialized recognition" use the title "health service provider"; this term is usually a further title designation once licensure has been obtained. Typically, the clinical, counseling, and school specialties qualify for such a designation.

Also, most psychology boards will license only doctoral-trained psychologists. Where two levels, master and doctoral, are licensed, it may be to distinguish master's/specialist degree psychologists within one specialty, such as school psychology. A *title* will usually distinguish between the two types of licensees, with the scope of practice for the psychologists with a master's degree either restricted and/or associated with supervision.

Psychology boards typically reflect the make-up of psychologists they license and include a public member(s). The members are often appointed by the governor, with input from state psychological organizations. The law itself is often supplemented by the rules of the board operation, which tend to be quite a bit more detailed. Finally, licensure often requires renewal, which may or may not be associated with a continuing education requirement. While many licensing acts have adopted the APA Code of Ethics by which licensees' behavior can be judged in instances of complaints, boards have also written their own codes because of the vagaries of the pre-1992 APA Code, which resulted in difficulty in sanctioning psychologists found in violation of the code.

The first psychology licensure law in the United States was passed in 1945 (1960 in Canada), but it was not until 1977 that all 50 states had such a statute. At that time it was estimated that there were 28,000 licensed psychologists. In 1967, the American Psychological Association adopted a Model for State Legislation to assist states in planning new legislation or considering amendments. A model licensing law that updates the 1967 APA model was published in 1987 (APA, 1987b). That proposal was followed in 1992 by the Association of State and Provincial Psychology Boards' (ASPPB) *Model Act for Licensure of Psychologists* (ASPPB, 1992), which included a definition of the practice of psychology. By 1996, the number of doctoral psychologists licensed for independent practice was 91,149 in the United States, and 3,410 in Canada (ASPPB, 1998).

Obviously, the conditions existing in each state, such as manpower needs and issues of a state's sovereignty, have led to less uniformity in compliance with licensure laws than some would like or expect. Because compliance with federal standards is required before insurance reimbursement is realized, there has been some standardization.

Licensing laws are generally administered by an independent board staffed by the profession for its own regulation; in other instances the board operates within another state agency such as a department of licensing and regulation or department of health. Usually the board is composed of licensed psychologists and public members. Most laws place the responsibility for selecting board members with the governor. Because some type of formal or informal input from the profession is also involved, the state psychological associations exert a certain degree of influence. Generally, then, the charge to the board is to insure that the statute is carried out as protection of the public rather than as advocacy for the profession or licensed professional.

Examination for Professional Practice in Psychology

Psychology boards are members of the Association of State and Provincial Psychology Boards, whose purposes involve promoting sound administration and facilitating communication among member boards. The ASPPB has also begun recommending policy to its member boards. However, the primary task of the organization is the semiannual preparation of two, essentially nonoverlapping, forms of the *Examination for Professional Practice in Psychology* (EPPP) for administration in April and October. The EPPP is a multiple-choice exam of approximately 200 items. It is standardized for use by licensing boards, and measures knowledge of basic psychology relevant to professional practice, ethics, and professional affairs. (All states use at least one complementary assessment procedure.) A separate ASPPB brochure, *Information for Candidates,* is available from the ASPPB (1997) or the state licensing board and explains how to prepare for

the exam. The content of the examination, beginning with the 1987 adminis-
trations, is based on the results from three projects that were undertaken to
ensure the content validity of the EPPP.

1. The first project assembled a "blue ribbon panel of psychologists who defined
   the scope of professional practice in psychology in terms of performance
   domains, roles, and the knowledge required to perform the roles" (Myers &
   Rosen, 1986, p. 8).
2. A job analysis of professional psychologists' work completed by 1,585
   licensed psychologists was the next project and resulted in an "inventory
   consisting of 59 responsibilities and 61 procedures, techniques, and
   resources" (Myers & Rosen, 1986, p. 12). A 23-member panel of psychologists combined the data from the job dimensions and the domains of practice into five dimensions.
3. In 1995 another practice analysis was conducted to examine "what licensed
   psychologists do and need to know to practice in the United States and
   Canada" (ASPPB, 1997, p. 4). Roles and responsibilities performed by psychologists were outlined along with the content areas and knowledge
   required in practice. A survey was then sent to 7,500 psychologists in both
   countries to validate that information. First, *roles* that licensed psychologists
   perform in their work emerged. Those roles involved (a) direct service (e.g.,
   diagnosis, problem identification, and designing, offering, and evaluating
   interventions); (b) outreach and consultation (planning and offering educational programs, consultation and collaboration in research, evaluation
   and psychological information to individuals, groups, and systems); (c) academic preparation and professional development (e.g., teaching, supervision, and curricula design and administration); (d) research and evaluation
   (e.g., use of results to expand and refine knowledge or improve programs and
   research). While not to be used as a guide to construct the EPPP, the exam
   writers are instructed to use the four roles in producing job-relevant examination questions. The survey also yielded eight *content* domains, which are
   used in writing the exam. The eight domains, plus definitions and percentage representation on the EPPP, are presented in table 5.1.

Items for the exam are constructed semiannually by subject-matter experts in
psychology and then reviewed and validated by other expert teams; the entire
process is described in the publication for candidates. Specific feedback to the
candidates on their EPPP performance is available as well as transfer of scores
from an administration taken in one state to another state. Finally, a booklet
containing 350 items used on past versions of the EPPP along with 100 new

Table 5.1
CONTENT AREAS OF THE EPPP WITH PERCENTAGE REPRESENTATION

1. *Assessment and diagnosis (14%)*. Knowledge of (a) psychometrics, (b) assessment models, (c) methods for assessment of individuals and organizations/systems, and (d) diagnostic classification systems and issues
2. *Biological bases of behavior (11%)*. Knowledge of (a) neuroscience, (b) the physiological bases of behavior and illness and psychopharmacology
3. *Cognitive-affective bases of behavior (13%)*. Knowledge of (a) cognitive science, (b) theories of learning, memory, motivation, and emotion, and (c) factors that influence an individual's cognitive performance and/or emotional experience
4. *Ethical/Legal/Professional issues (15%)*. Knowledge of (a) the ethical code, (b) professional standards for practice, (c) legal mandates, (d) guidelines for ethical decision-making, and (e) professional training and supervision
5. *Growth and life-span development (13%)*. Knowledge of (a) age-appropriate child, adolescent, and adult development, (b) atypical patterns of development, and (c) the protective and risk factors that influence developmental outcomes for individuals
6. *Research methods (6%)*. Knowledge of (a) research design, methodology, and program evaluation, (b) statistical procedures, and (c) criteria for accurate interpretation of research findings
7. *Social and multicultural bases of behavior (12%)*. Knowledge of (a) social cognition, social interaction processes, and organizational dynamics, (b) theories of personalities, and (c) issues in diversity (multiethnic, multicultural, gender, ageism, sexual orientation, and disability)
8. *Treatment/Intervention (16%)*. Knowledge of (a) individual, group, or organizational interventions for specific concerns/disorders, (b) treatment theories, and (c) consultation models and processes

From ASPPB, 1997, pp. 5–7. Reprinted with permission from the Association of State and Provincial Psychology Boards.

questions, answer key, and reference list is available from the ASPPB (1996a). The publication notes that this is not a "sample" test and it should not be used for study or other preparation; it merely serves to give applicants a sense of what test items are like.

The EPPP has become the accepted examination for entry into the profession, so that it must be passed in order for one to become eligible for licensure. While each jurisdiction sets its own passing point, the ASPPB has recommended that 70% be set as a passing point, which would set a national criterion. There is also a French version of the EPPP. An interesting use of the EPPP scores provides some insight into what may be a difference in the priorities of the different degree programs, although other variables such as recruitment factors and outcome criteria may be a factor. Nevertheless, in a study of 1988–1995 clinical psychology program graduates' EPPP scores, it was found that higher scores correlated with larger faculty-to-student ratios, smaller clinical programs, and Ph.D. (versus professional) program orientation (Yu et al., 1997). The specific clinical psychology programs' standing is also available in a separate publication (Herring, 1997).

It is important to recognize that since its inception in 1961, the ASPPB has been independent of the APA, and therefore represents the group of psychologists (i.e., state psychology boards) legally charged with regulation of the profession. Consequently, issues will be addressed from that perspective.

Elements of Licensing Laws

Six elements seem to recur in professional licensing laws or acts (Rubin, 1980):

1. The state psychology licensing board, as described in previous paragraphs, is appointed by the governor. Because licensing boards are generally self-sustaining bodies (receiving no funds from the state), their expenses and those of the staff are compensated through applications and annual license fees.
2. The act defines minimum fitness, education, and experience qualifications for licensure. Usually regional accreditations of the university from which the graduate has received his or her degree are required. Transcripts are reviewed for documentation of psychology as the major field of study.
3. During the initial stages of state licensure, "grandparenting" provisions also have been included.
4. A code of ethics is stated, either by referencing to the APA Ethical Principles or restating those concepts and others in a state code.
5. The act states the disciplinary action to be taken in accordance with the ethical code and in other instances, such as committing an illegal act. Due-process mechanisms, normally from the state's administrative code or other reference, are employed in such instances.
6. Provision is made for prohibition of professional practice by unlicensed individuals.

The addresses of state and provincial licensing boards can be found in each annual archival issue of the *American Psychologist* (usually the August issue), while the APA's Board of Professional Affairs summarizes the state licensure or certification laws regulating psychological practice on a periodic basis. Among the information included in this summary are the following items: educational and supervisory requirements, renewal policy, ABPP recognition, and continuing education renewal expectations. The ASPPB publishes the most comprehensive description of licensing information in the United States and Canada (ASPPB, 1986), including such information as the type of statutes that exist, levels of licensing (e.g., academic degree, exams, cut-off scores, etc.), and description of the board. In addition, it published similar information on the regulation of professional psychology in 54 countries (ASPPB, 1996b).

In Canada psychologists are registered, certified, or licensed by each of the Canadian Provinces and the Northwest Territories. The criteria and levels of the credentials that are available vary considerably, so psychologists are advised to contact the Canadian Psychological Association or the regulation body directly for a summary of those requirements. Credentialing in the United Kingdom is described in chapter 3.

Reciprocity

It is a fact that licensing statutes vary among states and provinces so that reciprocity agreements are few and far between. Usually, the state psychology board will accept the EPPP score if it meets the state's passing score during that same administration period. Similarly, ABPP board certification as a Diplomate in 1 of 11 specialties also facilitates mobility. There is a formal reciprocity agreement among several states/provinces. Nevertheless, as of 1998 the ASPPB established a mechanism to determine competence to practice by licensed doctoral psychologists. Documentation must include their training in psychology, five years of clinical experience, two years of supervised experience, as well as an established ASPPB passing score on the EPPP and an oral examination and/or interview. This service is provided through the ASPPB's Licensed Psychologists Data Service (LPDS). This Certificate of Professional Qualification in Psychology (CPQ) is voluntary and boards are encouraged to adopt the CPQ for *mobility purposes*. Thus, the certificate holder would presumably only need to present the CPQ validation. It is important to note that the CPQ is not a credential per se, and as noted in ASPPB literature "should not be represented as an additional qualification or as a superior level of psychological qualifications or service."

Psychology Specialty Credentials

Specialty professional credentials, which are nationally recognized, go beyond the degree and licensure demands for practice and directly assess the competency of the experienced psychology professional. The academic degree and licensure could, in one sense, be described as entry credentials that validate the beginning professional's training and competency. Only where continuing education requirements exist for the renewal of a license can it be said that professional growth is a criterion for continued possession of that credential. In contrast, the specialty credentialing bodies generally require licensure and several years of experience and/or specific training before applications are accepted. The criteria of these groups usually involve direct evidence of the applicant's professional behavior as part of the examination period.

The question has often been raised concerning the benefits and value of specialty professional credentials. Certainly, there is some prestige value associated with these credentials, given the rigor of the examination process and the judgment of senior colleagues regarding one's professional work. However, it might also be argued that the process of working toward and preparing for this credentialing serves as a sound professional development activity. To a certain extent, some of these credentials may aid in the licensure reapplication process needed when one moves from one state to another (i.e., reciprocity) and may increase the number of referrals of clients who are moving to new areas. Also, it is not unreasonable to expect trainers in professional psychology programs and, in particular, the director of such programs to represent the best attributes as professional role models. In fact, the APA accreditation criteria in the past suggested that the directors of the programs be recognized in some way by professional associations for their contributions (e.g., fellow in an APA division or possession of the ABPP diploma).

Following are examples of specialty credentials in psychology, including objectives of the credential, qualifications for application, and examination procedures.

Specialty Board Certification: Diplomate of the American Board of Professional Psychology

Established in 1947, the American Board of Examiners in Professional Psychology was incorporated and later renamed the American Board of Professional Psychology (ABPP). The ABPP "serves the public need by providing oversight certifying psychologists competent to deliver quality services in various specialty areas of psychology" (ABPP, 1996). Originally conceptualized as the credential for professional psychologists in lieu of the absence of state licenses, it has evolved from a credential promoting recognition of excellence (and thus, achievement) to a board certification credential for psychology specialty practice areas. "A specialty is a defined area in the practice of psychology that connotes special competency acquired through an organized sequence of formal education, training, and experience" (ABPP, 1996). There are currently eleven member specialty boards: health psychology, school psychology, behavior psychology, clinical psychology, counseling psychology, family psychology, forensic psychology, clinical neuropsychology, industrial/organizational psychology, rehabilitation psychology, and psychoanalysis in psychology. One additional board, group psychology, is in the final phase of the three-phase process of affiliation. Practice in each specialty area is seldom considered exclusive to that specialty by ABPP and most practice activities are shared with general professional practice areas. Practice activities patterns in the area plus the limiting of scope of practice and the nature of problems addressed, combined with advanced education and training as well as experience, are important to each specialty's definition.

Psychologists who have a doctoral degree in psychology as defined by the education and credentialing criteria (see chapter 4) and two years of supervised postdoctoral experience in a psychological practice area recognized by the ABPP may apply for the ABPP credential. The application must be in the candidate's area of specialty. A doctoral internship or field experience of a minimum of 1,500 hours of training is also required. The application process consists of a review to determine if the applicant meets the following criteria: (a) adequacy and extent of basic training, (b) amount, breadth, and quality of professional experience, (c) special competence, and (d) reputation among professional colleagues. A preliminary review in which would-be applicants submit only their educational and internship credentials is possible.

Following acceptance of the application, the ABPP candidate is asked to submit a written work sample representative of his or her professional practice, including assessment of individual(s), group(s), or situation(s), and professional efforts to effect or influence change. The last step of the process involves the ABPP examination, which is developed by the specialty board and conducted by a committee of board-certified examiners from the specialty. The examination is conceptualized as a "collegial process" and designed to allow the candidate to demonstrate the defining characteristics. By definition, the ABPP considers that all specialties are at an advanced level of competency and, thus, the purpose of the examination is to affirm the candidate has met the criteria of the specialty rather than reach a normative level. The format of the examination typically involves (a) discussion of the work sample, (b) exploration of the candidate's fundamental knowledge in the specialty along with situational content (in vivo, video, or simulation) representative of his or her specialty practice, and (c) knowledge of professional issues/ethical problem-solving capacity. The examination, which lasts four to five hours and uses the work sample as a springboard for discussion, is to cover the interrelated areas of (a) effectiveness of the candidate's efforts toward constructive intervention based on realistic assessment of the presented problems, (b) awareness of the relevance of research and theory, and (c) sensitivity to the ethical implications of professional practice. The nature of the examination varies from specialty to specialty, and objective examinations may also be part of the process.

In addition to the application and examination costs, annual fees are required for those holding the ABPP board certification. Diplomates receive the *Directory of ABPP Diplomates* and the ABPP semiannual newsletter, *The Diplomate*.

Guidelines for revocation of the ABPP diploma exist for failure "to maintain a reputation among professional colleagues for standards of personal integrity which are irreproachable as a representative of the profession of psychology in the community or failure to maintain affiliation with the American Psychological Association."

This voluntary credential for doctoral psychologists is significant for several reasons. First, the ABPP is the only unitary organization with quality controls on specialty boards recognized by the psychology profession. Second, board certification is the only *specialty* credential and the only doctoral credential based on a *competency* examination. Third, it is a credential recognized in over 40 licensing jurisdictions, serving as an endorsement for reciprocity. Fourth, it is recognized for listing in various professional directories, which reflects its growing recognition in various contexts. For example, Congress has provided the Veterans' Administration with the authority to pay a bonus to those clinical or counseling psychologists who hold the credential. A similar recognition is now approved by the Department of Defense. One state, Missouri, through its Department of Mental Health, provides automatic pay raises for psychologists who pass rigorous national examinations such as the ABPP. Fifth, the potential exists for school psychologists to advocate for such recognition through state departments of public instruction within the career development plans being adopted across the country. And sixth, it is an independent, rigorous verification that the standards and competencies required in a specialty area of psychology have been met, which, if nothing else, demonstrates a commitment to professional development values.

Most of the specialties have formed an academy of board-certified psychologists, who frequently hold a Fellow status in the membership organization. Mission statements of the academies usually involve a commitment to advancing the education and training standards of the specialty, advocacy for the services in benefit of clients, provision of mentors for applicant/candidates, and training of examiners.

http:www.ABPP.org

Certification: State Department of Public Instruction

Not to be confused with the type of psychology licensure discussed earlier and issued by a psychology board, this educational credential is issued by the state's education agency. It is created by legislative action similar to a licensure statute and pertains to the qualifications of the educational personnel working in the public schools, that is, teachers, administrators, and specialized personnel such as guidance counselors, school social workers, and school psychologists.

Initially, certification eligibility was determined by *course requirements*—submission of transcripts resulted in a documentation of successful completion of prescribed courses. Currently, certification may also involve *program approval*. Program-approval models require that training programs stand a review that has some of the characteristics of accreditation (see next section). If approved, graduates of the program are certified, pending satisfaction of any other requirements. Some states also require that applicants take the National Teachers' Examination or a similar state examination. Certification can be permanent or provisional, pending completion of a certain number of initial years of successful entry experience. Certification can also be time-related with a renewal procedure contingent on completion of continuing education requirements.

Psychologists who are interested in becoming full-time employees of a school system will be most interested in this type of credential. Certification for school psychologists requires criteria separate from those specified for other professionals. Again, as with the variability among psychology licensure laws, certification from state to state follows no standard criteria. There may be several levels of school psychology certification, for example, master's degree, specialist (60-hour master's or its equivalent), and doctorate. On the other hand, only one certification level may exist. As with licensure laws, there is no reciprocity among states.

A recent development has involved the separation of education personnel, mainly teachers and administrators, from noneducational personnel (e.g., school psychologists), and the adoption of the licensure terminology. In states where this has taken place or has been considered, the state education agency is directed to "license" teachers through a Professional Standards Board, while the credentialing of support personnel (e.g., school psychologists) is shifted to the disciplines board (e.g., psychology board).*

Listing: National Register of Health Service Providers in Psychology (Register)

The Register is a nonprofit organization, which is run separately from the APA. It publishes a list of psychologists who voluntarily apply for and meet the criteria as health service providers in psychology; it does not evaluate quality or com-

---

*The reader can refer to Pryzwansky (1999) for a more complete description of the process and the implications of this development for school psychologists.

petence of listed individuals. As such, then, it is not a credential per se, but rather a validation that the individual has met certain criteria of education and training and holds psychology credentials. A Health Service Provider in Psychology is defined by the Register "as a psychologist, currently and actively licensed/certified/registered at the independent practice level in a jurisdiction, who is trained and experienced in the delivery of direct, preventive, assessment, and therapeutic intervention services to individuals whose growth, adjustment, or functioning is impaired or to individuals who otherwise seek services" (Council for the National Register, 1998, p. I–8).

The criteria for listing also include the holding of a doctoral degree in psychology and at least two years of supervised experience in health services in psychology, of which at least one year is in an organized health service training program, and one year is postdoctoral. Guidelines for defining the doctoral degree in psychology are included if the applicant's program is not APA accredited. Specific guidelines for defining supervised experience of internships are spelled out and include a minimum of 1,500 hours completed within 24 months; 1,500 hours of supervised practice at the postdoctoral level is also required.

As of 1997, approximately 15,500 licensed as psychologists registrants were listed in the National Register. The information for each psychologist includes name, highest degree earned, preferred mailing address and telephone number, the state(s) in which he or she is licensed or certified, and ABPP board certification status. Optional characteristics that may be listed for registrants who so choose are their theoretical orientation, the health service offered, specialized services offered, ages served, and language fluency. Registrants are listed both alphabetically and by state.

The Register makes this list available to consumers of health services, health service organizations, health and welfare organizations, governmental agencies such as the National Institute of Mental Health, and the general public. A number of public and private insurers have informally recognized this registry for purposes of insurance reimbursement.

In addition to the application fee, there is an annual renewal fee. Guidelines exist for removal of a psychologist from the listing when there is significant violation of professional ethics or standards of practice.

The Register provides a directory to its registrants, a newsletter, and periodic legal update statements. In addition, registrants become part of a multidisciplinary credentials verification system run by a subsidiary of the Register. Additional available fee-based services include a legal consultation plan, which provides advice on matters arising in a member's professional psychology practice, and a retirement plan.

http://www.nationalregister.com

Proficiency Certificate: College of Professional Psychology

Established in 1994 by the APA, the College of Professional Psychology is charged with developing mechanisms for credentialing special proficiencies in psychology as recognized by the APA Council for the Recognition of Specialties and Proficiencies in Psychology (CRSPP). The College currently offers a proficiency certificate recognizing competency in the treatment of alcohol and psychoactive substance-use disorders based on a 150-item examination and documentation of training criteria. Three other proficiencies have been recognized: biofeedback, geropsychology, and applied psychophysiology. Examination-based proficiency certificates should be forthcoming.

http://www.apa.org

INSTITUTIONAL REGULATION: ACCREDITATION

One important individual credential that is sometimes overlooked is graduation from an *accredited* institution. The graduate degree, mentioned earlier, represents an individually oriented credential, which derives credibility indirectly from the quality review of the institution. These reviews are conducted by accrediting agencies and/or associations. The U.S. Commissioner of Education determines which agencies and associations are reliable authorities to evaluate the quality of training offered by educational institutions with programs.

An accrediting body is concerned with either the evaluation of educational entities as a whole or educational units or programs within institutions. Examples of the former include regional and national accrediting commissions, national institutional accrediting bodies (e.g., American Association of Bible Colleges; National Association of Trade and Technical Schools), and regional institutional accrediting bodies (e.g., Accrediting Commission for Senior Colleges and Universities/Western Association of Schools and Colleges; Commission on Colleges/Southern Association of Colleges and Schools). Specialized accrediting bodies include commissions on accreditation established by national professional organizations such as the APA (accredits doctoral programs in psychology), National Council for Accreditation of Teacher Education (baccalaureate and advanced degree programs), American Bar Association (law schools), and the Council on Social Work Education (baccalaureate and master's degree programs). In some instances, this group also evaluates freestanding professional or occupational schools. While these commissions or national accrediting agencies have no legal control over educational institutions or programs, "they promulgate standards of quality or criteria of institutional excellence and approve or admit to membership those institutions that meet the standards or criteria" (Department of Health, Education, and Welfare [DHEW], 1978). Most of the institutions attain eligibility for federal funds through accreditation by one of these recognized bodies. Accreditation is a voluntary process.

The Council on Postsecondary Accreditation (COPA) is a nongovernmental organization that "foster(s) and facilitate(s) the role of accrediting agencies in promoting and insuring the quality and diversity of American *postsecondary* education" (DHEW, 1978). The COPA performs three primary functions: They recognize the accrediting members as well as coordinate and periodically review the work of those groups to insure they serve the broader interests of society as well as their membership. A similar council exists for secondary education.

APA Accreditation

Graduate Programs

The APA began accrediting professional psychology programs in the 1940s, beginning with clinical psychology programs. Through its Office of Accreditation, the APA now accredits doctoral level programs in school, clinical, and counseling psychology, or appropriate combinations thereof, and lists them each year in the July or August and December issues of the *American Psychologist*. However, with the 1996 publication *Guidelines and Principals for Accreditation of Programs in Professional Psychology* (APA, 1996b) the focus was changed to include "board and general preparation for practice at the entry level" (p. 3). Thus, programs are now given broader latitude to define themselves. Accreditation still lists the above three specialties, but notes that "the program's philosophy of training or model of training may be identified through a national conference of psychologists" (APA, 1996b, p. 6) which can be interpreted as including those specialties recognized by CRSPP. More than 300 doctoral programs are currently accredited by the APA.

Recognized and consistent with the provisions of the Commission on Recognition of Postsecondary Accreditation, the APA's Committee on Accreditation (CoA) is a 21-person body representative of academic institutions and programs, practitioners, and publics served by the profession. The accreditation process is defined as an activity "to promote consistent quality and excellence in education and training in professional psychology and, thus, to provide tangible benefits for perspective students; the local, national and international publics that are consumers of psychological services; and the discipline of psychology itself" (APA, 1996b, p. 2). At a minimum, doctoral programs must be site-visited every seven years but accreditation can range from three to seven years. There are two categories of accreditation: "Accredited" means the program has met the guidelines and procedures (G & P) as determined by the CoA;

"accredited on probation" means that aspects of a formerly accredited program are not consistent with the G & P. The process includes voluntary application by the program through a written self-study addressing eight accreditation domains, which is then followed by a two-day site visit by a three-member team, two of which represent a declared specialty. The objective of the site visit is to verify the self-study report and to discover and report on unique characteristics of the program. The CoA then makes the final decision on accreditation, or reaffirmation in the case of programs already accredited.

Several important changes mark the 1996 revision of the guidelines. The accreditation review process now places greater emphasis on *outcomes* or products of the program's training efforts. Thus, the program's goals and objectives are evaluated not only in terms of "clarity, consistency and appropriateness," but also in terms of outcomes in relation to those aspirations along with the ability to achieve them and consistently maintain such productivity. Also, programs are given broader latitude in defining the philosophy or model of training and how to go about reaching that mission, a change that recognizes there are a number of valid approaches versus one preferred model. It is the program's responsibility to articulate its mission and procedures, and document that it can basically train to that goal(s).

The eight domains and significant standards, as briefly presented here, illustrate the guidelines and principles which make up the professional judgments required of the CoA—versus counting among a checklist of criteria.

- Domain A: *Eligibility* requires sponsorship by an accredited institution of higher education with a minimum of three full-time academic years of graduate study.
- Domain B: *Program Philosophy, Objectives, and Curriculum* is the most comprehensive area of the eight and calls for a publicly available statement of an explicit philosophy of training wherein psychological practice is influenced by the science of psychology and the professional practice of psychology. The breadth of scientific psychology (e.g., biological bases of behavior) along with the foundations of practice (e.g., ethics), assessment and intervention, and adequate/appropriate practicum experiences in preparation for the internship are expected.
- Domain C: *Program Resources* addresses the number and quality of the faculty, resources, administrative support, and characteristics of the student body.
- Domain D: A commitment to *Cultural and Individual Differences and Diversity.*
- Domain E: *Student-Faculty Relations* covers the manner in which interactions are collegial and facilitates students' educational experiences.
- Domain F: *Program Self-Assessment and Quality Enhancement* is a most impor-

tant area in terms of the outcome emphasis. It addresses the ongoing self-study approach(es) that is used.

- Domain G: *Public Disclosure* deals with the comprehensiveness of the program's public disclosure documents and, in particular, the details made available to prospective as well as current students.
- Domain H: *Relationship* is concerned with the program's commitment to APA policies and procedures as well as the cooperation and collaboration shown not only during the review process but also during the period of accreditation.

Internships

The APA also accredits more than 400 doctoral internship program through its Committee on Accreditation. Listed primarily as clinical, counseling, and school sites, they are listed in the July/August and December issues of the *American Psychologist*. The eight Domains are the same as those for graduate program accreditation, but the standards of each are, of course, different. Some of these standards include the following guidelines:

- The internship must be full-time and completed in no less than 12 months or no more than 24 months.
- The primary training must be experiential and include integrated modalities such as observation modeling.
- Interns must receive four hours of supervision, of which two hours must be individual supervision.
- The designated director should be a doctoral psychologist who is appropriately credentialed; supervisors should have similar credentials and training.
- There will be more than one intern at the site and they will receive at least semiannual written feedback on the extent to which they are meeting program requirements and expectations.

Postdoctoral Residencies

For the first time, with these 1996 guidelines and principles, training in preparation for practice at an advanced level in a substantive traditional or specialty practice area in professional psychology can be accredited through program application and review. It is important to note that the CoA can "adopt definitions, training models, goals, objectives and norms developed by certain professional psychology training communities or reference groups" (APA, 1996b, p. 17). Furthermore, under the *eligibility* domain, consistency with the training programs model "and the standards of the specialty practice area in which the program it provides its standard" (APA, 1996b, p. 17) has been included as a guide for CoA procedures at this level. Several years prior to adoption of these criteria, an Interorganization Council (IOC) of regulatory bodies, including the ABPP and representatives of its specialty boards, National Register, APPIC, ASPPB, Canadian National Register, and CPA, began meeting to explore mechanisms and criteria for the accreditation of postdoctoral residencies in psychology specialty areas. The CoA joined with that group and eventually adopted the IOC criteria and procedures. Consequently, when a residency program requests to be reviewed as a "specialty practice area" the CoA will refer to or "adopt definitions, training models, goals, objectives, and norms developed by certain professional psychology training communities or reference groups" (APA, 1996b, p. 17).

In order to facilitate accreditation, the IOC endorsed the formation of the Council of Specialties. This Council will consist of a representative from a broad constituency (e.g., APA Division Trainers) of each specialty. Furthermore, to meet the needs of the CoA, the Council will develop a template that specialties can use in developing their standards and then endorse the specialty-specific guidelines developed by each specialty council. The Council can also communicate these guidelines within the profession, mediate issues among specialties, and serve as an advisory body to the CoA.

The CoA domains used to categorize standards for the accreditation of postdoctoral residencies are the same as those for the doctoral internship programs. Differences include the recognition that training may cover a period of up to three years full-time, that residents demonstrate an advanced level of competency, that the program director's credentials and expertise be consistent with program's mission and goals and with the advanced substantive traditional or specialty practice area standards, and that at least two psychologists be among the formally designated supervisors.

NCATE/NASP Program Reviews

The National Association of School Psychologists (NASP), through its affiliation with the National Council for the Accreditation of Teacher Education (NCATE), has participated in the accreditation of master's and doctoral level school psychology programs located in schools of education. Because of the perceived overlap with APA accreditation of doctoral programs in psychology, an APA/NASP Task Force was established in 1979 to identify similarities and differences in the accreditation standards and process followed by the APA and NCATE. From this effort a Joint Accreditation Pilot Project between the APA and NCATE/NASP accreditation was implemented, which resulted in a recommended plan for future accreditation visits that could be held jointly. However, at this time, the NCATE has moved to focus its accreditation efforts at the unit level (e.g., schools of education) rather than the program level.

As a result, NASP automatically recognizes the APA accreditation of school psychology programs. For those doctoral school psychology programs that are not APA accredited, NASP will conduct a program folio review in which the NASP (1994) *Standards for Training and Field Placement Programs in School Psychology* are used as the criteria to award "program approval."

AN INTEGRATED REGULATORY SYSTEM FOR PROFESSIONAL PSYCHOLOGY

It does not take much more conceptualization to envision a model of an integrated regulatory system given the above discussion of accreditation and credentialing mechanisms (see figure 5.1). Such a model was first envisioned by the work of the IOC and later articulated again for the applied areas of psychology (Hall, 1997) and for a specialty (Pryzwansky, 1999). Essentially, it has involved students completing preservice doctoral programs and doctoral internships which meet at least minimum criteria as professional psychology training programs followed by either informal or formal supervised postdoctoral experience. The next step would include licensure from a state/provincial psychology board which, given the acceptance of the EPPP, becomes one index of the prior training preparation quality (i.e., the number of program graduates applying for licensure who obtain the license). This entry credential will then become one of several criteria for subsequent board certification in a specialty practice area (e.g., board certification in clinical psychology) and/or listing of emphasis in practice (e.g., health service provider) or proficiency competency recognition (e.g., substance abuse counselor). Some of the latter credentials also become outcome measures, particularly in the case of board certification. This system, as outlined in figure 5.1, in large measure exists in practice as well as, to a certain degree, the operations of the credentialing organizations. For example, data bases of individual credentialing are shared among the various credentialing bodies as are violation actions (e.g., revocation of license) taken by the agency/board against individual psychologists. The credentialing success of program graduates is less well developed, except in some states which report pass/fail rates of individuals by in-state programs who take the EPPP. Additionally, such information is not typically distributed widely. The status of program accreditation/designation is, of course, available in sources noted above.

For all the above concerns regarding professions developing more detailed structures and criteria for entry and sustained practice, it seems that the infor-

Figure 5.1
An Integrated Regulatory System for Professional Psychology

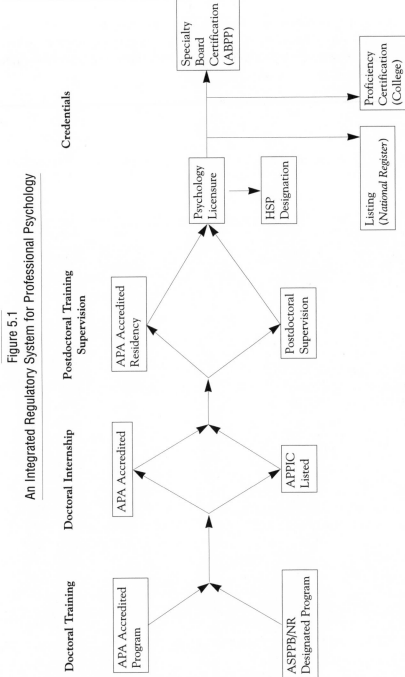

mation included in figure 5.1 serves to illustrate what benefits can accrue to the clients as well as the profession through an integrated regulatory system. This conclusion is particularly true in the realm of the relatively new professions, wherein students need assistance in selecting among training opportunities, and consumers on all levels need information and assurance that intelligence choices among providers can be made.

Chapter 6

Codes of Ethics for Psychologists

As discussed earlier, a code of ethics is typically a salient characteristic of a profession's definition. In this chapter a brief discussion of the emergence of ethics in professions will introduce a detailed description of the APA ethical code and promotion of its use in practice. In addition, the CPA Code will be presented, along with its unique application procedures.

The notions of standards and accountability seem to have emerged simultaneously with the description of physician activities (and other occupations) in ancient Egypt around 2000 B.C., as evidenced in the Code of Hammurabi (American College of Physicians, 1984). A fee structure was proposed, as well as punishments for poor results. Of course, the Hippocratic Oath, written about 400 B.C., is the most well-known example of a professional code of ethics. Written by members of the profession, the Oath mentions the obligations of the professional not only to the profession, but also to members of society. The Hippocratic Oath advocates for many of the ethical principles and values that are key concepts in modern codes of ethics (Sinclair et al., 1996). In their history of psychology's attention to its ethical responsibility, Sinclair and colleagues (1996) find the period following World War II as the time the psychology profession forcefully pressed forward with efforts to develop standards of professional behavior. They attribute this surge of interest to at least three factors: the success of psychology as a profession in providing war-related services, the resulting potential to apply psychological principles in various segments of society, and the publication of the *Nuremberg Code of Ethics in Medical Research* (Nuremberg Code, 1964). The development of ethical principles has been a continuous process since 1938, when the American Psychological Association formed a special committee to consider the adoption of an ethical code. Generally speaking, as the ethics of the psychology profession have evolved, so has the complexity of the ethical principles.

The 1938 committee investigated and resolved ethical complaints; most of its work was informal in nature. In 1940, the Committee on Scientific and Professional Ethics (CSPEC) was created as a standing committee to consider ethical complaints. However, the development of a formal code of ethics did not begin until 1947 when an incident involving the collection process was identified. In 1948, APA members were asked to submit incident reports detailing ethical problems. Based on over 1,000 reports, six ethical categories were derived: teaching, research, public responsibility, client relationships, professional relationships, and writing and publishing.

These reports were used to prepare a number of drafts of an ethical code, and designated for reactions and debate in psychology departments and at state, regional, and national professional meetings. This process has been reviewed extensively by Golann (1970) and reports by the Committee on Ethical Standards for Psychology appear in two issues of the American Psychologist (APA, 1951a, 1951b). According to Golann, the first formal code of ethics was adopted in 1953, with a revised version featuring 18 general principles published in 1959. The 1959 version was adopted for a 3-year trial period. In 1977, after numerous revisions, another version of the code evolved. A subsequent revision, entitled *Ethical Principles of Psychologists*, was adopted January 24, 1981, by the APA Council of Representatives and published in the June 1981 issue of the *American Psychologist* (APA, 1981a). This revision contained both substantive and grammatical changes in each of nine ethical principles, plus a new 10th principle, "Care and Use of Animals." The 1992 *Ethical Principles and Code of Conduct* will be discussed later in this chapter.

Essentially, the process of adopting new standards within the APA involves the Ethics Committee drafting revisions of present standards based on complaints and prevailing issues within the profession. The proposed changes are then given to the membership for reactions and comment. After several revisions are drafted, the final proposal is presented to the APA Council of Representatives for approval.

Additionally, given the complexity of the APA, there are numerous other committees, panels, and task forces that generate issues and policy statements that influence the work of the Ethics Committee in developing and monitoring standards and practices. Thus, through the APA office, members of one committee will generate policy statements and solicit comments and reactions from other committees. As a result, there are numerous influences operating with the APA that directly or indirectly influence the thinking relative to ethical codes and standards.

It is very important to understand that the ethical principles and standards of psychology are reviewed continuously. A number of areas may remain unclear and/or incomplete so that continual clarification and additions will need to be made to reflect the current ethical thinking and standards of the profession.

THE CONCEPTUALIZATION OF ETHICS

From a *legal* perspective, professionals assume a very special obligation with their clients that is distinct from those of one individual interacting with another individual. Known as a *fiduciary* obligation, it implies a "special duty to care for the welfare of one's clients or patients" (Haas & Malouf, 1995, p. 2). Thus, where a moral principle is involved, the professional's standard in terms of its application is much higher than the ordinary citizen's.

Psychology as a profession has a moral dimension relative to professional practice. It is embodied within the ethical code developed by the APA (1992a) and codes developed by virtually every national-level professional group providing treatment services to the public. Additionally, licensing and regulatory boards have adopted rules for professional conduct based upon the APA *Ethical Principles of Psychologists and Code of Conduct.*

Individual professionals may support their professional code for practical reasons, such as a desire for respect and enhanced reputation within the professional community, or the possible loss of license by the licensing boards. However, most professionals support their professional code because they believe it is good and justifiable. It must be kept in mind that mere acceptance of a code by professionals does not demonstrate that its principles are morally sound. One needs only to look to the past relative to the treatment of the mentally disabled to realize that ethical behavior is related to what is currently acceptable within the broader context of society, and existing standards will change as technologies advance and society changes.

It is indeed quite possible that an immoral code could be adopted much in the same manner that laws that discriminate against minorities have existed. If, then, an ethical issue is also a moral one, the specific questions relative to professional conduct and motivation are not nearly as important as the underlying moral principles of the professional code. Therefore, it well serves all psychologists to pause, read carefully, and reconsider the Preamble to the APA *Ethical Principles and Code of Conduct:*

> Psychologists work to develop a valid and reliable body of scientific knowledge based on research. They may apply that knowledge to human behavior in a variety

of contexts. In doing so, they perform many roles, such as researcher, educator, diagnostician, therapist, supervisor, consultant, administrator, social intervention-ist, and expert witness. Their goal is to broaden knowledge of behavior and, where appropriate, to apply it pragmatically to improve the condition of both the indi-vidual and society. Psychologists respect the central importance of freedom of inquiry and expression in research, teaching, and publication. They also strive to help the public in developing informed judgments and choices concerning human behavior. This Ethics Code provides a common set of values upon which psychol-ogists build their professional and scientific work.

This Code is intended to provide both the general principles and the decision rules to cover most situations encountered by psychologists. It has as its primary goal the welfare and protection of the individuals and groups with whom psychol-ogists work. It is the individual responsibility of each psychologist to aspire to the highest possible standards of conduct. Psychologists respect and protect human and civil rights, and do not knowingly participate in or condone unfair discriminatory practices.

The development of a dynamic set of ethical standards for a psychologist's work-related conduct requires a personal commitment to a lifelong effort to act ethical-ly; to encourage ethical behavior by students, supervisees, employees, and col-leagues, as appropriate; and to consult with others, as needed, concerning ethical problems. Each psychologist supplements, but does not violate, the Ethics Code's values and rules on the basis of guidance drawn from personal values, culture, and experience. (APA, 1992a, p. 1599)

Beauchamp and Childress (1994) assert that "ethics" is a generic term for "various ways of understanding and examining the moral life" (p. 4). The theo-ry or principles, rules, and virtues are based on fundamental assumptions or judgments. However, ethical theories/perspectives can differ in terms of the basic premises on which they are based. For example, in terms of consequences a *tele-ological* orientation, which is utilitaristic, promotes decisions wherein the great-est good for the greatest number is achieved. In contrast, a *deontological* orienta-tion assumes that certain discussions or actions are intrinsically right or absolute. Thus, deontological theories view rules as absolute regardless of the relationship with the person or the context. Meara, Schmidt, and Day (1996) argue for an orientation between absolutism and ethical or cultural relation, which they call "ethical objectivism" (p. 9) or "virtue ethics" (p. 24).

Principle Ethics

Many moral philosophers consider ethics to be based on universal principles from which the correct behavior can be reasoned (Haas & Malouf, 1995). Often referred to as *principle ethics,* this concept "encompasses five primary facie duties—nonmaleficience, fidelity, beneficence, justice, and autonomy" (Bersoff, 1996, p. 87). These principles are not hierarchically utilized in their application to dealing with an ethical dilemma, but rather assist in evaluating the different action options open to the psychologist and deciding on how to move forward. Kitchener (1984) has described these principles in the following manner. The principle of *autonomy* involves the professional's right to not only make his or her own decisions, but also to extend that right to others to make autonomous decisions. It is important to note that this does not imply unlimited freedom to do anything, and is based on the assumption the person is competent to make rationale decisions. The principle of *beneficence* involves not only acting to prevent harm to another, but also to promote the welfare of the client. Very often it involves a balancing act with the objectives underlying the autonomy principle. Above all, no harm should be influenced on others in the delivery of service as expressed by the principle of *nonmaleficience*. Kitchener points out that the ambiguity of the notion of harm will inevitably lead to some degree of choice. Another critical principle in the delivery of professional services is that fairness, that is, *justice*, characterizes the availability. All individuals should receive equal treatment as a result of this principle. Finally, the principle of *fidelity* (veracity) seems basic to all professionals so that loyalty and trustworthiness exist as the cornerstone of the professional-client relationship. These five obligations "provide an array of moral choices and can be applied flexibly in relations to the context of a dilemma" (Bersoff, 1996, p. 89).

Virtue Ethics

In contrast to principles, "virtues historically have been viewed neither as situation specific nor as universal maximus, but rather as character and community specific" (Jordon & Meara, 1995, p. 137). Virtue ethics, then, is a set of ideals to which professionals aspire and involve more than moral actions. It involves the professional's ideals, motivation, emotion character, and moral habits within the practices of a culture or other group. According to Meara and colleagues (1996), a virtuous professional would be characterized as an individual "who (a) is motivated to do what is good, (b) possesses vision and discernment, (c) realizes the role of affect or emotion in assessing or judging proper conduct, (d) has a high degree of self-understanding and awareness, and, perhaps most importantly, (e) is connected with and understands the mores of his or her community and the importance of community in moral decision making, policy setting and character development and is alert to the legitimacy of client diversity in these respects" (pp. 28–29). Meara and colleagues argue that four virtues are appropriate to the life of a professional psychologist: prudence, integrity, respectfulness, and benevolence. They view the perspectives of virtue ethics and principle ethics as complementary and, as such, both are critical to the ethical decision-making process; however, virtue ethics "focuses on the ideal rather than the obligatory and on the character of the agent or professional rather than on the solving of specific ethical dilemmas" (Meara et al., 1996, p. 47). In reality, however, they point out that the distinctions cannot be separated. Finally, they call for data-based research into professional ethics to learn how codes are written, how to proceed on policy issues, and, as suggested by Welfel and Lipsitz (1984), why ethical behavior occurs.

CRITIQUES OF ETHICAL PERSPECTIVES

While generally recognizing the construct of virtue ethics, Bersoff (1996) seems less impressed with its utility in terms of guiding ethical conduct. He has raised four issues regarding virtue ethics: "(a) The application of virtue ethics is irrelevant in deciding the majority of cases adjucated by the APA Ethics Committee; (b) there is substantial similarity between virtue and principle; (c) resolving ethics dilemmas is unavoidable, for which principle ethics is a valuable tool; and (d) the reliance on character and community wisdom, central tenets of virtue ethics, can lead to aberrant, if not problematic, resolutions of ethical conflicts" (p. 86).

In contrast, Jordan and Meara (1995) argue that professions need to embrace a virtuous orientation for the profession not only to continue to be maintained but also to develop as a positive-valued segment of society. The kind of person the professional becomes is important in a complex, diverse society where he or she increasingly interacts within organizational business-oriented contexts versus the past autonomous professional-client context. The use of ethical criteria (i.e., principles and rules) apart from one's moral theory can lead to idiosyncratic solutions. "Professional psychology is a discipline with a pervasive moral, as well as scientific, dimensions" (Jordan & Meara, 1995, p. 139).

THE APA ETHICAL PRINCIPLES OF PSYCHOLOGISTS AND CODE OF CONDUCT

The sixth version of the APA *Ethical Principles and Code of Conduct* (APA, 1992a) represents a major revision in terms of format in the sense that the highest ideals of psychology are presented separately from specified mandatory standards that contain enforceable rules. Thus, a Preamble and six General Principles are considered aspiration goals for the individual psychologist to strive toward and are followed by the eight categories of Ethical Standards. A number of new issues have been introduced since the last version, along with an expectation that psychologists will operate from a preventative set in order to minimize or eliminate the likelihood of harm to those with whom they are in contact professionally. Essentially, an educational tool for psychologists, they are used by the APA Ethics Committee to address complaints against members of the association (APA, 1992a). The *Principles and Code* has also been included in state statutes governing the practice of psychologists, and thus relied upon by states' psychology boards in adjucating complaints against psychologists licensed by that board. It should be noted that while the Preamble and Principles are not considered rules, individual psychologists are nonetheless encouraged to make use of them in deciding upon ethical courses of action. Similarly, ethics boards are invited to utilize these statements as they interpret the ethical standards in cases before them. A description of the APA *Principles and Code* follows, along with two additional codes for comparison. The next chapter will discuss the process of ethical practice, with an emphasis on problem-solving and ethical decision-making models.

APA Preamble

As noted earlier, the Preamble sets the goal for each psychologist as a member of the psychology community to act ethically according to the Principles and Standards set forth in the *Code* and to supplement (not supersede) these behaviors with those drawn from their own values as well as their own cultural and personal experience. It is important to recognize that the *Code* applies to all psychologists and not simply to psychologists in a "professional practice." It includes the dual objectives of expanding and applying knowledge. The welfare and protection of clients (individuals and groups) with whom the psychologist works are the primary responsibilities of the psychologist while encouraging such behavior by others. Thus, the Preamble sets the context for the Principles and Standards.

General Principles

Six General Principles provide many of the ethical concepts operationally defined in the Ethical Standards. Again, as noted earlier, while aspirational in intent and general in description, they exhort "psychologists to aim for the highest goals in their work" (Canter, Bennett, Jones, & Nagy, 1996, p. 20). The General Principles are: (1) competence, (2) integrity, (3) professional and scientific responsibility, (4) respect for people's rights and dignity, (5) concern for others' welfare, and (6) social responsibility.

Ethical Standards

Considered the heart of the document, 102 standards are presented within eight sections. The specific distribution is as follows: (1) General Standards (27 standards), (2) Evaluation, Assessment, or Intervention (10 standards); (3) Advertising and Other Public Statements (6 standards); (4) Therapy (9 standards); (5) Privacy and Confidentiality (11 standards); (6) Teaching, Training, Supervision, Research, and Publishing (26 standards); (7) Forensic Activities (6 standards), and (8) Resolving Ethical Issues (7 standards). The significant changes from the prior code include: for the first time, an entire section on forensic activities, a prohibition of sexual contact with students or supervisees, a more practical position on multiple relations while raising the threshold for what behavior should be followed, a reflection of the laws regarding advertising and public statements, an acceptance of bartering along with a discussion of fees and third party requests for services, more detailed consideration of teaching, research, and publication issues, and more stringent rules regarding record-keeping and assessment responsibilities (Canter et al., 1996). Also, it should be recognized that a range of issues may be addressed in each standard section. As one example, the General Standards section deals with boundaries of competence, maintaining expertise, respecting human differences, sexual harassment, barter and fees, consultations, and records.

A casebook is now also available as a resource for psychologists, which prepares them for issues before they develop, describes implications of each of the standards, and provides interpretations of all 102 Standards (Canter et al., 1996). In addition, *Ethical Conflicts in Psychology*, edited by Bersoff (1995), provides a number of stimulating pieces written around seven topical conflicts in ethics such as confidentiality and multiple relationships. A third excellent resource is the Koocher and Keith-Spiegel (1998) text, which confronts many ethical questions and issues psychologists deal with in everyday practice.

APA Ethics Committee Policy Statements

Since the publication of the 1992 APA *Principles and Code*, the Ethics Committee has encountered a number of issues and questions warranting additional guidance to the members. In 1994, four such policy statements were published in the July issue of the *American Psychologist* (APA Ethics Committee, 1994a, b, c, d), which addressed "take home" tests, advertisements and canned columns, internship applications and confidential materials, and military psychologists and confidentiality. Additional statements appeared in the August 1995 issue (APA Ethics Committee, 1995a, b) of the *American Psychologist*, which dealt with "Limitation on Teaching" (Standard 6.4) and "Referrals and Fees" (Standard 1.27). Finally, in the November/December 1996 *American Psychologist* (APA Ethics Committee, 1996a, b) two additional statements appeared, covering the topics of "Services by Telephone, Teleconferencing, and Internet" and "Policy on Barring Resignations During Ethics Investigations" (which was actually a Board of Directors resolution that effected the Ethics Committee policy).

The widespread interest in using technology to facilitate and even deliver services has astounded many of its advocates, but the application in the telehealth movement has been quite dramatic. As a result, a multitude of questions have arisen for which there is obviously little experiential base from which to formulate a response. What services (can, should) be offered and with what qualifications? Is answering questions over the internet unethical professional behavior? How much in-person contact should be planned? The APA Ethics Committee (1998) issued a statement on November 5, 1997, based on its 1996 statement on the same topic; because of the timeliness of such issues the statement is presented here in its entirety.

Services by Telephone, Teleconferencing, and Internet
The Ethics Committee can only address the relevance of and enforce the Ethical Principles of Psychologists and Code of Conduct and cannot say whether there may be APA Guidelines that might provide guidance. The Ethics Code is not specific with regard to telephone therapy or teleconferencing or any electronically provided services as such and has no rules prohibiting such services. Complaints regarding such matters would be addressed on a case by case basis.

Delivery of services by such media as telephone, teleconferencing and internet is a rapidly evolving area. This will be the subject of APA task forces and will be considered in future revisions of the Ethics Code. Until such time as a more definitive judgment is available, the Ethics Committee recommends that psychologists follow Standard 1.04c, Boundaries of Competence, which indicates that "In those emergency areas in which generally recognized standards for preparatory training do not yet exist, psychologists nevertheless take reasonable steps to ensure the competence of their work and to protect patients, clients, students, research participants, and others from harm." Other relevant standards include Assessment (Standards 2.01–2.10), Therapy (4.10–4.09, especially 4.01, Structuring the Relationship, and 4.02, Informed Consent to Therapy), and Confidentiality (5.01–5.11). Within the General Standards section, standards with particular relevance are 1.03, Professional and Scientific Relationship; 1.04 (a, b, and c), Boundaries of Competence; 1.06, Basis for Scientific and Professional Judgments; 1.07a, Describing the Nature and Results of Psychological Services; 1.14, Avoiding Harm; and 1.25, Fees and Financial Arrangements. Standards under Advertising, particularly 3.01–3.03, are also relevant.

Psychologists considering such services must review the characteristics of the services, the service delivery method, and the provisions for confidentiality.

Psychologists must then consider the relevant ethical standards and other requirements, such as licensure board rules.

CANADIAN CODE OF ETHICS FOR PSYCHOLOGISTS

The Canadian Code of Ethics is the longest code discussed in this book. It orga-
nizes 152 ethical standards around four ethical principles "ordered according to
the weight each generally should be given when they conflict (Canadian
Psychological Association [CPA], 1991b, p. 15). The CPA Committee on Ethics
identified the principles by sending hypothetical ethical dilemmas to psychologists in Canada; the psychologists indicated the four principles used most consistently in response. The four principles in order of the greatest weight are Respect
for the Dignity of the Person, Responsible Caring, Integrity in Relationships, and
Responsibility to Society. "The standards range from minimal behavioral expectations . . . to more idealized, but achievable attitudinal and behavioral expectations" (CPA, 1991b, 14–15). Each principle is defined by a values statement,
which describes a number of the values subsumed by the principle. This statement is then followed by several standards. "Key phrases" (e.g., minimize harm,
confidentiality) are used throughout the listing of standards and are provided as
an orientation to the user. The code is intended as both an educational tool and
an "umbrella" document to help in the construction of specific guidelines and
standards for particular specialty or proficiency areas of practice. Thus, its purpose is broader than simply to serve as a code of ethical behavior.

Perhaps the most unique and interesting feature of the CPA code is the fact that
it contains an ethical decision-making model. In addition, the publication contains a detailed example that illustrates the use of the code in addressing an ethical dilemma, and includes 111 ethical vignettes that can serve as practice material. A bibliography is also provided, which address standards within each principle.

In comparing the CPA and APA Codes, Sinclair (1996) finds that the APA
Code tilts more toward an emphasis on the integrity in relationship principle
while the CPA Code places a more balanced emphasis on the four principles.
She attributes this conclusion in part to the fact that the APA may have been
more influenced by the content of complaints against psychologists while the
primary objective of the CPA is to educate and guide psychologists' actions. Both
Codes acknowledge that personal conscience can play a role in ethical decision-
making and both seem to allow for some civil disobedience. Sinclair concludes
that the codes complement one another: The APA Code is more detailed and
gives examples of what to do in certain situations; the CPA Code provides a
framework and model for resolving dilemmas.

ASSOCIATION OF STATE AND PROVINCIAL PSYCHOLOGY BOARDS CODE OF CONDUCT

Prior to the publication of the most recent revision of the APA Code, the state regulatory boards experienced some difficulty in enforcing the 1981 version because of its aspirational quality and lack of specificity (Sinclair, 1996). A North Carolina case (*White v. North Carolina Board of Practicing Psychologists*, 1990) illustrates the challenge many boards faced in processing ethical complaints. In that case, state appeals court overturned the findings of the North Carolina psychology board against a psychologist judged to have violated the APA ethical code. The court found that the 1981 code was vague in terms of citing specific violations, which led the North Carolina board to write its own code. The North Carolina Code, which still exists today, takes precedent over the APA Code and is included in that state's psychology licensing act. Thus, the objective of the *Association of State and Provincial Psychology Boards Code of Conduct* (1991) was to provide statements of unacceptable conduct that are *legally* definable and defensible. The legal forum understandably was considered more important to the ASPPB member boards than the "guiding" or "educating" objectives of the professional associations. It is argued that the professional associations' ultimate purpose is to protect the welfare and integrity of the profession, although the APA and CPA Codes would take issue with that statement, asserting that their objective is to protect the client.

The ASPPB Code contains 48 rules, which are grouped under 10 areas of professional behavior: competence, impaired objectivity and dual relationships, client welfare, welfare of supervisees and research subjects, protecting confidentiality of clients, representation of services, fees and statements, assessment procedures, violations of law, and aiding illegal practice.

The codes of 14 of the 27 jurisdictions that had a regulatory code served as the beginning point in the task of writing the ASPPB Code. State psychology boards are not obligated to adopt the ASPPB rules; rather, they serve as a model if the boards choose to include rules in their statues. Nonetheless, it is important to note that delegates to the ASPPB annual meeting did accept the code for use if boards saw fit. These standards include definitive statements of behaviors that psychologists *should* or *should not* engage in, and standards by which psychologists can be judged. For example, under the section on aiding illegal practice, the psychologist "shall not delegate professional responsibilities to a person not appropriately credentialed or otherwise appropriately qualified to provide such services" (ASPPB, 1991). Or, under the client welfare section, the psychologist "shall make an appropriate referral of the client to another professional when requested to do so by the client." Also, this code does make reference to the utility of the APA and CPA

Codes when ambiguities arise in the use of the code. Finally, in her comparison of the ASPPB, APA, and CPA Codes, Sinclair (1996) stated that these three codes complement one another and that any "differences among the codes are ones of purpose, structure and underlying philosophy" (p. 69).

ETHICAL COMPLAINTS AND RESOLUTION

The CPA, APA, and state associations have jurisdiction only over their members, and provide enforcement through their ethics committees. However, all 50 states and the District of Columbia as well as Canadian Provinces and Territories also have statutory licensure or certification laws. Based on each law, rules of professional conduct are promulgated by the state licensing board and for the most part are identical to the APA *Ethical Principles*. As a result, the practicing psychologist choosing not to voluntarily join a professional organization matters little since he or she will, more than likely, end up being accountable to the APA/CPA Standards or a similar code.

The APA and CPA have put forth rules and procedures for dealing with ethical complaints. The APA has published *Rules and Procedures* (APA, 1992b) as has the CPA, which are included in an inclusive manual (CPA, 1991b). Following is a brief summary of some of the major points found in those procedures:

- Both the CPA and APA have policies regarding time limits as well as their operation procedure vis à vis other tribunals in their documents. The CPA limits complaints to a 12-month period from the time the alleged unethical conduct was discovered or the adjudication by another jurisdiction was completed.
- The CPA typically defers processing complaints until a decision is reached by the provincial/territorial/state regulatory body as specified in its agreement with those bodies (CPA, 1991b). Consequently, if a complaint is made against a CPA member who is also registered, the complainant will be asked to lodge the complaint with the appropriate regulatory body.
- The APA *Rules and Procedures* are much more detailed and complete than CPA's, perhaps due to the absence of such an agreement with other regulatory bodies.
- The APA ethics committee receives complaints from members only if made within one year after the alleged conduct is discovered or five years in the case of nonmembers. An absolute 10-year limit is placed on committee action.

The APA's official committee for handling complaints of members' unethical misconduct is the Ethics Committee. This committee has the power to investigate or adjudicate allegations of unethical behaviors that may be harmful to the public. This charge is provided for in the APA *Bylaws* (APA, 1998i), Rules of Council, Ethical Principles (APA, 1992a), and the *Rules and Procedures* (APA, 1992b). As stated previously, the most any professional association can do as a sanction for the violation of ethical principles is to expel an offending member although information is shared publicly with the members. Although that event seldom occurs, in light of the size of the APA's membership, lesser sanctions such as reprimand, censure, or stipulated resignation are more common.

When filing a complaint against a psychologist, one may choose to work through the Ethics Committee if the psychologist is a member of the APA, or with the respective state or provincial licensing board if legal violations are involved. The Ethics Committee determines if the behavior meets the criteria and falls within the jurisdiction of the committee. The complainee will then be sent the complaint form and asked to respond within 30 days. A final decision regarding formal case investigation will then be made. It should be noted that failure to cooperate "is a violation of sufficient gravity, posing danger of substantial harm to the profession, to warrant formal charges" (see section 7-4 of the APA *Rules and Procedures,* APA, 1992b). A detailed outline of procedures, due process actions, appeals, etcetera is spelled out in the document.

LEGAL ENFORCEMENT

Since the advent of licensing laws and the creation of state licensing boards with the explicit charge to protect the public, enforcement within the last five years has increasingly become a major function of state regulatory boards. As indicated in chapter 1, competence through the credentialing process is difficult to guarantee and has been a controversial issue within the profession during the last 15 years. However, the public deserves protection against incompetent and unethical behavior on the part of licensed psychologists.

During the 1970s and early 1980s, credentialing issues have occupied most of regulatory boards' time and resources. As the credential issues increasingly become resolved through modification in state laws, rules, litigation, and the national examination process, board activities have become increasingly investigative and enforcement-oriented. It may be safe to say that relative to enforcement, state boards have supplanted professional organizations and will continue to do so in the future. As a result, it is important for the professional psycholo-

gist to understand fully the state licensing board's role in the process of enforcement of regulations and standards.

The state regulatory board generally has jurisdiction over individuals who hold
a license or who, as a result of being registered with the board, are allowed to hold
the title of *psychologist* and to practice psychology. It is important to note again
that some states have "title" laws that regulate the title of *psychologist*, while other
states have "practice" laws that specify what is considered to be the practice of
psychology. The advantage of having practice provisions enables the boards to
prosecute, usually through civil or criminal court, those individuals who practice
psychology without a license either through the misuse of the title or involvement
in illegal practice (e.g., psychological testing). It should be noted that most laws
do provide an "exempt status" for specialties, such as a school psychologist certified by a state department of education and employed by a board of education, or
for disciplines, such as the pastoral counselor or social worker; these exemptions
vary from state to state. Some states also have jurisdiction over individuals who
are registered with the board under the supervision of the licensed professional
psychologist, such as interns, psychological assistants, or examiners.

Violations relative to licensed individuals are usually prosecuted by the state
attorney general; unlicensed individuals are prosecuted by local district attorneys. While it cannot be fully documented, initially boards were concerned with
pursuing the unlicensed person. As the public and practitioners have become
more knowledgeable, these situations have lessened considerably and boards
have become more concerned with regulating the profession.

It is very important to reiterate that boards have no authority to enforce standards of practice unless they are specified in statutes or rules and regulations. The
peer-imposed standards (e.g., APA *Ethical Principles*, Standards for Providers of
Psychological Services) are often embodied in state laws or regulations, usually
by paraphrasing them and occasionally by reference. In the latter situation, the
disadvantage is that standards might change and become more ambiguous and
thus more difficult to enforce, or even that such changes might not be in the best
interest of the consumer.

State licensing boards essentially respond to complaints from consumers or
professional psychologists. Occasionally, the board will respond to noted irregu-
larities with site review visits or formal investigations. In other instances, boards
will become involved when a court finds a psychologist guilty of, for example,
welfare or third-party payment fraud. Cases may also be referred to boards by
state ethics committees or third-party payers who review case procedures. While
the procedure is not systemized, it appears that consumers, professional psychologists, and others are becoming increasingly aware of the role of the licensing
boards in enforcement and are reporting violations (see table 6.1).

Table 6.1

WHEN ACTION BY LICENSING BOARDS IS DETERMINED TO BE RELEVANT

---

1. Violations of statute
    (a) Unlicensed practice of psychology as defined in the state statute
    (b) Violations related to the practice of psychology by licensed individuals (e.g., moral turpitude, fraud)
    (c) Laws such as felonies, unrelated to the practice of psychology (Note: Some states, such as California, require the felony to bear a substantial relationship to the licensed practice in order for the board to take action.)
2. Violations of rules and regulations
    (a) Rules of professional conduct
    (b) Gross negligence
    (c) Incompetence
3. Violations of other licensing boards and action taken by other boards
4. Disciplinary actions or denial of license by the psychology board of another state

---

A significant deterrent to reporting violations is the complainant's fear of legal action against him- or herself—particularly from a colleague. Most boards will not reveal the name of a complainant unless he or she will be involved in the actual hearing process; some states (e.g., California) have laws protecting persons who report suspected violations without malice. In some instances, boards who have an investigating process prefer to have complaints made directly to the board and are not concerned about having the psychologist first contact the offender.

Psychologists need to read and be very familiar with the laws and rules of the state in which they practice. Violations and subsequent penalties can be prevented through knowledge and consultation, along with understanding the potential seriousness for violations.

Investigations

When a violation is suspected, the licensing board will initiate a formal investigation. The investigation is performed either by board members or a designated state department of investigation, which assigns a state investigator to the case who, in turn, works closely with the board. The primary advantage of board members investigating a case is their intimate knowledge of the profession and the subsequent manner in which violations can be hidden. An added function is the commitment board members have to the maintenance of the integrity of the profession. This orientation may be contrary to public opinion, which often assumes that regulating boards operate to protect the profession from the public and will take little action.

State investigators have considerable expertise in investigating procedures, thereby eliminating the need to train new board members as investigators. However, they also serve on numerous other boards, are generally less knowl-edgeable about the profession, and sometimes are less committed to extending investigations when impasses are reached; the time commitment for any investi-gation can be quite extensive, a factor board members must consider when tak-ing on a case.

Some states have explicit due rights procedures spelled out in detail, while others are vague. In some instances, states may employ undercover investigators. Investigators and hearings are also expensive. States vary as to fiscal support and other resources for investigations and hearings, with some required to pay for such expenses solely from renewal and application fees and others supported from general revenue funds.

At any rate, clear guidelines for investigators are usually established. When a formal hearing results from an investigation, the investigator does not participate as a member of the panel if he or she is a board member. Likewise, board mem-bers who work with state investigators are not involved. Previous bias can be avoided in this way. Finally, whatever the resolution of the case, the originator of the complaint is given information about the disposition.

Hearings

If a complaint is found to have validity, formal charges may be filed with the board and the accused psychologist is notified of an opportunity for a formal hearing. To avoid the time and expense of further proceedings, agreements regarding guilt and punishment can sometimes be negotiated. When consent cannot be reached or either party does not want to reach an agreement, the case proceeds to a formal hearing.

Although procedures vary among states, the most common model is for hear-ings to be held by the board itself, usually with a presiding hearing officer who is familiar with legal procedures. Some boards have the authority to appoint a hear-ing officer; the drawback of using an outside hearing officer is that unless he or she is familiar with psychological practice, real issues relative to ethical practice and harm to the client may not be fully appreciated by the presiding officer.

During the hearing, the state's case is presented by the deputy attorney general of the state. The defendant is also represented by legal counsel. In some states, witnesses may be subpoenaed and sworn in so that cross-examination is permissible. The formal hearing is quite similar to a trial proceeding, but with more flexibility and leniency. The American Association of State Psychology Boards (AASPB), working with the Texas Board, has developed a videotape of a model hearing which makes both educational and interesting viewing and can be secured upon request from AASPB or state licensing boards.

Butler and Williams (1985) analyzed hearings of the Ohio Board of Psychology from 1972 to 1983, and concluded that when a complaint reached the hearing stage there was, in most instances, enough evidence to warrant a conviction. In most states, after weighing the evidence the board has the authority to reprimand, suspend, or revoke the license. Both suspension and revocation can be stayed, with a specified period of probation. If the terms of the probation are violated, the original punishment is activated. Combinations of these actions can be given (e.g., suspension of one year, stayed with 30 days actual suspension plus conditions of probation). The advantage of staying is that the board has both a surveillance and rehabilitation mechanism. The Psychology Examining Committee of California has issued a set of disciplinary guidelines to aid boards in reaching decisions. The guidelines were reproduced in the *AASPB Newsletter* (Psychology Examining Committee of California, 1979). Most boards believe that publicizing the actions taken may be useful, both as a deterrent and as evidence that the board is doing its job.

SUMMARY

This chapter has provided a basic introduction to the conceptualization and organization of professional ethics. Beyond the obvious need to develop familiarity with the specifics of the relevant code and practice guidelines, some experience with hypothetical cases in which application of the material is required is essential. The use of a problem-solving model with which the psychologist is comfortable is advisable. To that end, the following chapter presents a number of models that have been presented in the literature.

Chapter 7

Ethical Behavior

The ASPPB and the APA Ethics Committee have reported a significant increase in disciplinary and legal actions against psychologists (Peterson, 1996). The total number of active complaints at all stages handled by the APA ethics committee in 1996 was 921, and while slightly lower than the 1995 figure, it still reflects the increase of activity noticed since 1990, when the total was 563 (APA Ethics Committee, 1997). However, the total of 89 new complaints in 1996 was down from the average of 120 over the past three years (11% of the membership). Finally, it is interesting to note that 27 of the cases were opened as a result of a loss of licensure. The next highest category involved 10 cases of inappropriate practice on the part of psychologists in dealing with child custody cases.

In a random survey of APA members, respondents were asked to share examples of ethical dilemmas faced in their work (Pope & Vetter, 1992). The most frequently described dilemmas involved confidentiality (18%), with actual or potential risks to a third party constituting the crux of the issue. The second most frequently described incidents (17% of the incidents reported) involved blurred, dual, or conflictual relationships. The third most frequently mentioned area (14%) dealt with payment sources, plans, settings, and methods. Of the 20 remaining categories of ethically troubling incidents, the percentages ranged from 1–8.* The topics involved such behavior as becoming friends with a former client, telling a client you are angry with him or her, and accepting only male or female clients.

Peterson (1996) reported that the most common problems presented to the

---

*A somewhat related study involving therapists and their beliefs and behavior, while too specific for analysis here, is "Ethics of Practice: The Beliefs and Behaviors of Psychologists as Therapists" (Pope, Tabachnick, & Keith-Spiegel, 1987).

APA Ethics Committee involved matters of *competence*, such as misuse of tests, poor record-keeping, practicing outside one's areas of competence, or ineffectual professional judgment and/or practice due to a physical and/or mental impairment. Another problem area involved questions of *informed consent and confidentiality*. Although less prevalent than the issues related to competence, some psychologists did not provide adequate informed consent information or help their clients to understand and protect their confidentiality rights. *Dual relationships* continue to be guarded against along with the manner of arranging and implementing *financial arrangements*.

The above findings can be the result of a number of factors, for example, poor training, a general decline in society on the priority given to values and integrity, the fact that there has been an increase in the number of training programs and thus graduates, the emphasis on teaching contents of ethical codes without stressing the importance of using them (Bernard & Jara, 1996), and failure on the part of professionals to use consumer input or data reflecting critical incidents experienced by the psychology practitioner (Bersoff, 1996). Whatever the answer, the situation warrants the trainee's, trainers' and practitioner's attention.

Pettifor (1996) argues that while psychologists have a responsibility to provide ethical services to their clients, there is little that can insure compliance with ethical standards. Mandatory continuing education programs do not insure compliance. Pettifor offers professional organizations some practical strategies for supporting the psychologist's daily practice. First, a *self-evaluation* questionnaire, consisting of practice questions tied to the principles should be available to practitioners; the questions are of a generic or specialty orientation. Second, maintenance of a centralized resource library, containing up-to-date publications, standards, and guidelines would help keep psychologists current. Third, ethics workshops, focusing on refresher types of objectives as well as newer areas of proficiency should routinely be available. Fourth, peer support networks as well as informal, voluntary peer review should be developed.

Canter, Bennett, Jones, and Nagy (1996) discuss preventative steps that can be taken in day-to-day practice as well as when an ethical dilemma arises. The steps essentially comprise an ethical practice model:

1. Know the ethics code. It might be added that not only should the relevant national professional code (e.g., APA, CPA) be familiar to the practictioner, but also the state code if one exists.
2. Know the applicable state laws and federal regulations, including state licensure laws as well as other statues.
3. Know the rules and regulations where you work. Again, it is important to recognize the areas of potential as well as real discrepancy with ethical and

best-practice professional behavior. Taking steps to alert supervisors/employers to acceptable professional practice can lead to sanctioned written procedures.

4. Engage in continuing education in ethics. Many of the ideas presented by Pettifor (1996) above are relevant to this step.

5. Identify when there is a potential ethical problem. Easier said than done? Perhaps. Canter and colleagues (1996) encourage psychologists to know their "blind spots, prejudices, weaknesses, or ignorance" and boundaries of competence. Haas and Malouf's (1995) guidelines are particularly helpful in this regard. They note that competence is not a static concept and can "erode" or "decay" over time (p. 26). They encourage the practitioner to ask, "Do relevant standards exist? Is the approach being used grounded solidly in research or theory? What contextual constraints apply? Are you emotionally able to help the client? Could you justify your decision to a group of your peers?" (pp. 26–32).

6. Learn a method for analyzing ethical obligations in other complex situations. Six ethical decision-making models are presented in the next section of this chapter as a means of helping the reader begin to develop his or her own model.

7. Consult with professionals knowledgeable about ethics. Although this is perhaps the easiest, most sensible suggestion, it is often simply overlooked or avoided because of its self-exposure aspect. Common resources for the individual psychologist are former training program faculty and/or former or current supervisors. Supervisors can be a great resource for either brainstorming ideas or giving advice; after all, they probably know the psychologist well. Additional resources are state licensing boards and state psychological association ethics committees, who usually provide consultation on ethical issues. Of course, colleagues can be of great assistance, serving as neutral analyzers of a situation.

Increasingly there have been calls to improve the ethical training of psychologists (Eberlein, 1987). The APA's accreditation standards require the teaching of ethics (APA 1996a). Indeed, teaching students how to apply the codes in controlled situations emphasizes the value of a "routine" or "model" for approaching potential and emerging ethical dilemmas, which can facilitate professional development. At the very least, it would force the student to be objective and guided by neutral observers in attempting to deal with the situation in a good-faith manner.

The next section will present examples of such decision-making approaches. The reader is encouraged to adopt one and use it to analyze daily practice in order to get a feel for its utility, or to continue elements of two or more of the models for a more individual approach.

ETHICAL DECISION-MAKING MODELS

Ethical decisions can be conceptualized as occurring on at least three levels: "(a) ethical behavior that is virtually automatic, (b) choices that can be made relatively easily by reference to the Code, (c) dilemmas in which ethical principles seem to conflict" (Canadian Psychological Association, 1991a, p. 88). Ethical behavior does not require hours of deliberation; in fact, vigilance to this aspect of practice and early action may make such behavior routine. The automatic nature of some decisions, such as selection of assessment tools or the need to include a consent form, illustrate the almost routine way in which psychologists can act ethically. Similarly, when choices require some pause, a review of the code as a quick reminder or detailing of steps to be taken can be all the psychologist needs to proceed with confidence that he or she is acting professionally. It is the third level where there is ambiguity, or a conflict of principles, values, or obligations, that the psychologist is well served if he or she has a set of procedures in place to systematize the decision-making. While those procedures, or model, are not used every day, the fact that preparatory work has been done assures that problem-solving in the ethical decision area can proceed systematically. This model embraces Canter and colleagues' (1996) suggestion to have a method for analyzing situations. The following six models all have some common elements, but are unique enough to warrant a separate brief presentation.

Kitchner's Model of Ethical Justification

Kitchner's (1984) guidelines for decision-making represent a sophisticated blend of ideas regarding moral thinking and the use of ethical principals as a basis for ethical reasoning. In the model (figure 7.1), there are two levels of moral reasoning, the intuitive level and the critical-evaluative level. Reasoning at the intuitive level represents our immediate moral values and may be a strong influence on our reactions when time constraints require a decision. However, Kitchner argues that it may not always lead to sound, defensible results, so that we need to have a hierarchically-related external set of standards to call upon. This resource allows for a critical analysis to be employed in decision-making wherein evaluative problem-solving is likely to occur. The psychologist's first recourse then is to the ethical code(s) of his or her profession. However, when the code fails the professional, then he or she must refer to an even higher

Figure 7.1
A MODEL OF ETHICAL JUSTIFICATION

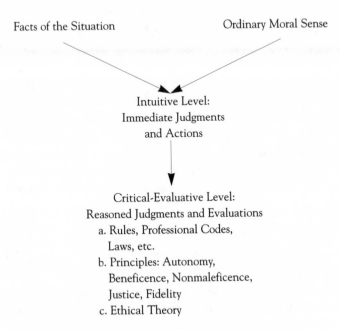

Facts of the Situation   Ordinary Moral Sense

Intuitive Level:
Immediate Judgments
and Actions

Critical-Evaluative Level:
Reasoned Judgments and Evaluations
a. Rules, Professional Codes,
   Laws, etc.
b. Principles: Autonomy,
   Beneficence, Nonmaleficence,
   Justice, Fidelity
c. Ethical Theory

Adapted from Kitchner, 1984, with permission from Sage Publications.

norm—ethical principles. Based on the work of Beauchamp and Childress (1979) and Drane (1982), Kitchner identified the principles of autonomy, beneficence, nonmaleficense, justice, and fidelity as most critical for psychologists The principle of *autonomy* involves the right of both the consultant and the consultee to act autonomously. Respect for others' rights, including that of choice, is valued. A professional's commitment to informed-consent policies is one practical application of this principle. However, as with all principles, there are limitations or restrictions on its application. For example, the competence of the consultee to make decisions and the prohibition against infringing on the rights of others constrain this principle so that it is not completely binding in each instance of its application (Kitchner, 1984). The principle of *beneficence* results in not just preventing harm but also promoting benefit for the client. Very often it requires an accommodation to the autonomy objective. Kitchner suggests that, above all, no harm should be inflicted on others in the delivery of service—this is the principle of *nonmaleficence*. While actions such as the use of diagnostic labels may illustrate the negative consequences of some services, Kitchner points out that "harm" is such an ambiguous term that there will always be dilemmas in situations where this principle is applied. Professionals are encouraged to offer services and, in general, to behave professionally with fairness, or *justice*. Equal treatment to all is among the most timely of the issues that face our society today. Finally, *fidelity* implies that loyalty and truthfulness become the cornerstone of a professional relationship; of course, confidentiality is more relevant here.

In response to the extreme positions that these principles are absolute, or not valid since morality is relative, or prima facie valid ("i.e., moral principles are neither absolute nor relative, but they are always ethically relevant and can be overturned only when these are stronger ethical obligations" [Kitchner, 1984, p. 52]), Kitchner takes the last position. Hence, the relevance of principles always needs to be considered in ethical situations as a framework or set of guidelines.

Haas and Malouf's Decision-Making Flowchart

Haas and Malouf (1995) describe their flowchart as a sequential approach, insuring that an ethical decision is reached (see figure 7.2). It begins by addressing the need to identify the issues or "dimensions" of the situation facing the psychologist. What may be discovered on the part of the practitioner is that the problem being faced may be more legal than ethical and/or involve technical challenges. On the other hand, the situation may actually pose one or multiple ethical questions. Beyond these critical questions Haas and Malouf (1995) point out that it is critical that the psychologist involve all of the individuals who may be affected, such as parents, family members, a clinic, third-party payers, and their legitimate stake in the outcome of the decision-making. The ideas and preferences of these stakeholders should be taken into account. Finally, the existing professional codes of ethics and standards for practice must be considered. The three underlying presumptions of the flowchart are as follows: "the dignity and freewill of the individual (autonomy), the obligation of professionals to respect the existing standards and expectations of the society that legitimizes their activities (responsibilities), and the duty to avoid special or self-serving interpretations or situations (universality)" (Haas & Malouf, pp. 12–13). Thus, these authors subscribe to a multifaceted model of Kitchner's type in their framework. In presenting their flowchart, they stress the importance of consultation with colleagues and professional units, such as the ethics committee of a professional association or the state licensing board. It has been argued elsewhere (Pryzwansky, 1993) that professional peer consultation is not only a viable response to a given dilemma, but such documented action is one example of the professional's sensitivity to the problems and attempt at objectivity. At the same time the contact with other

Figure 7.2
THE DECISION-MAKING FLOW CHART

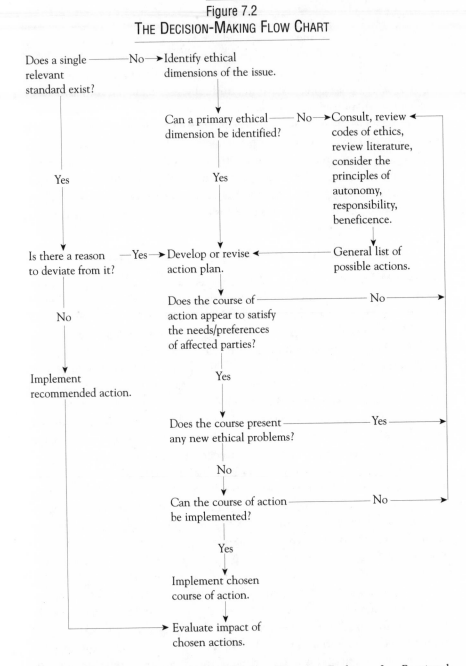

From Malouf, 1995. Copyright 1995 by Professional Resource Exchange, Inc. Reprinted by permission.

professionals reduces the feeling of isolation, of being under siege, or just the overwhelming burden that such circumstances can generate, even under relatively minor circumstances.

Finally, Haas and Malouf (1995) identify three limitations of their proposed flowchart, which in fact may apply to any of the models presented in this book. First, rationality is presupposed, but in fact there is no way to eliminate self-serving rationalization on the part of the practitioner. Second, the legal components of the situation must also be taken into account. Finally, the framework "makes no allowance for ambiguity or mistakes" (p. 19), although an evaluation component is incorporated into the recommended steps. They note that trying to do one's best is important since mistakes may happen, which is quite a different behavior than incompetence or intentional wrongdoing.

Problem-Solving Paradigms

There are at least three models of ethical decision-making that loosely follow what might be considered a problem-solving approach. They are Koocher and Keith-Spiegel's (1998) eight-step model (table 7.1), Nagle's (1987) process (table 7.2), and Packard's (1997) model (table 7.3). Koocher and Keith-Spiegel outline a sequence of practitioner-centered steps for consideration in deciding on a solution and/or course of action; their approach is adapted from Tymchuk (1981) and Haas and Malouf (1989). Similarly, Nagle has adapted other "procedural" approaches and encourages a more collective, collaborative approach with others that incorporates a continuation/obligation beyond the decision-making point. The notion of the professional's obligation to follow up on decisions has become much more salient in ethical decision-making discussions in this decade. Finally, Packard has provided a rather comprehensive set of "components," which he uses as a guide to ethical decision-making. He encourages each psychologist to develop a customized "model," incorporating personally meaningful steps from available models.

Canadian Psychological Association's Model

A truly unique feature of the CPA (1991a) Code of Ethics is the inclusion of decision-making steps with examples of their direct use with the Code. While basically a problem-solving approach of the type just described, it is recommended for use in resolving ethical difficulties when ethical principles appear in conflict. As noted earlier, a series of values are associated with each of the four principles. Consequently, a Canadian psychologist is urged to identify those values that are most relevant to the conflict at hand. These are arranged in a tabular format. The steps are listed in table 7.4 (CPA, 1991b). Note especially, step 3; the value of considering the positive and negative consequences of an action cannot be underestimated. Such a strategy generally facilitates efforts to maximize positive and minimize negative consequences. However, when the outcome is still not satisfactory, the psychologist is obligated to resolve the new dilemma.

Table 7.1
KOOCHER AND KEITH-SPIEGEL'S ETHICAL DECISION-MAKING PROCESS

1. Determine that the matter is an ethical one.
2. Consult the guidelines already available that might apply to a specific iden-tification and possible mechanism for resolution.
3. Consider, as best as possible, all sources that might influence the kind of decision you will make.
4. Locate a trusted colleague with whom you can consult.
5. Evaluate the rights, responsibilities, and vulnerability of all affected parties.
6. Generate alternative decisions.
7. Enumerate the consequences of making each decision.
8. Make the decision.

From Koocher & Keith-Speigel, 1998. Reprinted with permission from Oxford University Press.

Table 7.2
NAGLE'S SUGGESTED PROCESS FOR ETHICAL DECISION-MAKING

1. Gather information from individuals or parties involved and define poten-tial ethical issues involved in matter.
2. Consult appropriate ethical and legal guidelines, if available, that may apply to resolution of issues.
3. Determine the rights, responsibilities, and well-being of all parties involved.
4. Formulate possible alternative decisions for each issue raised.
5. Evaluate the various consequences possible of making each decision.
6. Estimate the probability of occurrence of each consequence.
7. Review information with affected parties.
8. Implement the decision.
9. Monitor, review, and follow up the decision.

From Nagle, 1987. Reprinted with permission from Guilford Publications.

Table 7.3
PACKARD'S COMPONENTS OF AN ETHICAL DECISION-MAKING MODEL

---

1. Identify the known facts of the situation.
2. Assess your personal response (i.e., Kitchner's "ordinary moral sense").
3. Review the APA Ethics Code carefully (giving thanks for the "user-friendly" nature of the 1992 revision).
4. Check for relevant state or federal laws.
5. Don't forget that institutional policies are often a factor.
6. Apply general moral principles as concretely as possible (the "Big 6").
7. Ask the deontological and teleological questions.
8. Consider how a "virtuous" person might respond to the situation (i.e., apply virtue ethics).
9. Identify and analyze possible conflicts between codes, laws, institutional policies, moral principles, and ethical theories.
10. Consult regularly with trusted and respected colleagues.
11. Be alert to relevant cultural and diversity issues.
12. Construct alternative courses of action.
13. Act by implementing the alternative that according to your thoughtful and reflective analysis seems most credible.
14. Review the consequences of your actions and be ready to reinvolve yourself in the decision-making process if the ethical issue is not resolved.
15. Keep in mind that the decision-making process is inevitably interactive, reciprocal, and systemic and not a set of linear steps as the above listing implies.

From Packard, 1997. Reprinted with permission from the author.

GUIDELINES FOR SPECIFIC PSYCHOLOGICAL PRACTICE

In addition to ethical codes, professions have begun to articulate statements of practice, which may range from minimal indicators of acceptable practice to "best practices" descriptions to aspirational documents. Recently, the term *guidelines* has been preferred to *standards*, since *standards* can be construed to represent a benchmark criterion and, thus, suitable in accountability-type proceedings. Guidelines, on the other hand, have the intent of providing the practitioner with a resource for developing and/or emerging behavior in a particular service. The guidelines can also be generic, that is, applied to the entire profession, or

Table 7.4
CPA's Ethical Decision-Making Process

1. Identification of ethically relevant issue and practices.
2. Development of alternative courses of action.
3. Analysis of likely short-term, ongoing, and long-term risks and benefits of each course of action on the individual(s)/group(s) involved or likely to be affected (e.g., client, client's family or employees, employing institution, students, research participants, colleagues, profession, society, self).
4. Choice of course of action after conscientious application of existing principles, values, and standards.
5. Action, with a commitment to assume responsibility for the consequences of the action.
6. Evaluation of the results of the course of action.
7. Assumption of responsibility for consequences of action, including correction of negative consequences, if any, or re-engaging in the decision-making process if the ethical issue is not resolved.

From CPA, 1991b. Reprinted with permission from the Canadian Psychological Association.

specialty- or proficiency-oriented. In any event, the number of such documents is growing and, as Sinclair (1993) has found, "making it difficult for the psychologist to have detailed knowledge of them all" (p. 191), let alone their very existence. In American psychology, various entities of the APA have developed such documents but there is no systematic way to inform the membership of guidelines that have been formalized. Nevertheless, the proliferation of such documents, no doubt reflecting needs within the various segments of the profession, has led APA to develop systematic procedures for review and approval of guidelines.

Guidelines typically offer advice on respectful and competent provision of services (Sinclair, Simon, & Pettifor, 1996). They can be used for training purposes and, to a certain extent, in the oversight of professionals, but with less force than ethical codes. However, many guidelines are written to be consistent with a specific ethical code.

Following are brief discussions of examples of guidelines primarily directed to specific aspects of practice, as well as a more general set of guidelines dealing with the delivery of services by clinical, counseling, industrial-organization, and school psychologists.

Specialty Guidelines for the Delivery of Services

Generic standards for providers of psychological services were adopted by the APA's Council of Representatives in 1977 (APA, 1977). They formed the basis for the subsequent *Specialty Guidelines* (APA, 1981), which described the practice of the four recognized professional specialties at that time—clinical, counseling, industrial-organizational, and school psychology. The content of each set of specialty guidelines reaffirms the same basic principles found in the 1977 *Standards*, and also reflects each specialty's consensus of its knowledge base, services provided, problems addressed, and clients served. The intent of the guidelines is to improve the quality, effectiveness, and accessibility of psychological services. For that reason, each set of guidelines provides information on the *definition* of providers of the service and descriptions of the services provided. Specifically, the four major guidelines address information about the providers, programs (policies and procedures), accountability, and environment. The providers of psychological services include the *professional psychologist* (psychologists who hold the doctoral degree) and all other persons who participate in the delivery of psychological services under the supervision of a professional psychologist. Information would be available on the program's plan of operation, including organization, objectives, and scope of services; delivery of services; procedures; and accountability. In addition, a documentation of services rendered would be maintained along with a file of practice documents, for example, code of ethics, standards for tests, etc. Finally, the guidelines would include a plan of services and obligations, such as promoting freedom of choice and confidentiality.

The *Standards* were revised in 1987 as *Guidelines* (APA, 1987). Based on six principles of understanding, the now 30 guidelines are grouped under the three domains of providers, programs, and accountability. The revision notes that these guidelines are aspirational in nature and, given that the professional practice of psychology is continually evolving, there is no intent to limit future revisions.

In 1989, The Canadian Psychological Association adopted their own *Practice Guidelines for Providers of Psychological Services* (CPA, 1989). These guidelines are directed to three levels of providers (the APA guidelines deal with two levels): the larger organization or employer; the psychologist administrator/supervisor; and the individual psychologists. The guidelines are taken from the CPA Code of Ethics.

Practice Guidelines

As already mentioned, both the APA and CPA have endorsed practice guidelines and the list is growing. Some relate to specialty areas; others, to psychological practice regardless of practice expertise and/or focus. Several major APA examples will be discussed, but the individual psychologist is advised to keep abreast of those that are endorsed and in the development phase for, to date, there is no systematic way for psychologists, whether members of a professional organization or not, to obtain lists, let alone descriptions or sources for accessing copies of these documents. References are provided for the guidelines presented here.

APA Record-Keeping Guidelines

The *Record-Keeping Guidelines* (APA, 1993a) are clearly presented as *aspirational* in nature, and specific applications require judgment wherein the intent, technology, and the current knowledge base are taken into account. The various purposes for record-keeping are noted, such as self-monitoring, helping to plan services, and state/federal laws requiring records and protection from professional liability. The *Guidelines* deal with five topics:

1. "Content of Records" outlines the minimum information that should be included in the record, for example, identifying data, dates of service, types of service, fees, and assessments or intervention plans, including consultations, reports, and release of information forms. Record maintenance and protection are also addressed.
2. "Construction and Control of Records" deals with confidentiality questions and the fact that psychologists have the ultimate responsibility for the content and control of client records.
3. "Retention of Records" guidelines may be superseded by laws or regulations and/or organizational policies, but three years is considered a minimum time period for retaining records after the last contact with the client, with a summary maintained for at least one additional year. In the case of minors, a three-year period of record maintenance following the age of majority is recommended.
4. "Outdated Records" addresses disposal of records and the cautions required in reporting outdated information.
5. "Disclosure of Record-Keeping Procedures" to clients may take place and include the nature and extent of the records as well as limits in confidentiality of records. As with the intent of all guidelines, these suggestions facilitate the decision-making of the psychologist as he or she pursues a "best practices" set of professional behaviors, as opposed to a learning process that takes place in the "school of hard knocks."

Guidelines for Child Custody Evaluations in Divorce Proceedings
Recognizing that psychologists are in a position to make significant contributions to child custody decisions, the goal of these guidelines is to "promote proficiency in using psychological expertise in conducting child custody evaluations" (APA, 1994a, p. 677). Sixteen specific guidelines are organized into three major sections (see table 7.5).

Guidelines for Psychological Evaluations in Child Protection Matters
Approved in 1998 (APA Committee, 1998) these guidelines consist of three major sections. The first addresses the purpose of such evaluations, the second describes steps to be taken in preparing the child for the evaluation, and the third describes procedures for conducting such evaluations. A total of 17 specific guidelines make up this document, along with a glossary of common terms that are used in child protection matters.

Guidelines for Providers of Psychological Services to Ethnic, Linguistic, and Culturally Diverse Populations
The nine statements making up this document (APA, 1990) present principles intended to be aspirational and provide psychologists with suggestions on how to work with culturally diverse populations. The guidelines encourage providers to obtain the knowledge and skills needed for multicultural assessment and intervention when required by issues related to mental health service; several counseling and therapy models are referred to. Specifically, psychologists are expected to educate clients to the processes of psychological intervention; to be aware of the relevant research and practice issues of the population they are serving, recognizing ethnicity and culture as significant parameters; to respect the client's cultural and religious and/or spiritual beliefs and values; to interact in the language requested by the client; to take into account the impact of adverse factors; to attend to and work to eliminate biases, prejudices, and discriminatory practices; and to document culturally and sociopolitically relevant factors in the record. While a reference section is a strength of this document, unless updated regularly the guidelines lose their utility and relevance.

Guidelines for Engaging in Contractual Provision of Psychological Services in Schools
These guidelines (APA, 1995) are endorsed by the National Association of School Psychologists (NASP) and were developed to provide guidance to state boards of education and psychology, school administrators, and individual providers. Where individual providers are school psychologists, they should be certified by the state board of education and, if not considered an employee of

Table 7.5
SUMMARY OF GUIDELINES FOR CHILD CUSTODY
EVALUATIONS IN DIVORCE PROCEEDINGS

I. Orienting Guidelines: Purpose
1. Purpose: to assess the best psychological interests of the child.
2. Child's interests and well-being are paramount.
3. Focus of the evaluation is on parenting capacity, psychological and developmental needs of the child, and the resulting fit.

II. General Guidelines: Preparing a Child for Child Custody Evaluation
4. Role of psychologist is a professional expert who strives to maintain an objective, impartial stance.
5. Psychologist gains specialized competence (child and family development, child and family psychopathology, family violence, impact of divorce on children, legal standards and laws, state laws).
6. Psychologist is aware of personal and societal biases and engages in nondiscriminatory practice.
7. Psychologist avoids multiple relationships (therapeutic role, any other involvement).

III. Procedural Guidelines: Conducting a Child Custody Evaluation
8. Scope is determined by the evaluator, based on nature of referral question.
9. Obtain informed consent from all adult participants and, when appropriate, child participants.
10. Inform participants about the limits of confidentiality and disclosure of information.
11. Use multiple sources of data gathering.
12. Do not overinterpret nor inappropriately interpret clinical or assessment data.
13. Do not give any opinion regarding psychology or functioning of any individual who has not been personally evaluated.
14. Recommendations are based on what is in the best psychological interests of the child.
15. Clarify financial arrangements.
16. Maintain written records.

the system, be licensed by a state regulatory board. Likewise, the services should be provided "within the context of a comprehensive service delivery system" with opportunities for follow-up and consultation. Furthermore, appropriate supervision of the provider is also considered to be important.

Guidelines for Identifying Appropriate Supervisors for Psychological Services in Schools

Recognizing the concern of psychologists working in the schools being supervised by nonpsychologists, the APA approved these guidelines in 1994 (APA, 1994b). They call for the supervision of school psychologists' services by qualified supervisory school psychologists and then define the qualifications for a supervisor.

Guidelines for the Evaluation of Dementia and Age-Related Cognitive Decline

Approved in 1998, the guidelines (APA, 1998j) outline a variety of factors practitioners should consider before assessing dementia and age-related cognitive decline. There are three general guidelines: familiarity with nomenclature and diagnostic criteria; ethical considerations; and procedural guidelines. Examples of the latter include: Psychologists should be sure of the current diagnostic nomenclature and criteria and they should gain specialized competence in the selection and use of psychological tests, and understand the tests' limitations and the context in which they may be used and interpreted. As are other guidelines, these are considered aspirational and not exhaustive. These guidelines also point out that assessments of these types are the core activity of the specialty of clinical neuropsychology. The appropriate training model to attain that specialty is specified in the Houston Conference on Specialty Education and Training in Clinical Neuropsychology (Hannay et al., in press). Important information that should help psychologists work with older adults is available from a recent APA publication on providing services to this age group (APA, 1998k).

Resolutions, White Papers, Task Force Reports

While not on the same level as standards and guidelines, there are other organizational products that help the individual practitioner think through issues and challenges associated with the provisions of service. For example, "Resolution on Lesbian, Gay and Bisexual Youths in the Schools" (APA, 1993b) (again supported by both the APA and NASP) calls for a commitment to a "safe and secure educational atmosphere" for all youth and for psychologists to "develop and evaluate interventions that foster . . . non-discriminatory environments, lower risk for HIV infection, and decrease self-injurious behaviors in lesbian, gay, and bisexual youths." Also, in the 1995 *American Psychologist* (pp. 674–676) there are three additional resolutions: "Firearm Safety and Youth"; "Violence in Mass Media"; and "Resolution on the Psychological Needs of Children Exposed to Disasters."

Statement on the Use of Anatomically Detailed Dolls in Forensic Psychology

Adopted in 1991 by the APA, this statement calls for psychologists to be competent in the use of such dolls and that they document (by videotape, audiotape, or in writing) the procedures used for each administration. Also, they should be prepared to provide clinical and empirical rationale for the procedures they use as well as the interpretation of results gained from their use. Koocher and colleagues (1995) provide a comprehensive review of the scientific and clinical knowledge base in the scholarly literature on use of these dolls, and discuss such topics and issues as doll features, ethical and methodological considerations, memory and suggestibility concerns, and narrative behavior with anatomically detailed dolls. Despite the debate on the use of such dolls use during sexual-abuse evaluations and/or treatments with children, Koocher and colleagues conclude they can be a useful communication tool provided practitioners realize that they are not psychological tests with productive validity; definitive statements cannot be made based simply on the results from play with the dolls. Particular caution must be taken when interpreting the reports of children aged 4 years or younger; the child's socioeconomic and cultural background should also be considered.

Statement on the Disclosure of Test Data

This statement was developed by the APA Committee on Psychological Tests and Assessment and approved in 1996 (APA, 1996b). As practice and legal mandates can differ depending on settings, the intended purpose, and use of testing, the statement is intended to enhance professional judgment where disclosure issues arise rather than preempt it; it was not intended to establish a guideline or standard of conduct. It provides guidance on 13 issues and/or questions that arise in this activity: (1) general issues, (2) access to test data, (3) informing the test taker of the purpose, use, and results of testing, (4) releasing data with or without the consent of the test taker, (5) release of data and test security, (6) releasing data to unqualified persons, (7) protecting copyright interests when releasing data, (8) conforming to federal and state statutes and rules, regulatory mandates, and institutional/organizational rules and requirements, (9) releasing test data to third party payers, (10) releasing test data when the organization is the client, (11) role of psychologists in forensic contexts, (12) role of psychologists in requesting or obtaining secure test data and test materials, and

(13) other issues (e.g., reprinting of test items, use of test items in teaching and training, and retention and maintenance of testing data). As can be discerned from this list, there are many considerations related to just this one topic, and familiarity with the perspectives and advice that is provided should only benefit the psychologist in both the trainer or practitioner role.

Terminating a Practice

While retirement is the typical reason given for terminating practice, it is not always the case. Regardless of the reason, termination needs to be done carefully with legal, ethical, and emotional factors taken into account. Freiberg (1998) recommends providing adequate notice to clients/patients, helping patients to identify another therapist, protecting records, and maintaining liability insurance after retirement. While there are no hard and fast timeframes, the psychologist should keep in mind that each client will have different needs. The APA Ethics Code can provide some information and *The Psychologist Legal Handbook* (Stromberg et al., 1988) is another resource in this regard.

Ethical codes and decision-making strategies have been presented in this and the previous chapter. The next chapter will address some ethical issues in professional practice.

Chapter 8

Professional Behavior and Accountability

This chapter will explore some of the more common ethical problems encountered during professional practice, with the underlying theme of accountability. While the previous chapters have focused on ethical codes and the ethical decision-making process, this chapter deals with the problems of competence, confidentiality, and dual relationships in clinical practice. Issues relevant to the media and clinical supervision are also explored, and empirically-based treatment guidelines are discussed. The chapter highlights the most problematic areas for practicing psychologists and dispels the common misconception that practice issues are clear and concise; in fact, most of the time ambiguity is prevalent. Psychologists are accountable to the public, to licensing boards, and to the profession regarding their professional behavior. It is difficult to protect the consumer and oneself at the same time; however, despite the complexity, psychologists are held accountable for the welfare of the public.

ACCOUNTABILITY

The *General Guidelines for Providers of Psychological Services* (APA, 1987a) discussed in chapter 6 has as its third guideline the obligation for *accountability*. It is explained in terms of the psychologist's commitment to promoting human welfare (see chapter 5), being a member of the independent, autonomous profession of psychology, conducting periodic, systematic, and effective evaluations of psychological service, and finally, being accountable to those people who are concerned with these services. Thus, accountability is broadly conceived and much more complex than the routine collection of data. A brief explanation of each point follows.

158

1. Practitioners are expected to interact with clients in an effective, considerate, economical, and humane manner and to protect the confidentiality of the relationship. Likewise, unit (i.e., agency, organization, practice) services are not withheld to potential clients on the basis of age, gender, religion, affectional orientation, or national or ethnic origin; should that happen, psychologists are to take appropriate corrective actions.

2. As members of an autonomous profession, psychologists are not to engage in self-serving behaviors that are not in the interest of the user. Psychologists are also expected to facilitate the development of and participate in professional standards review (APA, 1987a). Perhaps the most challenging implication of this statement involves the responsibility of psychologists to keep everyone they work with aware of the codes, guidelines, etc., that influence their work; the work setting obviously influences how and when this is accomplished.

3. Periodic, systematic, and effective evaluations of psychological services form the third point of this accountability guideline. Evaluations should be both internal and conducted by some independent party. The services (therapy, etc.), as well as the outcome measures, should be described thoroughly. The evaluation should take into consideration costs, in terms of time and money, and availability of professional and support personnel. Continuity of the service, as well as availability and adequacy, should also be considered. In all procedures, confidentiality of records and the privacy of clients need to be carefully guarded.

4. Professional psychologists should be accountable in all aspects of their service, so that clients are aware of their qualifications, the nature and the extent of the services offered or provided, and, where appropriate, financial costs and potential risks. Similarly, information about psychological services regarding evaluation, initiation, continuation, modification, and termination should be provided.

5. As a means of being accountable to more general societal needs, pro bono services are encouraged.

Not many examples appear in the literature of either individual or unit accountability plans. Jackson and Pryzwansky (1987) reported on an audit of a school psychological services unit. They used the *Specialty Guidelines* (APA, 1981b) as the basis for their review and found them user-friendly. However, even though the accountability review was externally initiated by the administration, there was very little in the way of expectations for how several questions posed to the auditor would be addressed and with what kind of data.

Miller's (1996) model deals with services provided in the managed care context and proposes that accountability be defined in terms of the economic efficiency and the quantity of services. He pointed to the lack of adequate information at the time for evaluating and comparing such plans.

Finally, accountability also refers to meeting the standards of professional practice. The legal statutes and ethical codes set the standards for practice; based upon these standards, psychologists are accountable to clients, licensing boards, and professional organizations relative to their professional behavior. What follows are some of the major issues facing psychologists in clinical practice.

COMPETENCE

While methods for adequately analyzing competence are not clear and precise, the issue regarding the professional responsibility to achieve and maintain competence is absolute. Psychology is an amalgamation of techniques, orientations, and approaches. For example, the outcome of therapy often depends upon a blend of the type of client, problem, method, and therapist; the measure of successful outcome is often difficult to determine. Given the psychologist's training and other factors, a psychologist can be competent in one setting and incompetent in another. Despite these difficulties, psychologists are expected to practice within the bounds of activities and settings they are qualified to conduct. Pope and Brown (1996) make a further distinction between having the prerequisite knowledge and skill base and the emotional competence, including the ability of the therapist to deal with the emotion-laden content and affect in the therapy session.

From the standpoint of the individual psychologist, competence involves the ability to honestly assess one's own professional strengths and limitations and often a willingness to refer or not to treat a client whose problem is beyond one's competence. This decision can be difficult. Presently, the psychologist is issued a general license and conceivably engages in any type of evaluative or therapeutic practice. Consumers are often uninformed about the differences in training and may assume that a psychologist who is well trained in individual psychotherapy, for example, would also have appropriate training and skills in marital or family therapy. It is unfortunate that some psychologists make the same erroneous assumption that their license allows them to practice in any applied area of psychology, regardless of training or supervised experience.

One method for dealing with this issue has been the development of specialty and subspecialty standards (see chapter 2). Through the archival descriptions of each of the recognized specialties, the APA has attempted to define the knowledge base and skills employed by each specialty. Therefore, degrees, titles, and practice should be related to the descriptions. These descriptions provide useful guidelines for competent practice, as well as protection for the psychologist should complaints arise relative to failure to follow professional standards. The APA, as well as other certification bodies (e.g., American Board of Professional Psychology), has attempted to alleviate the general confusion over what constitutes competency in a given practice area.

Because of the lack of clear identification by the public and self-limiting behaviors on the part of individual psychologists, licensing boards must deal with problematic relationships between competency and training in several ways. In attempting to determine relevant training, boards begin by specifying the degree(s) required: that is, master's or doctoral degree in psychology or an equivalent program. While the doctorate is essentially the entry-level requirement, content and standards of programs vary considerably, so that this does not provide a sufficient sole determiner of competence. While the doctoral degree was designed to develop high standards to protect consumers, some argue that the real issue is third-party reimbursement. The addition of a general examination was intended to test knowledge, but it more recently has begun to focus on general practice issues. An additional criterion is that of supervised experience, whereby a licensed professional endorses the psychologist's clinical abilities and clinical judgment. Some boards, such as California's, base oral examinations on clinical case vignettes to further assess competency.

Many malpractice suits involve competency issues, where both therapeutic ability and judgment are called into question. At this point, the psychologist most often defends him or herself, and licensing alone does not provide an adequate defense. The psychologist must be able to demonstrate adequate academic preparation, including didactic and practical training, as well as clinical supervision relative to this particular situation. A defense relative to the reasonable judgments made in a case begins with basic competence.

The major focus relative to competence has been discussed mainly in terms of psychotherapy; however, competence is also an issue in testing, teaching, research, and consultation. Basic coursework and supervised training in specific tests and techniques (e.g., Rorschach, WAIS-III) and report writing also involve a basic sensitivity about labeling. Teaching requires keeping abreast of new knowledge as well as ethical considerations of the course content. Research involves working within one's level of competence regarding designs and considering subject welfare, including obtaining valid consent from subjects. Consulting in schools, agencies, and industries requires different academic preparation and training for each area.

CONFIDENTIALITY

Confidentiality protects the privacy and welfare of clients. *Privilege* and *confidentiality* are frequently confused. Privilege (communication) is a legal term, granted by state laws to clients, which defines the type of relationships that prevent information learned as part of such relationships from being disclosed in legal proceedings or to third parties without the expressed consent of the client. While the psychologist (or other professional) is explicitly named in the statute, the privilege exists for the client. If the client waives the privilege, the psychologist may be compelled to release the information or testify. In these instances the client may not be selective relative to the waiver, that is, once the waiver is given the psychologist may testify regarding all aspects of the situation that directly pertains to the case. As a result, the client may not realize that by waiving privilege he or she may be putting him or herself at risk.

In some states, judges in criminal cases can overrule the privilege between the client and the psychologist if it is determined that the interests of justice outweigh the confidentiality. Some states may limit privilege to civil actions, while other states allow privilege in criminal cases with the exception of homicide.

Mandatory Reporting Laws

Privilege is rarely absolute, and in some situations, such as child abuse, the psychologist may be legally required to make a report to the authorities. The Child Abuse Prevention, Adoption, and Family Services Act of 1988 defines child maltreatment as "the physical or mental injury, sexual abuse or exploitation, negligent treatment, or maltreatment of a child by a person who is responsible for the child's welfare under circumstances which indicate that the child's health or welfare is harmed or threatened" (Pub.L. 100-294 §14). This law requires states to use the same definition in order to qualify for child protection funds.

Child welfare advocates have succeeded in getting all states to adopt mandatory child abuse reporting requirements. These requirements have been modified since the passage of federal law (The Public Health and Welfare Act, Pub.L. 93-247, 42 usc.) that made federal financial assistance contingent upon individual states' adopting laws requiring mandatory reporting by certain professionals of suspected child abuse. Typically, the list of professionals includes teachers, physicians, psychologists, social workers, and other healthcare and social service workers. The professional only needs to suspect child abuse; proof of the abuse is not required—the final determination rests with the child services agency. For psychologists there is little room for discretion relative to the initial reporting of suspected abuse. School psychologists, in particular, must be familiar with the clinical signs of abuse and neglect and the procedures for reporting suspected abuse.

There are substantial penalties for failure to report, including criminal fines and vulnerability to civil lawsuits. In addition, many state licensing laws have provisions for mandatory reporting; failure to report could result in disciplinary action, including suspension or revocation of a license to practice. Most states require that knowing and willing failure to report is necessary for liability to exist, which mitigates and protects against honest mistakes. In most instances, actually seeing the child is a necessary prerequisite for learning about the abuse in regards to the liability issue, which, at the same time, does not fully relieve the psychologist of the burden to report. At the same time, Pub.L. 93-247 (The Public Heath and Welfare Act) requires states to provide immunity to mandated professionals who make reports in good faith.

While all states and Canadian provinces have mandatory reporting laws for child abuse and elder abuse, only some have reporting requirements for handicapped abuse. In these instances, the laws are based upon the rationale that the needs of vulnerable individuals and society are more important than certain individual rights (Kalichman, 1993). Statutes vary as to waiver of privilege for criminal activity, whether perpetrator, victim, or even witness. Kalichman (1993) believes that reporting laws do not interfere with the therapeutic relationship, while Koocher and Keith-Speigel (1998) have concluded that the data indicate that the impact of reporting requirements on the therapeutic relationship are mixed. In some instances, the development of trust in the therapeutic relationship can override the legal need to breach confidentiality.

VandeCreek and Knapp (1993) give some guidelines relative to handling these types of clinical situations. It is important in borderline cases to document the rationale for reporting decisions and to consult with other professionals. If possible, family members should be persuaded to call the child welfare or family services agency themselves or the psychologist should make the call with the family present. This allows the psychologist to clarify the decision, process the feelings of the family, and explain the criminal and civil ramifications for the psychologist in not reporting. This can minimize the damage to the therapeutic relationship. Anonymous reporting, while allowed in many states, is not recommended because the family can usually guess the identity of the informant.

Because state laws do vary, it is the ethical responsibility of psychologists to make themselves aware of the nature and status of privileged communication in their own state. It is also their responsibility to fully inform clients of the limits of confidentiality.

Danger and Breaching Confidentiality

Confidentiality, in contrast to privilege, refers to a professional standard of conduct and, as such, is an ethical principle without a legal basis. Therefore, in ordinary situations, a professional is obligated through a professional code of ethics not to discuss information about a client with anyone. Regarding the disclosure of information, two types of problems can occur: (a) the psychologist, through carelessness, reveals confidential information; and (b) the psychologist makes a decision to reveal information. In the first instance, information can be revealed by, for example, a professor teaching classes and not sufficiently disguising case examples from his practice, a health psychologist maintaining open filing systems in her office, or a forensic psychologist consulting with other staff. These situations can easily occur and create problems if not monitored carefully by the psychologist.

The second problem, regarding the conscious decision to release information, creates the greatest controversy, especially in terms of situations that would justify this decision. The focus of this controversy involves the "clear danger to the person or to others" clause in the APA *Ethical Principles* (APA, 1992a). In some instances, a psychologist must make the decision to breach confidentiality when it seems that the client will move from talking about harmful situations to actually taking action. While physical harm to self or others may be obvious, insidious forms of harm, such as financial ruin, also necessitate the same decision.

The classic Tarasoff case (*Tarasoff v. Regents of University of California*, 1976) is discussed in detail in chapter 9 and raises the issue of whether or not the psychologist has a duty to protect all potential victims. Despite the fact that psychologists generally have not been found liable in *Tarasoff*-like situations, psychologists must still use reasonable caution and carefully assess the threat of harm to the patient and potential victim. Courts have not found psychologists liable for errors in judgment.

Another confidentiality issue relates to situations where the psychologist is working with clients infected with the human immunodeficiency virus (HIV) or who have acquired immunodeficiency syndrome (AIDS). The main concern is when the client is aware of the disease and fails to warn sexual partners or use safe sexual practices. Koocher and Keith-Speigel (1998) point out that therapists must be current regarding to medical information relative to transmission risks as well as state laws regarding professional relationships with HIV patients. Therapists need to speak openly to their clients about the dangers of transmission. Often, clients are conflicted on this issue and welcome the opportunity to resolve it. However, if the client continues to resist informing partners, the psychologist may need to breach confidentiality and warn identified partners. This should be done only after the psychologist has discussed the need to warn others with the client and, hopefully, gained his permission to do so. As usual, consultation with colleagues is essential, as well as the examination of personal attitudes toward the disease.

Suicide is never perfectly predictable; however, when the psychologist thinks it is a possibility, he or she must warn relatives or, in the case of minors, the parents. The suicide of a client can be extremely upsetting to the therapist responsible for the treatment. Client suicide results in a great deal of self-questioning about the treatment plan and second-guessing about what could have been done differently to prevent the suicide. Not only must the therapist work through personal feelings, which may range from anger and pain over the loss to self-doubt, but he or she must also deal with the feelings of the family. The reactions of the family may swing between anger at the client and the therapist to acknowledging and appreciating the efforts of the therapist. Malpractice suits from client suicides are not uncommon.

Generally, the courts have maintained that reasonableness of professional judgment is the determinant of liability. If the suicide was not foreseeable, as in the case of cooperative clients who did not discuss suicide or indicate having a definitive plan, liability has not been an issue. Unlike *Tarasoff*, there is no duty to warn the relatives of adult clients. Psychologists are held to a standard of taking reasonable precautions, and there is leeway in the determination of reasonableness.

In inpatient situations, therapists need to use reasonable professional judgment in assessing the risks of suicide and have written policies in place regarding the supervision of therapists who are dealing with dangerously suicidal patients. The courts have generally recognized that "an overly restrictive environment is as destructive as a permissive one and that professionals need to balance the benefits of treatment against the risks of freedom" (VandeCreek & Knapp, 1993, p. 26).

In outpatient situations, the reasonableness standard also prevails, and it is generally agreed that therapists need to take all threats or gestures of suicide seriously. The potential for suicide increases when the client has a definite plan, the plan includes a means that will likely result in death (e.g., a gun), and the client has the means to implement the plan. A sudden change toward impulsivity and a lightening of mood can also be serious indicators. Prior attempts and long-term chronic illness, including HIV infection, also increase suicide probability. The difficulty for the clinician is dealing with the complexity of issues involved in predictability, which include intent, method, previous attempts, depth of depression, manipulativeness of the gestures, and the social support system of the client. The decision of the psychologist not to recommend voluntary hospitalization or seek involuntary commitment is not, in itself, a determinant of negligence. Again, the courts are concerned about whether the suicide was foreseeable and if reasonable professional judgment was exercised in carrying out the treatment plan.

In the case of minors, involving the family in the treatment can be helpful in activating a support system to monitor the client. When a working relationship with the support system of any suicidal client has been established, the psychologist is in a better position to help the family work through the grief over the loss if it occurs. This is especially true with parents and siblings of children and adolescents. The likelihood of later litigation is also appreciably reduced.

It is imperative that agencies and schools have written policies for responding to suicidal gestures. Such a policy should include a referral to an individual trained in suicide prevention, such as a school psychologist, contacting and involving the parents in the treatment, and, if necessary, referral to an appropriate individual practitioner or agency (Poland, 1995).

A breach of confidentiality may also be considered relative to substance abuse in the schools. Some states (e.g., Virginia) have enacted legislation that requires that parents be notified of alcohol and/or substance abuse. In situations involving therapy with middle- and high-school students (where it is safe to say many of the students in treatment are involved in some level of drinking or drug use), it again becomes an issue of clinical judgment as to when it goes beyond experimentation or occasional social use to the level of dependence or abuse. Written policies relative to confidentiality and notification are necessary to protect both the student and the professional.

VandeCreek and Knapp (1993) further point out that laws relative to reporting and decisions to breach confidentiality are not a shield for inadequate clinical practice, but rather hold the professional to a realistic standard of care while protecting society from abusive behavior and foreseeable violence. These standards include:

1. Initially advise clients in writing on the limits of confidentiality.
2. Have knowledge about relevant state statutes and court decisions.
3. Consult with the client and appropriate legal and professional colleagues prior to finalizing a decision.
4. Clearly think through and document the rationale behind a decision to breach confidentiality.

Client Records

Psychologists need to be aware of the laws governing the release of records to clients. Clients generally have access to institutional records (e.g., school, clinic, agency), but private practitioner records and working notes are usually not covered by specific legislation. An overriding principle regarding records is that they belong to the institution or private practitioner and not the client. While clients may make a claim to the records because they "paid for the therapy sessions" or a psychological report, the fact is that the client only paid for the services rendered (Koocher & Keith-Speigel, 1998). Because the psychologist generated and is responsible for keeping the data, the information belongs to the practitioner or, in the case of institutions, to the organization according to their policy. Perhaps a copy of the report may be made available as part of the agreement; however, original working notes and protocols are property of the practitioner.

Institutional records belong to the institution, not the client or practitioner. That is, any record kept in a file that other members of the institution have access to is considered part of the institutional records. The exception is working notes kept by the psychologist, which are often speculative in nature relative to the psychological report or therapy. These notes should be kept in a private place by the psychologist and reviewed carefully for sensitive data. A safe assumption to make is that all records might be made available to the client at some point in time as a result of court action. Once a court action is initiated, the notes cannot be subsequently edited. Caution, therefore, is advised for the psychologist relative to working notes, because of the sensitive nature of the psychologist's impressions and the possibility of such speculation being subpoenaed in a court action. Regular reviews and summaries are recommended.

Psychologists need to have written permission from the client prior to releasing any records or information; they must also alert the client to any possible hazards involved. The client should consider both the how the information will be used and impact of such use on the client. Special exceptions exist when the notes affect the rights of confidentiality of other clients, such as in group or marital therapy, or in rare circumstances when access to the records may be detrimental to the client. In these situations, the records may have to be edited to eliminate any references to other individuals that would violate their rights. However, Koocher and Keith-Speigel (1998) point out that in such instances outside consultation is necessary to assist in determining that detriment is indeed an issue.

In presenting the records to the client, it is helpful to review the record with the client in order to explain technical terms and deal with his or her reactions. At any rate, it is helpful to have an established policy relative to these situations. Records are best kept in a factual manner, devoid of speculation, with appropriate documentation. When the records are carefully prepared, access to the records by clients usually does not have a negative impact on the client, nor does it create unusual problems for the psychologist.

Record Retention

The APA adopted guidelines relative to records in 1993. It is important that records be maintained in a fashion that documents clearly the reason for treatment, relevant history, medical information including current medications, diagnostic impressions, and a basic treatment plan. Progress notes relative to the treatment are also essential, and they should be developed in a professional manner that avoids speculation. These notes may, at some point, be subject to disclosure. Any assignments given to clients and follow-up procedures or referrals to other professionals or agencies also need to be documented. A summary at the end of therapy is important, as it reflects the clinical judgment of the psychologist as to the outcome of treatment. Generally speaking, the more dangerous, emotionally ill, or litigiously inclined the client, the more important it is to keep careful records.

The APA (1993a) recommends retaining full records for a minimum of three years and an additional 12 years for the summary of the record. In the case of a minor, the time frame should be extended to at least three years past the age of majority. However, most states have enacted legislation relative to the retention of medical records, which may or may not include psychologists' records. In some cases, the laws distinguish between agencies and private practice settings. It is extremely important for psychologists to be aware of their own state laws relative to the length of retention of business and clinical records. While the APA standards should be the minimum, a number of jurisdictions require more extended time. The time element begins with the termination of service.

Welfare of the client is also a consideration in the retention of records. On the positive side, the records can facilitate treatment at a future time, including when the records are transferred to another professional or agency. The documentation of past treatment outcomes can facilitate the development of current planning and decision-making. On the other hand, outdated or obsolete material can be harmful if it is not relevant to the current situation. For example, family dynamics or test data a decade old will not be relevant when the psychologist is performing an evaluation to determine if an applicant is currently suitable and employable for a specific job.

A final concern is what happens to the records in the case of retirement or death of the psychologist. In the instance of retirement, the psychologist can simply keep the relevant records in his or her personal possession and be available when further interpretation or forwarding requests are made. When a psychologist dies, it is extremely helpful if he or she has made prior arrangements for the disposition of his or her records. The usual method is to have them placed in the care of another psychologist for the management and processing of requests for information.

Subpoenas and Court Orders of Records

Subpoenas are usually issued at the request of an attorney to the clerk of courts for information and/or appearance in court. While the subpoena requires a response, it doesn't necessarily require the psychologist to divulge privileged communication unless there is a release of information by the client. If there is no release form, the psychologist should contact the client(s) regarding the signing of a release and discuss any aspects of the material that may be damaging to the client. If some of the notes are especially sensitive, then the psychologist may offer to release a summary. When a subpoena is received and questions exist relative to the impact of releasing the material, the psychologist should consult legal counsel before surrendering the information.

If the subpoena comes from an attorney opposing the case of the client, it is often helpful to contact the attorney and indicate that the material cannot be released without a signed consent of the client. In such instances, it is important to contact the client and explain the situation and ask for permission to contact the client's attorney. Then explain to the client's attorney the need to protect the rights of privilege. The attorney should work out the issues with the opposing attorney or work to quash the subpoena (Koocher & Keith-Speigel, 1998). At any rate, it is important to understand there is an obligation to respond to the subpoena. An excellent source for responding to subpoenas is provided by the APA's Committee on Legal Issues (1996).

Koocher and Keith-Speigel (1998) further suggest that it is appropriate to release notarized copies of files rather than the originals. If the court requires originals, then notarized copies should be kept by the psychologist, as records can be lost or misplaced in the court system.

Court orders, on the other hand, are issued by a judge on the basis of a hearing and require a disclosure unless appealed and affirmed by a higher court. In these instances, which are usually criminal cases, the court will decide what is considered to be privileged and protected information. As with subpoenas, the psychologist is obligated to respond to court orders.

DUAL RELATIONSHIPS

Dual relationships in psychotherapy arise when a connection exists with the client outside the therapeutic alliance, such as a friend, lover, student, family member, or business partner. Dual relationships distort the objectivity of therapy and compromise the therapeutic relationship. The issue of dual relationships is essentially a matter of maintaining appropriate boundaries between the psychologist and the client. On the one hand, Lazarus (1994) believes that boundaries have become too rigid and negatively impact the therapeutic process. He believes that therapists hide behind the role boundary and, as a result, the level of connection with the client is diminished. At the same time, boundary violations can lead to exploitation and harm to the client. In many instances, this occurs when the psychologist becomes oblivious to the feelings of the client when boundaries are allowed to blur. Sonne (1994) points out that over half of the ethical complaints to the APA involve problems resulting from boundary problems and that this is a problem that impacts all psychologists. A clear and guiding principle for the psychologist is never to enter into a multiple role relationship with a client, supervisee, or student. This includes any kind of business or sexual relationship, which sets the stage for loss of objectivity and exploitation on the part of both the client and the psychologist. Anger, miscommunication, and feelings of rejection and abandonment result in clients' looking for revenge through licensing boards or civil court action that can create havoc with the personal and professional life of the psychologist. The responsibility for maintaining appropriate boundaries rests with the psychologist. Lack of boundaries can result from the psychologist's poor training; using the therapeutic relationship to meet unresolved emotional needs for adoration, connection, or power; or embracing theoretical positions that promote physical contact designed to break down emotional barriers. Family stress, including marital difficulties or divorce, can also be contributing factors. Excessive self-disclosure is also seen as a common precursor to the development of sexual misconduct (Gutheil, 1994).

Sexually intimate behavior is a serious ethical violation that carries severe penalties with licensing boards. Prolonged suspension or revocation of the license are common penalties. In some states, it is a criminal action to have a sexual relationship with a patient. Clients also have found redress in civil malpractice actions. Moreover, the legal costs in terms of defense before boards and civil suits by clients can be astronomical. Legal fees and damages awarded in sexual malpractice suits are currently not covered by professional liability insurance. Financial and professional devastation notwithstanding, psychologists are advised to avoid sexual dual relationship situations because they always lead to an abuse of client's trust. Despite the multitude of sanctions aimed at discouraging sexual improprieties, complaints still come to licensing boards with regularity.

Training programs have in the past decade incorporated ethics into the curriculum, with the strong message that having sexual relations with clients is an ethical violation, and that it is the responsibility of the therapist to deal with his or her erotic feelings and attraction. Moreover, touching clients is usually a therapeutic mistake. It is important that students, supervisees, and practicing psychologists learn to openly deal with the myriad of feelings that arise in the therapeutic relationship (Pope & Tabachnick, 1993; Strasburger, Jorgenson, & Sutherland, 1992).

There have been instances of false allegations against psychologists. Borderline or narcissistic clients who are extremely vengeful can create years of personal and professional havoc in the lives of psychologists.

Koocher and Keith-Speigel (1998) list a number of precautions psychologists can take to protect themselves against unwarranted claims of sexual misconduct, some of which are summarized as follows (p. 218):

1. Before attempting any form of nonerotic touching or verbal compliment that could be considered flirtatious or suggestive, thoroughly know your client's psychological functioning. Some clients may remain unsuited to these types of displays in therapy.
2. If uneasy feelings about attraction dynamics are perceived as emanating from a client, consult a trusted, sensitive, and preferably experienced colleague about the proper course of action.
3. Avoid boundary violations of a nonsexual nature (such as taking a client to lunch, giving a client a gift, or writing an affectionate note), which licensing boards often take as corroborative evidence of sexual misconduct.
4. Avoid seeing clients outside of the professional setting. It is helpful to conduct therapy in a group practice setting where other people are around.

While psychologists who deal with clients in a professional manner need not be overly concerned about unwarranted accusations, the psychologist's feelings of sexual attraction should not be ignored. Often it is unwise to discuss these feelings in the therapy session; it is better to consult with a colleague, especially when the desire exists to act upon these feelings. In such instances, termination and referral are advisable.

Pope (1993), in his review of the survey literature, suggests that approximately 10% of therapists have had a sexual relationship with former clients. The APA *Ethical Principles and Code of Conduct* (1992a) is clear about a two-year limit after the termination of professional services. Psychologists need to be aware that numerous problems arise when they become involved with an ex-client, even after the two-year moratorium. Transference does not end when services cease, and a shift in the relationship can create damage even years later. Moreover, it prevents the client from returning for future therapy with a therapist who is familiar with the history and whose judgment is trusted.

While sexual relations are the most serious violation, other multiple relationships can be extremely problematic. For example, entering into a business relationship with a client or supervisee can lead to being or feeling exploited. These types of relationships are clearly ethical and state regulatory violations that could result in sanctions. Treatment of family members or close friends is also problematic, because the emotional involvement impairs clinical judgment. Similarly, seeing employees for therapy creates role confusion and can interfere with the economic well-being of both the client-employee and the psychologist. While emotional support given free of charge in an emotional crisis is acceptable, psychologists are well advised to refer friends and relatives to another professional for evaluation and treatment.

In some situations, for example, when living in a rural or small community such as a military base, psychologists need to be extra vigilant regarding professional boundaries. Often clients are seen in some sort of social context, where fears about confidentiality and boundary role confusion become evident. While these situations cannot realistically be fully avoided, psychologists are responsible for maintaining the appropriate role definition and being sensitive to the client's feelings and needs. Consultation with other professionals is helpful in avoiding situations where the psychologist rationalizes the multiple role conflicts. Dual relations of any kind need to be carefully avoided, because of the professional's inherent influence and power over the client.

ADVERTISEMENTS

Historically, until the mid-1970s, psychologists operated under the guidelines for telephone directory listings published in the *American Psychologist* (APA, Committee, 1969). Announcements or listings were limited to name, highest relevant degree, narrow area of specialization, address, and phone number. Announcements to colleagues regarding the establishment of the practice were also acceptable. In response to Federal Trade Commission (FTC) rulings based on the Supreme Court ruling (*Goldfarb v. Virginia State Bar*, 1975; *Bates et al. v. State Bar of Arizona*, 1977) relative to ethical codes in the legal profession that heretofore had prohibited advertising, price competition, and overall competitive practices, the APA Ethics Committee made some substantial shifts in its position. As a result, psychologists were allowed to advertise within narrow limits.

An interesting development occurred in 1989, when the APA declared an emergency and the board of directors amended the "Ethical Principles of Psychologists" section on advertising without notifying the Council of Representatives or the membership. The amendments, published in the *American Psychologist* (APA, 1990b), contained no explanation relative to the rationale for the changes. The new provisions removed prohibitions against testimonials from patients, unique or one-of-a-kind abilities, appeals to client's fears if services were not obtained, claims of comparative desirability of one service over another, or direct solicitation of individual clients. Another provision relative to preventing fee-splitting or kickbacks for referrals was also eliminated, because it had the effect of preventing the participation in legitimate referral businesses or managed care operations (Koocher, 1994). The emergency was related to ongoing and intense legal negotiations with the FTC over the APA prohibitions in the *Biographical Directory,* which is published every three years. Prior to the emergency declaration, the APA membership, through its various committees, had taken positions relative to retaining the various prohibitions. However, the APA Board of Directors decided that a compromise consent agreement with the FTC was preferable to the media embarrassment and protracted legal costs that would result from resisting the FTC. The Board of Directors action ended the negotiations, and the FTC carefully reviewed the new *Ethical Principles and Code of Conduct* (APA, 1992a) prior to its approval.

Many state licensing boards now carry more restrictive clauses relative to advertising than the APA ethics code. It is generally believed that the FTC has no interest in acting against state licensing boards that are more restrictive, as long they are well reasoned as a matter of "state's interest." It appears that state legislation, which is designed to "protect the public," can determine through its statutory regulatory boards that more restrictive limitations on advertising are in the best interests of the consumers in that state. In other words, state laws take precedence over rulings by the FTC as long as the state does not prohibit access to pertinent information. Therefore, it is extremely important for psychologists to be familiar with state licensing laws as well as the APA Code when making a decision on how to present oneself to the public.

Currently, the most controversial examples involve Yellow Pages listings. Disagreement exists relative to the style of advertising, ranging in most directories from simple name, address, and phone number to complex ads that display a long list of specialties. With the increased liberalization by the APA, it is now permissible to cite APA membership as well as other credentials recognized by the APA and earned through special requirements, such as a Diplomate from the American Board of Professional Psychology (ABPP) or a listing in the *National Register of Health Service Providers*.

Controversy exists as to what constitutes a "legitimate" diplomate or specialty. The APA recognizes in its directories the diplomates awarded by the ABPP and the American Board of Clinical Hypnosis. A number of other organizations unrecognized by the APA have developed various diplomas, such as "medical psychotherapy," but some question whether they truly represent specialty areas and whether the examination and credential review are valid. The APA Council of Representatives is currently working on developing specialty guidelines. At this point in time, while listing unrecognized specialties may not constitute an ethical or legal violation, we advise representing only specialties recognized by the APA in a factual manner in advertisements.

There are a number of points to consider in advertising. The basic elements include a listing of degrees and affiliations. Advertisements are considered appropriate if modesty, caution, and accurate representation of qualifications and credentials are exhibited. Simple factual statements are the most appropriate format to use. Exaggerated claims, direct solicitation of clients, testimonials, and evaluative comments range from illegal violation of some licensing laws to unprofessional misrepresentations.

Regarding degrees earned, it is important to be factual about the degree earned from an accredited institution and specialty area. Only earned degrees should be listed and specialties should reflect the academic content of the graduate program. For example, it is not a good idea to list oneself as a clinical psychologist when the academic program was in counseling, school, or another type of psychology program, despite what kinds of activities are engaged in by the practitioner. In the case of generic licensure it is appropriate to list oneself as a "psychologist"; however, in instances of limited or specialty licenses the title on the license is what should be listed. As a general rule, it is appropriate to advertise as long as the information is factual and the tone is professional. Despite the compromise in the APA ethics code, psychologists should refrain from using testimonials or claims of effectiveness; while not unethical they may violate licensing regulations—and they most certainly will invoke ridicule from one's professional colleagues.

Licensing boards constantly review telephone listings for appropriateness of the listing and to prevent nonpsychologists, including supervisees, from listing under "psychologist." Subtle misrepresentation is a real issue and difficult to prevent. Psychologists have been known to list services clearly beyond their areas of competency in order to attract clients. Other psychologists may list degrees (e.g., Ph.D.), when the degree was awarded in another field or from an unaccredited institution. The latter situation is usually a direct violation of state licensing laws and will result in charges being filed against the psychologist. The psychologist is accountable for how one is presented to the public; special care and thought are important and essential.

MEDIA RELATIONSHIPS

The entire field of mass media increasingly has become an area of concern for the psychology profession. On the one hand, as the profession matures, the media looks toward psychology for answers that, if handled correctly, can enhance the profession in the eyes of the public. On the other hand, some forms of mass media are geared to sensationalism, hype, and superficiality. This is sometimes related to poor journalism, while at other times it occurs just by virtue of the media's format, time allowance, and topic in a particular situation. Often psychologists are hard-pressed to avoid becoming involved in media situations where sensationalism, exaggeration, or superficiality, as defined in the APA *Ethical Principles*, are present.

Psychologists find themselves interviewed by newspaper journalists, making guest appearances on radio and television, or promoting books on psychological procedures. A particularly heated issue has been the "advice-giving" situations, in which media sometimes merges with psychotherapy. Prior to 1981, the APA prohibited psychologists from offering psychological services or products for the purpose of diagnosing, treating, or giving personal advice to individuals through the mass media. In 1981, the Code was modified so that, while individual diagnostic and therapeutic services still belong in a private professional context, personal advice-giving through public lectures, newspaper and magazine articles, and broadcast media is allowed as long as the psychologist uses current, relevant data and exercises a high level of professional judgment. The 1992 Code deals with the ethical issues related to social responsibility, competence, conflict of and the public image of psychology regarding public statements, but offers little guidance on how to handle the media.

A major problem in dealing with the media is the loss of control of what is finally printed or broadcast because of editing by the journalist or producer. Many psychologists have reported incidents where they were wildly misquoted or made to look foolish, as the media was only interested in sensationalistic reporting. Unfortunately, when this occurs this presents the psychologist and the profession in a bad light. Therefore, psychologists should be very cautious in dealing with unknown journalists or publications. Generally, the more control psychologists have over the content, the more accountable and responsible they are for the media content. The risks can be minimized, according to Koocher and Keith-Spiegel (1998), by first learning the purpose of the story and how the writer or producer is approaching it and then familiarizing oneself about the publication or program making the request. It is a good idea to pass on any situation that seems exploitive or superficial or if it is a topic that is beyond one's level of knowledge. Koocher and Keith-Spiegel suggest that, when a decision is made to participate in an interview, the psychologist prepare a brief written statement of the major points to considerably reduce misquotations. The APA Office of Public Affairs (n.d.) has a booklet entitled *Media Training for Psychologists* to help deal with representatives of the media. Avoid overgeneralizations and making statements that speak for the profession. Extra care should be taken when responding to questions that are designed to ameliorate particular problems. Ethics complaints can arise when statements or endorsements lack hard supporting data.

The APA change in position, while not totally satisfactory, is an attempt to begin to deal with an emerging problem in a positive manner. Deciding what distinguishes "personal advice" from diagnosis and therapeutic interpretation is extremely difficult. In addition, what constitutes current relevant data and sound professional judgment is, at best, open to interpretation and argument. Furthermore, these issues are compounded by the fact that psychology itself is hardly unified as to what constitutes a comprehensive and coherent body of knowledge that could be represented to the public. Moreover, there is a great deal of overlap between psychology and other mental health professions, such as psychiatry and social work. While we point the finger at the media for confusing the public, the profession needs to ultimately define itself in a more coherent manner.

This issue of media relations ultimately rests on the competence and expertise of the giver of advice in relationship to the welfare of the public. The impact of psychology on the public is the primary concern, but how the profession will ultimately proceed in handling this situation is still unclear.

It is clearly inappropriate for psychologists to endorse products or to be compensated for the endorsement. Koocher (1983) gives two reasons for this conclusion: (a) if the product is psychological in nature, it will stand on its own scientific merit; and (b) if the product is not psychological in nature, the psychologist is using his or her professional stature to endorse a product that is misleading the public. In a sense, the psychologist would be using undue influence to manipulate the public for personal financial gain.

In summary, psychologists need to exercise considerable caution when dealing with the media. Ultimately, the psychologist is responsible for how his or her name is used and the statements or advice given. It needs to be recognized that often the goals of the media may be in conflict with those of the individual psychologist and the profession.

SUPERVISION

An area of increasing concern for licensing boards has been the supervision of interns and other mental health professionals. Supervision can take two forms: (a) training in order to prepare the supervisee for licensure, or (b) work supervision, when the supervisee becomes, in essence, an extension of the psychologist.

In the first situation, training standards as well as licensing laws provide guidelines and rules; in the second, state licensing laws provide the parameters for supervision. With the increase of availability of third-party reimbursement, supervision has become a viable method for private practitioners and agencies to increase revenues. As a result, agencies may pressure psychologists to utilize "sign off" procedures on case reports and insurance forms for a large number of cases and supervisees. At the same time, private practitioners may actively seek supervisees but, because of time constraints, fail to provide adequate work or training supervision. In terms of most licensing laws, supervisees do not have any "professional status"; they are extensions of the psychologist, who is legally responsible for all of the psychological work of the supervisee. This legal responsibility extends to any malpractice or negligent action of the supervisee. Sloppy or inadequate supervision places the psychologist in a vulnerable position, both in terms of litigation and with the licensing board. Licensing boards are increasingly revising their rules relative to supervision and providing strict enforcement in this area.

The lack of quality supervision also affects the supervisee, especially in terms of training supervision, where the trainee depends upon the supervision to provide the foundation for future professional practice. One or two years of supervised experience is necessary for licensure in most states and, unfortunately, some students may end up in situations that provide inferior supervision and experience.

Quality supervision involves a complex relationship between the supervising psychologist and the supervisee. Vasquez (1992) describes the supervisor's responsibilities as involving ethical knowledge and behavior, clinical competency, and interpersonal sensitivity. The supervisor not only needs to know the supervisee's training and personal needs, but also the dynamics of the clients. The education of supervisees is a major responsibility requiring clinical and professional competence, the ability to deal with the problems of supervisees with sensitivity and tact, and the ability to communicate with honesty. Supervisors become powerful role models in the socialization process of the beginning professional. Sherry (1991) has concluded that supervision has elements of therapy and requires multiple roles. In many respects, it is a form of psychological intervention and, as such, it is vulnerable to ethical infractions.

In summary, psychologists who undertake supervision need to be familiar with state laws. They have a professional and legal obligation to provide quality supervision. They also need to make clear to clients, as well as supervisees, the nature and expectations relative to the supervisory relationship.

EMPIRICALLY VALIDATED TREATMENT GUIDELINES

With the accountability emphasis of the healthcare reform of the 1990s in the United States, there has been renewed interest in the development of psychological practice guidelines. Not to be confused with the guidelines discussed in chapter 6, these would prescribe a treatment shown by research to be efficacious. There are numerous therapies that psychologists can choose from that, at best, can be described as questionable. Psychologists are accountable for the decisions made relative to the course of treatment. Thus, practice guidelines that would provide sound support for clinical decision-making have some appeal. *Practice guidelines* deal with the conduct and issues in particular areas of practice. They tend to be based on expert and professional consensus of best practices in a service area. Often, they direct the practitioner in an area where there is a question or controversy. *Clinical guidelines* provide specific directions concerning client treatment that are client-focused and condition- or treatment-specific.

There have been a series of attempts since 1952 to identify such treatments, as well as several sets of recent clinical guidelines proposed; Nathan (1998) has provided a comprehensive critique of those efforts. He describes the debate that has arisen within the profession, given the potential of such guidelines to disenfranchise one or more groups of practicing psychologists depending on (a) the methodological approach that is used and (b) the criteria employed to judge the effectiveness or the background of the investigation(s). In many of the current proposed guidelines, the judgment is that behavioral or cognitive-behavioral treatments are most often the best established approaches (see Division 12 Task Force, 1995). Nathan supports the proposal made by the APA Template Task Force (1995) that the efficacy of a treatment as determined by a well-designed study must be equally effective in real-life clinical settings. The APA's Task Force has developed a template for psychological intervention that can be used to evaluate clinical rules that insurers, professional organizations, and governmental agencies urge or require providers to follow in offering a particular service. The template helps to examine the scientific validity of the treatment while leaving room for the practitioner's clinical judgment.

At this time controversy surrounds these types of guidelines. There is a lack of agreement among professions, let alone psychology, on the emphasis to place on clinical judgment versus research studies. The effect on training and practice, then, is likely to be inconsistent and variable. It would seem, therefore, that the time is ripe for some coherent response to the challenges presented by the expectations for effectiveness and accountability, which can best occur when both research and clinical experience are taken into account in an integrated manner.

SUMMARY

The issue of accountability involves in the broadest sense the profession's responsibility to provide quality services and define professional behavior that protects the consumer and the psychologist. The issues presented in this chapter relative to competence, confidentiality, and dual relationships define the essentials of the professional-client relationship. It is important to realize that many practice issues are ambiguous and that psychologists must continually keep up-to-date regarding changes in ethics codes and licensing board regulations.

Chapter 9

Legal Impact on Practice

The practice of psychology has become increasingly regulated. In fact, it appears that over the last 25 years federal legislation, state legislation, and court decisions have coalesced to actually control the practice of psychology. As a result, the professional organizations have been relegated to a less influential role than ever before in some areas of practice. This chapter explores the increasing impact the legal system has upon the practice of professional psychology. In many ways, the legal system essentially determines how applied psychology will be financed relative to healthcare and third-party payments, and ultimately the shape and scope of how psychologists will function.

Additionally, legislation related to the delivery of mental health and developmental disabilities services, as well as regulations governing access to records, have had an impact upon the profession. In all instances of federal regulation, the Department of Health and Human Services has published a series of complex and controversial regulations implementing these statutes. Adding to legislative regulation are court decisions relative to malpractice, testing and evaluation, and other areas that will continue to shape the functioning of the profession.

Whether this legal influence is beneficial to the profession is arguable. There was a time, as recently as the 1960s, when applied psychology functioned relatively independently of the legal system and was guided essentially by professional standards developed by the APA. In the 1970s, with the advent of state licensure laws, freedom of choice laws at the state level relative to third-party reimbursement, and federal legislation of a variety of health plans, psychology fully entered the arena of the provision of healthcare services. After the legislation of the 1970s, in the 1980s we witnessed mainly relevant state legislation and court decisions. In contrast to the previous two decades, the 1990s have been relatively quiet, especially with regard to federal legislation that directly impacts the practice of psychology. Therefore, it is important to see the evolution of the legal impact over the past 25 years or so.

In this chapter, state laws will be discussed first, as they have had the most direct influence on general practice, followed by a review of federal legislation, mostly related to federal programs and agencies. Mental health and developmental disabilities legislation and relevant court decisions will then be discussed. Inasmuch as psychologists most likely will at one time or another be involved in court hearings, the basics of being an expert witness are presented. Finally, specific issues pertaining to malpractice liability and insurance will be analyzed.

THE LEGAL SYSTEM AND LAWS AFFECTING PSYCHOLOGY

The legal system is governed by statutes and court decisions. Legislation is enacted in developing laws. However, because laws are often written in broad terms, the courts must often apply and interpret the statutes. When a court renders a decision that creates a new legal principle, that court and lower courts in the same jurisdiction are bound to apply the precedent to future cases with similar facts.

Statutory laws, like court decisions, exist in each of the 50 states as well as on the federal level. The statutes are binding only in the jurisdiction in which they are passed. Outside of the state, they do not have direct influence on any court. General compilations of statutes are called "codes," which are published by state agencies (e.g., state psychology boards) or contracted out to private publishers for publication. Federal statutes can be found in the *United States Code*, which is the official government publication. However, there are two unofficial popular publications—West Publishing Company's *United States Code Annotated* and Lawyers' Cooperative Publishing Company's *United States Code Service*—that are updated annually.

Another area of law comes from administrative agencies that have been delegated broad rule-making authority by Congress or state legislatures. These agencies (e.g., psychology boards) need to have specialized knowledge and time beyond the limits of legislation to develop and promulgate rules on all areas of government control. State governments usually have a manual or "redbook," which gives information about the various state agencies. However, the most expedient method of obtaining information may be to contact the state agency directly for a set of rules. At the federal level, since 1735, the federal government has published the *Federal Register*, which is a daily gazette of documents of the administrative and executive branches. The regulations collected for the *Federal Register* are arranged by subject and published in the *Code of Federal Regulations*.

Often the courts must apply, interpret, and fill in the gaps of the various statutes. The cumulative body of court decisions within a jurisdiction is called common (judgment) law. When a court lays down a decision that becomes a new principle of law, the court and lower courts in the same jurisdiction are bound to apply that precedent to future cases. In terms of other courts, however, depending on the reasoning, these decisions are only persuasive and not binding. Consequently, because of the volume and complexity of the legal decision-making process, it is virtually impossible for the practicing psychologist to be current with the precedent-setting cases relative to the profession. Professional organizations (state and national) regularly provide legal updates and are an invaluable resource to the practitioner.

Psychologists should be aware of the basic structure of the American judicial system. Cases can be decided in the trial, intermediate, appellate, or highest court levels within the state or federal systems. Typically, at the federal level, the court nomenclature in descending order is:

1. U.S. Supreme Court
2. U.S. Court of Appeals
3. federal district courts
4. specialized courts (e.g., court of claims)

At the state level, the various court levels are:

1. state supreme court
2. appellate court, superior court
3. county courts
4. district courts
5. court of common pleas
6. specialty courts (e.g., family court)

Initial case testimony is given in trial courts. The losing party may appeal to the appellate court, which does not receive new testimony, but, rather, decides if the law was applied properly at the lower level. A subsequent appeal is made to the supreme court, which has the right to decide if the case should be heard before considering the appeal itself.

STATE STATUTES

The professional practice of psychology is most directly affected by state laws. State licensure, in particular, has been the basis for the maturing of the profession. The insurance industry, influenced by the direct recognition of psychology as a health provider through freedom of choice laws, also falls under state jurisdiction. The regulation of health insurance through state laws and insurance plans has directly influenced the practice trends in psychology.

Licensing Laws

The first state to enact legislation in the form of a psychology law was Connecticut, in 1945, followed by Virginia, in 1946, and Kentucky, in 1948. Approximately half of the states and six of the Canadian provinces had adopted such statutes by 1970. In 1977 Missouri became the last state to include such provisions. Currently all Canadian provinces including the Northwest Territories have legislation governing the use of the title of "psychologist" and provide for the regulation of psychological services.

The relationship of these laws to credentialing and to disciplinary actions has been fully discussed in chapters 5 and 6. While most laws directly recognize psychologists and identify procedures to obtain a license, approximately 42 states and the Canadian provinces of British Columbia and Quebec also define the actual practice of psychology. These laws specify services or functions that can be legally performed by a psychologist. The range of practice includes, for example, diagnosis and treatment, biofeedback, hypnotherapy, psychological psychotherapy, and behavioral modification. However, many of these definitions are rather unclear and vary considerably from state to state.

In essence, the development of licensing laws has paralleled the growth of applied psychology. Licensure laws have allowed psychologists to be recognized as independent providers of services. Without state statute authority, and thus legislation aid at the state level regarding insurance benefits to clients for psychological services, psychology would not have been able to effectively enter the healthcare industry.

Freedom of Choice Laws

As of 1985, 40 states had passed "freedom of choice" legislation embracing 92% of the population (Dörken, Stapp, & VandenBos, 1986). Freedom of choice legislation essentially creates a choice for the consumer relative to mental health services. Directly changing state insurance laws, freedom of choice legislation requires insurance companies to recognize licensed psychologists as mental health providers and provide coverage at the same level as psychiatrists for the treatment of mental and emotional disorders. As a result, the consumer has a broader range of options when seeking services.

In states without freedom of choice laws, insurance companies' recognition of psychologists is strictly voluntary. Some major carriers have voluntarily recognized psychologists, especially for psychological testing at a physician's referral, while others such as Blue Shield (e.g., the extended litigation in the Virginia "Blues" case; Resnick, 1985), have been reluctant. Although psychologists' fees are comparatively lower than those of psychiatrists, when the number of providers is expanded, the costs for insurance companies are considerably increased.

Insurance laws apply to the state in which they are written. Basically, if an insurance carrier has a beneficiary in the freedom-of-choice state, it must reimburse psychological practice in that state. Conversely, if the beneficiary lives in a state without such legislation, the carrier will most likely not provide the reimbursement. Thus, for major insurance companies, reimbursement policies differ considerably from state to state. To further complicate the issue, in some instances reimbursement will depend upon the state in which the master contract was written. If the contract was written in a state requiring reimbursement for psychological services, then, for the most part, the company will retain the reimbursement policy regardless of the state of residence held by the provider. Often in these instances, and in states without specific provisions for licensed psychologists, the companies will utilize the *National Register for Health Care Providers in Psychology* (see chapter 2) to determine the qualifications of the provider (Council, 1985).

States that do have specific provisions for licensed psychologists, in terms of specific language and reference to licensed psychologists, include California, Maryland, Massachusetts, New Jersey, New York, and Ohio. In other instances, the legislation provides for mandatory coverage when the insurance group requests that psychology be recognized for reimbursement. In other situations, psychology reimbursement has been a negotiated issue. With insurance laws varying so much between states, beginning practitioners should study carefully the legislation in the state in which they plan to practice. State psychological associations are usually most helpful in this regard.

The prospective practitioner should be aware not only of the reimbursement procedures in a particular state, but also of the minimum standards required in that state for recognition as a healthcare provider. In some states, licensing itself is sufficient, while in others, as indicated previously, *National Health Care Provider* registration is a necessity. In the future, issues relative to training, degree, and type of supervision, as well as the setting of supervised experience, may play a larger and more specific role in the determination of eligibility as a reimbursable healthcare provider.

With most of the freedom of choice legislation having been passed since 1970, psychology will still have to keep up its efforts in this area. As counselors and social workers work extremely hard to get licensing recognition, and subsequently access to reimbursement, insurance companies will continue to fight the expansion of the providers' pool.

Already, there have been developments that negate state insurance laws. For example, large companies underwrite their own policies in collaboration with a major insurer, thus becoming "self-insured" programs. An example is the General Motors Corporation working with Blue Cross/Blue Shield to develop contracts in which psychological services are not included. Qualifying as a "self-insured" body, GM did not have to adhere to state insurance laws. The basis for such arrangements is found in the Employee Retirement Income Security Act (ERISA, 1974, Pub.L. 93-406), which takes precedence over state laws regarding employee benefit plans. However, the issue of the ERISA exemption status has been in litigation for some time, so long-term implications are unclear.

On June 3, 1985, the U.S. Supreme Court reached a decision in *Metropolitan Life Insurance Company v. Massachusetts* that upheld the freedom of choice laws. The case stemmed from a situation in Massachusetts involving the Travelers Insurance Company, where the court was asked to decide the issue of whether ERISA actually does preempt state insurance laws. The court's decision was limited and applied only to self-insured companies; such companies are almost always exempt from state regulation due to other federal court decisions related to ERISA. In essence, the court decided unanimously that states have broad powers to regulate health insurance offered by insurance companies. Specifically, states can mandate coverage by insurance companies for alcoholism, childbirth, mental health, and related benefits.

In regard to mandated benefits applied to third-party insurance carriers, the benefits are now on firm constitutional grounds. On a practical basis, if a state has a mental health mandate law that requires carriers to provide a minimum of mental health coverage and a freedom of choice law, then, for residents of this state, reimbursement is required for psychologists under both statutes, provided that the insured person's employer's home office is in the same state. If, however, the employer's home office is in another state, then only the freedom of choice law would apply. However, the *Metropolitan Life v. Massachusetts* Supreme Court decision applies only to situations not specifically covered by state law, including, in most states, health maintenance organizations, preferred provider organizations, and "self-insured" programs such as the GM plan. Thus, while the decision was vital and helpful, the increase in self-insured programs is still a critical matter.

Fortunately, now that all states have psychology licensing statutes, most states have been able enact freedom of choice laws. In fact, in some instances psychology has more recently found itself opposing other groups such as counselors and social workers in their attempts to seek reimbursement at the nondoctoral level. The freedom of choice issue has now, in fact, moved toward dealing with limitations to access on closed provider panels of managed care organizations. The issue of exclusion or underrepresentation of psychologists or being dropped from panels without explanation has become a serious concern of the profession. Freedom of choice legislation is slowly moving away from the direct recognition issue and billing for third-party reimbursement toward dealing with the issue of the consumer having greater choice in the selection of a provider.

Workers' Compensation

The area of workers' compensation and rehabilitation services involves disability evaluations and therapeutic services to job-injured or otherwise disabled workers. Nationally, the need for these services is quite extensive; however, psychology has not as yet become involved in this service area to any great extent. In 1971, Montana, and later, California (1978), became the only two states with recognized psychological services under workers' compensation laws. In 1974, Ohio became recognized in the state compensation fund. Federally, clinical psychologists were given recognition in 1975 with the passing of Public Law 93-416, which amended the Federal Employee Compensation Act for work injuries to federal employees.

Dörken (1979) provided a review of workers' compensation programs by state. Workers' compensation plans are casualty/liability insurance that cover all injury-related medical care. Dörken reported that this area is a major insurance market with over $1 billion paid in medical and rehabilitation expenses in 1970; premiums in California alone in 1976 exceeded $1.5 billion. According to the U.S. Department of Commerce (1997), the benefits paid in California amounted to over $7.1 billion in 1995. Meanwhile, nationally the annual benefits for workers' compensation have risen from $13.6 billion in 1980 to $43.5 billion in 1995. It is quite probable that psychological aspects of industrial disability will continue to increase in importance. Psychological services of an evaluative nature, rehabilitative therapy, and even case reviews by psychologists can become a viable market for psychologists. Psychologists interested in this market should assertively review opportunities within their respective states.

Psychologists have been recognized since 1975 as providers for rehabilitation services for the severely disabled, through the Rehabilitation Act of 1973, Public Law 93-112. Individual states receive a fixed dollar/formula amount to provide rehabilitation services when a disabled individual can become employable. Most states employ rehabilitation counselors and psychologists in either a direct service or consultative role. When contracting for psychological services, the rate of reimbursement is usually lower than the prevailing rate for similar services in the private sector.

FEDERAL LAW RELATIVE TO REIMBURSEMENT

Medicare

Medicare is that part of the Title XVIII of the Social Security Act that provides health insurance funds for all citizens 65 years of age and older. The plan is financed from Social Security revenues and includes Part A, *Hospital Insurance*, which covers the costs for inpatient hospital care and also certain skilled nursing facilities, hospice, home health, and other services, and a voluntary Part B, *Supplemental Insurance Coverage*, which covers physician services, outpatient hospital services, and certain other nonhospital services and medical supplies, and, to a limited extent, psychological services. Part A is an "entitlement" program and does not charge a premium, while Part B involves voluntary participation and requires eligible participants to pay a premium. Both A and B programs have deductibles and coinsurance requirements. As a matter of practicality most individuals participate in both A and B programs. The state can cover these deductible costs under Part B if they so choose. Many individuals also purchase private insurance to provide complete coverage.

In 1982, in order to control costs Medicare went to a prospective payment system (PPS), in which reimbursement for healthcare is fixed at a predetermined rate. However, due to extensive lobbying efforts, currently the treatment of mental and emotional episodes remains exempt from PPS and is funded on a modified fee-for-service basis. PPSs may well be a prototype for future funding of healthcare services.

The Budget Reconciliation Act of 1987 (Pub.L. 100-203) had four psychology-related Medicare provisions: (1) Psychology was formally recognized for the first time under the Rural Health Clinic provisions; (2) it was made expressedly clear that hospitals could bill for "psychological services" under the Part A (inpatient) provisions of Medicare; (3) another related provision requiring patients to be under the care of a physician was specific to only Medicare patients and no longer to all patients, which had important ramifications for psychologists in hospital practice; and (4) it enabled psychologists in community mental health centers to be directly reimbursable under Medicare (without physician involvement) and directed the Secretary of the Department of Health and Human Services to develop a psychology fee schedule.

Public Law 100-239 further recognized psychological services under Medicare (Pub.L. 100-239, 1989) by including provisions for psychologists providing and billing for inpatient (hospital and other appropriate health facility) services. The hospital component of this legislation was clarified the following year. This opened the door for services in hospitals and nursing homes for the elderly.

Psychologists have been limited to evaluative services when functioning as independent practitioners. They may bill for diagnostic evaluative services upon referral by a physician. Intervention services can also be provided when under the direction and supervision of a physician within the physician's facilities and when billed by the physician. When the psychologist is seen as a physician extender, there is no dollar or visit limit on services. When private supplementary insurance is purchased, some insurance plans do provide for psychological services in states with freedom of choice laws; however, reimbursement is usually considerably limited.

There has been considerable legislative effort by the psychology profession to gain recognition. There is still a great deal of work ahead.

Medicaid

Medicaid is the part of Title XIX of the Social Security Act that provides funds to states for healthcare to families with dependent children, the blind, aged, or disabled whose incomes are insufficient to meet the costs of health services. In order to assist families and individuals in attaining or retaining self-care capabilities, Medicaid further provides rehabilitation and other services.

States independently determine eligibility for services within fairly broad federal guidelines. The states also determine the types of assistance, reimbursement schedules, and provider eligibility. Thus, each state essentially has its own assistance programs with the freedom to determine the extent to which psychological services will be recognized. Therefore, when a state chooses to include psychological services in its plan, it has great latitude in determining the extent of services and the controls that are imposed.

As of 1982 (Resnick, 1983), 25 states had some form of reimbursement for psychological services. Testing and therapy were directly reimbursed as independent services in 13 states: California, Kansas, Maine, Massachusetts, Minnesota, Montana, New Hampshire, New Jersey, New Mexico, New York (except New York City), Ohio, Utah, and West Virginia. Physician referral for testing and therapy was required in Connecticut, Georgia, Hawaii, Indiana, Oregon, and Vermont. Illinois and Michigan recognized only testing and referral, while medical supervision was required in Arkansas and Nebraska. Tennessee also required a medical referral and physician billing. Wisconsin psychologists are recognized through state contracts. Dörken and Webb (1981) also indicated that testing is generally reimbursed—however, at levels lower than customary rates. A recent survey by the APA Practice Directorate (1995) found that the number of states offering reimbursement for psychological services has not changed since 1982.

Due to the striking differences between plans and the intermediary role of physicians, Medicaid and Medicare account for only a very small portion of claims submitted by psychologists (Dörken & Webb, 1980). Psychologists are required to be eligible as recognized professionals under the state plan and then apply to have a number assigned to them in order to bill for services. Currently, most states recognize some form of psychological service delivery; however, in some states, recognition and services change frequently, causing confusion to practitioners. As a result of the bureaucratic problems and low rates for reimbursement, psychological services to the poor are limited to public agencies, with independent practitioners having little involvement with this strata of society. DeLeon (1996) points out that the minuscule recognition by most state programs may well reflect the overall lack of involvement of the profession, and that most psychologists don't care if they are covered. He believes that as a result we may never be involved; yet, Medicaid is one of the most rapidly growing federal initiatives and costs the federal and state governments over $50 billion per year.

CHAMPUS

The U.S. Department of Defense instituted through congressional action the Civilian Health and Medical Program of the Uniformed Services (CHAMPUS) in 1956. The plan, which was broadened in 1966, provides civilian healthcare resources for active-duty and retired members of the armed services and their dependents, when services are delivered in the military treatment facilities and direct care system. This program has experienced tremendous growth over the past two decades, as the Department of Defense and Congress have recognized the healthcare needs of military families and have tied the development of national defense readiness to the health status and economic well-being of uniformed service beneficiaries. Not only is CHAMPUS one of the single largest health programs, but it also has excellent and comprehensive mental health benefits.

This program is modeled after private insurance programs and has an insurance orientation in providing healthcare reimbursement for civilian medical services. With over 8.6 million lives covered, this is the single largest healthcare plan in the country. Under administrative directive since 1974, formalized in Public Law 94-212 (1976), clinical psychologists have been recognized as independent healthcare providers. (In this instance, as in most federal laws, the term *clinical psychologist* is used generically to mean applied or specialty psychologist.) While the title itself is not defined, licensed psychologists with one or two years of supervision who have passed a national exam, as well as "grandparented" psychologists, are recognized providers. Thus, reimbursement is available for psychologists who meet certain qualifications: First, reimbursement is limited to qualified providers and to services that are, according to the law, "medically or psychologically necessary"; second, psychologists listed in the *National Register of Health Service Providers in Psychology* are recognized automatically, while others must apply and have a credential review by the fiscal intermediary, which is usually an insurance company such as Aetna or Blue Shield (Dörken, 1983).

An additional unique feature of this program has been the peer review plan initiated in 1977 with the American Psychological Association and the American Psychiatric Association. The actual processing of claims did not begin until the latter part of 1979. Essentially, dialogue between the professional organizations and the Department of Defense was necessary in order to develop peer review criteria and procedures regarding psychological and psychiatric outpatient services; treatment criteria, review protocols, and reviewer manuals needed to be developed. Administrative liaisons with each association and approximately 350 psychiatric and 400 psychological peer reviews had to be identified and prepared, as well as report forms and protocols designed (Claiborn, Biskin, & Friedman, 1982).

Rodriguez (1983) provides an excellent review of the issues that need resolution with such a peer review program. Considerable concern was expressed by both professions regarding the uses and possible misuses of clinical information that would be submitted for peer review. Bent (1982) described the need for additional control of confidential information, as third-party payers in general have increasingly asked for more information in their efforts to assure quality and cost control of healthcare. Despite the focus of concern, Rodriguez believes that records are maintained with strict care and respect for privacy. To date, there have been no known breaches of confidentiality; however, the issue of confidentiality and privileged communication resting with client and professional, excluding third-party payers, is still not fully resolved to everyone's satisfaction. Further concern has also been expressed about the validity of information from providers, the standards and types of services imposed relative to healthcare, quality, and theoretical orientation of the reviews, and financial costs for the entire system.

Reimbursement for services is contingent upon quality-review procedures to the extent that fees represent the usual, customary, and reasonable (UCR) rate for the profession within the practice area, as well as representing the provider's own UCR rate. The UCR rate is determined by the 75% level of the fees charged for services. The reimbursement level and individual UCR rates are adjusted annually.

The end result of this plan is that psychologists are required to demonstrate the benefit from services in order to have such services maintained in a treatment plan. Psychologists must also meet the standards of the profession. The system is designed to promote cost-effectiveness and accountability, and to limit services to those demonstrated as effective.

Another aspect of this program of practical interest is the element of benefit coordination provision with other insurance plans to prevent duplication of payments. When Medicare or other insurance is applied, the other insurance must be used before CHAMPUS benefits. CHAMPUS will cover psychological services not covered under other plans. The practitioner will have to bill the other plan prior to submitting for CHAMPUS reimbursement.

Federal Employee Health Benefit Act

Federal employees are covered for health insurance under the Federal Employee Health Benefit Act. In 1975 (Pub.L. 93-363), clinical psychologists were recognized as independent providers. The plan itself is authorized through independent insurance companies, with Blue Cross/Blue Shield being the largest and Aetna the second largest. In all, there are about 20 plans, each differing as to benefits involving psychological services. In all, these plans cover over 10 million individuals.

Clinical psychologists are recognized by Blue Cross/Blue Shield as having a license, doctoral degree in psychology, and at least two years of clinical experience in a recognized health setting. Listing in the *National Register* is also acceptable for direct recognition.

While reimbursement is generally consistent with private plans, group prepayment plans such as health maintenance organizations (HMO) and independent practices associations (IPA) are not required to recognize psychological services. Because of a general exclusion clause in Public Law 93-363, recognition of psychologists is not mandatory in group practice prepayment plans. For other traditional plans, reimbursement procedures are generally the same as when submitting any insurance claim.

LEGAL REGULATION OF PRACTICE

The legal system, especially the courts, has had a direct impact on the practice of psychology. Congress and federal administrative agencies have passed legislation related to handicapped children, including the Handicapped Children's Early Education Assistance Act of 1968, the Rehabilitation Act of 1973, the Education for the Handicapped Amendment of 1974 (Pub.L. 93-380), the Family Rights and Privacy Act of 1974 (the Buckley Amendment), and the Education for All Handicapped Children Act of 1975 (Pub.L. 94-142).

Federal and state courts have also been active, especially with decisions regarding the placement of minority children in special education classes and treatment of handicapped persons in general. The courts have also been protected with cases relative to licensing and malpractice by psychologists. Additionally, mental health laws have protected patient rights, as well as directly influencing the work of forensic psychologists. The last 25 years have seen increased legal regulation of the profession.

Psychological Assessment

Psychologists, especially school psychologists, have been most directly affected by the Education for All Handicapped Children Act of 1975 (EHA; Pub.L. 94-142). This act provides educational and "related" services for handicapped children. States that fail to meet this requirement are subject to the termination of federal funding. In 1986, Congress passed Public Law 99-457, an amendment to EHA, which introduced new directions in services to special children. The law reauthorized EHA and mandated services to 3- to 5-year-old children and their families. In addition, it established state grant programs for handicapped infants and toddlers (birth through 36 months) for the purpose of providing early intervention for all eligible children.

Since psychologists are directly involved with the identification and, to some extent, therapy of these children, practicing psychologists should be familiar with the provisions of this act, as well as relevant state regulations. States must have a system for the identification of all handicapped children in the state from birth to the age of 21. Schools must provide adequate identification procedures, which often include psychological assessment. The following are considered to be handicapping conditions: deafness, mental retardation, hearing impairment, speech impairment, visual handicap, orthopedic impairment, serious emotional disturbance, other health impairment, or special learning disabilities. Children who have learning problems that are primarily the result of cultural, economic, or environmental disadvantage are excluded.

The 1986 amendment defines developmental delays for birth through 36 months as reflected in the appropriate diagnostic instruments and procedures in one or more of the following areas: cognitive development, physical development, psychosocial development, language and speech development, or self-help skills. In addition, the following services need to be provided (100 stat. 1146):

1. family training, counseling, and home visits
2. special instruction
3. speech pathology and audiology
4. occupational therapy
5. physical therapy
6. psychological services
7. case management services
8. medical services only for diagnostic and evaluation services
9. early identification, screening, and assessment services
10. health services necessary to enable the infant or toddler to benefit from other intervention services

In 1990, the Education of the Handicapped Act Amendments of 1990 (Pub.L. 101-476) was signed into law, which changed the name of the Education of the Handicapped Act to Individuals with Disabilities Education Act or IDEA. Throughout IDEA the term *handicapped* is replaced by the term *disability*. The legislation includes definitions for eligibility, placement procedures, pupil evaluation procedures, individualized education programs, and least restrictive environments. IDEA provides funds to state and local educational agencies for services for children with disabilities aged 3 through 21 years.

Once a child is identified as having a suspected disability, schools are required to perform a multidisciplinary team evaluation of the child, which often includes an evaluation by a school psychologist. Extensive requirements also exist for involving parents in every step of their child's placement process, beginning with full and formal consent for the evaluation. Three-year evaluations are required for children placed in a special program, although they can be scheduled more frequently at the request of the parents. Often, these evaluations are performed by the school psychologist, although independent evaluations by outside psychologists may also be performed. When the latter's recommendation differs from that of the school team, this discrepancy must be considered by the multidisciplinary team.

Every child placed in a special education program must have an individual educational program (IEP) developed by special placement teams. Psychologists involved with the evaluation should also be involved in developing the IEP. In addition, there are provisions for psychological counseling for children and parents. This intervention may be done by school psychologists, or contracted privately by parents, and at public expense if recommended by the IEP team.

IDEA added the requirement for IEPs to include transition services with community agencies when the student leaves the school system, placing an emphasis on postsecondary education, employment, and adult education and services. Autism and traumatic brain injury were added as separate categories, and rehabilitation counseling and social work services were defined as "related services."

A number of concerns have been raised by school psychologists regarding IDEA regulations proposed by the Department of Education (DOE). These issues are complex. Fowler (1998), as Executive Vice-President and Chief Executive Officer of APA, delineated four areas of concern in a letter to the Office of Special Education and Rehabilitative Services of DOE: related services and personnel standards, access to services, assessment and evaluation, and other topics. Within each category the recommendations call for greater definition and clarity relative to the provision of psychological services. Kubiszyn and Oddone (1998) express concern that IDEA provides only limited protection for school psychological services and that state requirements can exceed federal requirements. As a result, psychologists need to work on the state level to ensure that children receive quality assessment and appropriate interventions.

A series of court decisions have been rendered regarding nondiscriminatory assessment of the handicapped. The most important decision by far has been *Larry P v. Riles*. The courts essentially maintained that the practice of placing children solely on the basis of an intelligence test resulted in a disproportionate and harmful impact on black children, in violation of the equal protection clause. The court issued a preliminary injunction and, in 1979, a permanent injunction against the administration of individual intelligence tests to place black children in educable mentally retarded classes. However, in 1980, in *PASE v. Hannon*, the Illinois district court determined that the WISC-R and Stanford-Binet tests, when used in conjunction with other criteria as defined in Public Law 94-142, do not discriminate against black children in the Chicago public schools. These cases, while narrow in scope and limited to specific jurisdictions, have not discouraged the use of intelligence tests; however, they do provide a warning against single factor assessment.

Psychological Records

The Family Education Rights and Privacy Act (Buckley Amendment) changed the tradition of limiting access to psychological reports. The 1976 regulations were incorporated into Public Law 94-142, which gave parents of handicapped children the right to inspect and review all educational records. Parents of handicapped children can also review all records pertaining to identification, evaluation, and placement in special education programs.

It is generally agreed that psychological reports are open to inspection by parents; however, whether the right of parental review extends to test questions and protocols is questionable. As of this date, there are no cases to answer this question. Excluded from the definition of educational records are those documents retained as personal records or notes by the psychologist. Therefore, the determining factor has been whether the test protocols have been made available to others. If not, then the protocols remain as personal notes and are not available for parental inspection. However, the situation reverses itself if the protocols are kept in a place where others have access to them or if they have been revealed to others in a case conference. Therefore, when test reports are shared in making placement decisions, they are considered to be part of the child's educational records. This affects the private practitioner functioning in an independent evaluation role, whose concerns may be different from those of the psychologist employed by the school system.

Informed Consent

A general legal principle involves not only consent for evaluation or therapeutic services, but also the understanding that the client must be fully informed about the evaluation and any treatment that is required. This requirement includes both the client and the parents or guardian in the case of children or adolescents. The court must be the provider in the case of mentally incompetent persons.

Children are basically considered incapable of fully understanding psychological evaluation and treatment, and the courts have determined that the parents need to give consent prior to any formal psychological services for their children. When there is evidence of direct physical and psychological abuse of the child, the psychologist might decide to initiate involvement without parental consent, although such action is very risky. The same procedure exists for adolescents; however, states increasingly have given them greater freedom to independently seek outside assistance for certain kinds of medical problems such as venereal disease and other sex-related problems. In general, the courts have consistently shown a preference for parental control where assistance to minors is concerned.

PRACTICE ISSUES IMPACTED BY THE LEGAL SYSTEM

Mental Health Legislation

The legal system accepts the medical model of mental disorder, which assumes that disordered behavior is symptomatic of underlying illness. As such, these behaviors are not subject to personal control and the patient is not responsible for his or her behavior. The legal system, therefore, has established a set of laws treating the mentally disordered person differently from normal persons, based upon the scientific study of these disorders.

As a result, scientific research in medicine and psychology has had considerable impact on the formulation of these laws. The legal system, in general, and lawyers, specifically, are not equipped to deal with the complexity of issues surrounding mental disorders; thus, they rely on mental health professionals to provide advice that is primarily psychological, rather than legal, in nature. Traditionally, in addition to claiming a scientific basis for special treatment of the mentally disabled, many experts have contended that decisions about competence, freedom, and responsibility for the mentally disabled should be made primarily by professional psychologists. Therefore, while decisions about individual cases are determined by the legal system, it has been argued that psychologists should have the major influence relative to treatment.

In this context, professional psychologists directly interface with the courtroom and lawyers in a diversity of fascinating cases. There are millions of such cases each year and, increasingly, psychologists are called on to perform psychological evaluations and serve as expert witnesses.

The field of forensic psychology is a specialty area served by the American Board of Forensic Psychology associated with the American Board of Professional Psychology, and one of the American Psychological Association divisions (41) is devoted to psychology and the law. However, most psychologists, even those without a forensic specialty, can expect to participate in some manner as a mental health expert and to provide expert testimony. Therefore, we present a brief overview of mental health laws, followed by a section discussing the role of an expert witness testifying in the courtroom situation.

Serious Mental Illness

It has been asserted that graduate programs in psychology typically do not give extensive training in dealing with individuals who have serious mental illness (Johnson, 1990). Traditionally, psychologists have seen this population as being relevant for psychiatry and social work. Additionally, there has been an economic disincentive to provide treatment to this population. Many are covered only by Medicaid and Medicare programs, and only with the recent inclusion in the Medicare program has there been an increased interest in working with the seriously mentally ill. In order to work with this group, psychologists need to understand the biological as well as the psychological etiological factors that comprise the diagnostic categories of serious mental illness (Torrey, Bowler, Taylor, & Gottesman, 1994). They must also understand the current approaches to treatment and rehabilitation, as well as research relative to prognosis (DeSisto, Harding, McCormick, Ashikaga, & Brooks, 1995). It is also helpful to understand the experience of mental illness from the perspective of the client (Hatfield & Lefley, 1993).

Manderscheid and Sonnenschein (1996) reported data from the Center for Mental Health Services that approximately 5.4 million or 2.7% of the adult population have a "severe and persistent" mental disorder, including schizophrenia and bipolar affective disorder. Symptoms of schizophrenia include signs of delusions, hallucinations, bizarre behavior, and disorganized thought and speech. Bipolar symptoms might involve a decline in normal thoughts and feelings; disturbances of mood, including severely depressed mood, unusually elevated mood, or extreme mood swings; potentially harmful or self-destructive behavior; socially inappropriate behavior; and poor daily living habits. It is useful to understand that there is a biological component to the above disorders.

The treatment of persons with serious mental disorders is becoming an increasingly important area of practice for psychologists. Bedell, Hunter, and Corrigan (1997) discuss the need for functional assessment. They point out that the following psychological treatments have been demonstrated to be effective: cognitive-behavioral social skills training, pragmatic supportive therapy, personal therapy, the multimodal functional model, therapeutic contracting, case management, and multiple family therapy. However, when acute symptoms are manifested, psychologists will be involved in voluntary or involuntary hospitalization. While many psychologists have staff membership at a hospital, this status does not include admitting privileges. Therefore, even in the case of voluntary hospitalization, collaboration with a physician is necessary if the psychologist wants to continue treatment on a inpatient basis. When involuntary commitment becomes necessary, the legal system becomes involved in the process.

Commitment

Civil commitment occurs when a person is admitted to a state hospital consistent with procedures defined in the state statutes. All states provide for voluntary or involuntary commitment, and psychologists interested in this area should consult the statutes for procedures and regulations for state-specific information. All such laws vary from state to state, but generally require that the admitted person have a mental disorder and behave in such a manner that he or she is deemed dangerous to self or others or otherwise in need of care and treatment. For involuntary commitment, this "in need of care and treatment" provision is becoming quite rare and may possibly be ruled unconstitutional (e.g., *Lessard v. Schmidt*, 1976).

Most standards for commitment have focused on the behavior of the individual, although what constitutes the standard for "dangerous" can be argued. Generally, the degree of danger and likelihood of dangerous behavior occurring must be specified as a prerequisite to the court deciding in favor of involuntary commitment. Despite the professional difficulties of making predictions, courts have upheld the constitutionality of "dangerous" commitment based on clinical prediction where no overt behavioral action had occurred (*Mathew v. Nelson*, 1978).

There are procedures in most state statutes for emergency and temporary commitment when imminent harm is demonstrated. In such instances, court hearings are bypassed and admissions can be made by a physician, police officer, or family member. Evaluation and treatment can be authorized for a specified period of time, ranging from 48 hours to 15 days in some states. This procedure is a tempting one to follow, as it bypasses cumbersome hearings. However, the civil rights of patients can easily be violated so that care must be exercised in these situations. Because some state laws do not require imminent harm, involuntary commitments can occur far too easily. Additionally, once hospitalized, the patient is at a distinct disadvantage in arguing against a full commitment. Emerging commitments, in general, should be used only after careful consideration, and when necessary.

Morse (1983) argued that commitment is far too easily accomplished, even in full hearings. Due process procedures are violated with informal hearings that do not follow legally established standards and procedures. Morse believed that far too often, judges respond to these cases in a rough, paternalistic, and intuitive manner, relying mainly on expert testimony given by the mental health professional. Moreover, there are few appeals to appellate courts that assure that state statutory standards are kept.

In contrast to adults, commitment of minors to mental hospitals is the statutory right of the parent or guardian. Such "voluntary" commitments are subject only to acceptance by the hospital. In essence, this provision gives parents absolute control over the custody or care of their child. The Supreme Court, in *J. R. v. Parham* (1979), held that the child's due process rights were adequately safeguarded by the parents' concern and the independent evaluation of the medical expert performing the evaluation for admittance. In most jurisdictions, there are no due process procedures and formal hearings afforded children.

In such cases of "voluntary" hospitalization, release can be made at the request of the parent or a decision of the hospital. In cases where the professional expert believes, contrary to the parents, that further hospitalization is necessary, a petition must be made to the court that the state declare the child a ward of the court and assure guardianship. The legal system places enormous responsibility on the psychologist within the hospital setting relative to the appropriateness of the admission. Involuntary hospitalization involves civil liberties issues and considerable social stigma for the child or youth. Hospitalization can be viewed as a method for some parents to scapegoat a behaviorally difficult child, and decisions to admit need to be made on the basis of the disorder and treatment efficacy. Moreover, the psychologist may be faced with administrative pressure to maintain the patient population. Psychiatric and mentally disabled children and youth are clear candidates for admission; however, the criteria for hospitalization of delinquent or behaviorally disordered children or youth are far less clear.

Least Restrictive Environment

In the last 20 years, commitment for institutionalization has dramatically decreased relative to length of stay. With the improvement of psychotropic medication treatment, community-based treatment has been shown to be as effective as institutionalization. At the same time, the community mental health movement has resulted in more outpatient services, so that mental health professionals no longer need to rely on inpatient hospitalization (Musto, 1975; Rappaport, 1977). From a legal perspective, attempts have been made to ensure that hospitalization is avoided or minimized, when appropriate, with the principle of "least restrictive alternative." This doctrine was amended by the United States Supreme Court in the 1960s through a number of cases and applies to psychology to civil commitment and placement of children in programs for the handicapped.

The least restrictive doctrine holds that when state regulations infringe on civil liberties that are guaranteed by the constitution in order to fulfill the state's purpose, they should only do so in the way that least restricts those rights and interests. It is fair to assume that the state has a legitimate right to protect individuals or society through involuntary commitment of dangerous persons or to place children in programs for the handicapped to provide quality education. However, such placements also impinge on the freedom of the individual. The doctrine emphasizes that the state must investigate all available options, and in order to ensure that the rights of the individual have been protected, any alternatives that are not deemed suitable to the individual must also be explored.

Hospitalization and placement should only be ordered when other alternatives are unavailable.

This doctrine was explored for the institutionalized retarded through a number of Supreme Court decisions (*Halderman v. Pennhurst*, 1979). Briefly, this case began in 1977 when Terri Lee Halderman, a mental patient in the Pennsylvania Pennhurst State School and Hospital, filed a complaint involving the inhumane conditions, dangerous overmedication, inadequate supervision, unrestricted use of constraints, and lack of rehabilitative programs he encountered. In 1977, the Federal Court determined that the allegations were true. This case is complex and has a number of interesting issues; for more detail, the reader is urged to consult Morse (1983). However, the most important fact for purposes of this discussion is that in 1981 the Supreme Court held that the federal Developmentally Disabled Assistance and Bill of Rights Act did not grant the mentally retarded the right to habilitation in the least restrictive environment. The Court decided the case strictly on the interpretation of the federal statutory language.

However, in another patients' rights case arising against the Pennhurst institution (*Youngberg v. Romero*, 1982), the U.S. Supreme Court decided that retarded persons are entitled to freedom from excessive restraint and staff members who have received training to ensure their physical safety. While the issue of institutionalization in a least restrictive environment for the mentally retarded has not been settled, the courts seem increasingly to be moving in that direction for all mental disorders.

The entire issue of hospitalization of patients who are mentally ill is highly relevant to psychology The National Institute of Mental Health reports that over 70% of mental health funds are spent on hospitalization. Kiesler (1982a) reasoned that this allocation is due to inappropriate insurance mechanisms. The President's Commission on Mental Health (Platman, 1978) stated, "The level and type of care given to the chronically mentally disabled is frequently based upon what services are fundable and not on what services are needed and appropriate" (p. 369).

Despite the legal impact on commitment procedures and the emergence of the community mental health movement, Kiesler (1982b), in an extensive study regarding hospitalization, found the following trends:

1. Hospitalization of the mentally ill is increasing well in excess of the population rate. This includes inpatient episodes in hospitals with and without psychiatric units.
2. The site of hospitalization has changed dramatically with the state mental hospital and private mental hospital now accounting for only 25% of the total incidence of mental disorders.

3. Length of stays at state and Veterans' Administration hospitals have decreased, but stays in general hospitals have remained stable.

Kiesler (1982a) suggested that the majority of patients treated for mental disorders could be treated more effectively and less expensively elsewhere. As Talbot (1981) indicated, the treatment modalities are available but specific programs do not exist. However, Bedell and colleagues (1997) point out that patients currently treated in outpatient settings have more serious symptoms and are more acutely symptomatic than in the past. They reason that this is related to a hospital's requirement for more severe symptoms before admission is granted, and shorter inpatient stays that necessitate discharge with less stabilized symptoms. Psychologists involved in the area of diagnosis and treatment of the mentally disabled need to fully understand the legal, moral, and social issues relative to this population.

Expert Testimony

Psychologists increasingly are being called upon to testify as expert witnesses in administrative and judicial proceedings. Typically, these might include child abuse and custody hearings, competency hearings with the elderly, or in criminal defense and handicap issues with children in Public Law 94-142 hearings. Conceivably, most psychologists at one time or another will be called as an expert witness.

There are two types of witnesses, lay and expert, with considerable differences between each in terms of the actual testimony that is allowable. While lay witnesses have no specialized knowledge or skill in the subject matter in the area of testimony, expert witnesses, because of their experience and/or training, are called to give testimony in their field of expertise. Expert witnesses can give their opinion testimony and draw inferences from the facts concerned with the situation. The legal definition of an expert witness, as set forth in Rule 702 of the *Federal Rules of Evidence* indicates:

> If scientific, technical, or other specialized knowledge will assist the findings of fact (the judge, hearing officer, or a jury) to understand the evidence or to determine a fact in evidence; a witness qualified as an expert by knowledge, skill, experience, or training, or educated may testify thereto in the form of an opinion or otherwise. Thereafter, judges will tend to look at two issues relative to the admission of expert testimony: whether the testimony is relevant to understanding the issue in a controversy; and whether the expert possesses the necessary qualifications to deal with the subject matter.

Initially, in most hearings the qualification of a witness will be established. Such documentation typically includes the educational background, skills, and experience of the witness. An expert need not be a nationally recognized authority; however, it must be demonstrated that his or her level of education and experience meets the standards of the profession. Similarly, the opinions of the witness need only to be consistent with those reasonably held by others in the field.

It is important to note that judges and juries expect expert witnesses to be unbiased educators who help them to understand technical information necessary for their deliberations, despite the fact that only one side pays for the service (Ackerman, 1995). Therefore, psychologists are cautioned to be thoughtful, cautious, nondefensive, and scientifically rigorous in their testimony (Koocher & Keith-Spiegel, 1998).

A common dilemma for psychologists giving testimony relates to privileged communications. Psychologists need to understand that, despite state statutes, privileged communication often is not required in some types of court hearings, especially when criminal action or child abuse is involved. In many instances, when a patient has received psychotherapy from the psychologist for a mental or emotional disorder, the court will respect the psychologist-client privilege. The privilege is waived where the patient is criminal or treated for legal purposes, or when a psychologist is involved in determining sanity in a criminal case. The difficulty arises in forensic situations where the psychologist must divulge information that is embarrassing and painful to the client. The forensic psychologist needs to understand that confidentiality is not consistent with the structure of the legal system.

More recently, however, the Supreme Court decision *Jaffee v. Redmond* (1996) held that communications between psychotherapists (including psychologists) are privileged in federal courts under certain circumstances. The court ruled that "the confidential communications between a licensed psychotherapist and the psychotherapist's patient in the course of diagnosis or treatment are protected from compelled disclosure under Rule 501 of the Federal Rules of Evidence" (*Jaffee v. Redmond* 1996, p. 338). This decision now sets a federal precedence, which states can work from in regard to their privileged communication statutes. The specifics of privileged communication vary from state to state and psychologists are advised to seek legal counsel regarding when testimony is required versus when one has the right to refuse testimony.

Generally speaking, an expert witness is appropriate when the subject matter is beyond the knowledge level of the layperson. Psychologists, when qualified by training and experience, testify in a number of areas. However, psychologists need to be concerned with two general questions before agreeing to provide testimony (Morse, 1983): Does their training and experience qualify them to be experts? Are the questions they are to address truly "scientific" or are they moral and social judgments presented under the guise of scientific conclusion? The legal system is adversarial in nature, designed to deal with conflict resolution in ways alien to a "scientific" or "client-centered" model. Thus, the psychologist is placed on one side or the other in a dispute, but with considerable pressure from each side to be placed in the role of an advocate. The psychologist may indeed have an opinion or even, at a more subtle level, a bias. It is appropriate at times, when representing a client, to become an advocate as long as the testimony remains within the bounds of scientific professionalism. In other words, opinions should always be based upon clinical and research evidence.

Before testifying, the psychologist should thoroughly prepare the testimony in order to alleviate nervousness. He or she should dress in a conservative style and use notes, if necessary, to remember facts and details. Once his or her qualifications for the case are established, the psychologist, in a narrative fashion, will offer testimony that lays the foundation for his or her conclusions. The testimony will review the evaluation procedures employed, including the nature and purposes of the tests or techniques involved. The psychologist will then be asked to form an opinion relative to the issue involved. It is helpful to relate the conclusion to the underlying facts as often as possible. It is also necessary to avoid the use of jargon or sweeping conclusions without sharing the reasoning process involved in reaching an opinion. When opinions are based on an ambiguous scientific foundation, the psychologist should take even more care to demonstrate how the conclusions were reached. In general, the responses should be straightforward and related to the psychological data. If personal beliefs or sympathies are involved in the situation, such as in a custody case, admitting beliefs and sympathies honestly with an explanation is the best procedure. Cross-examination follows direct examination, and is designed to probe and expose weaknesses in the testimony. Opposing counsel may attempt to undermine the expert's qualifications, the quality of the assessment, and/or the basis of the opinion. Attorneys practice various techniques of cross-examination, ranging from a "soft" to a hard and attacking manner. Trick questions in an innocuous style, complex questions involving several answers, misleading premises, provocative insinuations, and a bombardment of yes-no questions can be employed by the opposing attorney. However difficult or annoying this experience may be, the psychologist should not become argumentative or defensive. Careful preparation and/or well-laid-out testimony considerably reduces the attack in cross-examination. Testifying in court can be a fatiguing experience, but if one takes the time to be well prepared, it can also be quite satisfying and educational.

Malpractice Liability and Insurance

Insurance rates for malpractice liability have risen dramatically in the last 20 years for psychologists, a trend that is part of a national crisis involving general liability coverage. There certainly has been an increase in malpractice suits in medicine and other professions in cases involving harm, injury, or even dissatisfaction with the professional, regardless of fault. Psychologists have also seen an increase in frequency of claims and size of settlements. Losses for insurance companies in 1963 totaled $13,000; in 1973, the total was $34,000. By 1983 losses averaged $2 million (Gable, 1983). Unfortunatley, more current totals are unavailable. The American Psychological Association Insurance Trust (APAIT) maintains statistics on the number and types of lawsuits against the 36,000 psychologists who carry its insurance, and reported an average of 125 claims per year between 1976 and 1989, or a .5% liklihood of a psychologist being sued (Bennett, Bryant, VandenBos, & Greenwood, 1990).

The APAIT currently provides insurance for $1,000,000/3,000,000 (single/aggregate claims) at an average rate of $630, which is considerably lower than for psychiatry and other malpractice programs for healthcare providers. The cost of a psychiatrist's annual premium ranges from 4–24 times the cost of an APAIT policy, depending on the state. There are two types of coverage: occurrence-based and claims-based. In the first, if covered at the time of occurrence, then one is covered in perpetuity for that claim. This contrasts with a claims-made policy, in which one has to be covered both at the time of the alleged negligence and when the claim is lodged, even if one is in retirement.

Dörken (1990) reviewed 13 years of psychology's national malpractice claims and found that there has never been a court award for any insured practitioner for failure to refer to a physician when needed, failure to identify a medical problem, or failure to provide appropriate psychological care for a patient with medical complications. He believes this finding has implications for countering physicians' concerns about psychologists practicing in healthcare settings.

Malpractice suits result from a number of situations, including negligence, improper diagnosis, disclosure of information, sexual intimacy with clients, issues of informed consent, and suicide or homicide by clients. While other situations occur, these areas have provided the greatest potential for liability. Koocher & Keith-Spiegel (1998) suggest that psychologists need to be sensitive when treating high-risk clients. High-risk clients include litigious clients, clients with volatile psychopathology (e.g., borderline, paranoid, and delusional clients), clients who have experienced trauma, those involved in child custody conflict, and abuse victims.

Behnke and Hilliard (1998) point out that "a malpractice lawsuit is often said to consist of the four Ds, defined as the Dereliction of Duty Directly causing Damages. Each of the four Ds is an essential element of a malpractice claim—"if one is missing the lawsuit cannot succeed" (p. 10). In a malpractice suit the plaintiff who is bringing the suit must demonstrate with a preponderance of the evidence that each of the four Ds is present. Dereliction of duty in regard to the medical profession is based on what is considered reasonable care.

While legal claims can be made relative to any aspect of psychological practice, Stromberg and colleagues (1988) found that certain areas often produce litigation. These include:

- misdiagnosis
- practicing outside one's area of competence
- failure to obtain informed consent for treatment
- negligent or improper treatment
- physical or sexual relations with patients
- failure to prevent patients from harming themselves or others
- improper release of hospitalized patients
- failure to consult another practitioner or refer a patient
- failure to supervise students or assistants
- abandonment of patients

Gable (1983) offers a number of general comments to help practitioners avoid legal entanglements due to professional negligence. He points out four "elements" of liability:

1. The practitioner owed a duty to the patient to conform to a professional standard of care and skill.
2. There was a dereliction or breach of this duty by the practitioner.
3. Because of the dereliction of duty by the practitioner the patient suffered some injury or harm.
4. The practitioner's dereliction of duty was the direct or proximate cause of injury or harm suffered by the patient.

One form of negligence is the psychologist's failure to conform to a professional standard of care and skill. While the quality of care and the technical skills employed are often resolved through litigation, in such instances the "local" standard has been a ruling guide. However, while the practitioner must hold only to an "average" standard, those who claim to be specialists in a given area must reflect a higher standard of practice, regardless of specialized training. When claiming to be a specialist, the professional must demonstrate current knowledge and skills, obtained by attending workshops, national conferences, or training courses. The standards of care may be established through state licensing laws, as well as through national professional standards. Thus, a member of the APA also has to conform to the APA ethical principles and standards that would help the court determine the standard of care involved in the litigated case. Violations of ethical standards will, in most instances, increase the probability of liability. Individual practice, however, need only be reasonable to the particular case. As long as the practice is usable to a "respectable minority" within the profession and not experimental in value, the risk of liability is clearly lessened. Nevertheless, the court still determines the standard that will apply in each case in the final analysis.

The court has also determined there must be *informed* consent to treatment. It is commonly accepted that psychologists must provide information to the client about the psychological treatment to be undertaken and any potential risks involved. In general, the psychologist needs to be honest and straightforward about the diagnosis given, the purpose of the treatment, methods to be employed, and prognosis. Additionally, the professional should have reviewed the possible negative outcomes that will accrue if treatment is not undertaken, along with the other alternatives for treatment being given to the client, in order to minimize the legal risks.

While misdiagnosis is more a medical problem involving physical disorders, psychologists should exercise care in determining clients' mental diagnoses. Diagnostic error alone does not constitute liability, regardless of the harm. All of the diagnostic means available need to be utilized, and the lack of ordinary diligence and skill are the determining factors.

The most controversial situations have been when clients have committed suicide or homicide when under treatment; a typical situation is when the client is released from the hospital where care and prevention were possible. In determining liability, Gable (1983) indicates that three factors are important: (1) the foreseeability of the patient's suicide attempt; (2) the reasonableness of professional judgment in treatment; and (3) the client's compliance with the treatment.

Tarasoff Decision

Psychologists may be held liable for foreseeable harmful acts of their clients, especially when the lack of reasonable care can be demonstrated. The usual standard applied is based on the question, Did the hospital or practitioner follow the degree of care that a reasonably prudent person would have exercised under the same or similar circumstances? This standard can take into account the error variance in psychological diagnosis of client assessment. When learning of a client's potentially dangerous behavioral inclinations, psychologists should seek consultation and warn possible victims, since the courts may well render decisions that favor the protection of potential victims.

The most well-known case dealing with this matter is *Tarasoff v. Regents of the University of California* (1976). The legal action was for the recovery of damages resulting from the murder of the plaintiff's daughter. In July of 1969 Prosenjitt Poddar was seen by a psychologist, Dr. Larry Moore, for treatment at the University of California at Berkeley student health clinic. Poddar, a 25-year-old Indian graduate student, had come to the center at the urging of a friend because of his obsession with a 19-year-old undergraduate student of Russian lineage, Tatianna Tarasoff. Although the relationship was limited to only a brief flirtation and friendship, Poddar became increasingly obsessed with Tatianna. In the course of therapy, he made repeated references about purchasing a gun and threatened to use it against his former girlfriend whom he identified only as Tatianna. Poddar left therapy shortly thereafter, almost certainly in response to Dr. Moore's statement that he would have to detain Poddar if he was indeed serious. Recognizing the seriousness of the situation, the psychologist wrote a letter to the campus police, informing them of the situation and indicated that Podder should be committed for observation. The campus police took Poddar into custody. Being satisfied Poddar was rational, the police released him. Evaluation by the supervising psychiatrist apparently concluded that Poddar was sane and commitment was not needed, and directed that the psychologist's letter and notes be destroyed. Neither the campus police nor anyone from the health center warned Tatianna or her parents of Poddar's threat. A few weeks later Poddar killed his former girlfriend in her home.

Tatianna's parents brought a lawsuit against a number of individuals at the University of California at Berkeley, including Dr. Moore and his colleagues at the health center. Their claim was based on negligence, that the professionals failed to warn Tatianna of Poddar's threat, which resulted in her death. The therapists responded that they had no relationship with Tatianna and thus had no duty to warn her. In addition, they were restrained by therapist-patient confidentiality. They argued that the case was open and shut: What happened to Tatianna was tragic but "duty" was missing and because of confidentiality, the case had no business being decided in a court of law.

The case drew a great deal of attention because if the parents' case prevailed, therapists would have a duty to warn people with whom they had no relationship. Courts had previously held psychiatrists liable for releasing patients prematurely from an inpatient treatment facility; however, this case was different because Poddar was seen on an outpatient basis and Dr. Moore was a psychologist raising the concern that duty may apply to all mental health professionals.

Both the trials and appeals courts dismissed the complaint, holding that despite the tragedy, there was no legal basis in California law for the claim. The Tarasoff family appealed to the Supreme Court of California, and in 1974 the court ruled that the therapists indeed had a duty to warn Tatianna Tarasoff. It was decided that when, in fact, a therapist determines that a patient poses a serious danger of violence to others, he or she has a duty to exercise reasonable care to protect the foreseeable victim of the danger. While predicting violence is difficult, the court felt that the risk to potential victims outweighs the need of the client. The court concluded: "The public policy favoring protection of the confidential character of patient-psychotherapist communications must yield to the extent of which disclosure is essential to avert danger to others. *The protective privilege ends where the public peril begins*" [italics added] (p. 347).

An interesting footnote to the case is that Poddar was convicted of second degree murder and after five years in prison his appeal was granted because the judge failed to give the jury adequate instructions regarding Poddar's defense of "diminished capacity" and was subsequently convicted of voluntary manslaughter. He was released with the promise not to return to the United States and is today married and living in India.

In a civil case the Tarasoff family and the defendants reached an undisclosed financial settlement and the case never went to trial. Therefore, none of the professional defendants were found negligent by a court of law.

Practitioners need to be aware that the duty is to "protect" the potential victim, which does not necessarily mean directly warning the person. The protection conceivably includes other reasonable methods, such as notifying the police, removing instruments of harm (e. g., weapons), establishing continuous supervision by the family or community, modifying treatment, referral, or even commitment.

Other states are not bound by the California decision; however, they are free to follow the line of reasoning in cases of litigation and in the enactment of state laws. Many states have enacted laws stipulating a duty to protect with varying degrees of applicability in terms of when, whom, and how to warn potential victims. Stromberg, Schneider, and Joondeph (1993) reviewed statutes in a number of states that require the duty to warn and noted that several states, such as Ohio, have enacted statutes that specifically negate any legal claim based on a psychologist's duty to warn potential victims based on patient threats. Other states, such as Florida, New York, and Tennessee, have statutes that grant immunity to therapists from suits based on a breach of confidentiality when the purpose of such breach was to warn an identifiable victim. While permitting psychologists to warn, these statutes do not require such actions. Based on these statutes and a number of court decisions, Koocher and Keith-Spiegel (1998) strongly recommend that when faced with this type of situation psychotherapists consult a lawyer who is familiar with the statutes and standards in their particular jurisdiction.

The *Tarasoff* decision created considerable concern among professionals, because the duty to protect is not clearly defined. The decision to warn the victim is covered in the APA *Ethical Principles of Psychologists* (1992a) to the extent that psychologists are permitted to disclose information without the consent of the individual only as mandated by law for a valid purpose, one of which is to protect the patient or client or others from harm. The *Tarasoff* decision does not involve potential suicide victims, which the California Appellate Court in *Greenson v. Bellah* (1978) indicated in concluding that warning parents of a patient that she might commit suicide was not a logical extension of the *Tarasoff* decision.

The Health Care Quality Improvement Act

Generally, malpractice liability has become a real issue for psychology as well as other professions. The implications of litigation for psychologists are wide-reaching in regards to credentialing, membership in managed care panels, and loss of potential income. The Health Care Quality Improvement Act of 1986 establishes standards for peer review procedures and various reporting/notification requirements. "These include (1) malpractice damage payments or settlements by insurers, (2) disciplinary actions against physicians by licensing boards (reporting of actions against nonphysicians such as psychologists is optional), and (3) any action by a professional membership organization affecting a physicians status (once again, reporting is optional for nonphysicians such as psychologists)" (Stromberg et al., 1988, p. 218). A central registry for reporting has been established, which is used by hospitals and many healthcare organizations as part of the credentialing for staff membership, including psychologists. The law also provides immunity for professional peer review of alleged misconduct, including individuals who provide the information, unless, of course, the information is knowingly false.

Risks relative to liability can be reduced by adhering to the *Ethical Principles of Psychologists*, as well as state statutes and rules relative to the practice of psychology. Discussions with clients relative to confidentiality, physical contact, and the nature of the professional relationship are enormously helpful. Written information and consent relative to practices that might be used and possible risks in treatment are a further necessity. Misunderstandings and prolonged treatment difficulties should result in consultation with colleagues. Referral to another practitioner or the arrangement of alternative treatment can also considerably lessen the possibility of litigation. Behnke and Hilliard (1998) make a strong point in that a clinician can rarely find protection in a book of laws. "Rather, what protects a clinician from liability is her capacity to see what values are relevant to a particular circumstance, apply those values in a thoughtful manner to a problem that may have no clear answer, and document how she has come to decide on a particular course of action" (p. 23).

SUMMARY

Federal and state legislation have increasingly impacted the practice of psychology. State licensure and freedom of choice laws at the state level, federal legislation regarding service to individuals with disabilities, access to records, and reimbursement for mental health services are examples of how psychology has become shaped by the legal process. Moreover, court decisions have created concern relative to malpractice and other aspects of professional practice. The complexities of the delivery of psychological services includes the need to have knowledge about the legal system and the relevant laws and court decisions that determine present practice and the future of the profession.

Chapter 10

Changes in Service Delivery

Several movements within the profession and in connection with the changing healthcare system in general have had an impact on how the profession is defining itself and how services are being delivered to the public. Within the profession there has been the movement to create more diverse markets by seeking hospital privileges and practice and the movement toward prescription privileges for psychologists. Changes in government and private funding of healthcare have introduced managed care into the process of service delivery of all mental health professionals. The result is that psychology is in an increasingly competitive marketplace whereby marketing of services, responding to consumer need while appealing to business and industry, has become a recent and important phenomenon for psychologists to address. Not only must psychologists reconsider their traditional forms of service delivery, but they must also create markets for their specialized services, distinct from psychiatry and social work.

This chapter will examine the changes in the delivery of psychological services that have occurred in the past decade, and the movements within the profession that will influence the future thinking and role of applied psychology within the healthcare system. Efforts toward gaining hospital and prescription privileges and changes relative to managed care will be explored. Marketing issues for psychologists will also be discussed.

HOSPITAL PRIVILEGES AND PRACTICE

DeLeon, Pallak, and Hefferman (1982) reported that approximately 10% of the APA membership is employed in hospital settings. Gaining access to hospitals has been an ongoing struggle with the medical profession. For psychologists interested in healthcare delivery along with treatment of mental and emotional disorders, hospital privileges provide an important link with the medical community. This contact is especially important for referral resources as well as client access. Additionally, insurance reimbursement is greater for inpatient than outpatient services.

For the last 25 years, psychologists have worked with the Joint Commission on Accreditation of Hospitals (JCAH) and the reorganized Joint Commission on Accreditation of Health Care Organizations (JCAHO) on the issue of formal membership in the JCAH. Zaro, Batchelor, Ginsberg, and Pallak (1982) described psychologists' ongoing struggle over the previous 10 years, through formal and informal means, as having very limited results. At the same time, since approximately 1978, psychologists also have actively sought comparable legislation at the state level. Increasingly, the demand for psychological expertise in delivering quality medical services has provided the opportunity for psychology as a profession to become more systematically and intimately involved in a wide range of healthcare activities, including hospital practice (Frank, Gluck, & Buckelew, 1990). Increasing the scope of psychologists' practice in all jurisdictions of full medical staff membership including full clinical privileges has been called the "challenge of the 1990s" by a number of professional leaders (Enwright, Welch, Newman, & Perry, 1990).

The process of obtaining this status, however, has turned out to be a complex legal process. In 1978, California was successful in obtaining staff membership and/or clinical privileges for licensed psychologists. Then, with the passage of State Bill 259, California became the first state to recognize the independent and autonomous practice of psychology in hospital settings. In 1982, the District of Columbia City Council enacted legislation that extended to psychologists, as well as other licensed healthcare professionals, the right to admit patients to psychiatric hospitals and to provide therapy to clients admitted to hospitals. While still able to deny privileges to individual psychologists, the bill prohibited District of Columbia hospitals from denying access and privileges to psychologists, podiatrists, nurse midwives, nurse practitioners, and nurse anesthetists as a class. Currently, 15 states have enacted hospital privileges statutes that include psychologists.

State laws, as such, do not pose a problem for psychologists seeking medical staff recognition. Buklad and Ginsberg (1982) reported that many states have laws or regulations affecting hospital medical staffs. These state codes comprise four categories:

1. states with laws that do not address the specific issue of the terms of medical staff membership (5 states)

2. states with hospital laws defining "medical" staff in terms broad enough to include psychologists (9 states)
3. states with hospital laws requiring some physical supervision, but not limiting staff membership to physicians and dentists (8 states)
4. states with hospital codes or regulations that could permit the JCAH to dictate about matters of staff and governance organizations (28 states)

Therefore, considerable effort had been placed with both the JCAH by APA, as well as state legislative action on the part of state psychological associations.

In 1979, the Ohio Attorney General filed suit in federal court against the JCAH, the Ohio Medical Association, and the Ohio Psychiatric Association for alleged violations of federal and state antitrust laws. This action was the result of psychologists being denied full access to practice in JCAH-accredited facilities on the grounds that it represented a restraint of trade; that is, psychologists were prevented from practicing to the fullest extent of their licenses. While this suit was waiting to be heard, the JCAH developed a new set of standards in December 1983. The new standards were a clear relaxation of hospital staff privilege standards for psychologists, which prompted the Ohio Attorney General's office to dismiss the antitrust suit that had started four years earlier.

The JCAH standards have become part of the *Accreditation Manual for Hospitals* (JCAH, 1983). They allowed that psychologists licensed to practice independently may be on the staff of hospitals, and that clinical privileges for psychologists would be dealt with on an individual basis. This action left the issue of hospital privileges up to individual hospital boards. Part of the clarification is that psychologists are more interested in working in a clinical or consulting capacity within the hospital rather than having admitting privileges per se.

The JCAHO's *Accreditation Manual* (JCAHO, 1991) requires a single organized medical staff and specifically allows licensed nonphysican professionals to provide direct patient care without supervision by another discipline as long as they are practicing within the scope of their license. JCAHO standards are specifically referenced in a number of federal statutes (e.g., Medicare and Medicaid) and will, in all probability, be included in all future national healthcare legislation. This policy has opened the door for psychology to be formally recognized in the hospital environment as a bona fide healthcare profession.

The most important development facilitating the full participation by psychologists in hospitals was the 1990 California Supreme Court decision in the *CAPP v. Rank* lawsuit, which upheld the California psychologist hospital privilege statute by a 4-3 vote, thus granting psychologists the right to full participation on hospital staffs. This includes the right to admit, diagnose, and treat independently, with physicians serving in the role of consultants. Psychologists who chose to work in hospital settings seek to, or actually do, serve on medical staffs with full staff privileges. Individual psychologists also contract with hospitals and healthcare facilities for specific services such as pain control and stress management. McCarrick, Rosenstein, Milazzo-Sayre, and Manderscheid (1988) have reported an increase in the use of psychotherapy in public hospitals. Psychiatry, however, has continued to provide opposition in regard to legislative action because they perceive psychologists as economic and emotional threats rather than opportunities to enhance patient care though collaborative endeavors.

Psychologists interested in hospital practice are referred to in a primer prepared by the APA Committee on Professional Practice (COPP) that is specifically aimed at the hospital setting (APA, 1985). It covers such issues as staff privileges, organized staff membership, roles for psychologists in hospitals, and training for psychological work in hospitals.

PRESCRIPTION PRIVILEGES

An interesting and intense debate has developed regarding prescription privileges for psychologists. The issue is whether psychologists should be granted the right to prescribe psychotropic medications for their clients. As might be expected, psychiatrists and the medical community have voiced strong opposition; however, there is also considerable concern and debate within the profession of psychology about the implications for the profession.

Current Status

In 1994, The APA Committee for the Advancement of Professional Psychology (CAPP) created a Task Force on Prescription Privileges. The task force developed model curricula and legislation for state psychological associations to use in pursuit of prescription privileges. Subsequently, in 1995 the APA Council of Representatives passed an endorsement supporting prescription privileges for psychologists.

In 1990, the Hawaii Psychological Association with the support of U.S. Senator Daniel Inouye, was able to get the state legislature to pass a resolution authorizing a study into the feasibility of granting psychologists prescription privileges. Inouye was also instrumental in encouraging the creation of the Department of Defense Psychopharmacology Demonstration Project in 1991, which has graduated its first psychologists. The project has demonstrated that the profession of psychology can prescribe competently and safely, and viable training modules can be developed at the postdoctoral level (DeLeon, Sammons, & Sexton, 1995).

Sammons and Olmedo (1997) indicate that five states—California, Florida, Louisiana, Missouri, and Tennessee—had prescription privilege bills brought before their respective state legislatures in 1997. While all were subsequently defeated, it is reflective of the national movement of state association efforts to seek legislation. Clay (1997) reported that in Louisiana a bill granting psychologists prescription privileges made it through the Louisiana legislature's House, Health, and Welfare Committee, which is the first time this type of bill (which never came to a full vote) survived the committee process.

The bill proposed that psychologists with three years of practice, 300 hours of specialized training, and one year of supervised experience be granted prescription privileges for treating mental disorders. As a result of the movement, psychology training programs are considering adoption of curricula designed to train psychologists to prescribe medications.

Seppa (1997) notes that the American School of Professional Psychology (Chicago) was the first civilian program to prepare psychologists to prescribe medications. Clay (1997) also reports that Georgia State University and the University of Georgia have developed a program with courses based on a biopsychosocial philosophy rather than purely biologically-based courses. In regard to university training, the movement is still in the infancy stage, and changes most likely will occur after legislation.

Impact on the Profession

It has been proposed that prescription privileges are necessary for the enhancement of the profession and to more adequately meet the treatment needs of clients (Burns, Chemtob, DeLeon, & Welch, 1988; DeLeon, Fox, & Graham, 1991; DeLeon et al., 1995; DeLeon & Wiggins, 1996; Pachman, 1996; Wiggins, 1992). DeLeon and colleagues (1995) report that the general consensus of the APA Council of Representatives was that prescription privileges would lead to a higher quality of life for America's homeless, elderly, and rural populations. Fox (1994) believes that with prescription privileges, psychologists would have more treatment options and thus be able to help clients more effectively. Moreover, it would also result in making more services available to the general population at a lower cost. Forman (1992) feels it will generally enhance professional pride and prestige.

Saunders (1992a, 1992b) indicates, however, that psychologists must determine the specifics of the privileges. Issues regarding training and professional identity must be clarified. Massoth, McGrath, Bianchi, and Singer (1990) surveyed a total of 207 psychologists regarding prescription privileges and found that most believed prescription privileges would not interfere with therapy and assessment skills, and that they were neutral about it in general. Concern was raised about increased malpractice rates and the quality and expense of additional training. Generally, older psychologists and women psychologists were less in favor.

There are many psychologists that oppose prescription privileges (Butz 1994; Chamberlain, 1994; DeNelsky, 1992, 1996; Hayes & Heiby, 1996; Kingsbury, 1992; May & Belsky, 1992; Moyer, 1995; Saeman, 1992). DeNelsky (1991, 1992) believes that prescription privileges would have a negative effect on the course of psychology and would only serve to move psychology toward the medical model. With the medical approach also comes increased lawsuits and significantly higher malpractice rates. DeNelsky (1996) asserts that prescription privileges could change the basic direction in which psychology is evolving and that, in essence, psychologists would become junior psychiatrists. Hayes and Heiby (1996) point out that there is still an M.D./Ph.D. option, and that five contextual factors have led to the proposal that psychologists secure prescription privileges. These factors are:

1. *The overattachment of applied psychology to psychotherapy.* The practice of psychology is very much driven by market forces of cost, supply, and demand, and the overdependence on psychotherapy to provide an income for clinical and counseling psychologists. However, nondoctoral level professionals are now also delivering effective therapy services and in the past 10 years the healthcare system has created an expanded system while reducing reimbursement for services.

2. *The oversupply of doctoral level psychotherapists.* While psychiatry has failed to keep psychology out of psychotherapy, psychology has failed to limit the practice of psychotherapy to doctoral level practitioners (Humphreys, 1996). There is an ever-expanding list of practitioners trained to provide therapeutic services, including, for example, counseling, drug and alcohol counseling, nursing, marriage and family therapy, sex therapy, social work. While many of these professions also have state licensing laws, certification also exists for a host of fringe approaches such as rebirthing and sandplay therapy.

3. *The rise of managed care.* Managed care systems push to maintain costs while keeping consumers and businesses satisfied. This places tremendous pressure on practicing psychologists from health maintenance organizations and the competition from other professionals.

4. *The hegemony of syndromal classification.* The development of the American

Psychiatric Association's *Diagnostic and Statistical Manual of Mental Disorders* (*DSM*), despite its empirical approach, maintains the underlying disease model. The hegemony was advanced by third-party payers linking reimbursement to syndromal classification. Syndromal classification discourages the historical, developmental, and contextual view of behavior and, as a result, psychology has adopted psychiatry's approach to human problems.

5. *The weakening of the medical guild and the rise of drug companies' attention to psychopharmacology.* The ability and resolve of the medical guild to control access to medicine is weakening, and nurse practitioners and physician's assistants now have some measure of prescription authority. This is the result of physicians being under the same pressures as psychologists and needing to develop cost-effective services. Drug companies, on the other hand, have invested a great deal of money into the development of psychotropic medications and have a desire to see the expansion of prescription privileges.

Training

Prescription privileges will most likely change the training of psychologists. The APA Board of Directors established an ad hoc task force on psychopharmacology to explore prescription privileges, with one of its tasks being to explore a potential training curriculum that would allow psychologists to prescribe medication (Smyer et al., 1997). Three levels were proposed, which allow for increased authority and responsibility at each level:

- Level 1 training would include basic psychopharmacology and neurobiology and focus on brain function and cellular mechanisms. Level 1 would also include education about medications commonly used in the treatment of mental disorders. A three- to five-credit semester course in psychopharmacology and a course in biopsychology would be sufficient to cover the basics. Continuing education on psychotropic medication would also be mandated. Level 1 students would need to have an undergraduate background in biology or chemistry, which is not normally required of psychology undergraduates; this could make level 1 attainment somewhat difficult.
- Level 2 training is more in depth than level 1. It involves the application of knowledge into practice under supervision of a licensed psychologist. This would include a doctoral psychopharmacology practicum, a psychopharmacology emphasis in the predoctoral internship, and continuing education. At level 2, psychologists could have a major role in medication decisions without having full prescription privileges.
- Level 3 training would be the same as training for dentists, podiatrists,

optometrists, and nurse practitioners who have independent prescription privileges that are limited by the scope of their practice. This level of training would entail a two-year full-time training program, additional supervised clinical experience, and specialized training at the doctoral level.

Sammons, Meredith, and Sexton (1996), believe that the core competencies in psychopharmacology for psychologists should include:

- outcomes assessment
- principles of basic and applied psychopharmacology
- general knowledge of common medical illnesses
- knowledge of neurosciences and biological mechanisms of mental disease
- techniques of physical, psychological, and environmental assessment
- psychopharmacological treatment principles and patient management

These are in addition to basic competencies in psychological service provision, and similar to the proposed levels for psychopharmacologic providers. Sammons and colleagues further propose that in order to safeguard the training of the profession, the bulk of the training should be at the postdoctoral level. The basic premise is that while we need to rethink various educational policies, the acquisition of these skills should not overly disrupt existing graduate education.

Moyer (1995), however, raises the issue that by "giving psychologists the option to become trained prescribers, a division will be created among psychologists. It is possible that psychologists with the right to prescribe may consider themselves better than those without the right" (p. 587). If the right to prescribe results in greater third-party reimbursement benefits and greater access to hospital privileges, then psychologists without the right to prescribe may be appointed to second-class status within the profession (DeNelsky, 1991).

Conclusions and the Future

Saeman (1992) points out that psychologists will need to make a massive financial commitment in order to secure the necessary support for prescription privileges. It will have to be proven to legislators and the public that the training will produce highly skilled practitioners and that the public will receive substantial benefit. It is important not to have a public backlash by reports of poorly trained psychologists who miscalculate dosages. There will have to be a carefully crafted media campaign, a line-up of political allies, and a de-radicalization of the medical establishment in terms of their stated position against prescription privileges. There will need to be grassroots support, ideologically and financially, and the understanding that it will be a long, expensive haul to overcome powerful state licensing laws.

At this point in time, there is strong debate within the profession as to the need for prescription privileges. It has been emphasized that prescription privileges are a logical extension of the practice of psychology and would benefit the public. Concerns, however, have been raised about the movement toward the medical model. A great deal of effort has gone into curriculum development (Fox, Schwelitz, & Barclay, 1992); however, it may well be that only a minority of psychologists will qualify unless graduate training programs change their emphasis. Wiggins (1993) argues that psychology needs to maintain its uniqueness by providing services based on its own science, while Pachman (1996) maintains that despite these concerns the profession needs to move forward to develop a better model of mental health delivery.

Chamberlain (1994) poses a number of broad questions about psychology as a profession that need careful consideration:

1. What is the role of psychologists in the system of human interaction?
2. What are the consequences if psychologists embrace pharmacological "solutions" to human distress?
3. How comfortable are psychologists with chemically modifying personality?
4. What is the effect on our society if we pursue change without transformation?

Butz (1994) examined the motivation behind the psychopharmacology movement and concluded that chaos theory raises the question of whether psychopharmacological treatment should be used at all. The basis for psychopharmacological treatment is grounded in a mechanistic philosophy rather than one of self-organization. When examining the history of biological interventions there is reason to question whether pharmacological treatment has proven to be an effective treatment modality. The profession also needs to examine the financial and political motivations behind the movement. These and other questions have resulted in an intense debate and anxiety about the future of psychological service delivery as the movement itself, supported by the APA, continues to gain momentum at the national and state political levels.

The prescription privileges issue has created a forum whereby the profession is questioning its future. What is certain, however, is that the issue of prescription privileges has far-reaching implications for not only the role and practice of psychologists, but also the training and credentialing of future psychologists. The profession remains divided on the issue.

THE EFFECTS OF MANAGED CARE

Managed care is the term given for the cost containment strategies and financing arrangements governing health insurance policy and reimbursement throughout the country. Over the past decade there has been a proliferation of managed care organizations, and while the psychology profession has continually expressed concern, the public only recently has begun to question the healthcare system where cost containment is the primary determinant for care and profits are gained at the expense of patient care. The media has depicted numerous cases of treatment abuse and enormous profits of insurance company executives, prompting legislators to examine and attempt to regulate the system (Higuchi, 1994; Newman & Bricklin, 1991).

The managed care issue is part of the rapid revolution of healthcare that dramatically affected mental health services and the professional practice of psychologists. In essence, the evolution in healthcare, occurring over the past 20 years, largely as a result of spiraling health costs, has resulted in cost-containment efforts, including shifting the risk to patients and providers, an organizational restructuring of provider systems, and more market regulation. In many respects it is safe to say that as the healthcare industry continues to evolve, managed care is here to stay. Stromberg, Ratcliff, and Mathews-Schuetze (1997) quoted a 1996 Institute of Medicine report that by the end of 1995, the "behavioral health of nearly 142 million people was managed with 124 million in specialty managed behavioral health programs and [18] million with benefits managed by an HMO" (p. 5).

Organization and Delivery of Managed Care

Managed care companies have several different types of organizational structures, including mainly HMOs, preferred provider organizations (PPOs), ERISA plans, and networks and managed behavioral healthcare organizations (Stromberg et al., 1997). Each has a different structure; however, participating psychologists agree to provide services to any member of the organization at a set fee specified in the contract between the psychologist and the organization.

Health Maintenance Organizations

HMOs are the original model for cost-containment care and have been in existence for over 50 years. An HMO functions as a prepaid model so that people know their healthcare expenses in advance. The patients pay one set fee and in return are eligible to receive all services that are covered by their particular

HMO. Cost savings can be achieved through three basic mechanisms (Broskowski, 1991):

1. the diversion of patients from costly inpatient settings to just as effective, but less costly, outpatient care
2. reduction of hospital stays
3. price discounts by preferred providers who in turn receive an increased volume of patient referrals

HMOs also employ a case management system, which controls the utilization of services by the patient by requiring preauthorization of treatment and financial benefits for using preapproved lower-cost providers.

HMOs have been developed to produce a profit through effective control of utilization of services and healthcare costs. Over the years, substance abuse and mental health costs have substantially risen to the point where they can be some of the most expensive of all types of episodes (Broskowski, 1991). Substance abuse and psychiatric inpatient stays, in particular, dramatically increased during the 1980s. Generally speaking, currently there is less stigma regarding mental illness and the utilization of mental health services, and in the general population there has been an increase in drug and alcohol consumption. Along with the increase in the provider pool, increased competition between inpatient programs, and increased governmental support for community-based programs, there has been increased public awareness through program-building advertisement. The result has been, over the past 20 years, greater utilization by the public of mental health services. Managed care philosophy maintains that there is a need to reduce costs by shortening the length of outpatient services and inpatient treatment.

There are three types of HMOs: staff, group, and individual practice associations (IPA). In the staff/group models, providers of professional services contract with the HMO to provide care. Usually, there is a central facility for the staff, overhead is paid by the HMO, and providers are salaried employees. In the group practice model, a provider group contracts with the HMO for prepaid service delivery. Individual practice associations are made up of individual providers who work out of their own offices and set aside a percentage of their practice to see HMO patients. When working for an HMO, IPA providers are paid a salary that is independent of the number of patients seen or the types of services provided.

Under the group and IPA models, HMOs contract with providers based on a maximum fee schedule (usually lower than the prevailing fee) or on a capitation basis (i.e., the provider or group receives a specified dollar amount per subscriber covered, regardless of whether, or how often, the services might be used). Profits or losses are determined by the amount of services provided during a given year; profits occur when there are monies left over at the end of the year. Fewer services provided results in greater profits. Therefore, pressure exists to limit the number of sessions for clients regardless of the maximum number of visits allowed under the particular insurance policy.

The process in practice is fairly standardized with variations according to the insurance company and specific plan. Typically, when a referral is made by the primary care physician to a psychologist who is on a limited panel of providers, the physician must contact the managed care company, which usually authorizes one to six sessions. After the initial sessions a utilization review is required with a representative of the company, who may or may not have a mental health background. For example, The HMO may authorize three visits and then require extensive documentation in the utilization review before authorizing six additional sessions. Additional sessions are always subject to continued review. The documentation, either in writing or over the telephone, is extremely time consuming for the psychologist. It is interesting to note that federally controlled HMOs limit mental health services to 20 visits per year per patient.

Preferred Provider Organizations

Another alternative healthcare service that has grown in popularity is the PPO. The PPO is a limited group of practitioners who provide service to a specific community. Fees are negotiated by a fee schedule or relative value system and are discounted. Consumers pay lower deductibles and insurance payments for PPO services, yet maintain the option to use non-PPO providers at higher costs. Services are extensively reviewed with the aim of lowering healthcare costs in the long run. PPOs are usually administered by a board of directors who determine which providers in a given community will comprise the provider panel. Once the panel is selected, the panel is closed, thus, the opportunity to join an existing panel becomes difficult. This creates significant problems for psychologists who are attempting to develop a practice.

The selling point made to the providers is that while the fees paid to the provider are less than the normal fee rate, the provider has patients and the claims are processed rapidly. The utilization review process is the same as with HMOs. In reality, however, there have been complaints by psychologists that they receive only a few clients and that HMOs and PPOs delay payments in order to maximize the interest on the capitation money. The difference between HMOs and PPOs are that, for the latter, costs are reduced by discounting the fee for service. HMOs are controlled by capitation, that is, fees and services are predetermined regardless of individual need or utilization.

For both HMOs and PPOs there are several issues that are of concern to psychologists. The only mandated providers of HMOs are physicians, although psychologists are allowed to participate in an HMO. There are no federal and few state laws controlling HMOs and PPOs, and physicians may exclude psychologists. According to the Employee Retirement Income Security Act of 1974 (ERISA, 1974), HMOs and PPOs and self-insured companies are exempt from state insurance laws and, hence, state control. Thus, freedom of choice laws, which require third-party payers to reimburse for psychological services, may not apply to HMOs and PPOs.

ERISA Plans

ERISA plans (after the Employee Retirement Income Security Act, the federal law that regulates such plans) are neither HMOs nor PPOs; rather, they are self-funded by the employer who pays the majority of the cost. This type of plan is usually affordable by large companies. Many of the self-funded plans have a managed care arrangement with a closed network of providers and referrals by the company's employee assistance plan (EAP) or primary care physician (PCP).

Self-funded insurance plans are regulated primarily by ERISA, which was established by congress to create a uniform federal framework for benefit plans, and as such are not subject to state insurance laws. They must comply with federal ERISA rules governing benefit decisions and claims and appeal procedures. In large part they have been exempt from state insurance laws; however, the Mental Health Parity Act of 1996 mandates that covered plans offering mental health services to beneficiaries may not impose different lifetime or annual dollar limits on those services than are applied to medical services. Most ERISA plans do hire a third-party administrator to handle utilization reviews, acceptance or denial of claims, and payment arrangements with providers.

Networks and Managed Behavioral Healthcare Organizations

Another model, networks and managed behavioral healthcare organizations, has been established by groups of providers seeking contracts as self-managed care. They contract directly with businesses, thus bypassing the traditional managed care company. This allows for mental health professionals, rather than business-minded bureaucrats to set policy. One example is the Health New England provider-run system, which was established in 1991. The system features 15 specialty groups, each run by a psychiatrist. Another example is the Georgia Network of Psychologists (GNP), a for-profit company owned by the Georgia Psychological Association. Each has had mixed results. Health New England, while committed to high-quality care with healthcare professionals at the helm, has suffered from cost-containment pressures. The average mental health patient receives just five sessions per year, and there have been financial problems due to budget overruns. The Georgia Network was developed in 1996 and represents an effort to provide a managed care company that is patient- and psychologist-friendly. When a managed care company offers GNP a contract, GNP mails it to the 254 psychologists it has credentialed to provide care. Each of them decides whether to participate and authorizes GNP to sign the contract. GNP currently has all-psychologist panel contracts for 750,000 people (Clay, 1998).

Stromberg and colleagues (1988) nicely summarized the potential advantages and disadvantages of psychologists participating in an HMO, PPO, or other type of managed care contract (pp. 152–153):

1. *Expanded client base*. With the increase of providers it can be difficult for psychologists to maintain the size of their practice. By joining an HMO or PPO, psychologists become part of a preferred provider list and as such have a secure base of clients.
2. *Prompt and easy payment*. The organization pays the psychologist the amount in the contract and the client pays the copay at the time of service, which simplifies billing and eliminates collections.
3. *More stable and secure work environment for members of HMO staffs*. Working hours are reasonable, practice insecurities are lessened, and intrusion on personal lives minimized; consultation with other professionals is encouraged.

There are, however, also a number of disadvantages:

1. *Discounted fees*. The fee per session is significantly reduced, which has to be made up by an increase in volume in order to maintain the same level of income.
2. *Emphasis on short-term therapies*. Most HMOs and PPOs provide only a limited number of sessions per year and the emphasis is on short-term therapies. For example, the client may have only 20 sessions per year and in some cases it can be highly frustrating to the client and the psychologist when additional service is needed.
3. *Burdensome administrative procedures*. The psychologist can end up spending a great deal of time filling out forms justifying the need for additional treatment.
4. *Financial risks*. If the psychologist invests money in a network system, there is a risk of financial failure. When involved in a capitation method, the psychologist is at financial risk if the amount of care is greater than anticipated.
5. *Constraints on practice*. There is considerable pressure to treat and terminate clients after 8 to 12 visits, and to make records available to the insurance company and to other providers.

The decision to participate in an HMO or PPO depends on a number of factors, including the competitive environment, the reputation of the psychologist, and the ability to obtain referrals. Many psychologists sign up with as many plans as possible, which can be very time consuming. In addition, there is a great deal of instability as healthcare companies are continually being bought out or involved in a merger. Within this context, managed care has resulted in significant changes in the structure of psychological practices, especially private practice.

Changes in Practice Structure

Managed care has dramatically changed the nature of private practice of psychologists over the past 15 years. *Psychotherapy Finances* surveyed 741 psychologists and concluded that managed care organizations have made a major impact by paying psychologists lower fees than other third-party payers and by limiting the number of authorized sessions ("Fee," 1995). Psychologists in private practice indicated that they have had to adopt brief-therapy or problem-based approaches in order to be accepted or kept on a panel (65%), attend training in time-limited techniques (53%), have a reduced client load (48%), change their therapy approach (49%), shorten the length of therapy (64%), and have experienced a reduction in income (63%) and an increase in the number of disallowed claims (53%) ("Fee," 1995).

In many communities, with the increased numbers of practitioners of all specialties, including psychologists, a growing sense of competition has permeated the profession. Group practices have competed for managed care contacts, either as HMO or PPO providers, and solo practitioners have had to compete for clients and to remain on panels. The competition has forced private practitioners to work longer hours to maintain their level of income. Psychologists have reported that 85%–95% have evening hours and about 40% work on weekends ("Fee," 1995).

Partly because of the nature of contracting, group practices have been more responsive than solo practitioners to managed care requirements ("Fee," 1995). They will more likely get training and adopt brief therapy techniques. However, despite not having a reduced client load, two-thirds reported a reduction in income. This suggests that group practices will typically offer a wider range of services and see clients for fewer sessions than solo practitioners. With managed care companies the bottom line is profit, and the tendency is to favor group practices. Therefore, it will be increasingly difficult for private practitioners to maintain a solo practice and many will move into group practices.

Finally, some have questioned whether quality of service is also sacrificed in such service delivery models. The Practice Directorate of the APA, which was formed in 1987, has monitored the development of the managed care industry and has found that the efforts to control costs of providing mental heath services have produced a dramatic decrease in the quality of services; ironically, however, they have not controlled costs (APA, 1992).

Phelps, Eisman, and Kohout (1998) reported the most comprehensive study to date on the effects of managed care. In 1995, the Practice Directorate was commissioned by the APA Committee for the Advancement of Professional Practice (CAPP) to conduct a survey of current members regarding their current psychological practice and to determine the impact in the changes of the health-care system ("Practitioner Survey Results," 1996). It was felt that most existing studies (e.g., "Fee," 1995, etc.) were based on small samples that were limited in scope. The survey was sent to all 47,119 of APA's licensed psychologists, which resulted in a total of 15,918 usable questionnaires for a response rate of 34%. They found that over 50% indicated that their primary work setting was independent practice, either as a solo practitioner (43%) or in group practice (11%). In addition, 29% of the psychologists employed primarily elsewhere reported doing some private practice. Secondary settings for private practitioners were medical (15%), academic, (7%), government (3%), and other settings (19%), including a broad range with forensic (4%) being the largest group. Psychotherapy was the principal activity in all settings except academia. More than 75% of private practitioner's time and roughly only half the time of psychologists in medical and government settings was spent in psychotherapy.

The impact of managed care was significant across private practice and medical settings in contrast to academic and government settings where impact has been minimal. Almost 79% of all respondents indicated that the impact has been negative. Only 10% felt it was positive, and 11% indicated no effect. Of private practitioners, 68% believed that managed care is changing private practice. Psychologists in medical settings reported some of the same concerns, although they indicated problems with having fewer clients and precertification of services. Reduced income from managed care was highest in private practice.

Changes in Service Delivery

Phelps and colleagues (1998) believe that managed care has changed the nature of clinical practice and that independent practitioners are under enormous pressure from the changes in the healthcare delivery system. Traditional psychological practice is threatened by "market-place driven demands for integrated services, large and diversified group practices, and greater accountability [which] have created obstacles and declining market opportunities" (p. 35). However, despite the pressures toward group formation and the need for practice diversification for survival, over three-quarters of psychologists are delivering services in a traditional independent practice. Furthermore, new graduates are working in private practice more than any other professional setting. While it is increasingly becoming more difficult to receive reimbursement for psychological assessment, it remains a major feature of practice activity. Despite the changes, it appears that the majority of psychologists are adhering to their traditional role identity. Psychologists in private practice for the most part have not diversified into the areas of consultation, teaching, or research. In fact, in response to the decline in income they have chosen to spend more time performing traditional clinical activities. They have also begun to develop secondary settings, probably in response to financial pressures. The main area of growth has been in medical settings, where there seems to be a greater number of opportunities. Medical settings are also attracting more new graduates. This may indicate a shift in identity from the traditional and narrow role of mental health provider to the broader role of health service provider. APA has actively pursued the efficacy of health-care service in other settings through association policy, marketplace initiatives, and special projects.

New graduates are very concerned about entry into the marketplace where service delivery is dominated by organized managed care systems whose panels are closed to new providers. Wicherski and Kohout (1997) conducted a survey of doctoral graduates and found that most felt they needed additional training to equip themselves for dealing with the changes in the healthcare system. Training needed to include information about marketing, the medical culture, alternatives to long-term psychotherapy, integrated service delivery models, interdisciplinary teams, and the ethical and legal issues created by managed care organizations.

Murphy, DeBernardo, and Shoemaker (1998) surveyed 442 members of APA's Division 42 (Division of Independent Practice) and found a number of ethical concerns that were raised in dealings with managed care that were not covered by the APA ethics code. Two aspects of utilization review caused several concerns. The first concern was the belief that managed care companies would not safeguard the information given to them, and that, as a consequence, there is high potential for harm. The second relates to the loss of control by the provider relative to the quality of services. A third concern, related to the first two, has to do with diagnostic and coding practices of the providers. Patients are essentially put into the position of waiving their rights of confidentiality or not receiving insurance plan benefits. If the clinician is concerned about the confidentiality issue, then he or she is placed in the position of deciding what information to release, withhold, or edit in some manner when dealing with the insurance company during the utilization review. It is widely believed within the profession that in order to protect clients' confidentiality, obtain services, or gain reimbursement, psychologists will alter the diagnostic code. Mostly, however, altering the diagnosis is to protect client confidentiality, their future employment, or future insurance benefits. The tendency might be to submit the lowest level diagnosis that is reimbursable, and that psychologists might, for example, leave off an Axis II diagnosis when the client has an Axis I diagnosis that is reimbursable. This is a problem that has not been researched, and the legal, ethical, and clinical impact is substantial. Examples are diagnosing a client with an adjustment disorder when the indicators reflect a more serious diagnosis; another possibility is to code a mood disorder because other more accurate codes are not reimbursable. The profession needs to move forward in developing studies and addressing the ethical issues and providing guidelines.

Many psychologists have clients whose needs require continued services after reimbursement has lapsed or been denied. The psychologist has the responsibility to advocate on behalf of the client in order to assure appropriate care. When such efforts fail, most clinicians will work out a compromise with the client, usually involving a reduced fee, pro bono service, or termination until the services are again reimbursable in the next year. Rarely, however, are services terminated because of a failure by the managed care company to continue reimbursement.

Other concerns, such as greater use of nondoctoral providers, rejection of clients with certain diagnoses, and a greater use of medication in lieu of psychotherapy, have also been identified. Strong concerns have been expressed about the negative impact on the overall quality care (Murphy et al., 1998).

In regard to how practices are structured, only about 21% have moved from a solo to an integrated practice. About 88% are still in solo practice, with 68% of their income from the practice. However, many have had to hire additional clerical and professional staff.

The modal number of practice hours is 40, with 18% working 40–60 hours per week. Individual, couple, and family therapy and psychological assessment were identified as the most frequently provided services. However, marital and couple therapy and psychological testing presented the most difficulty in gaining reimbursement. Psychodynamic-oriented psychologists tend to see clients for more than 20 sessions while cognitive-behavioral- and family-therapy-oriented psychologists generally see clients for less than 20 sessions. Managed care companies tend to favor the latter orientations because of fewer sessions and treatment of multiple family members in a single session. Most managed care companies keep a running record of the average number of sessions per client, and have been known to drop psychologists from panels when the ratio becomes higher than the one they internally, and nonpublicly, set as the standard.

Increasingly, psychologists have joined hospital staffs in order to anticipate that provider-based networks will be organized around the hospitals. However, most do not provide any hospital-based service except on a part-time basis.

In conclusion, while managed care has had a strong impact on private practice, the structure of practices has essentially remained the same. Most psychologists belong to numerous managed-care panels, have hospital staff privileges, and many are forming provider networks. The numbers of clients covered by managed care has dramatically increased in the past decade and the percentage of income derived from managed care has correspondingly increased. The general perception is that managed care has negatively affected the business aspects of practice and, more importantly, the quality of care. Utilization review, limits on assessment and treatment, discounted fee structures, and reduced referrals are commonly expressed concerns. Income has been reduced because of the fee structures and decreased numbers of clients, and providers, in order to compensate, are working longer hours in more diverse settings (Murphy et al., 1998).

THE FUTURE OF PROFESSIONAL PRACTICE

In 1992, the APA practice directorate predicted there would be increased movement toward national healthcare, more cost control programs from state governments, and national regulation of the managed care industry. Kiesler and Morton (1996) further predicted that with the overall changes taking place "public and private cost-containment efforts, in tandem with rapid restructuring of industry and growing consensus about the limits of free marketplace competition should lead to declining provider autonomy, increasing integration of services, increased emphasis on treatment outcomes, increasing management purview, and (eventually) more consumer control via government and administrative decree" (p. 67). In the healthcare system revolution, mental health, by no means a small sector, will continue to have more providers, greater costs, and more users of mental health services.

Recent legislative efforts on the federal and state levels as well as the press suggest that the public is increasingly becoming dissatisfied with managed care, and that changes loom on the horizon. Various bills have been written to address issues related to the rights of individuals to appeal utilization review decisions, broaden requirements for panel providers, eliminate "gag" requirements of healthcare providers, and provide disclosure of financial incentives between participating physicians, insurance companies, and referral sources, to name a few. Newman (cited in Martin, 1997) indicated that in 1996 there were 1000 state legislative proposals aimed at regulating managed care, and 56 laws were enacted in 35 states. Toward the end of 1997 there were more than 1,000 legislative proposals with more than 100 laws enacted. Despite the changes in private practice dictated by managed care, it is reasonable to be guardedly optimistic over the long term that legislation will allow providers the ability to provide appropriate care and that clients will have the freedom to choose their therapist at a competitive fee.

Phelps and colleagues (1998) point out that despite the difficulties facing the profession, psychology has survived numerous changes throughout its history. Battles have been fought over licensure, freedom of choice, mandates for mental health treatment, and access to medical and hospital settings, with the result being that the profession has been able to redefine itself accordingly. The profession continues to seek hospital privileges, the debate over prescription privilege continues, and at a broader level the APA continues to seek to influence the changes in the healthcare system. Meanwhile, individual practitioners continue to accommodate and make changes, and as the marketplace continues to change so too will well-established practice patterns. Psychologists have adapted by maintaining their professional and practice integrity and making accommodations through working longer hours and in more diverse settings. They have been positioning themselves well for the future and continue the process of redefinition of both themselves and the profession.

New Opportunities for Practice

Traditionally, psychologists and other mental health professionals have provided clinical services to their clients in a fee-for-service model. Services have been paid for by the clients, insurance companies, or government resources such as Medicare or Medicaid. Within such a model, the individual practitioner has usually functioned autonomously as a "cottage industry." Clients were referred through the psychologist's establishment of a referral network and his or her reputation of responsibility and competence. Few constraints threatened the independence of the psychologist. Clients were free to choose the professional they wished and some reimbursement was provided by insurance companies to licensed professionals. Fees were competitive and largely dictated by what the market would bear, that is, what the consumer was willing to pay and the limits of reimbursement from third-party payers. At the same time there were few, if any, mechanisms in place to monitor the quality of professional service to the consumer. Prior to the past decade, this model had been accepted as the modus operandi. While some psychologists may continue service delivery as independent practitioners under this model, especially those with a market niche and/or an excellent reputation, with the advent of managed care it is no longer feasible for psychologists to assume that this model of service delivery will remain the most viable one for themselves personally, or for the profession in general.

At the same time, there has been an increased call for community-integrated health delivery services. In particular, schools provide a prime example of the future diversification of psychological practice. A major policy shift is the reform of education and health services into a comprehensive service delivery system (Talley & Short, 1995). Due to the increasing number of high-risk children, increased school-based violence, and shifts in cultural and economic patterns, schools are seeking innovations that will meet the mental health needs of children. Psychologists have expertise in development, learning, organizations, and systems research, as well as the traditional assessment and psychotherapy skills, which can provide the foundation for assisting schools in establishing a comprehensive system of services to children and families linking school-based and community-based models (Talley & Short, 1996). This would require a significant paradigm shift in the delivery of school-related psychological practice. Paavola and colleagues (1995) indicated that some of the major components of the shift would include a move from isolated service delivery to interagency service delivery in collaboration with other professionals and disciplines and service delivery at the client location, including the school and at home. They called for psychology practitioners to prepare for service delivery within new comprehensive family-centered models in settings that included schools, homes, healthcare and childcare sites, and social service agencies. There are a number of operational school-based community-linked models (Carlson, Tharinger, Bricklin, DeMers, & Paavola, 1996), along with a rapid expansion of school-based clinics that are administratively controlled by school districts, government agencies, or both. These programs are funded piecemeal through a variety of federal acts and agencies, including IDEA, Medicaid, Social Security, Head Start, the juvenile justice system, and the Public Health Services Act. However, these funds are insufficient and have, in fact, created barriers for efficient allocation and use (DeMers & Bricklin, 1995). These efforts toward reform address the need for professional psychology to become more involved in the creation of diversified service delivery; moreover, at the same time, government funding needs to respond to the needs of consumers.

As the philosophy and priorities of government funding have changed and the federal deficit is of paramount concern, healthcare delivery has been influenced in significant ways. Healthcare cost is such that in the past 25 years the percentage of gross national product (GNP) spent on healthcare has doubled, without major improvement in the health of Americans. As of 1992, there were 36 million non-elderly Americans, including 10 million children and 15% of low income working individuals and their families, not covered by private health insurance or federal healthcare programs (Frank, 1993). The United States is consuming far more healthcare than it is paying for in taxes or insurance premiums. In 1992, over 225 billion (or over 28%) was spent in deficit spending, which also provided a substantial contribution to the federal deficit. Moreover, the United States lags behind a number of other countries in services provided that are spending less per capita on healthcare than the United States (VandenBos, 1996). As a result, the public at large and the government appear to be concerned about the rising costs.

At the same time that the government and the public are looking for ways to reduce healthcare costs through reform, other demographic changes are taking place that also affect the profession. The number of physicians and mental health professionals is growing, and an oversupply of providers, especially at the non-doctoral level, is anticipated in the near future. Thus, a supply-and-demand issue is emerging.

While many psychologists may resist changing how they manage their practice economically (as well as being naive and uninterested in business management), it is becoming crucial that psychologists become aware of and respond to changes that are taking place in the healthcare industry. With the structure and powerbase of healthcare changing, the competition between mental health professionals growing, and the consumer responding to economic realities, psychologists need to be knowledgeable about these changes as well as more acutely aware of the need to develop marketing strategies and managerial acumen.

Marketing psychological services can follow the same general principles as the marketing of any product. The basic goal of a marketing strategy is to anticipate and satisfy the needs of the client, while at the same time meeting the goals of the provider. The provider needs to assess his or her resources and strengths in a realistic manner, as well as identify the clients he or she wishes to serve. Assessing resources is a comprehensive exercise that could include the social, political, economic, and legal climate, as well as examining personal and professional attributes. Once the resources and appropriate populations have been identified, marketing variables referred to as the four Ps—product, place, promotion, price—need to be examined. *Product* defines what the client will get for the service. The kind of services to be offered must be consistent with the needs of the marketplace and the strengths of the provider. *Place* involves where the services will be provided, which needs to be consumer-friendly and accessible by the client population. The third P, *promotion*, is how the client will partake of the services. In psychology, this means educating the public and referral sources about the service; strategies might include networking, advertising, or public speaking. Finally, *price* must be considered, in terms of financial costs and also emotional, social, and physical costs to the consumer.

As a final step in marketing, the process must be evaluated and flexible enough to be changed as needed. If psychology is to remain a viable profession, providing unique and needed services to society, then it must remain responsive to the needs of society. Marketing is a tool by which the profession can remain economically viable as well as socially responsible. It provides the means through which psychology can respond to changes in healthcare and government policies and communicate the changes in service delivery and the relevance of psychological services in meeting the mental health needs of individuals.

SUMMARY

In reflecting on the practice of psychology over the past decade, the profession has increasingly moved toward diversification. In response to managed care and the healthcare reform movement, there has been an increased emphasis on practice in healthcare settings. The traditional private practice has diversified into consultation, assessment, and therapy in hospitals, community health facilities, and nursing homes. At the same time, the profession has moved forward on the legal front with efforts to secure hospital staff membership and prescription privileges—the latter with intense debate about the how it will possibly redefine the profession. It is probable that the creation of new options for practice has in the broadest sense moved psychology to rethink how it presents itself to the public. Increasingly, psychology is looking toward schools, businesses, government facilities, and other settings to expand and redefine service delivery within the context of health and the amelioration of problems in individuals and families.

Chapter 11

Professional Horizons

Becoming a psychologist is more than the attainment of a degree and the license to practice. It is also more than learning the appropriate theories and skills in order to practice. In fact, it is a lifelong developmental process involving a complex interplay between personal development, professional development, and the personal and professional context.

This chapter begins by examining some aspects of personal and professional development, followed by the development of technology, which allows psychologists to communicate and learn in ways unheard of a decade ago. The role of psychology in regard to public policy is then examined, illustrating the need for the profession to have a role in how this country meets the psychological and health needs of its citizens and how it provides the mechanism for simultaneous paradigm shifts for the profession and the individual professional. Finally, an international perspective is presented, whereby the profession can access transcultural resources through the globalization of psychology, which may well provide the vehicle for the growth of the profession and enable it to deal with societal problems.

THE PERSON OF THE PSYCHOLOGIST

Beginning psychologists often assume that their graduate school training has taught them all they need to practice competently in their particular specialty. Instead, as they begin to understand and appreciate their knowledge base and skills, they also discover how much they really don't know. Moreover, they may be surprised to learn that a psychologist's professional development is a lifelong process of personal differentiation that allows for the integration of personal life experiences. Beginning psychotherapy students and professionals have difficulty incorporating their personal experiences into the process of their work; this may possibly be related to limited life experiences, the need to achieve a professional identity through a feeling of competency, and/or unresolved personal issues with their own families of origin and personal emotional blockages (Wendt, 1997).

Incorporating life experiences into psychological work appears to develop at mid-career or mid-life, when psychologists have accumulated life and professional experience, resolved personal issues, and evolved to higher levels of self-differentiation. Integrating the personal into the professional while maintaining appropriate boundaries between them so that each becomes a valuable resource for the other is a complex process.

A common perspective, however, about the the process of professional development appears to focus mainly on the professional side and the need to attain and maintain competence. Psychologists are trained in the appropriate theory, or theories, and then gain experience and develop some new ideas and techniques as they move through their professional careers. Despite becoming more competent with professional experience, psychologists—especially those who provide therapeutic services—encounter numerous situations where they feel that their work was a failure. Davison (1995) believes that failures in therapy result in the therapist taking a more integrative position regarding theory in order to prevent further failure. A clear example of theoretical integration and expanding of technique is the multimodal therapy of Lazarus (1976), who posits that as psychologists integrate theories they become more competent, flexible, and proficient in the application of techniques.

The expansion of theory and technique is obvious in the United States, where the emphasis on treatment often includes the documentation of success and a preoccupation with the competence and incompetence of therapists. Both Claiborn (1982) and Cummings (1991) reflect a general trend in pointing out that quality assurance is needed in order to protect the welfare of clients from incompetence along with the need to have mental healthcare plans that improve efficacy and quality of services.

A core assumption is that failure commonly results from clinical incompetence, incompetence of the institution, or resistance in the client, resulting in the view that failure and incompetence are synonymous. Considerable research is focused on the development and evaluation of clinical competence (Berman & Norton, 1981; Shaw & Dobson, 1988), emphasizing that theoretical orientation, knowledge and training, and clinical experience are the determinants of successful therapy. However, others have also seen that personal characteristics are also important (Corey, Corey, & Callahan, 1988; Herman, 1993). The main

point, however, is that the profession places a strong emphasis on the relationship between the competence of the psychologist and success in his or professional work.

Success versus Failure

In the United States, therapy is often linked to funding other than patient
resources, such as private insurance, where there is an increasing demand for
accountability and efficacy of various therapeutic approaches. For example, purely for economic reasons most insurance companies favor brief therapies that
involve multiple family members. Success is often measured by symptom reduction or elimination. As a result, success is often defined in reductionistic terms,
which ignores the complexity of the family, therapist, and the therapeutic process.

Failure is then seen as the antithesis of success and is the enemy of all psychologists. For many psychologists, failure is often viewed as failure of clients to
change, early termination of services, and, at a deeper level, personal incompetence and impotence. Despite the lack of a universal definition, each person constructs a personal reality of what constitutes failure. This personal construction is
defined by both the professional culture and the culture of one's family of origin.

In reality, most psychology-related work is a professional endeavor in which
success and failure often elude definition. Often when we think we have succeeded, we have failed, and when we think we have failed, we have succeeded.
In a world consisting of individual realities, individual family members, consul-
tees, and psychologists will have differing ideas about what was and was not beneficial, whether the work was helpful, and what changed in the individuals
and/or context. For example, a couple may believe the therapy was successful
because they stayed together while the therapist may deem it a failure for the
same reason. A psychologist's beliefs about success and failure reflect his or her
process of self-validation and level of honesty.

A possible result of achieving what is considered by the individual and the
culture of the profession as successful is an overinflated sense of grandiosity about
oneself and the importance and quality of one's work. By ignoring failures and
accentuating perceived success, an illusion of grandiosity and importance is created, which stifles the development and growth of the psychologist. In both
training and in the beginning years of professional work, it is often perceived that
both the clients and psychologists need to be protected from failure, as psychologists believe that professional validation comes from clinical success. However,
allowing oneself to live in a context and culture of failure can open the process
of self-validation from mentors and, even more importantly, from peers (Wendt,
1997).

In contrast to the emphasis on competence and the attainment of success, a number of psychologists have discussed the impact personal life experiences have had on their professional development (Kaslow, 1990). L'Abate (1990) specifically illustrated the importance personal crisis and failures have had in terms of shifts in his professional development. The evolution of the psychologist is affected not only by professional development, but also by life experiences. This complex process integrates such factors as training, relationships with mentors and colleagues, and resolution of personal family experiences, including those from childhood, marriage, divorce, remarriage, and deaths (Wendt & Dupuy, 1995).

Gender

Feminist psychologists have raised questions about how gender affects the process of one's professional work. Hare-Mustin and Marecek (1990) discuss the differences between men and women, asserting that the notions relative to symmetry and complimentarities need to be challenged in regard to division of labor by sex. In essence, society does not provide men and women with equal opportunities for culturally defined success. In addition, women live out their lives in both the dominant male culture and the female subculture and are thus able to see life from both perspectives, giving them a unique advantage in the development of gender theory.

Crawford and Marecek (1989), Harding (1986), Keller (1985), and Rose (1983) have raised the level of gender theory beyond the emotional intensity associated with inequities developed from the social structure in both the society and the family. Chodorow (1989) indicated that the "single cause" feminism of the 1970s does not take into account the complexity of women's experience and the diversity and complexity of gender issues. As a result, there has been considerable discussion regarding how the gender socialization process affects the beliefs, values and behaviors of an individual—that is, the very essence of how men and women perceive and relate to the world. Dupuy (1993), Miller (1976), and O'Neil (1986) have concluded that a result of these socialization processes is that men have a worldview that emphasizes autonomy and independence while women have a relationally oriented perspective. The autonomy orientation focuses on a sense of self that is separate from others and tends to be culturally defined as goal-, performance-, and success-oriented. The relational orientation focuses on a sense of connection, in which the relationship (e.g., with self, others, work) provides the context of personal identity. Both orientations tend to define an individual's experience and often lead to differences in how these experiences are perceived and communicated.

Tannen (1990) suggests that communication from each orientation often has different intentions and meanings. From an autonomy orientation, communication can be seen primarily as a way to share information. The content of the communication is of major importance and the communication style often reflects the knowledge-sharing purpose of verbal exchange. Communication is often directed toward suggesting solutions to problems, presenting ideas through debate and confrontation, and as a way of establishing oneself as an expert in particular areas. Within a relational context, communication is often seen as a way of connecting. The process of hearing with empathy and being heard rather than merely listening for the content of the communication is the primary importance. In this context, expert, solution-focused, and confrontational styles may be seen as counterproductive to the purpose of connection. Instead, a style of mutual communication (empathetic listening and a supportive exploration of differences) serves the individual's needs for connection and validation.

For psychologists, both styles and purposes of communicating are important. However, gender socialization may actually inhibit the development of both styles for men and women. Changing communication patterns often involves a redefinition of self. The fear of losing one's sense of self through relational communication for autonomy-identity individuals is just as great as the fear of losing one's relational identity in communication styles that value provocation and confrontation. Thus, from the fear of losing one's identity, psychologists often develop limitations in their communicative flexibility (Wendt, 1996). It will be especially interesting to see how training, professional success, and the definition of the profession will change over the next half century as a result of changing gender patterns.

Professional Crisis

As psychologists progress in their development through professional experience, common issues regarding their power, control, status, and professional competency seem to be of major concern. Mentors can provide some guidance regarding these issues, but as time goes on many psychologists experience an increase in their dissatisfaction with themselves as professionals and the models presented to them. It is important to note that this process is inevitable and is a result of the structure of the profession (i.e., the context) rather than a personal or pathological problem. Gender, again, seems to define how this professional crisis is experienced.

For most autonomy-oriented psychologists, the professional goal is to obtain some sort of "expert" status. Historically, most noted psychologists have been men, who worked from an expert position. This position influences the dynamics of power, control, status, and competency for the psychologist. As an expert, the psychologist retains control of his professional life and uses his own power and status as an expert to influence change within the profession. The very same process is involved in working with clients. Personal measures of competency are then based on the ability to control and successfully produce appropriate change in the client(s) by using one's power, authority, and status as a professional. The professional crisis occurs for autonomy-oriented psychologists when their fear of failure (their lack of control, power, and status) gets in the way of their ability to connect, deal with emotional intensity, and be of general help to their clients. This is often experienced as feelings of impotence.

From a relationally oriented position, power, status, control, and competency are based on one's ability to connect with, nurture, and parent the family toward change. Relationally oriented trainees (usually women) often find themselves supervised by autonomy-oriented therapists (usually male), who attempt to develop the expert model in their supervisees. Such women often have a difficult time adapting their relational sense of being into an expert position as therapists. This can often leave the women trainees feeling confused and may actually undermine the development and personal validation of their unique skills. In addition, the fear of disconnection with the client may limit the relationally oriented therapist's effectiveness. The expert stance of authority may be perceived as threatening to the therapist-family relationship and experienced as a loss of connection with oneself. When the fear of disconnection becomes great, the therapist may actually be stifled in her effectiveness and experience overwhelming feelings of "stuckness" (Wendt & Dupuy, 1995).

Personal Crisis

As psychologists gain experience with clients, they are able to create stronger links between their clinical work and their life experiences. Clinical work is such that experience is crucial to working through a sense of impotence or stuckness. As the psychologist moves through his or her own life-cycle transitions, the interplay between personal and professional experience takes on greater meaning in regard to understanding what clients are experiencing. Through professional experience one learns how dysfunction and psychological processes relate to theory in order to understand clinical observations. As psychologists gain life experiences, they are better able to integrate their own existential process, which creates new options for interventions with clients in consultation and therapy. However, in order to achieve this level of interpretation, the psychologist usually moves through an intense personal crisis whereby personal and emotional blockages are challenged. For those therapists who recognize their blockages and that they are in a personal/professional crisis, the impasse can become quite intense. The blockages emanate from the family of origin and inhibit the psychologist's work with feelings, imagery, and symbolic and metaphorical aspects of themselves and their clients.

Psychologists do not enter the profession as whole persons, and often use clients for self-growth and completion. For example, early in his career, one of the authors (RW) worked extensively with adolescents, and was able to work through many personal unresolved adolescent issues through the professional relationship.

Unresolved issues and relationships in the psychologist's family of origin will produce unconscious blockages in relationships with his or her current nuclear family as well as families seen in therapy. The psychologist struggles with feelings of closeness or distance, or with specific feelings, such as love, anger, or sexuality. It is not a matter of discussing these feelings in therapy, but rather how the psychologist experiences and expresses them on a nonverbal level that provides the context in which clients can experience the session with emotional and intellectual intensity (Wendt, 1996).

Experience, Synthesis, and Liberation

The psychologist resolves mythologies, relationships, and family-of-origin emotional issues through therapeutic experience, often with a high level of intensity. The therapeutic experience may result from an intense emotional crisis and experience with the family of origin or other meaningful relationship, formal psychotherapy, or structured emotional experience related to professional development. By resolving emotional conflicts, one can access issues that were previously blocked and unavailable, allowing the psychologist to expand his or her internal resources.

A psychologist's development continues throughout life. It seems possible that many issues are revisited at different levels at different life stages. However, it seems that later development takes on the characteristics of synthesis and expansion, which lead to and are generated by self-evaluation, self-confidence, competency, creativity, and personal liberation. The processes of creativity and personal liberation free the psychologist to relate to clients and him- or herself in ways that are genuine, in the moment, and life- and growth-enhancing. Personal liberation is a complex individual process, rooted in one's family-of-origin relationships. Gender is also an important defining factor. For example, if a man is drawn to the profession by past experiences of loneliness, liberation may involve giving up the the belief that professional work is the only way to fulfill one's needs for intimacy; in order to let go of such a myth he needs to resolve the sense of disconnectedness with various parts of his family of origin (Wendt & Dupuy, 1995).

Similarly, if a woman is drawn to psychology to combat emptiness, she would have to challenge the corresponding myth of selflessness (filling oneself with other's needs and experiences) in order to promote personal liberation and creativity. This liberation would entail a new, more expansive definition of connection, which would include what was previously perceived as disconnection. Also, her own sense of self could be utilized in a fuller way to engender a type of power to effect change based upon connection. The process of liberation would then enhance the woman's sense of competency and creativity.

Personal and Professional Validation

The process of personal and professional validation can be considered as a paradigm when developing critical theory (Wendt, 1997). Critical theories aim at the emancipation and enlightenment of people by making them aware of how they came to embrace their beliefs, values, norms, and attitudes (Guess, 1991), and explaining the conditions by which beliefs and worldviews are acquired— that is, how individuals make significant shifts in their personal and professional development.

In essence, the process of validation is a consciousness-raising process similar to what Habermus described as the "ideal speech situation, . . . a situation of absolutely uncoerced and unlimited discussion between completely free and equal human agents" (Guess, 1991, p. 65). That is, in a situation free of competition and grandiosity, the force of discourse guides the process. However, our profession has established a code that maintains a hierarchy of competence and incompetence and diminishes the possibility of the type of discourse that leads to validation. With this emphasis on success, the individual psychologist seeks validation by striving for greater "success" than his or her colleagues.

Validation by mentors has been the traditional mode of seeking validation. When the successful and/or famous psychologist "anoints" the student/professional as competent or exceptional, the professional is supposed to then feel internally validated. While this is a valuable part of training, it does not hold in the reality of practice, where the definition of success is nebulous and the complexity of the clients' problems and the process of consultation and therapy, more often than not, create feelings of inadequacy and failure. To compensate, professionals tend to seek more "expert" validation, more information, and to become more rigid about which theory or approach is necessary for success.

An overlooked process consistent with critical development theory and discourse is that of peer validation. Whitaker (1989) often discussed the need for a "cuddle group," mainly to diffuse and distribute the emotional intensity of psychotherapy in order to enable differentiation of the personal from the professional. At the same time, most of the advances in psychological theory occur in contexts that support ideal speech discourse among peers.

The need for validation through discourse among equals is crucial to the development of the psychologist. Peer discourse provides the opportunity to challenge our thinking, embrace new ideas, and confirm our thinking and emotional process. The outcome of this level of honesty with oneself is an increased capacity to be creative and take risks that will benefit our clients. Ironically, equality is created through one's failures rather than successes. The process of looking at one's professional work as a failure involves a level of personal honesty that is a strong antidote to both grandiosity and competition. It requires the psychologist to examine his or her own personal role in an unsuccessful therapy, rather than blame the client or institution. As the psychologist becomes experienced, the number of personal and professional failures becomes more important than the successes, in that more can be learned about oneself and one's work from a painful struggle than from an easy, predictable course.

This is not a new idea; groups of psychologists have always met with learning objectives or consultation in mind. However, as we learn more about the need for peer validation, professional connectedness, intellectual stimulation, and a context for finding solutions to problems, the number of information resources has increased. In addition, technology now permits such groups to be less reliant on face-to-face meetings. Consequently, a psychologist practicing in a rural area, a school psychologist in an organization with only a few colleagues, a psychologist in a small group practice or with a highly defined practice should all be able to arrange a context in which learning and/or feedback can take place in a systemic, continuous manner.

Professional Development

Professional development is a concept consistent with the notion of lifelong learning. While always an implicit obligation of the profession (some credentials require some level of continuing education activity for renewal purposes), the information-technological revolution has given the concept a particular urgency. Regardless of the practitioner's intent to practice at the generic or specialty level, he or she must have a system for keeping up-to-date. It is the personal responsibility of all psychologists, requiring "continued development of self-assessment techniques to . . . identify areas of strength and deficiency" (APA, 1995b, p. 13).

The ongoing learning experience must be supported by several programs of varying length, goals, content, format, and frequency. It can be formal or informal, self-generated or guided, involving readings, didactic experiences, activity-based experiences, or some combination of each. In all instances, there should be an evaluative component, with specific entry and exit criteria. Moreover, it needs to to be relevant and enhance professional conduct in daily practice.

Pettifor (1996) has argued that professional development "requires an ongoing commitment of the psychologist to an ethic of caring, self-evaluation, and validation of practice against effectiveness of client outcome" (p. 100). Haas and Malouf (1989) note that "practitioner decay" can be problematic in terms of professional knowledge and professional judgment. Staying current is a challenge; a good self-check question for the practitioner is, Can I identify the most recent significant works in a particular area of practice? Practitioners must examine the value of their resources; for example, what journals do they subscribe to? What books have been read? What was the source of the recommendation for the book? Reference guides such as the APA's *PsycSCAN* and the *Psychologists' Desk Reference* (Koocher, Norcross, & Hill, 1998) can be helpful. The latter groups 125 contributions in seven categories of practice (e.g., psychotherapy, treatment), including guides and essential information for practitioners.

Protecting Against Burnout

According to Haas and Malouf (1989), burnout and "life imbalances" can affect the quality of professional judgment over time. Burnout typically results from excessive demands on energy, strength, and personal resources, and can involve a loss of investment in clients. Koocher and Keith-Spiegel (1998) summarize many of the reactions that can result in aversion to or detachment from clients. Haas and Malouf (1989) suggest that at a minimum, a commitment to an objective self-monitoring of one's motivation as well as alertness to other feedback is necessary to help protect against such a personal drift. They also encourage a practitioner to systematically review his or her inner balance as the demands of work and social life are encountered. Koocher and Keith-Speigel (1998, p. 70) list the following factors that protect a practitioner against burnout: "(1) role clarity, (2) positive feedback, (3) an enhanced sense of autonomy at work, (4) opportunities for rehabilitation from stress at work, (5) social support in the workplace, (6) personal accomplishment, (7) realistic criteria for client outcome, (8) an accurate awareness of personal strengths and weaknesses, along with a good sense of internal control."

Pettifor (1996) recommends five steps psychologists can take following a monitoring and review of their own practice. The first step is to make a straightforward decision or take a direct action, such as changing a billing procedure or clarifying the limits of confidentiality. The second step is to identify strategies to remain current in the field, which will involve self-study. Third, when the practitioner feels isolated he or she needs to develop a peer support system or arrange to have regular contacts with colleagues. Fourth, when the practitioner experiences excessive health- and personal-related stress, she recommends consultation with a trusted colleague and perhaps even assistance with self-monitoring functions. The practitioner may need to change his or her lifestyle or even obtain treatment. Finally, if the psychologist desires to expand or change the scope of practice, he or she needs to develop a plan of action, which may include supervision and further training.

Taking Care of Oneself

A recent article in the *APA Monitor* (Shapiro, 1997a) summarized an APA symposium discussion that advocated noncompetitive exercise as well as controlling one's smoking and drinking behavior as basic ways to cope with stress-induced behaviors. More novel stress management techniques included turning off technological communication devices, such as the fax machine, answering machine, and e-mail, for a few hours. Not wearing a watch for a few hours was also recommended. Another suggestion involved developing friendships with people who have nothing to do with psychology as a way to gain perspective on our work. A different and absorbing vacation, even if for a few days, without reading psychology books, should definitely be planned. A similar strategy is to have a regular activity that requires focusing, such as painting, gardening, golf, or tennis; these activities can be a healthy distraction from work.

At the same time, psychologists should be prepared for the worst case scenarios in their practice. For example, dealing with ethics charges may not be as isolated a situation as it was ten years ago. Quoting Bruce Bennett of the APA Insurance Trust, Shapiro (1997b, p. 19) listed a number of strategies psychologists should consider to reduce the risk of a legal action, including do's and don'ts if in fact a psychologist faces a complaint or legal suit involving personal liability. The suggestions are as follows:

1. Identify areas of exposure and take the necessary precaution.
2. In these high-risk areas of practice, take pains to avoid not only impropriety, but also the appearance of impropriety.
3. Purchase personal liability coverage to insure against unintended outcomes.
4. Don't ever try to settle a malpractice suit on your own.
5. Never attempt to call the patient back; you'll only make the situation worse.
6. Don't even think about altering or destroying any documents.
7. Continue to protect the client's confidentiality.

8. Consider retaining your own attorney in addition to the attorney your insurance company has provided.

On the matter of issues involving ethics charges, some boards are more aggressive than others in pursuing disciplinary action. In any case, Shapiro (1997b) quotes Greg Gormanous's recommendation that the psychologist be well schooled in regulatory law and also retain a lawyer with such a specialty. The psychologist should also decide what's in the future professionally; if a commitment to psychological practice remains, he or she may have to accept some sanctions, therapy, or restricted practice (Shapiro, 1997b).

While the above discussion may be enough to scare off the individual who is exploring psychology as a career, it must be understood that the field is not rampant with lawsuits. Nevertheless, some degree of cautious awareness and preparedness is not unreasonable. Every occupation has to be seen in every perspective in order for it, and the professionals who practice in it, to be completely appreciated.

Assisting Impaired Psychologists

While psychology has always maintained in its code of ethics that psychologists should be concerned with colleagues' conduct, it has only been during the last two decades that the problem of impairment among psychologists has been systematically addressed. "Impairment refers to the objective change in a person's professional functioning. An impaired psychologist is one whose work-related performance has diminished in quality" (Schwebel, Skorina, & Schoener, 1994, p. 2). While the term *distressed psychologist* appears in the literature, it is important to know that this refers to a person's subjective state and can or cannot be associated with ineffective professional behavior. Impairment involves a number of conditions, including aggression, sexual abuse, or alcohol and substance abuse. The extent of impairment among psychologists is not well known, but in a study of one state's membership, with 20% of the members responding, one-third reported one or more problems had impaired their professional functioning at some point during their career (Schwebel, 1986). Of that group, 72% were able to resolve their problems with help, while 32% resolved their problems on their own. (Total percentage exceeds 100% because some checked more than one possible outcome.)

Case studies of six well-functioning psychologists and results from a survey of randomly selected licensed psychologists indicated three factors associated with well-functioning psychologists (Coster & Schwebel, 1997). The first is that they maintained self-awareness and performed self-monitoring; such interpersonal skills were engaged in a reasonably quick manner and kept the psychologists alert to transitions and stress. Second, there was considerable support from established peer(s) relationships as well as a spouse or companion and/or family and friends. Finally, they lived a balanced life, such as insuring they took vacations, were active in the community, and engaged in professional development. Recognizing that all psychologists are vulnerable to distress sometime during their career, Coster and Schwebel recommend developing self-awareness, using metacognitive skills, seeking the assistance of a trusted peer when necessary, and consulting with a therapist or a state association's colleague assistance committee. "An ideal set of actions consists of stress-reduction on one's own (e.g., lessening the workload, adding more recreation) combined with personal therapy" (p. 12).

A number of rehabilitative approaches are available, such as peer education, self-help groups, colleague assistance programs, voluntary or confrontative programs, and rehabilitation aftercare programs. Diversion programs, usually for first-time violations of state laws, typically involve a licensing board's being able to stay any disciplinary action pending a psychologist's willingness to participate and successfully complete a rehabilitation program. Preventative programs include graduate school selection and screening and, with students, graduate school socialization (Schwebel et al., 1994). In the latter, graduate departments are encouraged to alert students to the threats of impairment, train them to identify the precursors to impairment, and give them practice in dealing with problems both on their own and with the assistance of peers and others. The objective is to make them aware of their role in monitoring their colleagues' as well as their own behavior. Continuing professional inservice education workshops for faculty and supervisors on topics such as spotting and dealing with vulnerabilities of the supervisee, managing client dependency, and recognizing depression in one's colleagues increases their effectiveness as models for graduate students, interns, and young professionals. Finally, Koocher and Keith-Speigel (1998) provide information on self-help strategies, organizations, books, and autobiographies, and discuss questions dealing with recognizing, assisting, and reporting the impaired psychologist.

Approximately 33 states have some form of colleague assistance programs in place, many of which can be considered the equivalent of employee assistance programs. The programs can refer troubled colleagues for appropriate treatment, and monitor those individuals through the recovery process (Sleek, 1997) or advocate an intervention program designed to rehabilitate practitioners. They usually try to work closely with state licensing boards in that regard. In addition, they can offer continuing education programs dealing with stress management and burnout prevention. Such colleague assistance programs are available to psychologists when they need help recovering from many types of problems, in addition to offering advice on dealing with and avoiding burnout, depression, and other emotional difficulties. Finally, approaching a colleague who needs psychological help or who needs to be questioned about his or her professional skill or behavior can be as uncomfortable and vexing a challenge as confronting ethical issues of one's own. Again, such programs can be of great assistance to the psychologist considering that important but necessary obligation associated with responsible professional behavior.

TELEHEALTH DEVELOPMENTS

The delivery of healthcare services and information using telecommunications technology is already making an impact on the delivery of healthcare. Telehealth includes telephones, fax machines, computers, teleconferencing, interactive video transmissions, and direct links to healthcare instruments and transmission of images. Online services that address mental health issues have grown significantly in the past few years. This growth has the potential to significantly transform healthcare services. Information services discuss problems, and even include problem-solving recommendations. Chat forums provide valuable peer support. While the use of telecommunications is also promoted by some as an adjunct to treatment, counseling or therapy without personal contact with a professional is a questionable practice. However, while such resources truly can empower the consumer, reduce the need for an unnecessary treatment, and provide earlier contact with a qualified provider, the possibility of the opposite is quite true (Trabin, 1997).

Some professionals use the internet for group chat or questions and answers with their clients, to provide specific exercises for in-office clients, and to work with homebound clients (Levenson, 1997). Stamm (1997) has pointed out that the goals of telehealth are to improve access to care, decrease patient movement, offer provider utilization, and improve access to consults. She notes that it is a delivery system that is ideal for isolated areas, such as rural communities, or for populations that have been traditionally underserved. Nickelson (1996) advocates its use in behavioral healthcare in a variety of settings. For example, it has been used in correctional and forensic settings and in isolated rural settings for assessment, diagnosis, and consultation. He points to a 1995 report by the Office of Rural Mental Health Research at the Institute of Mental Health that describes 19 programs that provide behavioral telehealth services to rural areas. These programs provide assessment and consultation to primary care providers. Chavez & DeLeon (1997) report that, while 26 identifiable telehealth programs exist within medical schools, there are none in psychology training programs.

While enthusiasm grows for the many possibilities offered by the electronic revolution, myriad ethical, legal, treatment, and regulatory issues have yet to be identified and/or managed in a manner that keeps pace with the almost daily increase in possibilities. For example, questions of confidentiality and licensure issues related to interstate practice (Sleek, 1995), malpractice liability, and the potential for "cookbook medicine" (Chavez & Deleon 1997) need to be answered.

The APA is acting on a number of recommendations in relation to its ethical code, regulation at the licensure level, involvement at the federal level wherein legislation will develop education of practitioners and graduate students, as well as considering research and insurance questions (Board of Professional Affairs, 1996). Similarly, some professional associations are exploring the possibility of endorsing a standards document to deal with professional conduct in this domain (American Nurses Association, 1998). The National Board for Certified Counselors (NBCC) has already issued its own set of standards (NBCC, 1997).

While telehealth is a completely new service avenue, the opportunity for access to psychological services seems possible with new and developing technology. Unfortunately, pitfalls remain numerous and often are not readily apparent. The individual practitioner is advised to proceed cautiously, with consultation and training from knowledgeable resources.

PUBLIC POLICY

Frank and Callan (1996) define public policy as the "total of all the laws, regulations, court rulings, and administrative procedures that guide this nation in solving socially agreed-upon problems" (p. 23). Public policy can be subgrouped into a number of different areas such as education, defense, economic, health, and welfare policy. Psychology has become involved in the political and social policy-making process, which has increased policy-makers' and society's recognition of the profession and led to significant societal benefits in the area of scientific and clinical knowledge.

Psychology's trend toward the shaping of public policy has stemmed from two divergent viewpoints. The first is related directly to guild issues. If the science of psychology were to remain unknown to the general public, then insurance carriers, elected officials, and the local, state, and federal agencies that maintain service delivery would form policies that could inhibit the practice of professional psychologists. Therefore, public policy advocacy or political activism are vital to the growth of psychological practice. While applied interests have become distinct within the profession, outside the discipline a number of steps have been taken toward professionalism: A specialized body of knowledge has been defined, training programs have been established, and legal recognition and skills in the form of licensure/certification laws are secured.

The opposite viewpoint is a result of a number of psychologists' belief that the profession has moved too far in pursuing guild issues. In practice, this might mean overcharging clients, using professional associates to eliminate competition, perpetuating inequitable social situations for clients, and generally placing their own welfare ahead of those clients and society as a whole. Hence, public policy must address these concerns. Essentially, as the profession matures, so does the weight of professional responsibility.

The public policy movement, for the most part, is not consistent with the background and training of psychologists. To view individuals' psychological problems from a preventive context contrasts with the emphasis of some psychology training programs. This section will discuss public policy first from a political and professional organization format, and second from a political activism and practical perspective for the practicing psychologist.

Social Perspective

In 1974, the Association for the Advancement of Psychology was incorporated as a national lobbying organization. Its purpose was to "promote human welfare through the advancement of the science and profession of psychology by the promotion of the interest of all psychology, by the representation of psychology before public and governmental bodies, by seeking out and contributing to the passage of important social and psychological issues in current legislation and to advocate to the legislature, judicial, executive branches of government the ethical and scientific views of the American psychological community" (Association for the Advancement of Psychology, 1977, p. 1). At the state level, most psychological associations have organized committees, task forces, and communication networks, which have proven effective in influencing legislation and administrative policies. At the national level, psychologists have visibly contributed to public policy through participation in various national advising commissions.

A number of divisions within the APA have sporadically dealt with political policy issues, but usually on a crisis basis. Efforts in terms of systematic or active involvement are limited by change in elected officials, geographical distance, not enough meetings, and fiscal resources. The APA Division of Health Psychology (Division 38) probably has, at least more recently, been the most active in federal policy-making.

The commitment of the APA in the last decade toward public policy formation has been extensive. The *American Psychologist* has regularly devoted sections to the shaping of public policy in such areas as AIDS, gerontology, urban-rural mental health issues, child and adolescent health services, national policy relative to education, and numerous areas of health psychology. In response to the recent increase in insurance rates, public policy advocacy for applied psychology will increase significantly; it is hoped that the result will be greater visibility for the profession and changes for the betterment of society.

Implications for the Psychologist

Lorian and Iscoe (1996) argue for the necessity of organized psychology and for individual practitioners to become involved in public policy. Psychology has remained a popular field of study at the undergraduate and graduate levels, yet legislators are questioning professors' workloads and the cost of higher education. At the same time, political leaders question the relevance of the science of psychology in dealing with major issues such as limited gains in reading and math scores, community violence, and family instability.

Lorian and Iscoe (1996) further point out that psychology has made considerable gains in extended service to individuals, couples, and families, and has reduced longstanding negative attitudes toward the identification and treatment of emotional disorders. In the past several decades, psychologists have clearly established themselves as independent healthcare providers and expanded the range of services available to those experiencing individual, marital, family and other forms of distress. Psychologists have led or participated in the understanding of the etiology of emotional and mental disorders and developed interventions that, while effectively reducing health-care costs, enhance quality of life. Yet, in many respects the quality of our work has not been publicly recognized. Lorian and Iscoe believe that other disciplines have a distinct advantage over psychology in securing public support and public funds; thus, psychology needs to make explicit the advantages it has in responding to both mental health and public welfare needs.

However, this is not another call for public relations, but rather a message that needs to be heard inside the profession. Sampson (1993) has concluded that psychology itself has failed to hear the collective movements (e.g., women, gay men, lesbians, and ethic minorities). These movements have challenged how psychology defines human functioning and speaks to the issue of "voice" within the profession. There is a salient issue that the "haves" and "have-nots" are heard within a context of accommodation rather than a transformational framework.

Lorian and Iscoe (1996) conclude that within psychology there need to be shifts in the collective and individual self-concepts. These shifts will be "considerably easier to make if we understand and adopt the perspective of members of other collective movements" (p. 6) and engage in transformational discourse and collaboration that alter the perspective of everyone rather than a dominant group. Sampson (1993) further asserts that although diverse in their membership, collective movements share "what might be best termed an *identity politics;* a politics based on the particular life experiences of people who seek to be in control of their own identities and subjectivities and claim that the socially dominant groups have denied them this opportunity" (p. 1219; emphasis in original). Involvement in public policy is in part designed to confirm and retain control over one's professional identity and provide valuable insights into understanding oneself.

Practicing psychologists with a public interest should be involved in personal paradigm shifts, resulting in an increased diversity of activities that are more wide-ranging and far-reaching than those in traditional practice. For example, during the 1960s and 1970s, psychologists tended to respond to changing social needs by developing new techniques (e.g., drug counseling, emergency hotlines), by modifying old ones (e.g., nonbiased testing), and learning the culture and language of new and neglected client groups (Simon, 1983). As a result, psychologists with a patient advocacy viewpoint developed practices that met the needs of clients within a social context rather than rigidly adhering to prior training and traditional values of practice.

Essentially, psychologists are already seeing the need to function as client advocates with a commitment to service. As a result, the psychologists in these situations shift from a traditional role to a social role, which entails working with clients at a very practical level when necessary—for example, assisting the client in dealing with the social bureaucracy in terms of a complaint or hearing. This role also calls for active participation in social reforms on a community level. From a conceptual point of view, social action can be seen as a means of reducing psychological problems through the application of professional skills to community problems. As another example, psychologists increasingly are serving on local mental health or other social policy-making boards. From even another point of view, psychologists are providing some services without fee to individuals or social causes, which is consistent with the *Ethical Principles of Psychologists* (APA, 1992a), which clearly specifies that psychologists may willingly contribute a portion of their work with little or no financial return. It is essentially this provision that distinguishes psychology as a humanitarian profession.

Another perspective involving benefits to the practitioner is that the action of involving oneself as a professional in large arenas in everyday practice is an excellent method for battling burnout. Burnout, in effect, leaves the professional feeling uncaring, cynical, and sometimes angry, leading to an indifferent feeling about work. While not an answer for this problem, involvement in national, state, and local causes; listening to the voices that will create personal paradigm shifts; and developing an international perspective through professional associations or otherwise helps the practitioner retain a sense of perspective and growth.

INTERNATIONAL PERSPECTIVES

In the post-World War II decades, the growth of the APA and psychology in general in the United States created the mind-set in psychologists that psychology was largely an American profession, and that there was little to be learned from European, Asian, or developing nations of the world. In truth, psychology has developed as a global profession at a very rapid pace.

In contrast to the rest of the world, the United States still trains a disproportionate number of psychologists relative to the general population and produces the greatest number of publications. However, at the same time, psychology has become firmly established in Europe and most nations of the world. In fact, some countries are experiencing the same kind of explosive growth that has occurred in America over the past 30 years. Rosenzweig (1992) has calculated that there are 75,000 psychologists worldwide engaged in research. Lunt and Poortinga (1996), working from the assumption that 80% of all psychologists work as practitioners rather than in research and teaching, concluded that there are approximately 300,000 practitioners, of whom one-half can be estimated to be in Europe. In Asian countries the discipline is rapidly gaining a foothold (Blowers & Turtle, 1987). In Mexico, Central America, and South America, psychology is offered in most universities and, in comparison to other disciplines, comprises the largest work force providing mental health services. In South Africa, the training of psychologists has continued to flourish in the 1980s and the post-apartheid era.

Psychologists are not only increasing in number all over the world, but the variety and scope of applied psychology has also increased. The training emphasis certainly is reflected in the more traditional areas of specialization, such as school, clinical, and organizational psychology, but there is also an increasing interest in forensic, community, sports, traffic, counseling, and environmental psychology. In Mexico, for example, there is a movement toward the development of community social psychology which is searching for alternative models for community-based efforts in dealing with low income groups in both urban and rural areas (Reid & Aguilar, 1991). However, similar to the United States, there is considerable tension between the academic aspects of psychology and the interests of practitioners. For example, the launching of the journal *The European Psychologist* was delayed for several years because of the tensions between the two groups (Lunt & Poortinga, 1996).

Despite the worldwide expansion of psychology, the books and journals published in the United States continue to dominate the profession. There are two reasons for this: (1) English is the most accessible language, either as a first or second language of most psychologists, and (2) the economic and historical infrastructure of American psychology is the most highly organized in the world in regard to publications and visibility. While publication in American journals may still set the standard, it should be noted that books and journals in America are controlled through the editorial process largely by American psychologists. Ardila (1982) has written persuasively on the negative effect of the dominance by the United States, arguing that the worldview of psychology is limited to a specific culture in a specific moment in history. Smith (1983), however, proposes that the problem is that the "English-only" psychology may be the one that suffers the distinct disadvantage. While psychologists from other countries read English publications, the "English-only" psychologists are isolated from reading the significant publications of other countries. Moghaddam (1996) takes the even stronger view that mainstream training models of Western psychology are ineffective for training psychologists in developing countries. The point is that modern cognitive psychology has ignored culture, and made culture a personal construction of mental processes. The power inequities between nations have created a situation where developing countries depend on the value system of training in the developed countries—which ignores cultural differences.

Sexton (1983) has described American psychology as xenophobic, noting that journals published abroad cite American publications more frequently than vice versa. More than three decades ago, Berlyne (1968) issued the warning while many of the advances in psychology will take place out of the evolve of American psychology, many will also take place outside of America. American psychology has indeed suffered from its ignorance of theories and research other countries. The length of time it took to discover the work of Piaget and Vygotsky are two notable examples. A more current example is the furor around Herrnstein and Murray (1994) relative to the differences in intelligence. Many counter arguments were presented in an excellent book by Simon Biesheuvel, a South African psychologist, in 1943. Moreover, considering the debates in the 1970s over Jensen's (1969) monograph, Biesheuvel's work and position has been largely ignored by American psychology (Lunt & Poortinga, 1996).

Berry, Poortinga, Segall, and Dasen (1992) have suggested that most of psychology is ethnocentric. From a perspective emanating from cross-cultural psychology, they distinguish four levels of ethnocentrism: (a) the use of culturally inappropriate stimuli or items, (b) the use of inappropriate instruments and methods, (c) culture-specific generalizations, and (d) a choice of topics for research and application focused on the perceived needs of one's own society.

Similarly, therapeutic interventions and methods have been dominated by Western paradigms.

Gergen, Gulerce, Lock, and Misra (1996) also have strong reservations about implicit assumptions that (a) there is a universally acceptable conception of psychological science, and (b) all cultures should emulate what is done in North America. Rather than the traditional model of Western colonialism, where experts from developed nations conduct research in developing countries and formulate procedures and interventions to solve their problems, psychology needs to respond to the misgivings of non-American, non-Western, and third-world psychologists about the traditions of American psychology. Psychology must also be less conservative and develop greater cultural sensitivity.

At a practical level, rather than work toward more abstract formulations, the culturally engaged psychologist might help to appraise and intervene in various problems related to health, environment, and psychological problems in terms of the values, beliefs, and motives that are particular to the culture at hand. Such efforts are useful in exploring the unique role of cross-cultural psychology, whereby collaboration across cultures provides the means to deal with problems within a region or developed countries, or developing countries.

Education and Training

There are substantial differences around the globe in regard to university courses and length of training required for qualification as a psychologist. The time required to qualify as a psychologist ranges from four to eight years in different European countries (Newstead, 1994), and the diversity between countries can be summarized by the educational background required to practice.

In some counties the bachelor's degree is the entry level for practice, in others the master's degree is required, and still others require the doctoral degree. Within these parameters there is a great deal of variation. In Central America and South America, for example, universities offer a four- or five-year program leading to the licenciado degree. This degree has no counterparts in other countries. In contrast, in the USSR, the degree equivalent to the Ph.D. is labeled "candidate of psychological sciences." A further degree, "doctor of psychological sciences," is obtained only by a very small percentage of psychologists (Sexton & Hogan, 1992). South Africa requires the master's degree for registration. In fact, despite the the variations in degrees worldwide, the level of training equivalent to the master's degree in the United States provides entry into professional practice. The doctoral degree is the preferred degree for teaching and research, although many master's level psychologists may teach part-time at a university.

Licensing and Certification

There is considerable variation among countries relative to legal recognition of psychologists. Some countries, such as Israel, have strict licensing laws, while others have no form of licensure, or have licensure pending. In some countries licensure is not strictly enforced or even well defined, while still others have a purely voluntary system.

In Europe, only Ireland and Finland have no licensing laws, although some form of registration is projected for the future. In France, a psychology licensing law was passed in 1985 and finally implemented in 1990. In the United Kingdom, there is voluntary registration with the British Psychological Society. In Italy, registration laws were passed in 1989. In Spain, licenses are granted by the universities (similar to the licenciado degree model of Latin America), but requirements for licenses are not clearly established. The rest of Europe has some form of licensure, certification, or registration which provides legal recognition of the profession.

In eastern Europe, Hungary has the only clear legal regulation relative to practice. Romania has a certification exam. Although Greece passed a certification exam requirement in 1979, it has never been implemented. The rest of eastern Europe has no form of licensure.

In Australia, as of 1992, five of the six states require registration in order to practice. In New Zealand, registration is required only for government or specific educational or health-related positions.

In South America and Latin America, Argentina and Brazil have the strictest licensing laws and also seem to have the greatest number of private practitioners. In most other South American countries, the university degree indicates a practitioner who is usually employed in a government agency. Mexico has a system of certification but it is not strictly enforced.

In Africa, Egypt has had a leniently enforced law that regulates the practice of psychology since 1956. Most graduates are employed in civil service positions, and Ph.D.s hold academic positions. South Africa and Zimbabwe have mandatory registration. Private practice is limited in these countries and is traditionally available mainly to the White population. In the past decade, however, considerable efforts by government agencies and universities have extended services to the Black townships with community psychology gradually increasing in importance.

Asian countries appear to have the fewest licensing requirements; India and Hong Kong do not have any requirements. Japan and Pakistan work within their respective psychological associations toward a registration process.

Despite the differences, it appears that licensing and registration have definitely become a global trend. Most countries have moved toward legal recognition; only a few have not made any effort in that direction (Sexton & Hogan, 1992).

International Employment Trends

An interesting and important observation around the world is that, while academic research and training positions are largely male-dominated, the practice of applied psychology is dominated by women. Women are more likely to be employed in clinical work, school psychology, or teaching part-time at the college level. In Europe, 53% of all psychologists are women; in Central and South America, approximately 70% are female. In Asia, however, only 25% are women, with only Hong Kong reporting a greater number of female psychologists (Ribarich & Sexton, 1987).

Ribarich and Sexton (1987) also report that male psychologists exceed female psychologists only in Australia, Canada, Egypt, Japan, Korea, the Netherlands, New Zealand, Norway, South Africa, and the United States. However a decade has passed since the survey and some of the above countries, notably South Africa and the United States, report that a majority of the students are female, indicating that the ratios have changed. In some countries, such as India, Pakistan, and Turkey, females predominate as students, however, in these countries work opportunities are limited.

Employment is clearly an issue in some countries. In Spain, for example, it is difficult upon graduation to secure employment: 25% of the registered 30,000 psychologists are unemployed. Most of the available positions are with government agencies. In Brazil, there are over 60,000 psychologists, most of whom work part-time. In the Netherlands, employment is found in nationally supported regional mental health centers, in contrast to Argentina, where private practice is highly competitive and provides part-time to full-time income, especially in Buenos Aires. It is important to note that in contrast to the United States, in the rest of the world private practice is not the primary mode of delivery of psychological services.

A firm distinction remains between psychology as a science and as a practice. Psychology around the world is largely a practice-driven profession. In many countries, traditional psychoanalysis is the primary mode of practice, followed by systems-oriented approaches, which are particularly strong in Europe and Argentina. Cognitive-behavioral approaches have gained increased importance in the United Kingdom and Israel.

In many countries, economic forces and resources limit the amount of research and publications—indeed, research is a luxury. Even in more established countries in Europe and North America, greater numbers of beginning psychologists are moving into the practice arena. India and the USSR maintain an emphasis on scientific research, although there is considerable nonclinical application in the military and the schools.

The USSR traditionally has been strong in the area of neuropsychology (especially notable are the works of A. R. Luria), both in terms of diagnosis and the etiology of psychoneurological dysfunction. The application of psychology to industrial concerns has also been a historical emphasis. Oleinik (1996) points out that before its disintegration, the Soviet Union had a well-established system for training professional psychologists. Education maintained a rigorous single standard, was free, and employment was guaranteed by filling openings at research institutions, industry, and other organizations. At present, the professional training of psychologists is significantly altered, with the structure of education increasingly being transformed into Western models with diverse specialties. New private institutions now offer specialties in counseling psychology, educational psychology, and other fields. However, rather than intellectual ability, the ability to pay has become the major criterion to entering the field. Moreover, fewer students are interested in psychology because they are no longer guaranteed future job placement. These are difficulties faced by many of the Eastern European countries.

In some countries, educational settings provide the primary means for employment. This is especially the case in Australia, Egypt, Korea, and Pakistan. Oakland and Cunningham (1992) estimated that at least 87,000 psychologists worked in the schools with at least a 4000 rate increase per year. Ezeilo (1992) points out that important differences exist between developed and developing countries, such as Nigeria, where quality university training is problematic due to lack of resources. Another case in point is Guatemala, where the economy has forced universities to use discarded American textbooks that were published in the late 1960s and early 1970s. Despite differences in training and regulation, in most countries of the world psychology is practice-oriented.

Generally speaking, the growth of psychology worldwide over the past the two decades has been phenomenal. In some countries the growth has tripled in the past decade.

The Future of International Psychology

If the psychological community in the United States decides to recognize the significant contributions and potential of the psychology movement worldwide, an international psychology will emerge. This requires an end to relative isolation and a false sense of superiority, and the emergence of the notion that transworld resources are needed to deal with psychological issues and problems. What needs to be created is a dialogue among equals that would result in true collaboration in order to achieve advances in research and practice. However, a major concern is that because psychology is rapidly becoming a practice-oriented profession, the scientific base grounded by research will be eroded.

Based on some of the observations of Sexton and Hogan (1992), a number of trends need to be considered:

1. Psychology is going through a "cognitive" revolution with a decreased emphasis on behaviorism and psychoanalysis.
2. Psychology has found its greatest acceptance in the areas of applied psychology, which continue to develop diverse specializations.
3. Clinical psychology is the dominant specialty, although training is at the nondoctoral level. Increasingly, over the past decade clinical psychology in Australia, Europe, South America, and southern Africa has moved steadily toward sophisticated humanistic and systems approaches in individual, group, and family therapy.
4. Financial support for practitioners has not shown any significant gains.
5. Psychology is in many countries a "young" profession, which places many practitioners at the early stages of their career.
6. Most countries where unemployment is not a major issue have developed to the point where they are able to provide the necessary education and training without the need for students to go outside one's country.
7. Western models for research and training are being questioned as to their relevance for the cultural and political realities of developing countries.

International psychology has become an area of increased activity, where in many countries there already exists a great deal of cross-cultural dialogue. However, in other nations, like the United States, myopic ethnocentrism inhibits growth, while in others geography and/or lack of economic resources makes international participation prohibitive. This dichotomy must be overcome in order to enure an international psychology, which is certainly the future of psychology.

SUMMARY

The professional horizon for the psychologist involves the interplay between personal and professional development within a context of increasingly sophisticated technology. Additionally, the profession must become more flexible in order to meet the needs of a changing society as well as the internationalization of psychology. In essence, the foundation for the future of the profession lies in its ability to appreciate difference, incorporate new ideas, continually search for an ever-evolving identity, and to embrace new technologies to better meet the needs of the public.

References

Academy of Psychological Clinical Science. (1997). Organization Profile. *APS Observer, 10*(1), 42–43.

Ackerman, M. (1995). *Clinician's guide to child custody evaluations.* New York: Wiley.

Akey, D. S. (1983). (Ed.). *Encyclopedia of associations* (17th ed., Vols. 1-2). Detroit, MI: Gale Research.

American Board of Professional Psychology. (1985). *Policies and procedures for the creation of diplomates in professional psychology.* Columbia, MO: Author.

American Board of Professional Psychology. (1996). *Specialty certification in professional psychology.* Columbia, MO: Author.

American College of Physicians, Ad Hoc Committee on Medical Ethics. (1984). Part I: History of medical ethics, the physician and the patient, the physician's relationship to other physicians, the physician and society. *Annals of Internal Medicine, 101,* 129–137.

American Nurses Association, & American Psychological Association. (1998). *Interdisciplinary telehealth standards working group report.* Washington, DC: Author.

American Psychological Association. (1954). *Psychology and its relations with other professions.* Washington, DC: Author.

American Psychological Association. (1958). Committee on relations with psychiatry, 1958 annual report. *American Psychologist, 13,* 761–763.

American Psychological Association. (1977). Standards for providers of psychological services. *American Psychologist, 32,* 495–505.

American Psychological Association. (1981a). Ethical principles of psychologists, revised edition. *American Psychologist, 36,* 639–691.

American Psychological Association. (1981b). Specialty guidelines for the delivery of services by school psychologists. *American Psychologist, 36,* 639, 670–681.

American Psychological Association. (1986). Five-year report of the policy and planning board: 1985. *American Psychologist, 41,* 626–632.

American Psychological Association. (1987a). General guidelines for providers of psychological services. *American Psychologist, 42,* 712–723.

American Psychological Association. (1987b). Model act for state licensure of psychologists. *American Psychologist, 42*(7), 696–703.

American Psychological Association. (1990a). Ethical principles of psychologists (amended June 2, 1989). *American Psychologist, 45,* 390–395.

American Psychological Association. (1990b). *Guidelines for providers of psychological services to ethnic, linguistic and culturally diverse populations*. Washington, DC: Author.

American Psychological Association. (1992a). Ethical principles of psychologists and Code of conduct. *American Psychologist, 47*(12), 633-638, 1597–1611.

American Psychological Association. (1992b). Rules and procedures. *American Psychologist, 47*(12), 1612–1628.

American Psychological Association. (1993a). Record-keeping guidelines. *American Psychologists, 48*(9), 984–986.

American Psychological Association. (1993b). Resolution on lesbian, gay and bisexual youths in the schools. *American Psychologist, 50, 669*.

American Psychological Association. (1994a). Guidelines for child custody evaluations in divorce proceedings. *American Psychologist, 49*(7), 677–680.

American Psychological Association. (1994b). *Guidelines for identifying appropriate supervisors for psychological services in schools*. Washington, DC: Author.

American Psychological Association. (1995a). *Changing gender composition of psychology*. Washington, DC: Author.

American Psychological Association. (1995b). *Education and training beyond the doctoral degree: Proceedings of the APA National Conference on Postdoctoral Educational Training in Psychology*. Washington, DC: Author.

American Psychological Association. (1995c). Guidelines for engaging in contractual provision of psychological services in schools. *American Psychologist, 50*(8), 669.

American Psychological Association. (1996a). *Graduate study in psychology*. Washington, DC: Author.

American Psychological Association. (1996b). *Book 1: Guidelines and principles for accreditation of programs in professional psychology*. Washington, DC: Author.

American Psychological Association. (1996c). Statement on the disclosure of test data. *American Psychologist, 51, 644–648*.

American Psychological Association. (1998a). *Archival description of clinical psychology*. Washington, DC: Author.

American Psychological Association. (1998b). *Archival description of clinical health psychology*. Washington, DC: Author.

American Psychological Association. (1998c). *Archival description of clinical neuropsychology*. Washington, DC: Author.

American Psychological Association. (1998d). *Archival description of counseling psychology*. Washington, DC: Author.

American Psychological Association. (1998e). *Archival description of industrial/organizational psychology*. Washington, DC: Author.

American Psychological Association. (1998f). *Archival description of psychoanalytic psychology*. Washington, DC: Author.

American Psychological Association. (1998g). *Archival description of school psychology*. Washington, DC: Author.

American Psychological Association (1998h). *Graduate study in psychology: 1998 edition*. Washington, DC: Author.

American Psychological Association. (1998i). *Bylaws of the American Psychological Association*. Washington, DC: Author.

American Psychological Association. (1998j). *Guidelines for the evaluation of dementia and age-related cognitive decline*. Washington DC: Author.

American Psychological Association. (1998k). *What practitioners should know about working with older adults*. Washington, DC: Author.

American Psychological Association, Committee on Ethical Standards of Psychology. (1951a). Ethical standards for psychology. *American Psychologist, 6*, 427–452.

American Psychological Association, Committee on Ethical Standards of Psychology. (1951b). Ethical standards for psychology. *American Psychologist, 6*, 626–661.

American Psychological Association, Committee on Legal Issues. (1996). Strategies for private practitioners coping with subpoenas or compelled testimony for client records of test data. *Professional Psychology: Research and Practice, 27*, 245–251.

American Psychological Association, Committee on Professional Practice and Standards (1998). *Guidelines for psychological evaluations in child protection matters*. Washington, DC: Author.

American Psychological Association, Committee on Professional Practice of the Board of Professional Affairs. (1985). *A hospital primer for psychologists*. Washington, DC: Author.

American Psychological Association, Committee on Scientific and Professional Ethics and Conduct. (1969). Guidelines for telephone directory listings:. *American Psychologist, 24*, 70–71.

American Psychological Association, Committee on Scientific and Professional Aims of Psychology. (1967). The scientific and professional aims of psychology. *American Psychologist, 22*, 49–76.

American Psychological Association, Ethics Committee. (1994a). "Take home" tests. *American Psychologist, 49*, 665.

American Psychological Association, Ethics Committee. (1994b). Advertisements and canned columns. *American Psychologist, 49*, 664.

American Psychological Association, Ethics Committee. (1994c). Internship applications and confidential materials. American Psychologist, 49, 664.

American Psychological Association, Ethics Committee. (1994d). Military psychologists and confidentiality. *American Psychologist, 49*, 665.

American Psychological Association, Ethics Committee. (1995a). Limitation on teaching (Standard 6.04). *American Psychologist, 50*, 713.

American Psychological Association, Ethics Committee. (1995b). Referrals and fees (Standard 1.27). *American Psychologist, 50*, 713.

American Psychological Association, Ethics Committee. (1996a). Services by telephone, teleconferencing, and internet. *American Psychologist, 51*, 1285.

American Psychological Association, Ethics Committee. (1996b). Policy on barring resignations during ethics investigations. *American Psychologist, 51*, 1194.

American Psychological Association, Ethics Committee. (1997). Ethics Committee Report, 1996. *American Psychologist, 52*(8), 897–905.

American Psychological Association, Ethics Committee. (1998). Services by Telephone, Teleconferencing, and Internet. *American Psychologist, 53*(8), 979–980.

American Psychological Association, Office of Public Affairs. (n.d.). *Media training for psychologists: A comprehensive guide for interview preparation*. Washington, DC: Author.

American Psychological Association, Practice Directorate. (1992). *Integrated care*. Washington, DC: Author.

American Psychological Association, Practice Directorate. (1995). *State Medicaid reimbursement standards for psychologists*. Washington, DC: Author.

American Psychological Association, Template Task Force. (1995). *Template for developing guidelines: Interventions for Mental disorders and psychosocial aspects of physical disorders*. Washington, DC: Author.

American Psychological Society. (1998). *A decade of commitment to Psychology*. Washington, DC: Author.

Ardila, R. (1982). International psychology. *American Psychologist, 37*, 323–329.

Association for Advancement of Behavior Therapy. (1984). Bylaws of the Association for Advancement of Behavior Therapy. *1984 membership directory*. New York: Author.

Association for the Advancement of Psychology. (1977). *Bylaws of the American Association for the Advancement of Psychology*. Washington DC: Author.

Association for Behavior Analysis. (1985). *Eleventh annual convention program*. Kalamazoo, MI: Author.

Association of Psychology Postdoctoral and Internship Centers & American Psychological Association (1998). *APPI/APA Supply and Demand Conference, 1997*. Washington, DC: Author.

Association of State and Provincial Psychology Boards. (1986). *Handbook of licensing and certification requirements for psychologists in North America*. Washington, DC: Author.

Association of State and Provincial Psychology Boards. (1991). *ASPPB code of conduct*. Montgomery, AL: Author.

Association of State and Provincial Psychology Boards. (1992). *Model act for the licensure of psychologists*. Montgomery, AL: Author.

Association of State and Provincial Psychology Boards. (1996a). *Items from previous examinations*. Montgomery, AL: Author.

Association of State and Provincial Psychology Boards. (1996b). *Regulation of professional psychology: An international resource directory*. Montgomery, AL: Author.

Association of State and Provincial Psychology Boards. (1997). *Information for candidates*. Montgomery, AL: Author.

Association of State and Provincial Psychology Boards. (1998). *Handbook of licensing and certification requirements for psychologists in the U.S. and Canada*. AL: Author.

Bardon, J. I. (1981). A personalized account of the development and status of school psychology. *Journal of School Psychology, 19*, 199-210.

Barlow, D. H., Hayes, S. C., & Nelson, R. O. (1984). *The scientist practitioner*. New York: Pergamon.

Bates et al. v. State Bar of Arizona, 433 U. S. 350 (1977).

Beales, III, J. H. (1980). The economics of regulating the professions. In R. D. Blair & S. Rubin (Eds.), *Regulating the professions* (pp. 125–142). Lexington, MA: Lexington.

Beauchamp, T. L., & Childress, J. F. (1979). *Principles of biomedical ethics*. Oxford: Oxford University.

Beauchamp, T. L., & Childress, J. F. (1994). *Principles of biomedical ethics* (4th ed.). New York: Oxford University.

Bedell, J. R., Hunter, R. H., & Corrigan, P. W. (1997). Current approaches to assessment and treatment of persons with serious mental illness. *Professional Psychology: Research and Practice, 28*, 217–228.

Behnke, S. H., & Hilliard, J. T. (1998). *The essentials of Massachusetts mental health law*. New York: Norton.

Belar, C. D., Bieliaukas, L. A. Larsen, K. G., Mensh, I. N., Poey, K., & Roehlke, H. J. (1989). The National Conference on Internship Training in Psychology. *American Psychologist, 44,* 60–65.

Bennett, B. E., Bryant, B. K., VandenBos, G., & Greenwood, A. (1990). *Professional liability and risk management.* Washington, DC: American Psychological Association.

Bent, R. J. (1982). Multidimensional model for control of private information. *Professional Psychology, 13,* 27–33.

Berlyne, D. E. (1968). American and European psychology. *American Psychologist, 23,* 1091–1093.

Berman, J. S., & Norton, N. C. (1981). Does professional training make a therapist more effective? *Psychological Bulletin, 98,* 401–407.

Bernard, J. L., & Jara, C. S. (1996). The failure of clinical psychology graduate students to apply understood ethical principles. In D. N. Bersoff (Ed.), *Ethical conflicts in psychology* (pp. 67–71). Washington DC: American Psychological Association.

Bernstein, D. A., & Nietzel, M. T. (1980). *Introduction to clinical psychology.* New York: McGraw-Hill.

Berry, J. W., Poortinga, Y. H., Segall, M. H., & Dasen, P. R. (1992). *Cross-cultural psychology: Research and applications.* Cambridge, England: Cambridge University.

Bersoff, D. N. (1982). The legal regulations of school psychology. In C. R. Reynolds & T. Gutkin (Eds.), *The handbook of school psychology* (pp. 1043–1074). New York: Wiley.

Bersoff, D. N. (Ed.). (1995). *Ethical conflicts in psychology.* Washington, DC: American Psychological Association.

Bersoff, D. N. (1996). The virtue of principle ethics. *The Counseling Psychologist, 24*(21), 86–91.

Beuther, L. E., Williams, R. E., Wakefield, P. J., & Entwistle, S. R. (1995). Bridging scientist and practitioner perspectives in clinical psychology. *American Psychologist, 50,* 984–994.

Biesheuvel, S. (1943). *African intelligence.* Johannesburg: South African Institute of Race Relations.

Blau, T. (1984). Psychological tests in the courtroom. *Professional Psychology: Research and Practice, 15,* 176–186.

Blowers, G., & Turtle, A. (Eds.). (1987). *Psychology moving east.* Sydney, Australia: Sydney University.

Board of Professional Affairs Task Force. (1996). *Online psychotherapy and counseling task force report.* Washington, DC: American Psychological Association.

Boice, R., & Myers, P. E. (1987). Which is healthier and happier, academe or private practice? *Professional Psychology: Research and Practice, 18*(5), 526–529.

Brickman, L. B. (Ed). (1985). *Issues and concerns: Graduate education in psychology.* Washington, DC: American Psychological Association.

British Psychological Society. (1998). *General Information about the Society.* Leicester, England: Author.

Broskowski, A. (1991). Current healthcare environments: Why managed care is necessary. *Professional Psychology: Research and Practice, 22,* 6–14.

Buklad, W., & Ginsberg, M. R. (1982). *State law and medical staff privileges for psychologists.* Washington, DC: American Psychological Association, State Association Program.

Burns, S. M., Chemtob, C. M., DeLeon, P. H., & Welch, B. L. (1988). Psychotropic medication: A new technique for psychology? *Psychotherapy 25*, 508–515.

Butler, R. W., & Williams, D. A. (1985). Description of Ohio State Board of Psychology hearings in ethical violations: From 1972 to the present. *Standards for educational and psychological tests and manuals*. Washington, DC: Author.

Butz, M. R. (1994). Psychopharmacology: Psychology's Jurassic Park. *Psychotherapy, 31*, 692–699.

Canadian Psychological Association. (1989). *Practice guidelines for providers of psychological services*. Old Chelsea, PA: Author.

Canadian Psychological Association. (1991a). *Canadian code of ethics for psychologists*. Quebec: Author.

Canadian Psychological Association. (1991b). *Companion manual to the Canadian code of ethics*. Quebec: Author.

Canadian Psychological Association. (1998). *Bylaws*. Ottawa, Ontario: Author.

Canter, M B., Bennett, B. E., Jones, S. E., & Nagy, T. F. (1996). *Ethics for psychologists*. Washington, DC: American Psychological Association.

Capp v. Rank, 51 Cal.3d 1, 793 P.2d 2 (1990).

Carlson, C. I., Tharinger, D. J., Bricklin, P., DeMers, S. T., & Paavola, J. C. (1996). Healthcare reform and psychological practice in the schools. *Professional Psychology: Research and Practice, 27*, 14–23.

Chamberlain, L. (1994). Psychopharmacology: Further adventures in psychology's Jurassic Park. *Psychotherapy Bulletin, 29*, 47–50.

Chavez, N., & DeLeon, P. H. (1997). News from Washington DC: Telehealth—telemedicine. *Professional Psychology: Research and Practice, 28*(3), 203-204.

Child Abuse Prevention, Adoption, and Family Services Act of 1988 (Pub.L. 100-294, 42 U.S.C. §1501 (1988).

Chodorow, N. J. (1989). *Feminism and psychoanalytic theory*. New Haven, CT: Yale University.

Claiborn, W. (1982). The problem of professional incompetence. *Professional Psychology,13*, 153-158.

Claiborn, W. L., Biskin, B. H., & Friedman, L. S. (1982). CHAMPUS and quality assurance. *Professional Psychology, 13*, 40–49.

Clay, R. (1998, May) Psychologists seek to balance cost and quality care decisions. *APA Monitor*, p. 20.

Clay, R. A. (1997, August). Two states move closer to gaining Rx privileges. *APA Monitor*, p. 34.

Cobb, C. T. (1989). Is it time to establish the doctorate entry level? *School Psychology Review, 18*, 16–19.

Colgate, C., Jr. (Ed.). (1983). *National trade and professional associations of the U.S.* (18th annual ed.). Washington, DC: Columbia.

Conoley, J. (1992, August). *2042: A prospective look at school psychology*. Paper presented at the annual meeting of the American Psychological Association, Washington, DC.

Corey, G., Corey, M. S., & Callahan, P. (1988). *Issues and ethics in the helping professions*. Pacific Grove, CA: Brooks/Cole.

Coster, J. S., & Schwebel, M. (1997) Well-functioning in professional practice. *Professional Psychology: Research and Practice, 28*, 5–13.

Council for National Register of Health Service Providers in Psychology. (1985). *National register of health service providers in psychology.* Washington, DC: Author.

Council for the National Register of Health Service Providers in Psychology. (1998). *National register of health service providers in psychology* (16th ed.). Washington, DC: Author.

Council of State Governments. (1952). *Occupational licensing legislation in the states: A study of state licensing legislation licensing the practice of professionals and other occupations.* Chicago: Author.

Crawford, M., & Marecek, J. (1989). Feminist theory, feminist psychology: A bibliography of epistemology, critical analysis, and applications. *Psychology of Women Quarterly, 13,* 479–494.

Cummings, N. A. (1991). Ten ways to spot mismanaged mental health. *Psychotherapy in Private Practice, 9,* 79–81.

Cutts, N. E. (1955). *School psychologists at mid-century.* Washington, DC: American Psychological Association.

Davison, G. C. (1995). A failure of early behavior therapy (circa 1966): Or why I learned to stop worrying and to embrace psychotherapy integration. *Journal of Psychotherapy Integration, 5,* 107–112.

DeLeon, P. H. (1996). Public policy and public service: Our professional duty. In R. Lorion, I. Iscoe, P. H. DeLeon, & G. R. VandenBos (Eds.), *Psychology and public policy: balancing public service and professional need* (pp. 41–55). Washington, DC: American Psychological Association.

DeLeon, P. H., Fox, R. E., & Graham, S. R. (1991). Prescription privileges: Psychology's next frontier. *American Psychologist, 46,* 384–393.

DeLeon, P. H., Pallak, M. S., & Hefferman, J. A. (1982). Hospital healthcare delivery. *American Psychologist, 37,* 1340–1341.

DeLeon, P. H., Sammons, M. T., & Sexton, J. L. (1995). Focusing on society's real needs: Responsibility and prescription privileges? *American Psychologist, 50*(12), 1022–1032.

DeLeon, P. H., & Wiggins, J. G. (1996). Prescription privileges for psychologists. *American Psychologist, 51,* 225–229.

DeMers, S. T., & Bricklin, P. (1995). Legal, professional and financial constraints on the delivery of healthcare services in the schools. *School Psychology Quarterly, 10,* 217–235.

DeNelsky, G. Y. (1991). Prescription privileges for psychologists: The case against. *Professional Psychology: Research and Practice, 22,* 188–193.

DeNelsky, G. Y. (1992). The case against prescription privileges for psychologists. *Psychotherapy in Private Practice, 11,* 15–24.

DeNelsky, G. Y. (1996). The case against prescription privileges for psychologists. *American Psychologist, 51,* 207–211.

Denmark, F. L. (1998). Women and psychology. *American Psychologist, 53,* 465–473.

Department of Defense Appropriation Act of 1976. Pub.L. 94-212, 90 Stat. 153 (1976).

Department of Health, Education, and Welfare, Office of Education, Bureau of Higher and Continuing Education, Division of Eligibility and Agency Evaluation. (1978). *Nationally recognized accrediting agencies and associations.* Washington, DC: Author.

DeSisto, M. J., Harding, C. M., McCormick, R. V., Ashikaga, T., & Brooks, G. W. (1995). The Maine and Vermont three-decade studies of serious mental illness. *British Journal of Psychiatry, 167,* 331–342.

Division 12 Task Force (1995). Training in and dissemination of empirically-validated psychological treatments: Report and recommendations. *The Clinical Psychologist, 48,* 3–23.

Dörken, H. (1979). Workers' compensation: Opening up a major market for psychological practice. *Professional Psychology, 10,* 834–840.

Dörken, H. (1983). Health insurance and third party reimbursement. In B. Sales (Ed.), *The professional psychologist's handbook* (pp. 249–284). New York: Plenum.

Dörken, H. (1990). Malpractice claims experience of psychologists: Policy issues, cost comparisons with psychiatrists and prescription privilege implications. *Professional Psychology: Research and Practice, 21,* 150–152.

Dörken, H., & Rodgers, D. A. (1976). Issues facing professional psychology. In Dörken, H. and Associates, *The professional psychologist today* (pp. 264–292). San Francisco: Jossey-Bass.

Dörken, H., Stapp, J., & VandenBos, G. (1986). Licensed psychologists: A decade of growth. In H. Dörken & Associates (Eds.), *Professional psychology in transition* (pp. 247–282). San Francisco: Jossey Bass.

Dörken, H., & Webb, J. (1980). 1976 Third-party reimbursement experience: An interstate comparison by carrier. *American Psychologist, 35,* 355–363.

Dörken, H., & Webb, J. (1981). Licensed psychologists on the increase, 1974–79. *American Psychologist, 36,* 1419–1426.

Drane, J. F. (1982). Ethics and psychotherapy: A philosophical perspective. In M. Rosenbaum (Ed.), *Ethics and values in psychotherapy* (pp. 15–50). New York: Free Press.

Dupuy, P. (1993). Gender and psychological distress. *Journal of Counseling and Development, 68,* 371–380.

Eberlein, L. (1987). Introducing ethics to beginning psychologists: A problem solving approach. *Professional Psychology: Research and Practice, 18,* 353–359.

Education for All Handicapped Children Act of 1975. Pub.L. 94-142, 20 U.S.C. §1401–1461, (1975).

Education of the Handicapped Act Amendment of 1974. Pub.L. 93-380, §611–621, Stat. 484, 579-587 (1974).

Education of the Handicapped Act Amendments of 1986. Pub.L. 100 Stat. 1145 (1986).

Education of the Handicapped Act Amendments of 1990. Pub.L. 101-476 (1990).

Employee Retirement Income Security Act of 1974. Pub.L. 93-406, 88 Stat. 829 (1974).

Enwright, M. F., Welch, B. L., Newman, R., & Perry, B. M. (1990). The hospital: Psychology's challenge in the 1990s. *American Psychologist, 45,* 1057–1058.

Ezeilo, B. N. (1992). The international school psychology survey: Implications for Africa. *School Psychology International, 13,* 155–161.

Fagan, T. K., & Delugach, F. J. (1985). Literary origins of the term school psychologist. In L. K. Grimeley (Ed.), *Historical perspectives on school psychology* (pp. 14-21). Terre Haute, IN: School of Education, Indiana State University.

Fagan, T. K., & Wise, P. S. (1994). *School psychology: Past, present, and future.* Reading, MA: Addison Wesley.

Family Rights and Privacy Act of 1974. Pub.L. 93-380, 88 Stat. 571 (1974).

Federal Employee Compensation Act of 1974. Pub.L. 93-416, 88 Stat. 1143 (1974).

Federal Employee Health Benefit Act of 1976. Pub.L. 93-363, 88 Stat. 398 (1974).

Fee, practice and managed care survey. (1995, January). *Psychotherapy Finances*, 1–8.

Flexner, A. B. (1915). Is social work a profession? In *Proceedings of the National Conference of Charities and Corrections*. Baltimore, MD: Social Work.

Forman B. D. (1992). Prescription privileges for psychologists: The case against. *Psychotherapy Bulletin, 27*, 14.

Fowler, R. (1998, Spring). APA's letter regarding IDEA. *The School Psychologist, 52*(2), 40–43.

Fox, R. E. (1994). Training professional psychologists for the twenty-first century. *American Psychologist, 49*(3), 200–206.

Fox, R. E., Barclay, A. G., & Rodgers, D. A. (1982). The foundations of professional psychology. *American Psychologist, 37*, 306–312.

Fox, R. E., Schwelitz, F. D., & Barclay, A. 0. (1992). A proposed curriculum for psychopharmacology training for professional psychologists. *Professional Psychology: Research and Practice, 23*, 216–219.

Frank, R. G. (1993). Health-care reform: An introduction. *American Psychologist, 48*, 258–260.

Frank, R. G., & Callan, J. E. (1996). Public policy—a process with a purpose. In R. P. Lorian, I. Iscoe, P. H. DeLeon, & G. R. VandenBos (Eds.), *Psychology and public policy: Balancing public service and professional need* (pp. 23–28). Washington, DC: American Psychological Association.

Frank, R. G., Gluck, J. P., & Buckelew, S. P. (1990). Rehabilitation: Psychology's greatest opportunity? *American Psychologist, 45*, 757–761.

Frankford, D. M., & Konrad, T. R. (1998) Responsive medical professionalism: Integrating education, practice, and community in a market driven era. *Academic Medicine, 73*(2), 138–145.

Freiberg, P. (1998). Closing shop: Steps psychologists should consider when leaving practice. *Monitor, 29*(3), 22.

Gable, R. K. (1983). Malpractice liability of psychologists. In B. Sales (Ed.), *The professional psychologist's handbook* (pp. 457–491). New York: Plenum.

Gergen, K. J., Gulerce, A., Lock, A., & Misra, G. (1996). Psychological science in cultural context. *American Psychologist, 51*(5), 496–503.

Glidewell, J. C., & Livert, D. E. (1992). Confidence in the practice of clinical psychology. *Professional Psychology: Research and Practice, 23*(5), 362–368.

Golann, S. E. (1970). Ethical standards for psychology: Development and revision, 1938–1968. *Annals of the New York Academy of Sciences, 169*, 398–405.

Goldfarb v. Virginia State Bar, 421 U. S. 773 (1975).

Greenson v. Bellah, 146 Cal. Rptr. 535 (Cal App. 1978).

Guess, R. (1991). *The idea of critical theory: Habermus and the Frankfort school*. New York: Cambridge University.

Gutheil, T. G. (1994). Discussion of Lazarus's "How certain boundaries and ethics diminish therapeutic effectiveness." *Ethics and Behavior, 4*, 295–298.

Haas, L . J., & Malouf, J. L. (1989). *Keeping up the good work: A practitioner's guide to mental health ethics*. Sarasota, FL: Professional Resource Exchange.

Haas, L . J., & Malouf, J. L. (1995). *Keeping up the good work: A practitioner's guide to mental health ethics* (2nd ed.). Sarasota, FL: Professional Resource Exchange.

Halderman v. Pennhurst State School and Hospital, 446 F Supp. 1295 (E.D. pa. 1977), 451 F Supp. 223 (F.D. pa. 1978), modified 612 F 2'd. 84 (3d Cir. 1979).

Halderman v. Pennhurst, 451 U.S. 1 (1981).

Hall, J. E. (1997). The executive officer's desk. *Register Report, 23*(2), 2, 12–13.

Hannay, H. J., Bieliauskas, L. A., Crosson, V. A., Hammeke, T. A., Hamsher, K., & Koffler, S. P. (in press). Proceedings: The Houston Conference on Specialty Education and Training in Clinical Neuropsychology. *Archives of Clinical Neuropsychology.*

Harding, S. (1986). *The science question in feminism.* Ithaca, NY: Cornell University.

Hare-Mustin, R. T., & Marecek, J. (Eds.). (1990). *Making a difference: Psychology and the construction of gender.* New Haven, CT: Yale University.

Hatfield, A. B., & Lefley, H. P. (1993). *Surviving mental illness.* New York: Guilford.

Hayes, S. C., & Heiby, B. (1996). Psychology's drug problem: Do we need to fix or should we just say no? *American Psychologist, 51,* 198–206.

Health Care Quality Improvement Act of 1986. Pub.L. 99-660, 42 U.S.C. §11111, et seq. (1986). with Disabilities Education Act of 1990, Pub.L. 101-76, 104 Stat. 1103 (1990).

Hellman, I. D., Morrison, T. L., & Abrahamowitz, S. I. (1987). Therapist experience and stresses of psychotherapeutic work. *Psychotherapy, 24*(2), 171–177.

Henderson, P. H., Clarke, J. E., & Reynolds, M. A. (1996). *Summary report 1995: Doctorate recipients from United States universities.* Washington, DC: National Academy.

Herman, F. C. (1993). Reassessing predictors of therapist competence. *Journal of Counseling and Development, 72,* 29–32.

Herring, L. (1997). How do professional schools' graduates compare with traditional graduates? *APS Observer, 10*(5), 7–9.

Herrnstein, R. J., & Murray, C. (1994). *The bell curve: Intelligence and class structure in American life.* New York: Free

Higuchi, S. A. (1994). Recent managed-care legislation and legal issues. In R. L. Lowman & R. J. Resnick (Eds.), *The mental health professional's guide to managed care* (pp. 83–118). Washington, DC: American Psychological Association.

Hoch, E. L., Ross, A. O., & Wender, C. L. (1966) *Professional preparation of clinical psychologists.* Washington, DC: American Psychological Association.

Hogan, D. B. (1979). *The regulation of psychotherapists, Volumes I–IV.* Cambridge, MA: Ballinger.

Howard, A., Pion, G. M., Gottfredson, G. D., Flattau, P. E., Oskamp, S., Pfafflin, S. M., Bray, D. W., & Burnstein, A. G. (1986). The changing face of American psychology: A report from the Committee on Employment and Human Resources. *American Psychologist, 41,* 1311–1317.

Hughes, E. C. (1963). *Professions.* Daedalus, 63, 655–668.

Human Factors Society. (1985). *The Human Factors Society should be your professional society.* Santa Monica, CA: Author.

Humphreys, K. (1996). Clinical psychologists as psychotherapists: History, future and alternatives. *American Psychologist, 51,* 190–197.

International Society for Developmental Psychology. (1986). *Application for membership.* Denver, CO: Author.

J. R. v. Parham, 422 U.S. 584(1979). (412 F Supp. 112 [M.D. Ga. 19761]). (Reversed and remanded).

Jackson, J. H., & Pryzwansky, W. B. (1987). An audit-evaluation of a school psychological services unit utilizing professional standards: An example. *Professional School Psychology, 2*, 125–134.

Jaffee v. Redmond, 135 L.Ed.2d. 337 (S. Ct. 1996).

Jensen, A. R. (1969). How much can we boost IQ and scholastic achievement? *Harvard Educational Review, 39*, 1–123.

Johnson, D. L. (Ed.). (1990). *Service needs of the seriously mentally ill: Training implications for psychology*. Washington, DC: American Psychological Association.

Joint Commission for Accreditation of Healthcare Organizations. (1991). *Accreditation manual for hospitals*. Chicago: Author.

Joint Commission for Accreditation of Hospitals. (1983). *Accreditation manual for hospitals*. Chicago: Accreditation Council for Hospitals.

Jordon, A. E., & Meara, N. M (1995). Ethics and the professional practice of psychologists: The role of virtues and principles. *Professional Psychology: Research and Practice, 21*, 107–114.

Kalichman, S. C. (1993). *Mandated reporting of suspected child abuse*. Washington, DC: American Psychological Association.

Karras, D., & Berry, K. (1985). Custody evaluations: A critical review. *Professional Psychology: Research and Practice, 16*, 76–85.

Kaslow, F. (Ed.). (1990). *Voices in family psychology* (Vols. 1, 2). Newbury Park, CA: Sage.

Keller, E. F. (1985). *Reflections on gender and science*. New Haven: Yale University.

Kiesler, C. A. (1981). Mental health policy: Research site for social psychology. In L. Wheeler (Ed.), *Review of personality and social psychology* (Vol. 2, pp. 273–295). Beverly Hills, CA: Sage.

Kiesler, C. A. (1982a). Mental hospitals and alternative care: Noninstitutionalization as potential public policy for mental patients. *American Psychologist, 37*, 349–360.

Kiesler, C. A. (1982b). Public and professional myths about mental hospitalization: An empirical reassessment of policy-related beliefs. *American Psychologist, 37*, 1323–1337.

Kiesler, C. A., & Morton, T. L. (1996). Psychology and public policy in the "healthcare revolution." In R. Lorion, I. Iscoe, P. H. DeLeon, & G. R. VandenBos (Eds.), *Psychology and public policy: Balancing public service and professional need* (pp. 57–79). Washington, DC: American Psychological Association.

Kilburg, R. R., & Pallak, M. S. (1978). A professional's guide to the American Psychological Association. In B. D. Sales (Ed.), *The professional psychologist's handbook* (pp. 157–184). New York: Plenum.

Kingsbury, S. J. (1992). Some effects of prescribing privileges. *American Psychologist, 47*, 426–427.

Kitchner, K. S. (1984). Intuition, critical evaluation and ethical principles: The foundation for ethical decisions in counseling psychology. *The Counseling Psychologist, 12*, 43–55.

Knapp, S. J., & Vandercreek, L. (1982). Tarasoff: Five years later. *Professional Psychology: Research and Practice, 13*, 511–516.

Knapp, S. J., Vandercreek, L., & Zirkel, P. (1985). Legal research techniques: What the psychologist needs to know. *Professional Psychology: Research and Practice, 16*, 363.

Kobocow, B., McGuire, J. M., & Blau, B. I. (1983). The influence of confidentiality conditions on self-disclosure of early adolescents. *Professional Psychology: Research and Practice, 14,* 435–443.

Kohout, J. L. (1991, August). *Changes in supply: Women in psychology.* Paper presented at the 99th Annual Convention of the American Psychological Association, San Francisco.

Koocher, G. P. (1979). Credentialing in psychology: Close encounters with competence? *American Psychologist, 34,* 696–702.

Koocher, G. P. (1983). Ethical and professional standards in psychology. In B. D. Sales (Ed.), *The professional psychologist's handbook* (pp. 77–109). New York: Plenum.

Koocher, G. P. (1994). APA and FTC: New adventures in consumer protection. *American Psychologist, 49,* 322–328.

Koocher, G. P., Goodman, G. S., White, C. S., Friedrich, W. N., Sivan, A. B., & Reynolds, C. R. (1995). Psychological science and the use of anatomically detailed dolls in child sexual-abuse assessments. *Psychological Bulletin, 118*(2), 199–222.

Koocher, G. P., & Keith-Speigel, P. (1998). *Ethics in psychology: Professional standards and cases* (2nd ed.). New York: Oxford University.

Koocher, G. P., Norcross, J. C., & Hill, III, S. S. (1998). *Psychologists' desk reference.* New York: Oxford University.

Korman, M. (Ed.). (1974a). *Levels and patterns of professional training in psychology: Conference proceedings, Vail, Colorado, July 25–30, 1973.* Washington, DC: American Psychological Association.

Korman, M. (1974b). National conference on levels and patterns of professional training in psychology. *American Psychologist, 29,* 441–449.

Korman, M. (Ed.). (1976). *Levels and patterns of professional training in psychology.* Washington, DC: American Psychological Association.

Kubiszyn, T., & Oddone, A. (1998, Winter). IDEA Update: (1) URGENT-Immediate grassroots response needed to practice threat under IDEA, and (2) Clarification issued on short term suspensions. *The School Psychologist, 52*(1), 4–5, 27.

Kultgen, J. (1988). *Ethics and professionalism.* Philadelphia: University of Pennsylvania Press.

L'Abate, L. (1990). Reconciling personal and professional priorities. In F. Kaslow (Ed.), *Voices in family psychology* (Vol. 1, pp. 139–155). Newbury Park, CA: Sage.

Lambert, N. M. (1993). Historical perspective on school psychology as a scientist-practitioner specialization in school psychology. *Journal of School Psychology, 13,* 163–193.

Larry P. v. Riles, 343 T. Supp. 1306 (N.D. Cal. 1982) Aff'd 502 F 2d. 963(9th Cir. 1974); 495 F. Supp. 926 (N.D. Cal. 1979).

Larsen, K. G., Belar, C. D., Bieliaukas, L. B., Klepac, R. K., Stigall, T. T., & Zimet, C. N. (Eds.). (1993). *Proceedings: National conference on postdoctoral training in professional psychology.* Washington, DC: Association of Postdoctoral and Internship Centers.

Lazarus, A. A. (1976). *Multimodal behavior therapy.* New York: Springer.

Lazarus, A. A. (1994). How certain boundaries and ethics diminish therapeutic effectiveness. *Ethics and Behavior, 4,* 253–261.

Lessard v. Schmidt, 349 F Supp. 1078 (E.D. Wis. 1972). Vacated and remanded on procedural grounds, 414 U.S. 473, new j'mt. entered, 379 F Supp. 1376 (E.D. Wjs. 1974). Vacated and remanded, 421 U.S. 957 (1975), prior j'mt. reinstated, 413 F Supp. 1318 (E.D. Wis. 1976).

Levenson, D. (1997, September). Online counseling: Opportunity and risk. *NASW News*, p. 3.

Lorian, R. P., & Iscoe, I. (1996). Introduction: Reshaping our views of our field. In R. P. Lorian, I. Iscoe, P. H. DeLeon, & G. R. VandenBos (Eds.), *Psychology and public policy: Balancing public service and professional need* (pp. 1–19). Washington, DC: American Psychological Association.

Lunt, I., & Poortinga, Y. H. (1996). Internationalizing psychology: The case of Europe. *American Psychologist, 52*, 504–508.

Manderscheid, R. W., & Sonnenschein, M. A. (Eds.). (1996). *Mental health United States, 1996.* Rockville, MD: Substance Abuse and Mental Health Services Administration, Center for Mental Health Services.

Martin, S. (1997, October). Partnerships are key to psychologists' success. *APA Monitor*, p. 28.

Massoth, N. A., McGrath, R. B., Bianchi, C., & Singer, J. (1990). Psychologists' attitudes toward prescription privileges. *Professional Psychology: Research and Practice, 21*(2), 147–149.

Matarazzo, J. D. (1998). President's message. *American Psychological Foundation, 15,* 2–5.

Mathew v. Nelson, 461 F Supp. 707 (N.D. III, 1978).

Maurer, C., & Sheets, T. E. (1998). *Encyclopedia of associations.* Detroit, MI: Gale Research.

May, W. T., & Belsky, J. (1992). Response to "Prescription privileges: Psychology's next frontier?" or The siren call: Should psychologists medicate? *American Psychologist, 47,* 427.

McCarrick, A. K, Rosenstein, M. J., Milazzo-Sayre, L. J., & Manderscheid, R. W. (1988). National trends in use of psychotherapy in psychiatric inpatient settings. *Hospital and Community Psychiatry, 39*(8), 835–841.

McClellan, III., J. E. (1985). *Science reorganized: Scientific societies in the eighteenth century.* New York: Columbia University.

Meara, N. M., Schmidt, L. D., & Day, J. D. (1996). Principles and virtues: A foundation for ethical decisions, policies and character. *The Counseling Psychologist, 24*(1), 4–77.

Mental Health Parity Act of 1996, Pub.L. 104-204 Tit. VII, 110 Stat. 2874 (1996).

Metropolitan Life Insurance Company v. Commonwealth of Massachusetts, 471 U.S. 724 (1985).

Michigan United Food and Commercial v. Baerwaldt, 767 F 2d. 308 (1985).

Miller, I. J. (1996). Managed care is harmful to outpatient mental health services: A call for accountability. *Professional Psychology, 27,* 349–363.

Miller, J. B. (1976). *Toward a new psychology of women.* New York: Beacon.

Millon, T. (1983). The DSM III: An insider's perspective. *American Psychologist, 38,* 804–814.

Moghaddam, F. M. (1996). Training for developing-world psychologists: Can it be better than psychology? In S. C. Carr, & J. F. Schumaker (Eds.), *Psychology and the developing world.* Westport, CT: Praeger.

Moore, W. E. (1970). *The professional: Roles and rules.* New York: Russell Sage.

Morse, S. J. (1983). Mental health law. In B. Sales (Ed.), *The professional psychologist's handbook* (pp. 339–442). New York: Plenum.

Moyer, D. M. (1995). An opposing view on prescription privileges for psychologists. *Professional Psychology: Research and Practice, 26,* 586–590.

Murphy, M. J., DeBernardo, C. R., & Shoemaker, W. E. (1998). Impact of managed care on independent practice and professional ethics: A survey of independent practitioners. *Professional Psychology: Research and Practice, 29,* 45–51.

Musto, D. F. (1975). Whatever happened to "community mental health?" *The Public Interest, 39,* 53–79.

Myers, R. A., & Rosen, G. A. (1986, August). *Research digest: The examination for professional practice in psychology.* Montgomery, AL: American Association of State Psychology Boards.

Nagle, R. J. (1987). Ethics training in school psychology. *Professional School Psychology, 2*(3), 163–171.

Napoli, D. S. (1981). *Architects of adjustment: The history of the psychological profession in the United States.* Port Washington, NY: Kennikat.

Nathan, P. E. (1998). Practice guidelines: Not yet ideal. *American Psychologist, 53,* 290–299.

National Association of School Psychologists. (1994). *Standards for training and field placement programs in school psychology.* Washington, DC: Author.

National Association of School Psychologists. (1997). *Leadership directory.* Bethesda, MD: Author.

National Board for Certified Counselors. (1997). *Standards for the ethical practice of web counseling.* Washington, DC: Author.

Nelson, P. D. (1995, April). *Education and training of psychologists: History and emerging trends.* Paper presented at the First International Congress on Licensure, Certification, and Credentialing of Psychologists, New Orleans.

Newman, R., & Bricklin, P. P. (1991). Parameters on managed mental healthcare: Legal, ethical, and professional guidelines. *Professional Psychology: Research and Practice, 22,* 26–35.

Newstead, S. (1994). The psychology curriculum and the training of psychologists in Europe. *News from EFPPA, 8,* p. 4.

Nickelson, D. W. (1996). Biohavioral telehealth: Emerging practice, research, and policy opportunities. *Behavioral Sciences and the Law, 14,* 443–447.

Norcross, J. C., Hanych, J. M., & Terranova, R. D. (1996). Graduate study in psychology: 1992–1993. *American Psychologist, 51*(6), 631–643.

Nuremberg Code of Ethics in Medical Research. (1964). *Science, 143,* 553.

Oakland, T. D., & Cunningham, J. J. (1992). A survey of school psychology in developed and developing countries. *School Psychology International,13,* 99–129.

Oleinik, Y. N. (1996). Russian psychology at present: Trends and paradoxes. In V. A. Koltsova, Y. N. Oleinik, A. R. Gilgen, & C. K. Gilge (Eds.), *Post-Soviet perspectives on Russian psychology.* Westport, CT: Greenwood.

Omnibus Budget Reconciliation Act, Pub.L. 100-239, 103 Stat 2106. (1989).

O'Neil, J. (1986). Male sex role conflicts, sexism, and masculinity: Psychological implications for men, women, and the counseling psychologist. *The Counseling Psychologist, 9,* 61–80.

Paavola, J. C., Cobb, C., Illback, R. J., Joseph, H. M., Jr., Torruella, A., & Talley, R. C. (1995). *Comprehensive and coordinated psychological services for children: A call for service integration.* Washington, DC: American Psychological Association.

Pachman, J. S. (1996). The dawn of a revolution in mental health. *American Psychologist, 51*, 213–215.

Packard, R. (1997). An *interactive model for ethical decision-making*. Paper presented at the Division 17 New Fellows Program at the annual meeting of the American Psychological Association Convention, Chicago, IL.

PASE v. Hannon. No. 74-C-3586 (N.D. 111.1980).

Perry, N. W. (1979). Why clinical psychology does not need alternative training models. *American Psychologist, 34*, 603–611.

Peterson, C. (1996). Common problem areas and their causes in disciplinary actions. In L. J. Bass, S. T. DeMers, J. R. P. Ogloff, C. Peterson, J. L. Pettifor, R. P. Reaves, T. Retfalvi, N. P. Simon, C. Sinclair, & R. M. Tipton. *Professional conduct and discipline in psychology* (pp. 71–89). Washington, DC: American Psychological Association.

Peterson, D. R. (1976). Need for the doctor of psychology degree in professional psychology. *American Psychologist, 31*, 792–798.

Peterson, D. R. (1985). Twenty years of practitioner training in psychology. *American Psychologist, 40*, 441–551.

Peterson, D. R. (1995). *The reflective educator*. American Psychologist, 50, 975–983.

Peterson, R. L., Abrams, J. C., Peterson, D. R., & Stricker, G. (1997). The National Council of Schools and Programs of Professional Psychology Educational Model. *Professional Psychology: Research and Practice, 28*(4), 373–386.

Peterson, R. L., Peterson, D. R., & Abrams, J. C. (1994, December 12). *Draft of the standards for education in professional psychology: The integrated resolutions of the conferences of the National Council of Schools and Programs of Professional Psychology.*

Pettifor, J. L. (1996). Maintaining professional conduct in daily practice. In L. J. Bass, S. T. DeMers, J. R. P. Ogloff, C. Peterson, J. L. Pettifor, R. P. Reaves, T. Retfalvi, N. P. Simon, C. Sinclair, & R. M. Tipton. *Professional conduct and discipline in psychology* (pp. 51-70). Washington, DC: American Psychological Association.

Phelps, R., Eisman, E. J., & Kohout, J. (1998). Psychological practice and managed care: Results of the CAPP practitioner survey. *Professional Psychology: Research and Practice, 29*, 31–36.

Platman, S. R. (Coordinator). (1978). *Report of the task panel on deinstitutionalization, rehabilitation and long-term care* (President's Commission on Mental Health, Vol. 2). Washington, DC: U.S. Government Printing Office.

Poland, S. (1995). Best practices in suicide prevention. In A. Thomas & J. Grimes (Eds.), *Best practices in school psychology: III* (pp. 459–468). Washington, DC: National Association of School Psychologists.

Pope, K. S. (1993). Licensing disciplinary actions for psychologists who have been sexually involved with a client: Some information about offenders. *Professional Psychology: Research and Practice, 24*, 374–377.

Pope, K. S., & Brown, L. S. (1996). *Recovered memories of abuse: Assessment, therapy, forensics*. Washington, DC: American Psychological Association.

Pope, K. S., & Vetter, V. A. (1992). Ethical dilemmas encountered by members of the American Psychological Association: A national survey. *American Psychologist, 47*, 397–411.

Pope K. S., & Tabachnick, B. G. (1993). Therapist's anger, hate, fear, and sexual feelings: National survey of therapist responses, client characteristics, critical events, formal complaints, and training. *Professional Psychology: Research and Practice, 24*, 142–152.

Pope, K. S., Tabachnick, B. G., & Keith-Spiegel, P. (1987). Ethics of practice: The beliefs and behaviors of psychologists as therapists. *American Psychologist, 42*, 993–1006.

Practitioner survey results offer comprehensive view of psychology practice. (1996, June). *APA Practice Directorate Practitioner Update, 4*, 1–4.

Pryzwansky, W. B. (1993). Ethical consultation practice. In. J. E. Zins, T. R. Kratochwill, & S. N. Elliott (Eds.), *Handbook of consultation services for children* (pp. 329–348). San Francisco: Jossey-Bass.

Pryzwansky, W. B. (1998). Individual psychologist: Specialty board certification. In A. S. Bellack & M. Hersen (Series Eds.) & A. N. Weins (Vol. Ed.), *Comprehensive clinical psychology: Vol. 2. Professional issues.* (pp. 231–240). New York: Elsevier.

Pryzwansky, W. B. (1999). Accreditation and credentialing systems in school psychology. In C. Reynolds & T. Gutkin (Eds.), *Handbook of school psychology* (3rd ed., pp. 1145–1158). NY: Wiley.

Pryzwansky, W. G., & Wenger, R. D. (1979). The role of state school psychology organizations in the promotion of professional organizations in the promotion of professional ethics. *Psychology in the Schools, 16*, 540–543.

Psychology Examining Committee of California. (1979, March). Disciplinary guidelines. *AASPB Newsletter, 15*, 38–43.

Psychonomic Society. (1997). *About the psychonomic society*. TX: Author.

Raimy, V. C. (Ed.). (1950). *Training in clinical psychology*. Englewood Cliffs, NJ: Prentice-Hall.

Rappaport, J. (1977). *Community psychology*. New York: Holt, Rinehart & Winston.

Reaves, R. (1993, February 20). *Disciplinary data bank: 8th midwinter meeting.* Montgomery, AL: Association of State and Provincial Psychology Boards.

Rehabilitation Act of 1973, 29 U.S.C. §794, (1973).

Reid, A., & Aguilar, M. A. (1991). Constructing community social psychology in Mexico: Latin America [special issue]. *Applied Psychology: An International Review, 40*, 181–199.

Resnick, R. J. (1983). Medicaid, direct provider recognition. *Professional Psychology: Research and Practice, 74*, 368–373.

Resnick, R. J. (1985). The case against the blues: The Virginia challenge. *American Psychologist, 40*, 975–983.

Ribarich, M. T., & Sexton, V. S. (1987). The status of women psychologists around the world: Report of a survey. *International Psychologist, 29*, 22–24.

Rodriguez, A. R. (1983). Psychological and psychiatric peer review at CHAMPUS. *American Psychologist, 38*, 941–947.

Roe, A., Gustad, J., W., Moore, B. W., Ross, S., & Skodak, M. (Eds.). (1959). *Graduate education in psychology*. Washington, D.C.: American Psychological Association.

Rose, H. (1983). Hand, brain, and heart: A feminist epistemology for the natural sciences. *Signs, 9*, 73–90.

Rosen, C. E. (1977). Why clients relinquish their rights to privacy under sign-away pressures. *Professional Psychology, 8*, 17–24.

Rosenzweig, M. R. (1992). Resources for psychological science around the world. In M. R. Rosenzweig (Ed.), *International psychological science: Progress, problems and prospects* (pp. 17–74). Washington, DC: American Psychological Association.

Rubin, S. (1980). The legal web of professional regulation. In R. D. Blair & S. Rubin (Eds.), *Regulating the professions* (pp. 20–60). Lexington, MA: Lexington.

Saccuzzo, D. P., & Kaplan, R. M. (1984). *Clinical psychology*. Boston: Allyn & Bacon.

Saeman, H. (1992). What price prescription privileges? *Psychotherapy in Private Practice, 11*, 9–13.

Sales, B. D. (Ed.). (1983). *The professional psychologist's handbook*. New York: Plenum.

Sammons, M. T., Meredith, J. M., & Sexton, J. L. (1996). Basic science training in psychopharmacology: How much is enough? *American Psychologist, 51*, 230–234.

Sammons, M. T., & Olmedo, E. (1997). The prescription privileges agenda in 1997: Forward progress, future goals. *Professional Psychology: Research and Practice, 28*, 507–508.

Sampson, E. E. (1993). Identity politics: Challenges to psychology's understanding. *American Psychologist, 48*, 1219–1230.

Sanford, F. H. (1951). Annual report of the executive secretary. *American Psychology, 6*, 664–670.

Sarason, S. B. (1982). *The culture of the school and the problem of change* (2nd ed.). Boston: Allyn & Bacon.

Sarason, S. B. (1996). *Revisiting the culture of the school and the problem of change*. New York: Teachers College Press.

Saunders, T. R. (1992a). Psychopharmacology: Decisions, decisions. *Psychotherapy Bulletin, 27*, 29–30.

Saunders, T. R. (1992b). Some conceptual issues linking pharmacotherapy and psychotherapy. *Psychotherapy Bulletin, 27*, 22–23.

Schwebel, M. (1986, Summer). Task force report survey about impaired psychologists. *New Jersey Psychologist*, 17–19.

Schwebel, M., Skorina, J. K., & Schoener, G. (1994). *Assisting impaired psychologists* (Rev. ed.). Washington, DC: American Psychological Association.

Seppa, N. (1997, April). First prescription program at university is launched. *APA Monitor*, p. 37.

Sexton, V. S. (1983). *Is American psychology xenophobic?* Presidential address at the annual meeting of the eastern psychological association, Baltimore, MD.

Sexton, V. S., & Hogan, J. D. (Eds.). (1992). *International psychology: Views from around the world*. Lincoln, NE: University of Nebraska.

Shakow, D. (Ed.). (1947). *Recommended graduate training program in clinical psychology*. Washington DC: American Psychological Association.

Shapiro, A. E., & Wiggins, J. G. (1994). A Psy.D. degree for every practitioner. *American Psychologist, 49*, 207–210.

Shapiro, B. (1997a, October). Have you been taking your own advice lately? *APA Monitor*, p. 19.

Shapiro, B. (1997b, October). Practitioners must prepare for the worst-case scenario. *APA Monitor*, p. 19.

Shaw, B. F., & Dobson, K. S. (1988). Competency judgements in the training and evaluations of psychotherapists. *Journal of Consulting and Clinical psychology, 56*, 666–672.

Sheldon, G. F. (1995). The health work force, generalism, and the social contract. *Annals of Surgery, 222*(3), 215–228.

Sherry, P. (1991). Ethical issues in the conduct of supervision. *Counseling Psychologist, 19*, 566–584.

Simon, G. (1983). Psychology, professional practice, and the public interest. In B. Sales (Ed.), *The professional psychologist's handbook*. New York: Plenum.

Sinclair, C. (1993). Codes of ethics and standards of practice. In Dobson, D. K. & Dobson, D. (Eds.), *Professional psychology in Canada*. Toronto: Hogrefe & Huber.

Sinclair, C. (1996). A comparison of codes of professional conduct and ethics. In L. J. Bass, S. T. DeMers, J. R. P. Ogloff, C. Peterson, J. L. Pettifor, R. P. Reaves, T. Retfalvi, N. P. Simon, C. Sinclair, & R. M. Tipton (Eds.), *Professional Conduct and Discipline in Psychology* (pp. 53–70). Washington, DC: American Psychological Association.

Sinclair, C., Simon, N. P., & Pettifor, J. L. (1996). The history of ethical codes and licensure. In L. J. Bass, S. T. DeMers, J. R. P. Ogloff, C. Peterson, J. L. Pettifor, R. P. Reaves, T. Retfalvi, N. P. Simon, C. Sinclair, & R. M. Tipton (Eds.), *Professional Conduct and Discipline in Psychology* (pp. 1–15). Washington, DC: American Psychological Association.

Sleek, S. (1997, October). Psychologists help one another survive in today's challenging times. *APA Monitor*, p. 20.

Sleek, S. (1995, November). Online therapy services raise ethical questions. *APA Monitor*, p. XX.

Smith, R. J. (1983). On Ardila's "international psychology" [Comment]. *American Psychologist, 38*, 122–123.

Smyer, M. A., Balster, R. L., Egli, D., Johnson, D. L., Kilbey, M. M., Seppa, N. (1997, February). More states pursuing prescription privileges: 1997 promises to be a year many states will vote on psychologists' right to prescribe. *APA Monitor*, p. 31.

Sonne, J. L. (1994). Multiple relationships: Does the new ethics code answer the right questions? *Professional Psychology: Research and Practice, 25*, 336–343.

Stamm, B. H. (1997, November,). *Improving caregiving with telecommunications technology*. Presentation to the American Psychological Association Board of Professional Affairs Institute on Telehealth, Washington, DC.

Stedman, J. M. (1997). What we know about pre-doctoral internship training? *American Psychologist, 28*, 475–485.

Stewart, A. E., & Stewart, E. A. (1998). Trends in postdoctoral education: Requirements for licensure and training opportunities. *Professional Psychology: Research and Practice, 29*, 273–283.

Stigall, T. (1983). Licensing and certification. In B. Sales (Ed.), *The professional psychologist's handbook* (pp. 285–337). New York: Plenum.

Stone, G. C. (Ed.). (1983). Proceedings of the National Conference on Education and Training in Health Psychology. *Health Psychology, 2*(5, suppl.), 153.

Strasburger, L. H., Jorgenson, L., & Sutherland, P. (1992). The prevention of psychotherapist sexual misconduct: Avoiding the slippery slope. *American Journal of Psychotherapy, 45*, 544–555.

Stricker, G., & Trierweiler, S. J. (1995). The local clinical scientist. *American Psychologist, 50*, 995–1002.

Stromberg, C. D., Haggarty, D. J., Liebenluft, R. F., McMillian, M. H., Mishkin, B., Rubin, B. L., & Trilling, H. R. (1988). *The psychologist's legal handbook*. Washington, DC: The Council for the National Register of Health Service Providers in Psychology.

Stromberg, C., Ratcliff, R., & Mathews-Schuetze, J. (1997, January). Surviving the minefield of managed care contracting. In J. E. Hall (Ed.), *The psychologist's legal update* (pp. 1–19) Washington, DC: National Register of Health Service Providers in Psychology.

Stromberg, C., Schneider, J., & Joondeph, B. (1993, August). Dealing with potentially dangerous patients. *The psychologist's legal update (2)*. Washington, DC: The Council for the National Register of Health Service Providers in Psychology.

Strother, C. R. (Ed.). (1956). *Psychology and mental health*. Washington, DC: American Psychological Association.

Talbot, J. A. (1981). The national plan for the chronically mentally ill: A programmatic analysis. *Hospital and Community Psychiatry, 32*, 699–713.

Talley, R. C., & Short, R. J. (1995). *Reforming America's schools: Psychology's role: A report to the nation's educators*. Washington, DC: American Psychological Association Center for Psychology in Schools and Education.

Talley, R. C., & Short, R. J. (1996). Social reforms and the future of school practice: Implications for American psychology. *Professional Psychology: Research and Practice, 27*, 5–13.

Tannen, D. (1990). *You just don't understand: Men and women in conversation*. New York: William Morrow.

Tarasoff v. Regents of the University of California, 551 P 2d, 334, Cal. Rptr. 14 (1976).

Tocqueville, Alexis de. (1966). *Democracy in America*. J. P. Mayer, & M. Lerner (Eds.), G. Lawrence (Transl.). New York: Harper & Row. (Original work published 1835)

Torrey, E. F., Bowler, A., Taylor, E., & Gottesman, I. (1994). *Schizophrenia and manic-depressive disorder*. New York: Basic.

Trabin, T. (1997, December). Dialogue: Will online services for consumer self-help improve behavioral healthcare? *Behavioral Healthcare Tomorrow, 32–38*.

Tymchuk, A. J. (1981). Ethical decision making and psychological treatment. *Journal of Psychiatric Treatment and Evaluation, 3*, 507–513.

United States Code. Washington, DC: United States Government Printing Office.

United States Code Annotated. St. Paul, MN: West.

United States Code Appendix, Title 28, Federal Rules of Evidence 702.

United States Code Service. Rochester, NY: Lawyers' Cooperative Publishing Co.

United States Department of Commerce, Bureau of the Census. (1997). *Statistical abstract of the United States* (p. 383). Washington, DC: Author.

VandeCreek, L., & Knapp, S. (1993). *Tarasoff and beyond: Legal and clinical considerations in the treatment of life-endangering patients*. Sarasota, FL: Professional Resource.

VandenBos, G. R. (1996). U.S. mental health policy: Proactive evolution in the midst of healthcare reform. In R. Lorion, I. Iscoe, P. H. DeLeon, & G. R. VandenBos (Eds.), *Psychology and public policy: Balancing public service and professional need* (pp. 305–322). Washington, DC: American Psychological Association.

Vasquez, M. J. T. (1992). Psychologist as clinical supervisor: Promoting ethical practice. *Professional Psychology: Research and Practice, 23*, 196–202.

Voorde, C. (1986). Association for the advancement of psychology. *American Psychology, 41*, 709–711.

Watson, N, Caddy, G. R., Johnson, J. H., & Rimm, D. C. (1981). Standards in the education of professional psychologists: The resolutions of the Conference of Virginia Beach, *American Psychologist, 36*, 514–519.

Welfel, E. R., & Lipsitz, N. E. (1984). The ethical behavior of professional psychologists: A cultural analysis of the research. *The Conseling Psychologist, 12*(3), 31–42.

Wendt, R. (1996). The gender of the therapist: Resource or handicap? In M. Andolfi, C. Angelo, & M. de Nichilo (Eds.), *Sentimenti e sistemi (Systems and feelings)* (pp. 103–114). Milan Italy: Cortina.

Wendt, R. (1997). Fallimento, perdita ed emarginazione: Verso la trasformazione del-terapeuta e l'onestà terapeutica (Failure, loss, and marginalization: Toward therapist trans-formation and therapeutic honesty). *Terapia Familiare (54), Luglio-lissue: Famiglie a rischio in una società multietnica. (Family Therapy [54], Special issue: Families in a multicultural society)*, 75–84.

Wendt, R., & Dupuy, P. (1995). Toward creativity in the family therapist: The evolv-ing influences of family, gender, and personal crisis. In J. van Lawick, & M. Marjet (Eds.), *Gender and beyond* (pp. 321–330). Hemsteed, The Netherlands: LS Books.

Whitaker, C. (1989). *Midnight musings of a family therapist.* New York: Norton.

White v. North Carolina Board of Practicing Psychologists, 388 S. E. 2d 148 (N. C. App. 1990).

Wicherski, M., & Kohout, J. (1997). *1995 doctorate employment survey.* Washington, DC: American Psychological Association.

Wiens, A. N. (1993). Post-doctoral education—training for specialty practice. *American Psychologist, 48,* 415–422.

Wiens, A. N., & Baum, C. G. (1995). Characteristics of current postdoctoral pro-grams. In American Psychological Association, *Education and training beyond the doctoral degree* (pp. 27–46). Washington, DC: American Psychological Association.

Wiggins, J. G. (1992). The case for prescription privileges for psychologists. *Psychotherapy in Private Practice, 11,* 3–8.

Wiggins, J. G. (1993). National healthcare reform: Implications for psychotherapy and psychopharmacology. *Psychotherapy Bulletin, 28,* 24–26.

Wilensky, H. L. (1964). The professionalization of everyone. *The American Journal of Sociology, LXX(2),* 137–158.

Youngberg v. Romero, 102 5. Ct. 2452 (1982).

Yu, L. M., Rinaldi, S. A., Templer, D. I., Colbert, L. A., Siscoe, K., & Van Patten, K. (1997). Score on the examination for professional practice in psychology as a function of attributes of clinical psychology graduate programs. *Psychological Science, 8(5),* 340–350.

Zaro, J. S., Batchelor, W. F., Ginsberg, M. R., & Pallak, M. S. (1982). Psychology and JACH: Reflections on a decade of struggle. *American Psychologist, 37,* 1342–1349.

Appendix

Ethical Principles of Psychologists and Code of Conduct

CONTENTS

Effective date December 1, 1992. Copyright © 1992 by the American Psychological Association. Reprinted with permission.

INTRODUCTION

The American Psychological Association's (APA's) Ethical Principles of Psychologists and Code of Conduct (hereinafter referred to as the Ethics Code) consists of an Introduction, a Preamble, six General Principles (A-F), and specific Ethical Standards. The Introduction discusses the intent, organization, procedural considerations, and scope of application of the Ethics Code. The Preamble and General Principles are aspirational goals to guide psychologists toward the highest ideals of psychology. Although the Preamble and General Principles are not themselves enforceable rules, they should be considered by psychologists in arriving at an ethical course of action and may be considered by ethics bodies in interpreting the Ethical Standards. The Ethical Standards set forth enforceable rules for conduct as psychologists. Most of the Ethical Standards are written broadly, in order to apply to psychologists in varied roles, although the application of an Ethical Standard may vary depending on the context. The Ethical Standards are not exhaustive. The fact that a given conduct is not specifically addressed by the Ethics Code does not mean that it is necessarily either ethical or unethical.

Membership in the APA commits members to adhere to the APA Ethics Code and to the rules and procedures used to implement it. Psychologists and students, whether or not they are APA members, should be aware that the Ethics Code may be applied to them by state psychology boards, courts, or other public bodies.

This Ethics Code applies only to psychologists' work-related activities, that is, activities that are part of the psychologists' scientific and professional functions or that are psychological in nature. It includes the clinical or counseling practice of psychology, research, teaching, supervision of trainees, development of assessment instruments, conducting assessments, educational counseling, organizational consulting, social intervention, administration, and other activities as well. These work-related activities can be distinguished from the purely private conduct of a psychologist, which ordinarily is not within the purview of the Ethics Code.

The Ethics Code is intended to provide standards of professional conduct that can be applied by the APA and by other bodies that choose to adopt them. Whether or not a psychologist has violated the Ethics Code does not by itself determine whether he or she is legally liable in a court action, whether a contract is enforceable, or whether other legal consequences occur. These results are based on legal rather than ethical rules. However, compliance with or violation of the Ethics Code may be admissible as evidence in some legal proceedings, depending on the circumstances.

In the process of making decisions regarding their professional behavior, psychologists must consider this Ethics Code, in addition to applicable laws and psychology board regulations. If the Ethics Code establishes a higher standard of conduct than is required by law, psychologists must meet the higher ethical standard. If the Ethics Code standard appears to conflict with the requirements of law, then psychologists make known their commitment to the Ethics Code and take steps to resolve the conflict in a responsible manner. If neither law nor the Ethics Code resolves an issue, psychologists should consider other professional materials* and the dictates of their own conscience, as well as seek consultation with others within the field when this is practical.

The procedures for filing, investigating, and resolving complaints of unethical conduct are described in the current Rules and Procedures of the APA Ethics Committee. The

---

*Professional materials that are most helpful in this regard are guidelines and standards that have been adopted or endorsed by professional psychological organizations. Such guidelines and standards, whether adopted by the American Psychological Association (APA) or its Divisions, are not enforceable as such by this Ethics Code, but are of educative value to psychologists, courts, and professional bodies. Such materials include, but are not limited to, the APA's *General Guidelines for Providers of Psychological Services* (1987), *Specialty Guidelines for the delivery of Services by Clinical Psychologists, Counseling Psychologists, Industrial/Organizations Psychologists, and School Psy-*

actions that APA may take for violations of the Ethics Code include actions such as reprimand, censure, termination of APA membership, and referral of the matter to other bodies. Complainants who seek remedies such as monetary damages in alleging ethical violations by a psychologist must resort to private negotiation, administrative bodies, or the courts. Actions that violate the Ethics Code may lead to the imposition of sanctions on a psychologist by bodies other than APA, including state psychological associations, other professional groups, psychology boards, other state or federal agencies, and payors for health services. In addition to actions for violation of the Ethics Code, the APA Bylaws provide that APA may take action against a member after his or her conviction of a felony, expulsion or suspension from an affiliated state psychological association, or suspension or loss of licensure.

PREAMBLE

Psychologists work to develop a valid and reliable body of scientific knowledge based on research. They may apply that knowledge to human behavior in a variety of contexts. In doing so, they perform many roles, such as researcher, educator, diagnostician, therapist, supervisor, consultant, administrator, social interventionist, and expert witness. Their goal is to broaden knowledge of behavior and, where appropriate, to apply it pragmatically to improve the condition of both the individual and society. Psychologists respect the central importance of freedom of inquiry and expression in research, teaching, and publication. They also strive to help the public in developing informed judgments and choices concerning human behavior. This Ethics Code provides a common set of values upon which psychologists build their professional and scientific work.

This Code is intended to provide both the general principles and the decision rules to cover most situations encountered by psychologists. It has as its primary goal the welfare and protection of the individuals and groups with whom psychologists work. It is the individual responsibility of each psychologist to aspire to the highest possible standards of conduct. Psychologists respect and protect human and civil rights, and do not knowingly participate in or condone unfair discriminatory practices.

The development of a dynamic set of ethical standards for a psychologist's work-related conduct requires a personal commitment to a lifelong effort to act ethically; to encourage ethical behavior by students, supervisees, employees, and colleagues, as appropriate; and to consult with others, as needed, concerning ethical problems. Each psychologist supplements, but does not violate, the Ethics Code's values and rules on the basis of guidance drawn from personal values, culture, and experience.

GENERAL PRINCIPLES

Principle A: Competence

Psychologists strive to maintain high standards of competence in their work. They recognize the boundaries of their particular competencies and the limitations of their expertise. They provide only those services and use only those techniques for which they are qualified by education, training, or experience. Psychologists are cognizant of the fact that the competencies required in serving, teaching, and/or studying groups of people vary with the distinctive characteristics of those groups. In those areas in which recognized

chologists (1981), *Guidelines for Computer Based Tests and Interpretations* (1987), *Standards for Educational and Psychological Testing* (1985), *Ethical Principles in the Conduct of Research With Human Participants* (1982), *Guidelines for Ethical Conduct in the Care and Use of Animals* (1986), *Guidelines for Providers of Psychological Services to Ethnic, Linguistic, and Culturally Diverse Populations* (1990), and *Publication Manual of the American Psychological Association* (3rd ed., 1983). Materials not adopted by APA as a whole include the APA Division 41 (Forensic Psychology)/ American Psychology–Law Society's *Specialty Guidelines for Forensic Psychologists* (1991).

professional standards do not yet exist, psychologists exercise careful judgment and take appropriate precautions to protect the welfare of those with whom they work. They maintain knowledge of relevant scientific and professional information related to the services they render, and they recognize the need for ongoing education. Psychologists make appropriate use of scientific, professional, technical, and administrative resources.

Principle B: Integrity

Psychologists seek to promote integrity in the science, teaching, and practice of psychology. In these activities psychologists are honest, fair, and respectful of others. In describing or reporting their qualifications, services, products, fees, research, or teaching, they do not make statements that are false, misleading, or deceptive. Psychologists strive to be aware of their own belief systems, values, needs, and limitations and the effect of these on their work. To the extent feasible, they attempt to clarify for relevant parties the roles they are performing and to function appropriately in accordance with those roles. Psychologists avoid improper and potentially harmful dual relationships.

Principle C: Professional and Scientific Responsibility

Psychologists uphold professional standards of conduct, clarify their professional roles and obligations, accept appropriate responsibility for their behavior, and adapt their methods to the needs of different populations. Psychologists consult with, refer to, or cooperate with other professionals and institutions to the extent needed to serve the best interests of their patients, clients, or other recipients of their services. Psychologists' moral standards and conduct are personal matters to the same degree as is true for any other person, except as psychologists' conduct may compromise their professional responsibilities or reduce the public's trust in psychology and psychologists. Psychologists are concerned about the ethical compliance of their colleagues' scientific and professional conduct. When appropriate, they consult with colleagues in order to prevent or avoid unethical conduct.

Principle D: Respect for People's Rights and Dignity

Psychologists accord appropriate respect to the fundamental rights, dignity, and worth of all people. They respect the rights of individuals to privacy, confidentiality, self-determination, and autonomy, mindful that legal and other obligations may lead to inconsistency and conflict with the exercise of these rights. Psychologists are aware of cultural, individual, and role differences, including those due to age, gender, race, ethnicity, national origin, religion, sexual orientation, disability, language, and socioeconomic status. Psychologists try to eliminate the effect on their work of biases based on those factors, and they do not knowingly participate in or condone unfair discriminatory practices.

Principle E: Concern for Others' Welfare

Psychologists seek to contribute to the welfare of those with whom they interact professionally. In their professional actions, psychologists weigh the welfare and rights of their patients or clients, students, supervisees, human research participants, and other affected persons, and the welfare of animal subjects of research. When conflicts occur among psychologists' obligations or concerns, they attempt to resolve these conflicts and to perform their roles in a responsible fashion that avoids or minimizes harm. Psychologists are sensitive to real and ascribed differences in power between themselves and others, and they do not exploit or mislead other people during or after professional relationships.

Principle F: Social Responsibility

Psychologists are aware of their professional and scientific responsibilities to the community and the society in which they work and live. They apply and make public their knowledge of psychology in order to contribute to human welfare. Psychologists are concerned about and work to mitigate the causes of human suffering. When undertaking research, they strive to advance human welfare and the science of psychology. Psychologists try to avoid misuse of their work. Psychologists comply with the law and encourage the development of law and social policy that serve the interests of their patients and clients and the public. They are encouraged to contribute a portion of their professional time for little or no personal advantage.

ETHICAL STANDARDS

1. General Standards

These General Standards are potentially applicable to the professional and scientific activities of all psychologists.

1.01 Applicability of the Ethics Code.

The activity of a psychologist subject to the Ethics Code may be reviewed under these Ethical Standards only if the activity is part of his or her work-related functions or the activity is psychological in nature. Personal activities having no connection to or effect on psychological roles are not subject to the Ethics Code.

1.02 Relationship of Ethics and Law.

If psychologists' ethical responsibilities conflict with law, psychologists make known their commitment to the Ethics Code and take steps to resolve the conflict in a responsible manner.

1.03 Professional and Scientific Relationship.

Psychologists provide diagnostic, therapeutic, teaching, research, supervisory, consultative, or other psychological services only in the context of a defined professional or scientific relationship or role. (See also Standards 2.01, Evaluation, Diagnosis, and Interventions in Professional Context, and 7.02, Forensic Assessments.)

1.04 Boundaries of Competence.

(a) Psychologists provide services, teach, and conduct research only within the boundaries of their competence, based on their education, training, supervised experience, or appropriate professional experience.

(b) Psychologists provide services, teach, or conduct research in new areas or involving new techniques only after first undertaking appropriate study, training, supervision, and/or consultation from persons who are competent in those areas or techniques.

(c) In those emerging areas in which generally recognized standards for preparatory training do not yet exist, psychologists nevertheless take reasonable steps to ensure the competence of their work and to protect patients, clients, students, research participants, and others from harm.

1.05 Maintaining Expertise.

Psychologists who engage in assessment, therapy, teaching, research, organizational consulting, or other professional activities maintain a reasonable level of awareness of current scientific and professional information in their fields of activity, and undertake ongoing efforts to maintain competence in the skills they use.

1.06 Basis for Scientific and Professional Judgments.

Psychologists rely on scientifically and professionally derived knowledge when making scientific or professional judgments or when engaging in scholarly or professional endeavors.

1.07 Describing the Nature and Results of Psychological Services.

(a) When psychologists provide assessment, evaluation, treatment, counseling, supervision, teaching, consultation, research, or other psychological services to an individual, a group, or an organization, they provide, using language that is reasonably understandable to the recipient of those services, appropriate information beforehand about the nature of such services and appropriate information later about results and conclusions. (See also Standard 2.09, Explaining Assessment Results.)

(b) If psychologists will be precluded by law or by organizational roles from providing such information to particular individuals or groups, they so inform those individuals or groups at the outset of the service.

1.08 Human Differences.

Where differences of age, gender, race, ethnicity, national origin, religion, sexual orientation, disability, language, or socioeconomic status significantly affect psychologists' work concerning particular individuals or groups, psychologists obtain the training, experience, consultation, or supervision necessary to ensure the competence of their services, or they make appropriate referrals.

1.09 Respecting Others.

In their work-related activities, psychologists respect the rights of others to hold values, attitudes, and opinions that differ from their own.

1.10 Nondiscrimination.

In their work-related activities, psychologists do not engage in unfair discrimination based on age, gender, race, ethnicity, national origin, religion, sexual orientation, disability, socio-economic status, or any basis proscribed by law.

1.11 Sexual Harassment.

(a) Psychologists do not engage in sexual harassment. Sexual harassment is sexual solicitation, physical advances, or verbal or nonverbal conduct that is sexual in nature, that occurs in connection with the psychologist's activities or roles as a psychologist, and that either: (1) is unwelcome, is offensive, or creates a hostile workplace environment, and the psychologist knows or is told this; or (2) is sufficiently severe or intense to be abusive to a reasonable person in the context. Sexual harassment can consist of a single intense or severe act or of multiple persistent or pervasive acts.

(b) Psychologists accord sexual-harassment complainants and respondents dignity and respect. Psychologists do not participate in denying a person academic admittance or advancement, employment, tenure, or promotion, based solely upon their having made, or their being the subject of, sexual harassment charges. This does not preclude taking action based upon the outcome of such proceedings or consideration of other appropriate information.

1.12 Other Harassment.

Psychologists do not knowingly engage in behavior that is harassing or demeaning to persons with whom they interact in their work based on factors such as those persons' age, gender, race, ethnicity, national origin, religion, sexual orientation, disability, language, or socioeconomic status.

1.13 Personal Problems and Conflicts.

(a) Psychologists recognize that their personal problems and conflicts may interfere with their effectiveness. Accordingly, they refrain from undertaking an activity when they know or should know that their personal problems are likely to lead to harm to a patient, client, colleague, student, research participant, or other person to whom they may owe a professional or scientific obligation.

(b) In addition, psychologists have an obligation to be alert to signs of, and to obtain assistance for, their personal problems at an early stage, in order to prevent significantly impaired performance.

(c) When psychologists become aware of personal problems that may interfere with their performing work-related duties adequately, they take appropriate measures, such as obtaining professional consultation or assistance, and determine whether they should limit, suspend, or terminate their work-related duties.

1.14 Avoiding Harm.
Psychologists take reasonable steps to avoid harming their patients or clients, research participants, students, and others with whom they work, and to minimize harm where it is foreseeable and unavoidable.

1.15 Misuse of Psychologists' Influence.
Because psychologists' scientific and professional judgments and actions may affect the lives of others, they are alert to and guard against personal, financial, social, organizational, or political factors that might lead to misuse of their influence.

1.16 Misuse of Psychologists' Work.
(a) Psychologists do not participate in activities in which it appears likely that their skills or data will be misused by others, unless corrective mechanisms are available. (See also Standard 7.04, Truthfulness and Candor.)
(b) If psychologists learn of misuse or misrepresentation of their work, they take reasonable steps to correct or minimize the misuse or misrepresentation.

1.17 Multiple Relationships.
(a) In many communities and situations, it may not be feasible or reasonable for psychologists to avoid social or other nonprofessional contacts with persons such as patients, clients, students, supervisees, or research participants. Psychologists must always be sensitive to the potential harmful effects of other contacts on their work and on those persons with whom they deal. A psychologist refrains from entering into or promising another personal, scientific, professional, financial, or other relationship with such persons if it appears likely that such a relationship reasonably might impair the psychologist's objectivity or otherwise interfere with the psychologist's effectively performing his or her functions as a psychologist, or might harm or exploit the other party.
(b) Likewise, whenever feasible, a psychologist refrains from taking on professional or scientific obligations when pre-existing relationships would create a risk of such harm.
(c) If a psychologist finds that, due to unforeseen factors, a potentially harmful multiple relationship has arisen, the psychologist attempts to resolve it with due regard for the best interests of the affected person and maximal compliance with the Ethics Code.

1.18 Barter (With Patients or Clients).
Psychologists ordinarily refrain from accepting goods, services, or other nonmonetary remuneration from patients or clients in return for psychological services because such arrangements create inherent potential for conflicts, exploitation, and distortion of the professional relationship. A psychologist may participate in bartering only if (1) it is not clinically contraindicated, and (2) the relationship is not exploitative. (See also Standards 1.17, Multiple Relationships, and 1.25, Fees and Financial Arrangements.)

1.19 Exploitative Relationships.
(a) Psychologists do not exploit persons over whom they have supervisory, evaluative, or other authority such as students, supervisees, employees, research participants, and clients or patients. (See also Standards 4.05-4.07 regarding sexual involvement with clients or patients.)
(b) Psychologists do not engage in sexual relationships with students or supervisees in training over whom the psychologist has evaluative or direct authority, because such relationships are so likely to impair judgment or be exploitative.

1.20 Consultations and Referrals.
(a) Psychologists arrange for appropriate consultations and referrals based principally on the best interests of their patients or clients, with appropriate consent, and subject to other relevant considerations, including applicable law and contractual obligations. (See also Standards 5.01, Discussing the Limits of Confidentiality, and 5.06, Consultations.)

(b) When indicated and professionally appropriate, psychologists cooperate with other professionals in order to serve their patients or clients effectively and appropriately.

(c) Psychologists' referral practices are consistent with law.

1.21 Third-Party Requests for Services.

(a) When a psychologist agrees to provide services to a person or entity at the request of a third party, the psychologist clarifies to the extent feasible, at the outset of the service, the nature of the relationship with each party. This clarification includes the role of the psychologist (such as therapist, organizational consultant, diagnostician, or expert witness), the probable uses of the services provided or the information obtained, and the fact that there may be limits to confidentiality.

(b) If there is a foreseeable risk of the psychologist's being called upon to perform conflicting roles because of the involvement of a third party, the psychologist clarifies the nature and direction of his or her responsibilities, keeps all parties appropriately informed as matters develop, and resolves the situation in accordance with this Ethics Code.

1.22 Delegation to and Supervision of Subordinates.

(a) Psychologists delegate to their employees, supervisees, and research assistants only those responsibilities that such persons can reasonably be expected to perform competently, on the basis of their education, training, or experience, either independently or with the level of supervision being provided.

(b) Psychologists provide proper training and supervision to their employees or supervisees and take reasonable steps to see that such persons perform services responsibly, competently, and ethically.

(c) If institutional policies, procedures, or practices prevent fulfillment of this obligation, psychologists attempt to modify their role or to correct the situation to the extent feasible.

1.23 Documentation of Professional and Scientific Work.

(a) Psychologists appropriately document their professional and scientific work in order to facilitate provision of services later by them or by other professionals, to ensure accountability, and to meet other requirements of institutions or the law.

(b) When psychologists have reason to believe that records of their professional services will be used in legal proceedings involving recipients of or participants in their work, they have a responsibility to create and maintain documentation in the kind of detail and quality that would be consistent with reasonable scrutiny in an adjudicative forum. (See also Standard 7.01, Professionalism, under Forensic Activities.)

1.24 Records and Data.

Psychologists create, maintain, disseminate, store, retain, and dispose of records and data relating to their research, practice, and other work in accordance with law and in a manner that permits compliance with the requirements of this Ethics Code. (See also Standard 5.04, Maintenance of Records.)

1.25 Fees and Financial Arrangements.

(a) As early as is feasible in a professional or scientific relationship, the psychologist and the patient, client, or other appropriate recipient of psychological services reach an agreement specifying the compensation and the billing arrangements.

(b) Psychologists do not exploit recipients of services or payors with respect to fees.

(c) Psychologists' fee practices are consistent with law.

(d) Psychologists do not misrepresent their fees.

(e) If limitations to services can be anticipated because of limitations in financing, this is discussed with the patient, client, or other appropriate recipient of services as early as is feasible. (See also Standard 4.08, Interruption of Services.)

(f) If the patient, client, or other recipient of services does not pay for services as agreed, and if the psychologist wishes to use collection agencies or legal measures to collect the fees, the psychologist first informs the person that such measures will be taken and provides that person an opportunity to make prompt payment. (See also Standard 5.11, Withholding Records for Nonpayment.)

1.26 Accuracy in Reports to Payors and Funding Sources.
In their reports to payors for services or sources of research funding, psychologists accurately state the nature of the research or service provided, the fees or charges, and where applicable, the identity of the provider, the findings, and the diagnosis. (See also Standard 5.05, Disclosures.)

1.27 Referrals and Fees.
When a psychologist pays, receives payment from, or divides fees with another professional other than in an employer-employee relationship, the payment to each is based on the services (clinical, consultative, administrative, or other) provided and is not based on the referral itself.

2. Evaluation, Assessment, or Intervention

2.01 Evaluation, Diagnosis, and Interventions in Professional Context.
(a) Psychologists perform evaluations, diagnostic services, or interventions only within the context of a defined professional relationship. (See also Standards 1.03, Professional and Scientific Relationship.)
(b) Psychologists' assessments, recommendations, reports, and psychological diagnostic or evaluative statements are based on information and techniques (including personal interviews of the individual when appropriate) sufficient to provide appropriate substantiation for their findings. (See also Standard 7.02, Forensic Assessments.)

2.02 Competence and Appropriate Use of Assessments and Interventions.
(a) Psychologists who develop, administer, score, interpret, or use psychological assessment techniques, interviews, tests, or instruments do so in a manner and for purposes that are appropriate in light of the research on or evidence of the usefulness and proper application of the techniques.
(b) Psychologists refrain from misuse of assessment techniques, interventions, results, and interpretations and take reasonable steps to prevent others from misusing the information these techniques provide. This includes refraining from releasing raw test results or raw data to persons, other than to patients or clients as appropriate, who are not qualified to use such information. (See also Standards 1.02, Relationship of Ethics and Law, and 1.04, Boundaries of Competence.)

2.03 Test Construction.
Psychologists who develop and conduct research with tests and other assessment techniques use scientific procedures and current professional knowledge for test design, standardization, validation, reduction or elimination of bias, and recommendations for use.

2.04 Use of Assessment in General and With Special Populations.
(a) Psychologists who perform interventions or administer, score, interpret, or use assessment techniques are familiar with the reliability, validation, and related standardization or outcome studies of, and proper applications and uses of, the techniques they use.
(b) Psychologists recognize limits to the certainty with which diagnoses, judgments, or predictions can be made about individuals.
(c) Psychologists attempt to identify situations in which particular interventions or assessment techniques or norms may not be applicable or may require adjustment in administration or interpretation because of factors such as individuals' gender, age, race, ethnicity, national origin, religion, sexual orientation, disability, language, or socioeconomic status.

2.05 Interpreting Assessment Results.
When interpreting assessment results, including automated interpretations, psychologists

take into account the various test factors and characteristics of the person being assessed that might affect psychologists' judgments or reduce the accuracy of their interpretations. They indicate any significant reservations they have about the accuracy or limitations of their interpretations.

2.06 Unqualified Persons.

Psychologists do not promote the use of psychological assessment techniques by unqualified persons. (See also Standard 1.22, Delegation to and Supervision of Subordinates.)

2.07 Obsolete Tests and Outdated Test Results.

(a) Psychologists do not base their assessment or intervention decisions or recommendations on data or test results that are outdated for the current purpose.

(b) Similarly, psychologists do not base such decisions or recommendations on tests and measures that are obsolete and not useful for the current purpose.

2.08 Test Scoring and Interpretation Services.

(a) Psychologists who offer assessment or scoring procedures to other professionals accurately describe the purpose, norms, validity, reliability, and applications of the procedures and any special qualifications applicable to their use.

(b) Psychologists select scoring and interpretation services (including automated services) on the basis of evidence of the validity of the program and procedures as well as on other appropriate considerations.

(c) Psychologists retain appropriate responsibility for the appropriate application, interpretation, and use of assessment instruments, whether they score and interpret such tests themselves or use automated or other services.

2.09 Explaining Assessment Results.

Unless the nature of the relationship is clearly explained to the person being assessed in advance and precludes provision of an explanation of results (such as in some organizational consulting, pre-employment or security screenings, and forensic evaluations), psychologists ensure that an explanation of the results is provided using language that is reasonably understandable to the person assessed or to another legally authorized person on behalf of the client. Regardless of whether the scoring and interpretation are done by the psychologist, by assistants, or by automated or other outside services, psychologists take reasonable steps to ensure that appropriate explanations of results are given.

2.10 Maintaining Test Security.

Psychologists make reasonable efforts to maintain the integrity and security of tests and other assessment techniques consistent with law, contractual obligations, and in a manner that permits compliance with the requirements of this Ethics Code. (See also Standard 1.02, Relationship of Ethics and Law.)

3. Advertising and Other Public Statements

3.01 Definition of Public Statements.

Psychologists comply with this Ethics Code in public statements relating to their professional services, products, or publications or to the field of psychology. Public statements include but are not limited to paid or unpaid advertising, brochures, printed matter, directory listings, personal resumes or curriculum vitae, interviews or comments for use in media, statements in legal proceedings, lectures and public oral presentations, and published materials.

3.02 Statements by Others.

(a) Psychologists who engage others to create or place public statements that promote their professional practice, products, or activities retain professional responsibility for such statements.

(b) In addition, psychologists make reasonable efforts to prevent others whom they do not control (such as employers, publishers, sponsors, organizational clients, and representatives of the print or broadcast media) from making deceptive statements concerning psychologists' practice or professional or scientific activities.

(c) If psychologists learn of deceptive statements about their work made by others, psychologists make reasonable efforts to correct such statements.

(d) Psychologists do not compensate employees of press, radio, television, or other communication media in return for publicity in a news item.

(e) A paid advertisement relating to the psychologist's activities must be identified as such, unless it is already apparent from the context.

3.03 Avoidance of False or Deceptive Statements.

(a) Psychologists do not make public statements that are false, deceptive, misleading, or fraudulent, either because of what they state, convey, or suggest or because of what they omit, concerning their research, practice, or other work activities or those of persons or organizations with which they are affiliated. As examples (and not in limitation) of this standard, psychologists do not make false or deceptive statements concerning (1) their training, experience, or competence; (2) their academic degrees; (3) their credentials; (4) their institutional or association affiliations; (5) their services; (6) the scientific or clinical basis for, or results or degree of success of, their services; (7) their fees; or (8) their publications or research findings. (See also Standards 6.15, Deception in Research, and 6.18, Providing Participants With Information About the Study.)

(b) Psychologists claim as credentials for their psychological work, only degrees that (1) were earned from a regionally accredited educational institution or (2) were the basis for psychology licensure by the state in which they practice.

3.04 Media Presentations.

When psychologists provide advice or comment by means of public lectures, demonstrations, radio or television programs, prerecorded tapes, printed articles, mailed material, or other media, they take reasonable precautions to ensure that (1) the statements are based on appropriate psychological literature and practice, (2) the statements are otherwise consistent with this Ethics Code, and (3) the recipients of the information are not encouraged to infer that a relationship has been established with them personally.

3.05 Testimonials

Psychologists do not solicit testimonials from current psychotherapy clients or patients or other persons who because of their particular circumstances are vulnerable to undue influence.

3.06 In-Person Solicitation.

Psychologists do not engage, directly or through agents, in uninvited in-person solicitation of business from actual or potential psychotherapy patients or clients or other persons who because of their particular circumstances are vulnerable to undue influence. However, this does not preclude attempting to implement appropriate collateral contacts with significant others for the purpose of benefiting an already engaged therapy patient.

4. Therapy

4.01 Structuring the Relationship.

(a) Psychologists discuss with clients or patients as early as is feasible in the therapeutic relationship appropriate issues, such as the nature and anticipated course of therapy, fees, and confidentiality. (See also Standards 1.25, Fees and Financial Arrangements, and 5.01, Discussing the Limits of Confidentiality.)

(b) When the psychologist's work with clients or patients will be supervised, the above discussion includes that fact, and the name of the supervisor, when the supervisor has legal responsibility for the case.

(c) When the therapist is a student intern, the client or patient is informed of that fact.

(d) Psychologists make reasonable efforts to answer patients' questions and to avoid apparent misunderstandings about therapy. Whenever possible, psychologists provide oral and/or written information, using language that is reasonably understandable to the patient or client.

4.02 Informed Consent to Therapy.

(a) Psychologists obtain appropriate informed consent to therapy or related procedures, using language that is reasonably understandable to participants. The content of informed consent will vary depending on many circumstances; however, informed consent generally implies that the person (1) has the capacity to consent, (2) has been informed of significant information concerning the procedure, (3) has freely and without undue influence expressed consent, and (4) consent has been appropriately documented.

(b) When persons are legally incapable of giving informed consent, psychologists obtain informed permission from a legally authorized person, if such substitute consent is permitted by law.

(c) In addition, psychologists (1) inform those persons who are legally incapable of giving informed consent about the proposed interventions in a manner commensurate with the persons' psychological capacities, (2) seek their assent to those interventions, and (3) consider such persons' preferences and best interests.

4.03 Couple and Family Relationships.

(a) When a psychologist agrees to provide services to several persons who have a relationship (such as husband and wife or parents and children), the psychologist attempts to clarify at the outset (1) which of the individuals are patients or clients and (2) the relationship the psychologist will have with each person. This clarification includes the role of the psychologist and the probable uses of the services provided or the information obtained. (See also Standard 5.01, Discussing the Limits of Confidentiality.)

(b) As soon as it becomes apparent that the psychologist may be called on to perform potentially conflicting roles (such as marital counselor to husband and wife, and then witness for one party in a divorce proceeding), the psychologist attempts to clarify and adjust, or withdraw from, roles appropriately. (See also Standard 7.03, Clarification of Role, under Forensic Activities.)

4.04 Providing Mental Health Services to Those Served by Others.

In deciding whether to offer or provide services to those already receiving mental health services elsewhere, psychologists carefully consider the treatment issues and the potential patient's or client's welfare. The psychologist discusses these issues with the patient or client, or another legally authorized person on behalf of the client, in order to minimize the risk of confusion and conflict, consults with the other service providers when appropriate, and proceeds with caution and sensitivity to the therapeutic issues.

4.05 Sexual Intimacies With Current Patients or Clients.

Psychologists do not engage in sexual intimacies with current patients or clients.

4.06 Therapy With Former Sexual Partners.

Psychologists do not accept as therapy patients or clients persons with whom they have engaged in sexual intimacies.

4.07 Sexual Intimacies With Former Therapy Patients.

(a) Psychologists do not engage in sexual intimacies with a former therapy patient or client for at least two years after cessation or termination of professional services.

(b) Because sexual intimacies with a former therapy patient or client are so frequently harmful to the patient or client, and because such intimacies undermine public confidence in the psychology profession and thereby deter the public's use of needed services, psychologists do not engage in sexual intimacies with former therapy patients and clients even after a two-year interval except in the most unusual circumstances. The psychologist who engages in such activity after the two years following cessation or termination of treatment bears the burden of demonstrating that there has been no exploitation, in light of all relevant factors, including (1) the amount of time that has passed since therapy terminated, (2) the nature and duration of the therapy, (3) the circumstances of termination, (4) the patient's or client's personal history, (5) the patient's or client's current mental status, (6) the likelihood of adverse impact on the patient or client and others, and (7) any statements or actions made by the therapist during the course of therapy suggesting or inviting the possibility of a post-termination sexual or romantic relationship with the patient or client. (See also Standard 1.17, Multiple Relationships.)

4.08 Interruption of Services.
(a) Psychologists make reasonable efforts to plan for facilitating care in the event that psychological services are interrupted by factors such as the psychologist's illness, death, unavailability, or relocation or by the client's relocation or financial limitations. (See also Standard 5.09, Preserving Records and Data.)
(b) When entering into employment or contractual relationships, psychologists provide for orderly and appropriate resolution of responsibility for patient or client care in the event that the employment or contractual relationship ends, with paramount consideration given to the welfare of the patient or client.

4.09 Terminating the Professional Relationship.
(a) Psychologists do not abandon patients or clients. (See also Standard 1.25e, under Fees and Financial Arrangements.)
(b) Psychologists terminate a professional relationship when it becomes reasonably clear that the patient or client no longer needs the service, is not benefiting, or is being harmed by continued service.
(c) Prior to termination for whatever reason, except where precluded by the patient's or client's conduct, the psychologist discusses the patient's or client's views and needs, provides appropriate pretermination counseling, suggests alternative service providers as appropriate, and takes other reasonable steps to facilitate transfer of responsibility to another provider if the patient or client needs one immediately.

5. Privacy and Confidentiality
These Standards are potentially applicable to the professional and scientific activities of all psychologists.

5.01 Discussing the Limits of Confidentiality.
(a) Psychologists discuss with persons and organizations with whom they establish a scientific or professional relationship (including, to the extent feasible, minors and their legal representatives) (1) the relevant limitations on confidentiality, including limitations where applicable in group, marital, and family therapy or in organizational consulting, and (2) the foreseeable uses of the information generated through their services.
(b) Unless it is not feasible or is contraindicated, the discussion of confidentiality occurs at the outset of the relationship and thereafter as new circumstances may warrant.
(c) Permission for electronic recording of interviews is secured from clients and patients.

5.02 Maintaining Confidentiality.
Psychologists have a primary obligation and take reasonable precautions to respect the confidentiality rights of those with whom they work or consult, recognizing that confidentiality may be established by law, institutional rules, or professional or scientific relationships. (See also Standard 6.26, Professional Reviewers.)

5.03 Minimizing Intrusions on Privacy.
(a) In order to minimize intrusions on privacy, psychologists include in written and oral

reports, consultations, and the like, only information germane to the purpose for which the communication is made.

(b) Psychologists discuss confidential information obtained in clinical or consulting relationships, or evaluative data concerning patients, individual or organizational clients, students, research participants, supervisees, and employees, only for appropriate scientific or professional purposes and only with persons clearly concerned with such matters.

5.04 Maintenance of Records.

Psychologists maintain appropriate confidentiality in creating, storing, accessing, transferring, and disposing of records under their control, whether these are written, automated, or in any other medium. Psychologists maintain and dispose of records in accordance with law and in a manner that permits compliance with the requirements of this Ethics Code.

5.05 Disclosures.

(a) Psychologists disclose confidential information without the consent of the individual only as mandated by law, or where permitted by law for a valid purpose, such as (1) to provide needed professional services to the patient or the individual or organizational client, (2) to obtain appropriate professional consultations, (3) to protect the patient or client or others from harm, or (4) to obtain payment for services, in which instance disclosure is limited to the minimum that is necessary to achieve the purpose.

(b) Psychologists also may disclose confidential information with the appropriate consent of the patient or the individual or organizational client (or of another legally authorized person on behalf of the patient or client), unless prohibited by law.

5.06 Consultations.

When consulting with colleagues, (1) psychologists do not share confidential information that reasonably could lead to the identification of a patient, client, research participant, or other person or organization with whom they have a confidential relationship unless they have obtained the prior consent of the person or organization or the disclosure cannot be avoided, and (2) they share information only to the extent necessary to achieve the purposes of the consultation. (See also Standard 5.02, Maintaining Confidentiality.)

5.07 Confidential Information in Databases.

(a) If confidential information concerning recipients of psychological services is to be entered into databases or systems of records available to persons whose access has not been consented to by the recipient, then psychologists use coding or other techniques to avoid the inclusion of personal identifiers.

(b) If a research protocol approved by an institutional review board or similar body requires the inclusion of personal identifiers, such identifiers are deleted before the information is made accessible to persons other than those of whom the subject was advised.

(c) If such deletion is not feasible, then before psychologists transfer such data to others or review such data collected by others, they take reasonable steps to determine that appropriate consent of personally identifiable individuals has been obtained.

5.08 Use of Confidential Information for Didactic or Other Purposes.

(a) Psychologists do not disclose in their writings, lectures, or other public media, confidential, personally identifiable information concerning their patients, individual or organizational clients, students, research participants, or other recipients of their services that they obtained during the course of their work, unless the person or organization has consented in writing or unless there is other ethical or legal authorization for doing so.

(b) Ordinarily, in such scientific and professional presentations, psychologists disguise confidential information concerning such persons or organizations so that they are not individually identifiable to others and so that discussions do not cause harm to subjects who might identify themselves.

5.09 Preserving Records and Data.

A psychologist makes plans in advance so that confidentiality of records and data is protected in the event of the psychologist's death, incapacity, or withdrawal from the position or practice.

5.10 Ownership of Records and Data.

Recognizing that ownership of records and data is governed by legal principles, psychologists take reasonable and lawful steps so that records and data remain available to the extent needed to serve the best interests of patients, individual or organizational clients, research participants, or appropriate others.

5.11 Withholding Records for Nonpayment.

Psychologists may not withhold records under their control that are requested and imminently needed for a patient's or client's treatment solely because payment has not been received, except as otherwise provided by law.

6. Teaching, Training Supervision, Research, and Publishing

6.01 Design of Education and Training Programs.

Psychologists who are responsible for education and training programs seek to ensure that the programs are competently designed, provide the proper experiences, and meet the requirements for licensure, certification, or other goals for which claims are made by the program.

6.02 Descriptions of Education and Training Programs.

(a) Psychologists responsible for education and training programs seek to ensure that there is a current and accurate description of the program content, training goals and objectives, and requirements that must be met for satisfactory completion of the program. This information must be made readily available to all interested parties.

(b) Psychologists seek to ensure that statements concerning their course outlines are accurate and not misleading, particularly regarding the subject matter to be covered, bases for evaluating progress, and the nature of course experiences. (See also Standard 3.03, Avoidance of False or Deceptive Statements.)

(c) To the degree to which they exercise control, psychologists responsible for announcements, catalogs, brochures, or advertisements describing workshops, seminars, or other non-degree-granting educational programs ensure that they accurately describe the audience for which the program is intended, the educational objectives, the presenters, and the fees involved.

6.03 Accuracy and Objectivity in Teaching.

(a) When engaged in teaching or training, psychologists present psychological information accurately and with a reasonable degree of objectivity.

(b) When engaged in teaching or training, psychologists recognize the power they hold over students or supervisees and therefore make reasonable efforts to avoid engaging in conduct that is personally demeaning to students or supervisees. (See also Standards 1.09, Respecting Others, and 1.12, Other Harassment.)

6.04 Limitation on Teaching.

Psychologists do not teach the use of techniques or procedures that require specialized training, licensure, or expertise, including but not limited to hypnosis, biofeedback, and projective techniques, to individuals who lack the prerequisite training, legal scope of practice, or expertise.

6.05 Assessing Student and Supervisee Performance.

(a) In academic and supervisory relationships, psychologists establish an appropriate process for providing feedback to students and supervisees.

(b) Psychologists evaluate students and supervisees on the basis of their actual performance on relevant and established program requirements.

6.06 Planning Research.

(a) Psychologists design, conduct, and report research in accordance with recognized standards of scientific competence and ethical research.

(b) Psychologists plan their research so as to minimize the possibility that results will be misleading.

(c) In planning research, psychologists consider its ethical acceptability under the Ethics Code. If an ethical issue is unclear, psychologists seek to resolve the issue through consultation with institutional review boards, animal care and use committees, peer consultations, or other proper mechanisms.

(d) Psychologists take reasonable steps to implement appropriate protections for the rights and welfare of human participants, other persons affected by the research, and the welfare of animal subjects.

6.07 Responsibility.

(a) Psychologists conduct research competently and with due concern for the dignity and welfare of the participants.

(b) Psychologists are responsible for the ethical conduct of research conducted by them or by others under their supervision or control.

(c) Researchers and assistants are permitted to perform only those tasks for which they are appropriately trained and prepared.

(d) As part of the process of development and implementation of research projects, psychologists consult those with expertise concerning any special population under investigation or most likely to be affected.

6.08 Compliance With Law and Standards.

Psychologists plan and conduct research in a manner consistent with federal and state law and regulations, as well as professional standards governing the conduct of research, and particularly those standards governing research with human participants and animal subjects.

6.09 Institutional Approval.

Psychologists obtain from host institutions or organizations appropriate approval prior to conducting research, and they provide accurate information about their research proposals. They conduct the research in accordance with the approved research protocol.

6.10 Research Responsibilities.

Prior to conducting research (except research involving only anonymous surveys, naturalistic observations, or similar research), psychologists enter into an agreement with participants that clarifies the nature of the research and the responsibilities of each party.

6.11 Informed Consent to Research.

(a) Psychologists use language that is reasonably understandable to research participants in obtaining their appropriate informed consent (except as provided in Standard 6.12, Dispensing with Informed Consent). Such informed consent is appropriately documented.

(b) Using language that is reasonably understandable to participants, psychologists inform participants of the nature of the research; they inform participants that they are free to participate or to decline to participate or to withdraw from the research; they explain the foreseeable consequences of declining or withdrawing; they inform participants of significant factors that may be expected to influence their willingness to participate (such as risks, discomfort, adverse effects, or limitations on confidentiality, except as provided in Standard 6.15, Deception in Research); and they explain other aspects about which the prospective participants inquire.

(c) When psychologists conduct research with individuals such as students or subordinates, psychologists take special care to protect the prospective participants from adverse consequences of declining or withdrawing from participation.

(d) When research participation is a course requirement or opportunity for extra credit, the prospective participant is given the choice of equitable alternative activities.

(e) For persons who are legally incapable of giving informed consent, psychologists nevertheless (1) provide an appropriate explanation, (2) obtain the participant's assent, and (3) obtain appropriate permission from a legally authorized person, if such substitute consent is permitted by law.

6.12 Dispensing With Informed Consent.

Before determining that planned research (such as research involving only anonymous questionnaires, naturalistic observations, or certain kinds of archival research) does not require the informed consent of research participants, psychologists consider applicable regulations and institutional review board requirements, and they consult with colleagues as appropriate.

6.13 Informed Consent in Research Filming or Recording.

Psychologists obtain informed consent from research participants prior to filming or recording them in any form, unless the research involves simply naturalistic observations in public places and it is not anticipated that the recording will be used in a manner that could cause personal identification or harm.

6.14 Offering Inducements for Research Participants.

(a) In offering professional services as an inducement to obtain research participants, psychologists make clear the nature of the services, as well as the risks, obligations, and limitations. (See also Standard 1.18, Barter [With Patients or Clients].)

(b) Psychologists do not offer excessive or inappropriate financial or other inducements to obtain research participants, particularly when it might tend to coerce participation.

6.15 Deception in Research.

(a) Psychologists do not conduct a study involving deception unless they have determined that the use of deceptive techniques is justified by the study's prospective scientific, educational, or applied value and that equally effective alternative procedures that do not use deception are not feasible.

(b) Psychologists never deceive research participants about significant aspects that would affect their willingness to participate, such as physical risks, discomfort, or unpleasant emotional experiences.

(c) Any other deception that is an integral feature of the design and conduct of an experiment must be explained to participants as early as is feasible, preferably at the conclusion of their participation, but no later than at the conclusion of the research. (See also Standard 6.18, Providing Participants With Information About the Study.)

6.16 Sharing and Utilizing Data.

Psychologists inform research participants of their anticipated sharing or further use of personally identifiable research data and of the possibility of unanticipated future uses.

6.17 Minimizing Invasiveness.

In conducting research, psychologists interfere with the participants or milieu from which data are collected only in a manner that is warranted by an appropriate research design and that is consistent with psychologists' roles as scientific investigators.

6.18 Providing Participants With Information About the Study.

(a) Psychologists provide a prompt opportunity for participants to obtain appropriate information about the nature, results, and conclusions of the research, and psychologists attempt to correct any misconceptions that participants may have.

(b) If scientific or humane values justify delaying or withholding this information, psychologists take reasonable measures to reduce the risk of harm.

6.19 Honoring Commitments.
Psychologists take reasonable measures to honor all commitments they have made to research participants.

6.20 Care and Use of Animals in Research.
(a) Psychologists who conduct research involving animals treat them humanely.

(b) Psychologists acquire, care for, use, and dispose of animals in compliance with current federal, state, and local laws and regulations, and with professional standards.

(c) Psychologists trained in research methods and experienced in the care of laboratory animals supervise all procedures involving animals and are responsible for ensuring appropriate consideration of their comfort, health, and humane treatment.

(d) Psychologists ensure that all individuals using animals under their supervision have received instruction in research methods and in the care, maintenance, and handling of the species being used, to the extent appropriate to their role.

(e) Responsibilities and activities of individuals assisting in a research project are consistent with their respective competencies.

(f) Psychologists make reasonable efforts to minimize the discomfort, infection, illness, and pain of animal subjects.

(g) A procedure subjecting animals to pain, stress, or privation is used only when an alternative procedure is unavailable and the goal is justified by its prospective scientific, educational, or applied value.

(h) Surgical procedures are performed under appropriate anesthesia; techniques to avoid infection and minimize pain are followed during and after surgery.

(i) When it is appropriate that the animal's life be terminated, it is done rapidly, with an effort to minimize pain, and in accordance with accepted procedures.

6.21 Reporting of Results.
(a) Psychologists do not fabricate data or falsify results in their publications.

(b) If psychologists discover significant errors in their published data, they take reasonable steps to correct such errors in a correction, retraction, erratum, or other appropriate publication means.

6.22 Plagiarism.
Psychologists do not present substantial portions or elements of another's work or data as their own, even if the other work or data source is cited occasionally.

6.23 Publication Credit.
(a) Psychologists take responsibility and credit, including authorship credit, only for work they have actually performed or to which they have contributed.

(b) Principal authorship and other publication credits accurately reflect the relative scientific or professional contributions of the individuals involved, regardless of their relative status. Mere possession of an institutional position, such as Department Chair, does not justify authorship credit. Minor contributions to the research or to the writing for publications are appropriately acknowledged, such as in footnotes or in an introductory statement.

(c) A student is usually listed as principal author on any multiple-authored article that is substantially based on the student's dissertation or thesis.

6.24 Duplicate Publication of Data.
Psychologists do not publish, as original data, data that have been previously published. This does not preclude republishing data when they are accompanied by proper acknowledgment.

6.25 Sharing Data.
After research results are published, psychologists do not withhold the data on which their conclusions are based from other competent professionals who seek to verify the substantive claims through reanalysis and who intend to use such data only for that purpose, provided that the confidentiality of the participants can be protected and unless legal rights concerning proprietary data preclude their release.

6.26 Professional Reviewers.
Psychologists who review material submitted for publication, grant, or other research proposal review respect the confidentiality of and the proprietary rights in such information of those who submitted it.

7. Forensic Activities

7.01 Professionalism.
Psychologists who perform forensic functions, such as assessments, interviews, consultations, reports, or expert testimony, must comply with all other provisions of this Ethics Code to the extent that they apply to such activities. In addition, psychologists base their forensic work on appropriate knowledge of and competence in the areas underlying such work, including specialized knowledge concerning special populations. (See also Standards 1.06, Basis for Scientific and Professional Judgments; 1.08, Human Differences; 1.15, Misuse of Psychologists' Influence; and 1.23, Documentation of Professional and Scientific Work.)

7.02 Forensic Assessments.
(a) Psychologists' forensic assessments, recommendations, and reports are based on information and techniques (including personal interviews of the individual, when appropriate) sufficient to provide appropriate substantiation for their findings. (See also Standards 1.03, Professional and Scientific Relationship; 1.23, Documentation of Professional and Scientific Work; 2.01, Evaluation, Diagnosis, and Interventions in Professional Context; and 2.05, Interpreting Assessment Results.)

(b) Except as noted in (c), below, psychologists provide written or oral forensic reports or testimony of the psychological characteristics of an individual only after they have conducted an examination of the individual adequate to support their statements or conclusions.

(c) When, despite reasonable efforts, such an examination is not feasible, psychologists clarify the impact of their limited information on the reliability and validity of their reports and testimony, and they appropriately limit the nature and extent of their conclusions or recommendations.

7.03 Clarification of Role.
In most circumstances, psychologists avoid performing multiple and potentially conflicting roles in forensic matters. When psychologists may be called on to serve in more than one role in a legal proceeding—for example, as consultant or expert for one party or for the court and as a fact witness—they clarify role expectations and the extent of confidentiality in advance to the extent feasible, and thereafter as changes occur, in order to avoid compromising their professional judgment and objectivity and in order to avoid misleading others regarding their role.

7.04 Truthfulness and Candor.
(a) In forensic testimony and reports, psychologists testify truthfully, honestly, and candidly and, consistent with applicable legal procedures, describe fairly the bases for their testimony and conclusions. (b) Whenever necessary to avoid misleading, psychologists acknowledge the limits of their data or conclusions.

7.05 Prior Relationships.

A prior professional relationship with a party does not preclude psychologists from testifying as fact witnesses or from testifying to their services to the extent permitted by applicable law. Psychologists appropriately take into account ways in which the prior relationship might affect their professional objectivity or opinions and disclose the potential conflict to the relevant parties.

7.06 Compliance With Law and Rules.

In performing forensic roles, psychologists are reasonably familiar with the rules governing their roles. Psychologists are aware of the occasionally competing demands placed upon them by these principles and the requirements of the court system, and attempt to resolve these conflicts by making known their commitment to this Ethics Code and taking steps to resolve the conflict in a responsible manner. (See also Standard 1.02, Relationship of Ethics and Law.)

8. Resolving Ethical Issues

8.01 Familiarity With Ethics Code.

Psychologists have an obligation to be familiar with this Ethics Code, other applicable ethics codes, and their application to psychologists' work. Lack of awareness or misunderstanding of an ethical standard is not itself a defense to a charge of unethical conduct.

8.02 Confronting Ethical Issues.

When a psychologist is uncertain whether a particular situation or course of action would violate this Ethics Code, the psychologist ordinarily consults with other psychologists knowledgeable about ethical issues, with state or national psychology ethics committees, or with other appropriate authorities in order to choose a proper response.

8.03 Conflicts Between Ethics and Organizational Demands.

If the demands of an organization with which psychologists are affiliated conflict with this Ethics Code, psychologists clarify the nature of the conflict, make known their commitment to the Ethics Code, and to the extent feasible, seek to resolve the conflict in a way that permits the fullest adherence to the Ethics Code.

8.04 Informal Resolution of Ethical Violations.

When psychologists believe that there may have been an ethical violation by another psychologist, they attempt to resolve the issue by bringing it to the attention of that individual if an informal resolution appears appropriate and the intervention does not violate any confidentiality rights that may be involved.

8.05 Reporting Ethical Violations.

If an apparent ethical violation is not appropriate for informal resolution under Standard 8.04 or is not resolved properly in that fashion, psychologists take further action appropriate to the situation, unless such action conflicts with confidentiality rights in ways that cannot be resolved. Such action might include referral to state or national committees on professional ethics or to state licensing boards.

8.06 Cooperating With Ethics Committees.

Psychologists cooperate in ethics investigations, proceedings, and resulting requirements of the APA or any affiliated state psychological association to which they belong. In doing so, they make reasonable efforts to resolve any issues as to confidentiality. Failure to cooperate is itself an ethics violation.

8.07 Improper Complaints.

Psychologists do not file or encourage the filing of ethics complaints that are frivolous and are intended to harm the respondent rather than to protect the public.

Index